LESSONS FROM HISTORY

CAROLYN HOLBROOK is a historian in the Contemporary Histories Research Group at Deakin University and the Director of Australian Policy and History. This is her third book with NewSouth, having published *Anzac: The unauthorised biography* in 2014 and *The Great War: Aftermath and commemoration*, edited with Keir Reeves, in 2019. Her current research is on the history of Australian federalism, public health care and national security. She has previously worked as a policy adviser in the Department of Prime Minister and Cabinet, and as a freelance journalist.

LYNDON MEGARRITY has enjoyed a varied career as a researcher, author and tertiary educator. He was the inaugural history lecturer at the Springfield Campus at the University of Southern Queensland (2012–13) and has since taught at James Cook University in Townsville, where he is currently an adjunct lecturer at the College of Arts, Society and Education. He is the author of *Northern Dreams: The politics of northern development in Australia*, 2018.

DAVID LOWE is Chair of Contemporary History at Deakin University and co-founder of the Australian Policy and History Network. His research focuses on modern international history, including Australia's role in the world, and the remembering of prominent events. Recent books include (with Carola Lentz) *Remembering Independence*, 2018 and (edited, with Cassandra Atherton and Alyson Miller) *The Unfinished Atomic Bomb*, 2017.

In memory of Stuart Macintyre
(1947–2021)

'Know the past to change the future. Insightful essays by leading historians on the complex back stories of some of our most vexed policy challenges.' –
JUDITH BRETT

'*Lessons from History* makes a formidable case for the contemporary real-world relevance, in both national and international policymaking, of deep historical understanding. Hugh White's account of the lessons of 1914 and 1939 for today's would-be warriors – just one of twenty-four invariably thought-provoking essays – is alone worth the purchase price. A rich and rewarding collection which should be read by anyone concerned for Australia's future.'
– GARETH EVANS

'For several decades now our national mentality has been dominated by economists and culture warriors. Few dare stand up to them. In this book, our top historians begin the fightback. As the pandemics, recessions, extremism and wars of the twentieth century return, the history profession announces its intention to re-enter the public sphere to help create a better future – and not a moment too soon. *Lessons from History* is the statement of intent all believers in the importance of this crucial discipline have been waiting for.' **– DENNIS GLOVER**

'When devising policies to address everything from climate change to racial justice and gender equality, to war and conflict, history and historical thinking are not only relevant, this book shows they are essential.'
– PHILLIPA McGUINNESS

'A book for the times – an astute contribution to public debate. In twenty-two lively and eminently readable essays leading historians present a compelling case for the importance of history to add span, depth, context and above all wisdom to our policy making repertoire.' **– HENRY REYNOLDS**

LESSONS FROM HISTORY

LEADING HISTORIANS TACKLE AUSTRALIA'S GREATEST CHALLENGES

EDITORS: CAROLYN HOLBROOK,
LYNDON MEGARRITY, DAVID LOWE

NEWSOUTH

A NewSouth book

Published by
NewSouth Publishing
University of New South Wales Press Ltd
University of New South Wales
Sydney NSW 2052
AUSTRALIA
https://unsw.press/

© Carolyn Holbrook, Lyndon Megarrity & David Lowe 2022
First published 2022

10 9 8 7 6 5 4 3 2 1

This book is copyright. While copyright of the work as a whole is vested in Carolyn Holbrook, Lyndon Megarrity and David Lowe, copyright of individual chapters is retained by the chapter authors. Apart from any fair dealing for the purpose of private study, research, criticism or review, as permitted under the *Copyright Act*, no part of this book may be reproduced by any process without written permission. Inquiries should be addressed to the publisher.

 A catalogue record for this book is available from the National Library of Australia

ISBN: 9781742237473 (paperback)
        9781742238425 (ebook)
        9781742239323 (ePDF)

Design Josephine Pajor-Markus
Cover design Peter Long
Cover image Tom Steventon / Alamy Stock Photo
Printer Griffin Press, part of Ovato

All reasonable efforts were taken to obtain permission to use copyright material reproduced in this book, but in some cases copyright could not be traced. The editors welcome information in this regard.

Contents

Contributors   viii

Introduction: Seeing the world *with* the past.
A call to historians and policymakers   1
Carolyn Holbrook, Lyndon Megarrity and David Lowe

PART I: HOW A KNOWLEDGE OF HISTORY MAKES BETTER POLICY

1. Writing the history of the future   10
   Graeme Davison

2. Learning the right lessons? Two policy stories   25
   Frank Bongiorno

3. Historians: Bridging the divide with policymakers   40
   James Walter

PART II: LESSONS FROM HISTORY

4. Making time for history: Climate change and detoxing from progress   56
   Yves Rees

5. Urban water policy in a drying continent   69
   Andrea Gaynor, Margaret Cook, Lionel Frost, Jenny Gregory, Ruth Morgan, Martin Shanahan and Peter Spearritt

6. War with China: What can history teach us?   83
   Hugh White

7. Past as prologue: Repairing Australia's trade relationship with China   97
   Philip Chang, Jeffrey Hole and Kieran Brockman

8. Foreign aid: Australia's reputation at stake?   117
   David Lowe

9	An open door? Foreign investment and multinational companies *Simon Ville*	131
10	Tackling inequality: Lessons from the postwar reconstruction *Andrew Leigh*	148
11	Electricity problems? Call a historian. Learning from the history of electricity reform in Australia *Jeffrey Hole*	166
12	Governing during economic crisis: The importance of memory *Joan Beaumont*	184
13	We need to hear the voices of refugees: Citizen engagement for reforming refugee policy *Niro Kandasamy*	200
14	The 'Muslim Problem' in Australia: The role of political leadership *Mahsheed Ansari*	215
15	Why soldiers commit war crimes – and what we can do about it *Mia Martin Hobbs*	227
16	How can we fight the far right? *Evan Smith*	239
17	The genie is out of the bottle: Self-determination and First Nations peoples of Australia *Laura Rademaker and Ian Anderson*	256
18	Pipelines and catalysts: Lessons from the history of women in corporate leadership *Claire E.F. Wright*	270
19	Beyond productivity: Working mothers and childcare policy *Carla Pascoe Leahy*	283
20	Too much talk, not enough action? Federal government responses to domestic violence *Ann Curthoys, Catherine Kevin and Zora Simic*	298

| 21 | The neglected north: Developing Northern Australia from the south since 1901 | 314 |

Lyndon Megarrity

| 22 | How to fix our federation | 332 |

Carolyn Holbrook

Conclusion: The history of the future   346

Carolyn Holbrook, Lyndon Megarrity and David Lowe

Acknowledgments   350

Notes   352

Index   401

Contributors

Professor Ian Anderson has been the Deputy Vice-Chancellor (Student and University Experience) at the Australian National University since 2020. He was previously Deputy Secretary, Department of Prime Minister and Cabinet and Deputy CEO, National Indigenous Australian Agency. Professor Anderson's background is in medicine and social sciences and he worked in Aboriginal Health and education for more than 30 years as a health worker, educator, general practitioner, policymaker and academic. He has written widely on Indigenous health and development and maintains an active research portfolio. His family are Palawa Lutrawita with traditional ties to Tebrakunna on the north-east coast of Tasmanian which includes connections to Pairrebenne, Trawlwoolway and Plairmairrenner and related clans.

Dr Mahsheed Ansari is a Senior Lecturer at the Centre for Islamic Studies & Civilisation, Charles Sturt University. She is a reader in Islamic thought and a community activist working in the areas of interfaith dialogue, social harmony and leadership-mentoring programs with Muslim youth and Muslim women. Her research interests include the history of Islamic thought, spirituality and culture. She is currently in the final stages of completing her book titled: *Modern Debates in Prophecy and Prophethood in Islam: Muhammad Iqbal and Said Nursi*. She has been working on an oral history project – Muslim Pioneers Post WWII – and is currently focused on writing the biography of Dr Ashfaq Ahmad.

Professor Joan Beaumont (Professor Emerita at the Australian National University and Honorary Professor at Deakin University) is an internationally recognised historian of Australia during the two world wars, the history of prisoners of war and the memory and heritage of war. Her publications include the multi-award-winning *Broken Nation: Australians in the Great War* (Allen & Unwin, 2014), and *Australia's Great Depression* (Allen & Unwin, 2022).

PROFESSOR FRANK BONGIORNO teaches history at the Australian National University. He has been a member of the Australian Policy and History Network since its foundation. Frank is the author of *The Sex Lives of Australians: A history* (2012) and *The Eighties: The decade that transformed Australia* (2015), and is a regular contributor to the media, including *The Conversation*, *Inside Story*, the *Sydney Morning Herald* and the *Age*. He is a Fellow of the Academy of the Social Sciences in Australia and the Australian Academy of Humanities.

KIERAN BROCKMAN is an economics analyst with the Department of Industry, Tourism and Trade (DITT) in the Northern Territory. He undertakes detailed research, investigation and analysis of complex economic, statistical and demographic issues, and provides advice on current economic, statistical and demographic developments relevant to the Northern Territory. He has extensive expertise in data analysis and data visualisation. Prior to joining DITT in 2013, Kieran held various positions with the Department of Treasury and Finance in the Northern Territory.

DR PHILIP CHANG is an economist with extensive trade and development experience in Asia and the Pacific. He is currently a director with a state government agency. He was previously an executive director at the Northern Territory Department of Industry, Tourism and Trade and the Senior Regional Economist for the East Asia and Pacific region with the International Finance Corporation. Prior to this role, he was Head of the Programs Unit at the Asian Development Bank (ADB), based in Beijing, where he led the formulation of ADB's Country Partnership Strategy 2016–20 for China. He has also worked at the World Trade Organization, APEC and the Australian Treasury.

Dr Margaret Cook is a history lecturer at the University of the Sunshine Coast and Honorary Research Fellow at the University of Queensland and La Trobe University. She specialises in the history of 'natural' disasters in Australia, especially floods and earthquakes. The history of floods in the Brisbane River catchment was the subject of her PhD (UQ, 2018) and is now a book, *A River with a City Problem: A history of Brisbane floods* (UQP, 2019). With Dr Scott McKinnon, Margaret is also co-editor of *Disasters in Australia and New Zealand: Historical approaches to understanding catastrophe* (Palgrave, 2020). Her broad academic areas of interest are environmental and social history and cultural heritage.

Professor Ann Curthoys is one of Australia's most respected historians, and her books include *Freedom Ride: A Freedom Rider remembers* (2002); with John Docker, *Is History Fiction?* (2005, rev. 2010) and, with Jessie Mitchell, *Taking Liberty: Indigenous rights and settler self-government in colonial Australia, 1830–1890* (2018). She is currently undertaking an ARC-funded history of domestic violence in Australia, 1850–2020 with Catherine Kevin and Zora Simic.

Professor Graeme Davison is an emeritus professor of history at Monash University. He has written widely on Australian history, especially urban and public history where his publications include *The Rise and Fall of Marvellous Melbourne, Car Wars, The Use and Abuse of Australian History*, and, as co-editor, *The Oxford Companion to Australian History*. He is a former president of the Australian Historical Association, chairman of the Heritage Council of Victoria and a prominent adviser and commentator on museums, heritage and urban policy. In 2011, he was made an Officer in the Order of Australia.

Associate Professor Lionel Frost is an Associate Professor in the Department of Economics, Monash University and is head of the Monash Business School, Peninsula Campus.

Contributors

PROFESSOR ANDREA GAYNOR is an Australian Research Council Future Fellow at the University of Western Australia. An environmental historian, her research seeks to use the contextualising and narrative power of history to assist transitions to more just and sustainable societies. Her current research encompasses histories of nature in Australian urban modernity, water in Australian urbanisation and community-led land management in Australia.

EMERITUS PROFESSOR JENNY GREGORY AM is based at the University of Western Australia. Her research focuses on urban history, primarily town planning and heritage. With her co-writers, she recently completed *Cities in a Sunburnt Country: Water and the making of urban Australia* (Cambridge University Press, in press 2022). Among her many books and edited collections are *City of Light: A history of Perth since the fifties* (2003) and, as editor-in-chief, the *Historical Encyclopedia of Western Australia* (2009).

JEFFREY HOLE has a background in economics, particularly economic history, and is currently undertaking a PhD at Deakin University on Australia's experience with microeconomic reform since the 1980s. Previously, Jeff held senior policy advising roles with several government agencies, including the Victorian Competition and Efficiency Commission, the Australian Productivity Commission and the Queensland Productivity Commission. He is also an Honorary Research Fellow in the School of Economics at Deakin University.

DR NIRO KANDASAMY is a lecturer in History in the School of Philosophical and Historical Inquiry (SOPHI), University of Sydney, where she teaches International and Global Studies and researches the historical dimensions of forced migration, international relations, and transnational activism. She holds a BSocSci (Honours Class 1) from the University of New South Wales and a PhD in History from the University of Melbourne. Before joining the University of Sydney, she was teaching in

Melbourne and held senior research roles in non-government organisations. She is currently working on several research projects, including her first manuscript on Tamil refugee resettlement in Australia, and an exploration of Indian Ocean state and civil society responses to the Cold War.

Associate Professor Catherine Kevin is based at Flinders University, where she teaches and researches Australian and gender histories. She has published on the histories of pregnancy, migration, feminism and domestic violence and is the author of the book *Dispossession and the Making of Jedda: Hollywood in Ngunnawal Country* (2020). Catherine is currently undertaking an ARC-funded history of domestic violence in Australia, 1850–2020, with Ann Curthoys and Zora Simic.

Dr Carla Pascoe Leahy is a lecturer in Family History at the University of Tasmania, an Honorary Fellow at the University of Melbourne, an honorary associate at Museums Victoria and joint editor of *Studies in Oral History*. She is an internationally recognised expert in the recent history of women and children in twentieth- and twenty-first-century Australia, with a particular focus on motherhood and family; children and youth; place, environment and sustainability; and oral history and qualitative research. She is the author of *Spaces Imagined, Places Remembered: Childhood in 1950s Australia* (2011) and co-editor of *Children, Childhood and Cultural Heritage* (2013), *Children's Voices from the Past: New historical and interdisciplinary perspectives* (2019) and *Australian Mothering: Historical and sociological perspectives* (2019). Carla has worked in government and the not-for-profit sector and remains committed to connecting historical research to contemporary policy and public debates.

Hon. Dr Andrew Leigh is the Shadow Assistant Minister for Treasury and Charities, and Federal Member for Fenner in the ACT. Prior to being elected in 2010, Andrew was a professor of economics at the Australian National University. He holds a PhD in Public Policy from Harvard, having graduated from the University of Sydney with first-class honours in Arts and Law. Andrew is a Fellow of the Australian Academy of Social Sciences. His books include *Disconnected* (2010), *Choosing Openness: Why global engagement is best for Australia* (2017) and *What's the Worst That Could Happen? Existential risk and extreme politics* (2021).

Dr Mia Martin Hobbs is an oral historian of war and conflict. Her research interests include the Vietnam War, the War on Terror, memory, trauma, peace and security. Mia completed her PhD at the University of Melbourne in 2018. Her doctoral project was a transnational oral history with American and Australian Vietnam veterans who returned to Viêt Nam after the war. Her book, *Return to Vietnam: An oral history of American and Australian veterans' journeys*, was published by Cambridge University Press in 2021. She is undertaking a second transnational oral history project with women and minorities who served in the British, American and Australian armed forces in the so-called War on Terror, supported by the Freilich Project and Contemporary Histories Research Group 'History and Policy Award'. She is currently a Research Fellow at Deakin University.

Associate Professor Ruth Morgan is an environmental historian and historian of science, based at the Australian National University, where she is Director of the Centre for Environmental History. She has a particular research focus on Australia, the British Empire, and the Indian Ocean world, living and working on the unceded lands of the Ngunnawal and Ngambri peoples. Her research has been generously supported by the Australian Research Council, the Alexander von Humboldt Foundation, and the Rachel Carson Center for Environment & Society. She was previously based at Monash University (2012–20) and completed her doctoral studies at the University of Western Australia.

Dr Laura Rademaker is an ARC DECRA Senior Research Fellow in the School of History at the Australian National University. She is the author of *Found in Translation: Many meanings on a north Australian mission* (University of Hawai'i Press, 2018) on language and cross-cultural exchange at Christian missions to Aboriginal people, which was awarded the 2020 Hancock Prize. Her work explores the possibilities of 'cross-culturalising' history, interdisciplinary histories as well as oral history and memory. At present, she is working on the history of self-determination in the Northern Territory. She is also working on a book about the Tiwi Islands and Aboriginal encounters with Catholicism as well as researching the closing of Christian missions, secularisation and Indigenous self-determination. Laura is co-editor of the *Journal of Religious History* and associate monographs editor for Aboriginal history Monographs.

Dr Yves Rees (they/them) is a writer and historian based on unceded Wurundjeri land. They are a Lecturer in History at La Trobe University, the co-host of Archive Fever history podcast, and the author of *All About Yves: Notes from a transition* (Allen & Unwin, 2021). Rees was awarded the 2020 ABR Calibre Essay Prize and a 2021 Varuna Residential Fellowship. They are a historian of Australia in the world, with particular interests in gender, modernity, mobility and whiteness. Their current research examines Australian women's transpacific careering and the impact of United States interwar immigration restriction upon white British subjects.

Professor Martin Shanahan is Professor of Economic and Business History in the School of Business, University of South Australia, and Elof Hansson Visiting Professor in International Business and Trade at Gothenburg University, Sweden. Professor Shanahan holds degrees in economics, politics and law and is a specialist in Australian economic and business history. His PhD was awarded the Butlin Prize in economic history in Australia and

Contributors

New Zealand. Professor Shanahan has written over a hundred peer-reviewed articles, book chapters, books and conference papers on historical aspects of wealth and income distribution, business cartels, trade practice law and water use.

Dr Zora Simic is a senior lecturer in History and Gender Studies at UNSW. She has published widely on past and present feminisms, as well as Australian migration history. Zora is currently undertaking an ARC-funded history of domestic violence in Australia, 1850–2020, with Catherine Kevin and Ann Curthoys.

Dr Evan Smith is a lecturer in History in the College of Humanities, Arts and Social Sciences at Flinders University. He is also a visiting research fellow in the School of Humanities at the University of Adelaide. He has published widely on political extremism, social movements, national security and borders in Australia, Britain and South Africa.

Emeritus Professor Peter Spearritt is an urban and environmental historian based at the University of Queensland. His *Sydney's Century: A history*, won the NSW Premier's prize in 2000, and the third edition of his *The Sydney Harbour Bridge: A life* was published in 2011. His *Where History Happened: The hidden past of Australia's towns and places* was published in 2018. Peter is the co-editor of the websites victorianplaces.com.au and queenslandplaces.com.au and the co-author of *The Twentieth Century Historic Heritage Framework: A tool for assessing heritage places*, published by the Getty Conservation Institute in 2021.

Professor Simon Ville is Senior Professor of Economic and Business History and Associate Dean Research in the Faculty of Business and Law at the University of Wollongong. Ville is an internationally recognised economic and business historian who has worked with scholars in a broad range of disciplines including economics, history, management, sociology, engineering and museum science. He is a Fellow of the Academy of Social Sciences in Australia and has served on the Australian Research Council in various roles, particularly as a member of the College of Experts. In 2022–23 he will be the Whitlam–Fraser Professor of Australian Studies at Harvard University.

PROFESSOR JAMES WALTER is Emeritus Professor of Political Science in the School of Social Sciences at Monash University. He has published widely on Australian politics, history, biography and culture. His latest book is *The Pivot of Power: Australian prime ministers and political leadership 1949–2016* (with Paul Strangio and Paul 't Hart, 2017). He maintains broad interests in political leadership, political psychology, political biography, public policy and the history of Australian political institutions.

PROFESSOR HUGH WHITE AO is Emeritus Professor of Strategic Studies at the Australian National University. His work focuses primarily on Australian strategic and defence policy, Asia-Pacific security issues, and global strategic affairs, especially as they influence Australia and the Asia-Pacific.

DR CLAIRE E.F. WRIGHT is a business historian at the University of Technology Sydney. She is interested in the ways that interpersonal connections affect knowledge, markets and business strategy, focusing on Australian corporate networks and diversity in leadership. She has contributed widely to national and international journals in history, economics, urban studies and management, and is the author of *Australian Economic History: Transformations of an interdisciplinary field* (ANU Press, 2022). Claire is currently an Australian Research Council Discovery Early Career Researcher Award (DECRA) Fellow (2022–25), working on the first history of Australia's corporate women across the twentieth and early twenty-first centuries.

Introduction:
Seeing the world *with* the past.
A call to historians and policymakers

Carolyn Holbrook, Lyndon Megarrity
and David Lowe

'Seeing the world without the past would be like visiting a city after a devastating hurricane and declaring that the people there have always lived in ruins', wrote the American historian Steven Stoll in his 2017 study of Appalachia.[1] Stoll's observation evocatively describes the belief that motivated us – a group of concerned academic historians – to write this book. Today, the world appears more volatile than it has been for many decades and our problems more intractable. Besides our descent into irreversible climate change, there is the threat of major conflict between the West and Russia and China, and the unthinkable truth that the United States might soon no longer be a democracy. Our politicians and policymakers need at their disposal the best information in order to make decisions of untold consequence. This includes a sound knowledge of history. Politicians and policymakers must see the world *with* the past.

Lessons from History provides a roadmap for this vital knowledge, laying bare how history can and, indeed, should inform public debate. It is a book for politicians, policymakers, community workers, journalists and engaged citizens, as well as historians. Far from seeking to offer crude historical 'lessons' or rigid templates that might be imposed upon contemporary problems, instead, we are interested in history's capacity to enlarge and contextualise public debates. At the very least, we expect that those engaged in policymaking and policy debate will agree that rich context is a desirable ingredient in good policy and decision-making. Historical literacy may not always lead to better policy, but we maintain that history is fundamental to understanding *context* – which, from its Latin roots, means weaving together or drawing on surrounding circumstances.

Historians have traditionally been reluctant to engage in debates on policy. There are various reasons for this. For one, the historical profession has legacies and characteristics, many of them admirable, which have traditionally inhibited our capacity to participate in policy debates. At the same time, policymakers often lack the time to read our books and scholarly articles for their present-day lessons. And academic performance measures do not reward us for writing concise material that would better suit a policy audience, though universities are trying to devise ways to respond to government pressure to measure 'impact and engagement'. *Lessons from History* responds to the challenge of condensing rigorous historical research in ways that make it useful to time-pressed practitioners.

In addition, academic historians can be suspicious of any approach that has them wedded too closely to the 'state'. They are also wary of 'instrumentalism', the notion that the value of their work can be reduced to simple, often government-defined, objectives that come and go easily, in contrast to the bolder idea of contributing to knowledge. As the examples presented in this book suggest, such tensions might be real but they can be managed. We hope that they provide inspiration for other historians.

In recent times, there has been a clear turn towards policy history. The United States has led efforts to highlight the significance of history for international relations. The Kennedy School at Harvard has long been a focus for government–academic exchanges. In 2002, the American Historical Association founded the National History Center in Washington DC, which allows historians to speak directly to politicians and their staffers. The Luskin Center for History and Policy at the University of California in Los Angeles and the Albert Lepage Center for History in the Public Interest at Villanova College were both established in 2017.

In the United Kingdom, the History and Policy Network, established in 2002, continues strongly. And in Australia, the Australian Policy and History network, founded in 2010 and directed from Deakin University, with partners ANU and the University of Melbourne, is highly active in the intersection between history and public policy. Among our many activities are annual conferences where historians, policymakers and journalists have the chance to rub shoulders and exchange ideas.

Taken together, these efforts across the world suggest that historians are increasingly willing to make their voices heard in the public forum. *Lessons from History* builds on this momentum by presenting a unique and accessible collection of historical reflections on vital policy issues for Australia.

Our opening three chapters tackle questions about the role of history in politics and policy. They are intended to provoke both historians and policymakers to think about how they can work profitably together. Graeme Davison stresses that the history discipline's tendency to study a large range of factors, and their complex relationships to one another, serves as a useful corrective to the limitations of policymakers viewing issues in splendid isolation. Frank Bongiorno shows how politicians, bolstered by think tanks and elements of the media, have frequently used an overly simplified, decontextualised version of past events to justify their policies. Throwing down the gauntlet, Bongiorno calls on fellow historians to play their part in fostering contextualised historical literacy by engaging with the public and presenting alternative perspectives in various mediums. In relation to this task, James Walter suggests that historians 'seize the moment': accelerated by COVID-19, the assumptions of neoliberalism and the 'historical narrative' it is based on are now being widely questioned. What then, can, historians bring to policies and debates?

The ensuing chapters rove widely across politics and economic, social, civic and security policy. They set topical issues in their historical context and, based on the lessons of history, provide recommendations for policymakers and citizens.

Yves Rees' chapter challenges basic concepts of growth and progress. Rees urges historians to champion non-linear ways of thinking about time in order to detach ourselves from the progressive narratives that have abetted climate destruction. Similarly, in tracing the extent to which a mindset of growth and development has determined water policy, Andrea Gaynor, Margaret Cook, Lionel Frost, Jenny Gregory, Ruth Morgan, Martin Shanahan and Peter Spearritt demonstrate the urgent need to conceive water as a life-giving resource rather than a commodity.

Australia's relations with the rest of the world are a major theme of this collection. In response to rising tensions with China, Hugh White suggests that Australia might find more valuable historical lessons among the causes of the First World War than the Second, while cautioning against clumsy misappropriations of history, especially those assuming that all adversaries can be treated the same. In their chapter on Australia–China trade, Philip Chang, Jeff Hole and Kieran Brockman highlight the danger of megaphone diplomacy. David Lowe argues that government has failed to capitalise on popular interest in Australia's international reputation in ways that can build public support for its foreign aid program.

Economic themes feature prominently in this volume. In his analysis of multinational companies in Australia, Simon Ville finds that these corporations have, on balance, made a positive contribution, although striking the right balance between economic benefit and national security can challenge policymakers. Andrew Leigh tackles the issue of rising wealth inequality. He argues that Australian political culture needs to discard the values of neoliberalism and rebuild a consensus around fairness and compassion. Jeff Hole's chapter traces the history of electricity reform, underlining the need for long-term leadership and planning by government, and the importance of reaching consensus on emissions reduction. Joan Beaumont considers the legacy of the Great Depression in popular, political and policy memory. While the Depression no longer serves as a source of policy inspiration, its status as the worst economic crisis ever faced by Australia has been frequently invoked in order to justify the drastic policies implemented during the COVID-19 pandemic.

This book also considers the history of policymaking in relation to migrant communities in Australia. Examining the experiences of Sri Lankan refugees, Niro Kandasamy demonstrates that when governments have sought input from refugee and migrant communities about settlement services, outcomes have been stronger and fairer. Mahsheed Ansari's chapter acknowledges the pervasiveness of anti-Muslim sentiment in Australian history, but also finds much more than survival amid fear. Ansari argues that recent anti-Muslim behaviour is easily stirred by internal political and external factors, but with strong leadership, is replaced by more affirming stories of Muslim Australia. Mia Martin Hobbs analyses war crimes by Australian soldiers and our allies, arguing that atrocities committed in war are deeply entrenched expressions of society, culture and politics.

The interaction between policy and community organising is also explored in this volume. In his chapter, Evan Smith shows how coalitions of grassroots activists have been effective in the past in combating racism, fascism and white supremacy. He proposes effective ways to respond to the concerning increase in recent years of far right–wing activism. Laura Rademaker and Ian Anderson reveal that the history of Indigenous self-determination in Australia has, in its persistence and vitality, surmounted the efforts of governments since the 1970s to define and prescribe self-determination with limitations attached.

Several contributors explore the theme of gender using an historical lens. Claire E.F. Wright's chapter praises the increasing representation of women in corporate leadership, though her analysis underlines the need for greater diversity among the women who are rising through the ranks. Using oral history interviews, Carla Pascoe Leahy shows that policies assisting working mothers have emphasised narrow economic goals such as productivity without sufficiently acknowledging the broader societal objectives of parental and child wellbeing. In their review of domestic violence policy, Ann Curthoys,

Catherine Kevin and Zora Simic distinguish between a decades-long tradition of admirable policy and the far patchier story of its implementation.

The final two chapters look at areas of civic policy vital to the nation's future. Lyndon Megarrity finds that plans to develop Australia's north have suffered from persistently abstract grandiosity, at the expense of evidence-based need. Finally, Carolyn Holbrook examines the history of civic apathy in Australia and implores political leaders to resist the appeal of Anzackery and dedicate public funding to the kind of civics education that might motivate Australians to reform the federation.

While history might not provide quick-fixes, the twenty-two essays contained in *Lessons from History* add span, depth, context and, above all, *wisdom*, to our policymaking repertoire. This book joins a rising tide of civic activism among exasperated historians. As 'citizen-historians', we will not stand by while the stumps of democratic governance are white-anted, while wealth inequality reaches the grotesque levels of previous eras, and while vested interests block necessary action on climate change.[2] We present this collection to politicians and policymakers in the hope it can help to improve our degraded system of political decision-making. We also hope that it encourages more historians to lend their expertise to the major public issues of our time. Yes, historians study the past. But we are passionately concerned about the present and the future. And we know that an awareness of history is one of the best ways to understand the present and prepare for the future.

PART I:

HOW A KNOWLEDGE OF HISTORY MAKES BETTER POLICY

CHAPTER 1
Writing the history of the future

Graeme Davison

'Histories make men wise', the Elizabethan essayist Francis Bacon declared.¹ He was repeating the wisdom of the ancients: that the past furnished lessons for both leaders and citizens. The study of history long remained an essential part of the preparation of politicians, soldiers and many professions. Only in the last half-century has it been sidelined by other disciplines such as economics, law and political science in the university curriculum and the halls of power. When the Australian government in 2020 introduced reforms to make university graduates more 'job ready', it actually increased the cost of history degrees; ironically, the minister was himself a history graduate!

Now historians have begun to fight back. In *The History Manifesto* (2014) David Armitage and Jo Guldi issue a rousing call to arms. Historians, they suggest, have only themselves to blame for their marginalisation. They 'hardly ever consider how history might promote human flourishing, nor do we debate whether some forms of historical work would advance it better than others'. Too much academic history is too narrowly framed and too inwardly directed. Meanwhile many of the most urgent questions of our time, from climate change to rising social inequality, cry out for the big-picture knowledge and long-term thinking that only historians can provide. 'Historians of the world, unite!' they urge. 'There is a world to win – before it's too late.'[2]

The History Manifesto drew enthusiastic support from some historians, scorn and scepticism from others.[3] Some objected to its apocalyptic tone, others to the naivety of the authors' belief that big history and big data could unlock the great problems of the age. Not all the most urgent issues of our time are global in scope, others insisted: what about the more intimate histories of race, sexuality and identity that inspired the liberationist causes of the past half-century and drew so much of the political and intellectual energy of contemporary historians – was this of no account?

Behind the divided responses to *The History Manifesto* lies a fundamental question, one that scholars and policymakers have often debated but never conclusively settled. They agree that history has – or ought to have – lessons for present-day decision-makers, but they are unsure about what they are. Is historical knowledge integral to the resolution of current policy dilemmas? Or is it, at best, useful background information? Can the techniques that explain events in the past be applied to planning the future? Or is the past such a foreign country that the traveller who knows its terrain best is also unable to venture into the future?

The wisdom of hindsight

Historians enjoy the benefit – or is it the handicap? – of hindsight. How often have you heard a politician, reminded of a policy gaffe, reply with irritation: 'Well, of course, with the benefit of 20:20 hindsight …' Prime Minister Scott Morrison, who has had more than a few such reminders during the COVID-19 pandemic, even labelled his critics 'hindsight heroes'.[4] There's a subtext here: only those in the room where it happened can really appreciate the push and pull of contending forces, the clash of opinions and arguments, and the intrinsic risks of politics. Those who dissect decisions after the event are mere spectators; wise but impotent. Yet when they write their memoirs, becoming historians of their own actions, only a rare politician – Barack Obama might be an example – acknowledges these uncertainties. More often, hindsight kicks in to justify, rather than explain, their actions.

My old friend, the economic historian John McCarty, used to compare the roles of the historian and the football pundit. In his retirement, the famous Collingwood footballer Lou Richards wrote a popular column for the *Sun* newspaper. Every Friday he reviewed the form and picked his winners, summarising the reasons for their expected success. If he felt particularly confident, he would say: 'If Collingwood doesn't win on Saturday, I'll sweep Swanston Street with a feather duster.' And sure enough, if Collingwood lost, the *Sun*'s front page on Monday would show Lou on his knees in the middle of the intersection. In his column he would explain, as confidently as he had previously explained why Collingwood was going to win, why it had actually lost. All the reasons that had pointed to the team's success were forgotten and replaced by factors he hadn't even considered on Friday. Historians, McCarty observed, are like football pundits who only write on Mondays. They never have to subject their explanations to the test of prediction or get on their knees with a feather duster.

Predicting the future, even when you have mastered the playbook of the past, is much harder than predicting next week's football results. Perhaps that's why claims for the value of history in current politics are often made tentatively or in the negative. George Santayana's famous aphorism 'Those who cannot remember the past are condemned to repeat it' is an example.[5] History, it implies, may save us from repeating some past errors, even if it can't tell us what we *should* do or what *will* actually happen. Historians tend to be less comfortable in the role of policy advisers than social scientists trained in positivist disciplines like economics. 'History is a discipline infused with particularity, irony and contingency', some British historians of public policy shrewdly observe.[6] Our intellectual bias is towards complication rather than simplification. In policy debates we prefer the role of critic, of dousing the overly confident prognoses of other social scientists with the cold water of historical experience, to that of the futurist or prophet.

Santayana's aphorism rests on the assumption that yesterday's mistakes are recognisable enough for the historian to spot them when they reappear. But does history actually repeat itself? The distinguished war historian Michael Howard concludes his book *The Lessons of History* (1989) on a sceptical note: 'Each new generation is presented with new problems and new challenges, and analogies drawn from the past are likely to be more of a hindrance than a help in solving them ... If the past has anything to teach us', he writes, 'it is *humility* – and suspicion of glib formulae for improving the lot of mankind'.[7]

As a military historian, Howard challenged an old tradition in which old battles were dissected in the classroom to prepare future commanders for the field. He widened the perspective beyond battlefield tactics to take in the wider array of forces – social and political as well as strategic – that influenced the outcome of conflicts. But such interpretative breadth comes at a cost; for the richer and more complex the story, the harder it is to extract easy lessons from it. The only lessons history has to teach, Howard decided, were the negative ones, of exploding myths and denouncing false prophets who put history at the service of ideology.

He may have been thinking of Marxists or other believers in what the philosopher Karl Popper called 'historicism' – the possibility of reading the future from the past. But by the end of the twentieth century few Marxists were still historicists. 'We do not know where we are going', the most famous Marxist historian of his generation, Eric Hobsbawm, wrote in the conclusion of *The Age of Extremes* (1994).[8] While he could plot the contours of change across the twentieth century, and held onto his socialist faith that capitalism was doomed, Hobsbawm could not tell when or how it would end. This did not mean, he insisted, that the historian could have no influence on the future. Indeed, he argued, 'we alone in the field of human studies *must* think in terms of historical change, interaction and transformation'. The historian's understanding of the 'limits, potentialities and consequences of human action', Hobsbawm suggested, was essential for good public policy.[9]

Some seasoned politicians and policymakers have been less reluctant than historians to draw lessons from the past. Students in Harvard's Kennedy School of Government once sought solutions to current policy dilemmas in the history of past crises.[10] In *Great Planning Disasters* (1980), the distinguished town planner Peter Hall reviewed a selection of failed plans – from London's Motorways Concorde to the Sydney Opera House – seeking 'rules of thumb' for present-day planners.[11] Why do historians hold back from such experiments? They may rightly fear that analogies will mislead rather than inform current decision-makers, pointing to cases like George W. Bush's invocation of the Munich appeasement crisis in his decision to invade Iraq in 2003. Yet, since policymakers cannot refrain from historical analogies, it may be all the more important for scholars with a more complete knowledge of history, and a more subtle grasp of historical contingency, to be in the room where decisions are made. And while historical precedents may not tell us what to do, or what will happen, they may prompt fruitful questions.

The truth of the past

Michael Howard's image of the historian as a myth-slayer or impartial witness calls to mind one of the most significant contemporary scenes of historical inquiry: the law court or tribunal. Any historian who has appeared as an expert witness is likely to have been struck by the similarities and profound differences between the protocols of the law and of the historical profession.[12] Critical to both are concepts of evidence, truth-telling, contestation and balanced judgment. Yet historians, especially over the past 30 years, with the advent of postmodernism and critical literary studies, have often felt disabled by 'the vertigo of relativity'.[13]

'In academia', notes Tom Griffiths, 'we often rightly focus on the elusiveness and contestability of truth, but historians also have a civic responsibility to insist on the possibility of truth.'[14] In his book *In Defence of History*, the distinguished British historian Richard Evans reflects on his experience as an expert witness in the courtroom battle between the Holocaust-denying historian David Irving and his American critic

HOW A KNOWLEDGE OF HISTORY MAKES BETTER POLICY

Deborah Lipstedt. History, he concedes, may be an uncertain form of inquiry, in which rival value systems and limited knowledge influence the investigator's conclusions, but it is not so uncertain that some propositions, such as that Hitler bore no responsibility for the Holocaust, cannot be objectively ruled out.[15] Like many other historians, Evans sought a middling position that acknowledged the contingency of historical inquiry but upheld its powerful probative value.

Telling the truth about history becomes more onerous in an era of 'alternative facts' and 'fake news'. Academic history was shaped by the assumptions and protocols of a civic realm where opinion was tested by evidence and robust public debate. But as the channels of communication have multiplied, the sources of reliable information have shrunk along with the civic space for reasoned debate. Myths and lies – medical, religious, political and historical – circulate on the wild frontier of cyberspace, apparently unchecked by evidence or reasoned debate. 'Honest History', the website 'supporting balanced and honest history' created by David Stephens, Peter Stanley and their Canberra colleagues, is a valiant local attempt to wrestle this rampaging Goliath to the ground.[16]

When they lost faith in grand narratives of emancipation and progress, historians often turned to the past, either for consolation, or, increasingly, to settle accounts with its victims. In Australia, where the sins of the past were grievous and long buried, that task has been especially pertinent and burdensome. Australian historians have led the still-unfinished task of reckoning with the colonial legacy of dispossession, murder and exploitation of the First Peoples. 'Truth-telling' – one of the three main themes of the Uluru Statement from the Heart – is also the title of a recent book by Henry Reynolds (NewSouth,

2021), who has devoted his 40-year career to the historical encounter between the European and Aboriginal people.[17]

According to the Uluru Statement, telling the truth about the past is a prerequisite for healing, reconciliation and restitution in the present.[18] Only when we know the truth, will we all – Black and White – be truly free. This assumption shapes other narratives of 'truth and reconciliation', such as the victim statements given in court proceedings or the pursuit of 'historical' cases of child abuse or sexual exploitation. Academic historians continue to play a significant role in these inquiries, although the bigger challenge may be to persuade other Australians of the truth of what is already well known. There is a risk, moreover, when the truths are hard, that telling them may reinforce fatalism rather than hope. Henry Reynolds is well aware of this trap and in celebrating the heroes of the 'First Land Rights Movement' – the humanitarian reformers of the early nineteenth century – he lays a foundation for a narrative of hope.[19]

Telling the history of the future: Hugh Stretton

Our overdue reckoning with the sins of the past cannot absolve historians from thinking about the challenges of the future. We are aware – perhaps more conscious than any recent generation – that we live in turbulent times. What can historians contribute to the task of navigating them? The twentieth century taught us the hazards of attempting to predict the future from the past; yet policies made in ignorance of the past are surely even more hazardous. Modern managers were often explicitly trained to root out institutional memory.[20] Is there a middle path that acknowledges the perils of hindsight, the uncertainty of historical knowledge and the burdens of the past, yet enables us to play a constructive, as well as a critical, role in policy debates?

No Australian historian has thought as deeply about these questions as Hugh Stretton (1924–2015).[21] He was regarded in his time as one of Australia's leading public intellectuals and a social democratic thinker of international stature. With the rise of neoliberalism, his reputation declined. Now, as COVID-19 and climate change challenge the neoliberal paradigms that have governed public policy for the past 40 years, his writings may attract renewed interest.

Stretton was born and educated in Melbourne and served in the Australian Navy during the Second World War before winning a Rhodes Scholarship to study history at Balliol College, Oxford. 'It is the more immediate and material function of history to make ready the tests and lessons of the past for application to the problems of the future', he wrote in his scholarship application. 'I learn what I can of the history of ancient and modern civilisations so that I may better understand the tasks that lie ahead of my generation in the troubled and perilous future.'[22] This high-minded declaration was no platitude. His father, Judge Leonard Stretton, had demonstrated the perils of historical amnesia in a famous Royal Commissioner's report on the 1939 bushfires. Hugh's interest was further stimulated by his studies at Melbourne University, where his teacher Max Crawford's 1946 paper 'History as a Science' became a lively subject of debate.

In Oxford, Stretton was an academic star, winning a college fellowship even before he sat his final examinations. He respected some Oxford historians but they did not share his urgent interest in the political uses of history. In 1954, aged just 30, he returned to Australia as Professor of History at the University of Adelaide. He had not written a doctoral thesis, entered an archive or published a history monograph. Only in his forties did he begin to publish, and then not history books but a series of strikingly original works on social philosophy and urban planning, such as *The Political Sciences* (1969), *Ideas for Australian Cities* (1970), *Capitalism, Socialism and the Environment* (1976), *Urban Planning in Rich and Poor Countries* (1978) and (his final book) a mammoth textbook titled *Economics: A New Introduction* (2015). Many readers may not have guessed he was a historian. Even Stretton himself sometimes doubted it. Yet, from first to last, his thinking about public policy was deeply historical. He was not a policy wonk who taught history on the side; everything he wrote about public policy drew on his understanding of history.

In 1992 Stretton accepted an invitation to address the 'Ideas Summit' in Canberra convened by his friend Donald Horne in an effort to lift the quality of public debate. He took the opportunity to advocate the value of history for policymakers. Three qualities, scarce in modern social science, were characteristic of history: it was holistic, uncertain and eclectic.

> Who study societies of every kind, study them whole, know most about how they conserve or change their ideas and institutions, write in plain language, and generally know how uncertain and selective their knowledge is at best? Historians do. Their vocation is – roughly speaking – to give as good foundation as scholarship can to the kind of selective-but-holistic discourse about society that politicians, public servants, journalists and citizens use every day to arrive at their political judgments and

policies. We should stop tagging historians as the people who study the dead past, and see them as the people who do their best — at whatever cost in certainty and precision — to study how whole societies conserve and change their social life.[23]

The value of studying history, Stretton suggests, is not in the specific information it imparts, or even the analogies it offers with contemporary problems, but something more elusive: a way of reasoning, an intellectual style, a trained capacity to think about problems in a distinctive way. His students were not trained to become cogs in an economic or political machine. They had acquired something more valuable, an ability to think historically about the future.

History and planning, Stretton argued, are kindred activities. In explaining events in the past, we employ a similar combination of values and skills that we can apply in planning the future. History is a corrective to narrowly technical approaches to planning. In telling us how things came to be, it illuminates the taken-for-granted, and potentially changeable, assumptions behind our way of life. By reviewing the chains of historical causation, it gives us a grasp of the complex, and often unforeseen, interactions between facets of society often studied separately. It illuminates the causes and effects of policies and decisions that seemed sound at the time but turned out to be flawed. It attends to the importance of different time scales in the process of planning. And it tells us something of what the present owes to the past and, in turn, what it might owe to the future.

Stretton's boldest experiments in applying history to public policy took the form of scenarios — attempts to foresee the consequences of different policy choices by constructing imaginary, but realistic, narratives of their outworking. In the final chapter of his *Political Essays* (1987) he writes: 'A long utopian tradition teaches that the best way to look forward is to look back. To foretell futures, set yourself a generation or a century ahead and tell your future as histories.'[24] He first attempted such scenarios in *Capitalism, Socialism and the Environment*. The book appeared in 1976, in the aftermath of the oil price hike, as policymakers were debating how to deal with the likely rapid depletion of oil and other natural resources, but well before awareness of climate change deepened the sense of crisis. Which policies – far right, moderate right or moderate left – were likely to produce the best outcomes for different classes and for society as a whole? His scenarios, he emphasised, were not predictions, or even good fictions. 'But they start from here and now and try to deal in real types of social interest and conflict and realistic mechanisms of historical change … This is a useful way to judge programs. If the history which seems to be required to fulfill a program is implausible, that may prompt second thoughts about the program.'[25] Because you can't foresee everything, he suggests, it doesn't mean that you shouldn't try to foresee as much as you can. If you want an example of the folly of a policy without a plan, look no further than Brexit. Only when the referendum passed did it become apparent how little consideration its supporters had given to the obstacles in their path.

After the longest period of peace and prosperity in the history of the planet, once again we face a 'troubled and perilous future'. A season of catastrophic bushfires, more terrifying even than those of 1939 and 2009, brought home the perils of climate change for the inhabitants of the driest continent over the summer of 2019–20. Inverting the history of seventeenth-century London, fire was followed by plague, a global pandemic whose end is not yet in sight as I write. Simultaneously, tectonic changes in the global balance of power have unsettled Australia's external security. As they grapple with the consequences of these events, politicians and journalists often reach for the word which topped the *Australian National Dictionary*'s 2020 popularity poll: we are living, they say, in 'unprecedented times'. Historians may quibble. Yes, indeed, there are features of this virus, and these historical circumstances, that are new, but not so new that the past has nothing to teach us.

Lessons from history: Thinking historically about the future

How might historians, following Stretton's lead, contribute to policies for a post-COVID-19 Australia? 'We need history because some things cannot be recognised as they happen,' Tom Griffiths shrewdly remarks.[26] We are more likely to recognise where we are, and what we are up against, if we place ourselves in historical perspective. In the first phase of the pandemic, many people hoped that the plague would quickly pass and our world would simply 'snap back' to 2019. The longer it continues, and the more its costs accumulate, the less likely that seems. Already it has lasted twice as long as the 1919 Spanish flu and, while the mortality in Australia is barely one-quarter of the previous pandemic, its impact on our more mobile, affluent and globally connected society is likely to be more enduring. If the country escaped relatively lightly during the first phase of this pandemic, it was because of historical advantages also apparent in 1919: strong borders (our restrictive immigration and quarantine policies sprang from a common root) and a utilitarian rather than libertarian approach to public health policy. Most of the conflicts that appeared in 2020–21 – between the Commonwealth and the states, hard and soft quarantine, rich and poor suburbs – also occurred in 1918. But there were big differences too: the Spanish flu killed more young people, there was no effective vaccine and – crucially – their protected agricultural–manufacturing economy was less vulnerable to shocks than our open trading service-oriented economy.

In 2006–2007, in anticipation of a future influenza pandemic, the distinguished American medical historian Howard Markel and his colleagues undertook a study of the effectiveness of the non-pharmaceutical interventions in the 1918 pandemic.[27] During the first phase of the COVID-19 pandemic, journalists and public officials often turned to Markel for advice. But by 2021, with the arrival of the Delta strain, and growing resistance to traditional public health measures, Markel had concluded that the lessons of 1918 were exhausted. 'We need to stop thinking back to 1918 as a guide to how to act in the future,' he warned. '*This* is the pandemic I will be studying and teaching to the next generation of doctors and public health officials.' His change of mind appeared in *The Atlantic* review under the title 'History Won't Help Us Now'.[28] Yet Markel was not abandoning history at all, but simply recognising that COVID-19 was now part of it. As the past changes, so must our histories, and so will their lessons.

For a stimulating example of someone thinking historically about a post-COVID-19 future, I recommend Janet McCalman's essay 'It's possible' (2020). In 1945, McCalman reminds us, Australia and the world faced a future scarcely less 'troubled and perilous' than our own: millions of people dead, displaced, homeless and unemployed, many of the cities and economies of Europe in ruins, and over all the looming global threat of nuclear war. Yet, as we know now, ordinary people were on the threshold of the most remarkable period of prosperity in the history of the planet. What saved them was the heroic work of national and international reconstruction undertaken by the Attlee administration in Britain, the Curtin and Chifley governments in Australia and by the international agencies. 'This story is important to retell,' says McCalman, 'because it gives us hope and a model.'[29] COVID-19 has suddenly forced governments to abandon financial austerity and assume larger responsibilities for public health and welfare – might they now 'return' to something like the ambitions and values of postwar reconstruction? McCalman's narrative of hope is something like one of Hugh Stretton's scenarios – a vision of a better future inspired and informed by history.[30]

History and historians have a critical part to play in the conversation about what comes next. The past may be a different country, but not so foreign that it has no lessons for us. Critical reflection on the paths we have followed in the past is essential if we are to think beyond the straightjacket of current policy choices. Occasionally historians will be in the room where the big decisions are made. Much more often they will write the books and lead the debates that shape the politicians' and policymakers' thinking. As Hugh Stretton recognised, it may be more important for historians to educate the decision-makers to think historically than to participate in the decisions themselves.

CHAPTER 2

Learning the right lessons?
Two policy stories

Frank Bongiorno

Can historians influence policy? Should they? And, if so, what kinds of historical knowledge should they produce?

Those who make policy perhaps only rarely think of historians as a first port of call when seeking the expertise that might guide them. And historians, for their part, do not often have policymakers in mind as a primary audience, even when their subject is the history of public policy. But historians in Australia – as elsewhere – have long been involved in policy debate. Some of the very earliest histories of Australia – written from around 1820 – were intended to influence British policy towards the colonies.[1] University-trained academics and teachers have also provided such commentary, sometimes amid considerable controversy, such as the early professor of history at the University of Sydney, George Arnold Wood, opposing the British Empire's participation in the South African War (1899–1902).[2] But there are traps for historians: their kind of knowledge does not usually form a solid basis for solving the problems of the present or predicting the future. Interpreting the past might offer clues and insights, but it does not normally present clear lessons that can be mechanically applied by policymakers to a present-day problem. Historians who have managed to delude themselves that it does have sometimes damaged both their own reputations and, where they have been sufficiently prominent, the standing of the profession as a whole.

The most dangerous trap for those who seek to use history in the context of policy is the taste for simple explanations of complex processes. History is a contextualising discipline: when we seek to explain the thoughts and actions of the past, we immediately search for those contexts that are most likely to be helpful in offering a convincing account of how and why something happened. Historians know that policy actors – indeed, any actors – make their choices from a relatively limited range of possibilities shaped by the past: social scientists call this 'path dependency'. To explore the limited nature of that range, and why one course might be selected over another, is to examine context and its influence.

Historians have also long understood the shadow that often falls between motivation and intention, on the one hand, and outcomes and consequences, on the other. Again, this kind of inquiry depends on an appreciation of context: that when actions have been undertaken in certain circumstances, they have produced one set of results rather than some other, whatever the motivations or goals of those concerned. These are essential aspects of historical thinking. And they are ways of understanding the world that are potentially useful in a range of decision-making situations. But historians should not deceive themselves that this is how everyone thinks: if it were, we should not need to worry over historical literacy, or how history is taught in schools, or the lack of institutional memory in our institutions.[3]

Appeals to history have been central to political contestation in Australia. Such appeals often express the interests of particular classes or groups, but the place of history in such debate raises ethical responsibilities for professional historians. Frequently the priorities of political actors and historians have been brought into tension, with history misused in policy debate. Two recurring examples illustrate this well. One is the allegation that Australia's economic decline in the twentieth century was caused by an interventionist state which the governments of the 1980s and 1990s reversed. The other is the failure of appeasement in relation to the Second World War, which has provided enduring lessons for Australian policymakers in their decisions about war and peace. In both examples, professional historians have produced careful and accessible research on the issues at stake. And yet in each instance, simplistic and decontextualised understandings have been circulated within media, think tanks and government, with little or no regard for evidentially based historical research. This is not a happy story for historians; it suggests that their careful scene-setting and qualified conclusions are poor instruments for challenging deeply entrenched myth. Whereas academic economists and political scientists have been able to produce, from their complex research, relatively simple and digestible ideas with deep influence on policymaking, historians generally do not produce this kind of knowledge. The historian's obligation to evidence-based inquiry and truth-telling often stands in stark contrast to the standards observed in the wider public sphere.

The changing fortunes of a rich country

The idea that Australia, probably the richest country in the world in the second half of the nineteenth century, went into economic decline in the twentieth because of excessive government economic interference is much more than a simplistic reading of the nation's economic history. It is integral to the identity of much of the modern Australian political class. The thesis has its more thoughtful proponents as well as its thoughtless ones, and it has its hard-line advocates on the free-market libertarian right along with proponents among those who would consider themselves social democrats. It is also arguably the dominant public narrative, which is disturbing given how poorly it is supported by historical scholarship.

A thesis with such political buttressing is not liable to easy displacement by academic research because it evidently serves a range of political and economic interests, and functions as a component of identity among people with formidable power. The inference to be drawn from their story of the past is that free markets create prosperity, countries should concentrate on their 'comparative advantage', and 'open' economies and societies are the key to progress, freedom and peace. Geoffrey Blainey, with a sceptical eye on some of its assumptions, has called it 'the Manchester creed', since the ideas are most closely associated with that great industrial city, and with nineteenth-century English liberalism in its classical form.[4]

How has such an interpretation been circulated in Australia? Its best-known expression in modern Australian writing came packaged in 'The Australian Settlement', a term coined by the journalist Paul Kelly in his book *The End of Certainty: The story of the 1980s* (1992). Kelly used the phrase to describe the major policies adopted in the early years of the Australian federation – a framework, he suggested, that survived until the last third of the twentieth century. These policies were the White Australia policy, Tariff Protection, Wage Arbitration, State Paternalism and Imperial Benevolence. Importantly, Kelly believed that their adoption was a wrong turn; Australia's economic decline in the twentieth century was the result of the flawed policies embraced in the early Commonwealth.[5]

In this understanding of Australia's political economy, Free Trade Party Prime Minister, George Reid, rather than the Protectionist, Alfred Deakin, was the hero. But in the arguments taken up by think tanks such as the Centre for Independent Studies and the Institute of Public Affairs, and intellectuals, columnists and publicists further to the right than Kelly was in the early 1990s, there is movement towards the political fringes of Australian history. In the 1980s, a right-wing industrial relations ginger group called itself the H.R. Nicholls Society in honour of a Tasmanian newspaper editor, Henry Nicholls, who was charged with contempt of court for his criticisms of the early Arbitration Court judge H.B. Higgins, a hated figure among Australia's modern free-market right because of his pioneering of the living wage and award system.[6] Bruce Smith, a minor figure in the history of the early Commonwealth, almost alone as a critic of the White Australia policy in the first federal parliament, and an extreme libertarian in his economic ideas, has been elevated to a heroic status among proponents of the anti-Deakinite interpretation of Australian policy history. Other heroes include Edward Shann, a former socialist who published an economic history of Australia in 1930 condemning the many departures of Australia's economic policy from a properly free-market course, and Bert Kelly, an energetic parliamentary critic of Australia's policy of protectionism through the 1960s and 1970s.[7]

Professional economic historians have not enthusiastically endorsed this interpretation of Australian history. They have generally understood economic prosperity as shaped by a range of influences; government decision-making forms only part of the story. Their comparative perspectives disclose that the state has often played a major role in shaping economic development in mixed economies. They are aware that decision-makers have had to choose from among a limited range of possibilities; that the choice was never simply between a free market, on the one hand, and state intervention, on the other, or between 'efficient' rural enterprise and 'inefficient' manufacturing. No Australian government ever faced such stark alternatives.

The work of economic historians such as Ian W. McLean suggests that after the 1840s, an economy based on pastoralism – mainly wool-growing – would not have been capable of sustaining rising living standards for the settler population in the way it had before. Based fundamentally on the seizure of land from Aboriginal people, and sometimes also drawing on their labour, the pastoral economy could generate large profits, but it was less capable of sharing wealth around or stimulating other economic activities. The gold rushes came just in time to provide the basis for population growth and economic diversification. Australia's new land laws and new democratic institutions were part of the story of Australia's rising prosperity: they ensured enough sharing of land to establish the family farm as central to the rural economy, but not so much as to strangle older, larger and more lucrative pastoral enterprises. Population growth, political stability and economic optimism also stimulated urbanisation, construction, manufacturing, services and borrowing. This order came crashing down in the 1890s, and Australia's experience of depression and drought brought what had possibly been the wealthiest people in the world back to the field.[8]

In the twentieth century, Australia industrialised partly in response to this series of shocks, which had exposed the country's vulnerability to capital flight and plunging commodity prices. An industrial economy would create a more stable prosperity: it was equated with modernity and was necessary for security. Australians also mostly agreed that a larger white – and predominantly British – population was essential to keeping the continent out of the hands of supposedly covetous Asians. Finally, a consumer-based and more diverse economy created demand that could only be satisfied through a mixture of imported and locally made goods. Governments used various forms of state intervention to develop such an economic order, including tariffs to help manufacturers, subsidies for farmers, government factories to promote defence industry, authorities to produce power, manage water and run transport, and minimum wages and modest social security to support the working class.[9]

Australia created these arrangements over about 50 years between 1895 and 1945 that saw global crises – depressions and wars – on an unprecedented scale. Governments around the world – including even famously free-trade Britain itself – responded to the economic instability of the interwar years by resorting to tariffs and other economic controls. Businesses responded through mergers that reduced competition. In the real world of decision-making, Australian governments were powerfully constrained by the force of the past and the present contexts in which they operated. They increased protection in the early 1920s to ensure that industries which grew up under the natural protection of the war would not die, and the jobs they had created along with them. They increased protection in the early 1930s to reduce the gap between what Australia was earning by selling its goods to the world, and what it was paying to buy imported goods and to cover the interest charges from its debts. Other borrowing and trading countries were doing much the same, in a process of mutual infliction of harm all round. At every stage, government decision-making about the economy was influenced by the information available to it, the political feasibility of various courses of action, and the limited choices presented by what decision-makers had inherited from the past. Furthermore, the economy itself was only ever partly amenable to these state interventions because it was overwhelmingly shaped by the forces of global capitalism and Australia's place, as a relatively small economy, in that order.[10] Such explanations, drawing on the best economic theory and economic history research, make explanations of economic decline based on high tariffs or wage regulation look as facile as they are.

In most tellings, the story of Australia's supposed economic failure in the twentieth century has a happy ending. In the 1980s, a far-seeing group of politicians, wise public servants, responsible unionists and business leaders, and economically literate journalists rescued the country from this descent into economic squalor, from the status of what Singaporean Prime Minister Lee Kuan Yew called 'the poor white trash of Asia'. This is a genuinely bipartisan political legend: the Labor government of Bob Hawke was supposedly supported every step of the way by the opposition of the day, with John Howard in particular being a great enthusiast. When his time as prime minister came, Howard continued this historic work of reform, if not quite at the same pace or with the same panache as Bob Hawke and Paul Keating.[11] At least until the Global Financial Crisis (GFC) of 2008, Australia's rising prosperity was attributed to the market reforms of the 1980s and 1990s – called economic rationalism at the time and now more commonly neoliberalism. As Carolyn Holbrook and James Walter have remarked, this became 'the received history of the 1980s and 1990s … a story of remarkable success'.[12]

When a story of the past so obviously affirms the positive self-image of those telling it, there are good reasons for caution. Holbrook and Walter have themselves pointed to the narrow focus of the celebratory narrative – it tends to be preoccupied with matters of economic management such as the floating of the dollar and the winding back of tariffs. It is little concerned with unintended consequences of action: for instance, that policies designed to transform and reinvigorate manufacturing had limited success; despite a desire to move away from dependence on commodity exports, Australia ended up as Asia's quarry anyway. It remains remarkable that the massive scale of financial losses experienced by both state and private banks, the corporate collapses, and the devastating recession of the early 1990s are so tenuously linked in cheery stories of the era to economic decisions of government. The stories of reform 'success' and economic 'failure' run along separate tracks: alternatively, the 1990s recession, which ended the working lives of many Australians prematurely, is absorbed into the happy story of how Australia conquered inflation.[13]

Neither is the declining trust in politics, including the turn away from the major parties to minor parties and independents, conventionally linked to the economic order that emerged from these years. Reduced federal government capacity is bemoaned when it results in a failure to deliver an efficient vaccination system in the middle of the worst pandemic for a century, yet such failures are rarely attributed to ideologies and policies of the 1980s and 1990s that deliberately wound back the state on the grounds that it was the role of the 'efficient' market rather than 'inefficient' government to meet most of people's needs. The GFC did, however, lead to some reassessment of this narrative, with the Labor prime minister of the day, Kevin Rudd, declaring the age of neoliberalism over, while even some of the principal architects of those policies on the Labor side, Keating included, have recognised the redundancy of the neoliberalism they ushered in.[14]

A narrative such as this can only work by omission, by a calculated forgetting. It ignores the ambivalence and even hostility that greeted many of the policies of the era. The story that is told is really one about the policymakers themselves: the people on whom they acted barely figure. When the veteran journalist Kerry O'Brien asked Paul Keating in an interview for a TV series and book about those whose jobs were forever wiped out by industry restructuring under Labor: 'And do you know what they found?' Keating answered, 'A better job a week later, in a growing economy with big employment growth'. 'You make it sound so simple', countered a sceptical O'Brien.[15]

It is context that is perhaps the gravest omission from the reform narratives. Again, McLean is helpful here: the reason for the shift in policy in the 1980s was that the economic costs of the more inwardly focused, industrially based strategy of the earlier part of the century had, since the end of the long boom especially, come to outweigh the benefits. It was not because there was some earlier 'wrong turn'. Rather, taking into consideration the unfavourable global circumstances of the first half of the century, with its slow growth, barriers to trade, currency instability and two world wars, 'the pursuit of a policy of economic diversification emphasizing an expansion in manufacturing was a defensible choice'. There is no evidence, McLean suggests, that living standards would have been higher if governments had not resorted to protection to promote such industrial growth. By the 1980s, however, there were greater benefits to be delivered by a more open trading order with an Asian orientation. Government acted accordingly.[16] Here, McLean promotes historical thinking informed by economic theory. It is the kind of insight infrequently encountered in Australian policy debate which is dominated, in these matters, by economists and policy specialists with a heavy investment in the 1980s reform narrative.

The long shadow of the Munich narrative

The failure of the policy of appeasing Hitler in the 1930s has been a favourite among politicians wishing to make war ever since. In this story, Neville Chamberlain is a villain because he favoured concessions to Nazi Germany in a vain effort to achieve 'peace in our time'. He is supported by 'the guilty men' who supported the Munich Agreement of 1938, which both betrayed Czechoslovakia and encouraged the next fateful step: the invasion of Poland the following year. Winston Churchill, as an opponent of such policies, is seen as a far-seeing prophet and then as a heroic national leader. It is the stuff of Hollywood, all there in the melodrama of a film such as *Darkest Hour* (2017).

Seemingly harmless when providing such entertainment, this telling has arguably been the costliest instance of historical illiteracy in the modern world. Its example stretches from Korea in 1950 and the Suez crisis of 1956 through the Vietnam War in the 1960s, down to the 'war on terror' and its manifestations in Afghanistan and Iraq. In each instance, 'Munich' is treated as the ultimate 'symbol of weakness in the face of aggression'.[17] But as Margaret Macmillan has shown, the problem with historical analogy of this kind is that policymakers will not necessarily appeal to the most relevant or illuminating analogy.[18] Political leaders use the example of Munich selectively and opportunistically. The United States did not exercise its military power in support of Hungary in 1956, Czechoslovakia in 1968 or Afghanistan in 1980, yet the customary crude reading of Munich should have dictated military intervention in each case against the Soviet Union. In reality, the United States was constrained by its appreciation of the Cold War rules of engagement and its balance of power with the Soviets. Historians have important work to perform in exposing this opportunism, as well as in explaining the contexts that gave rise to appeasement in the 1930s, and the very different contexts that decision-makers have faced in the lead-up to every other conflict since. As Macmillan points out, 'We can learn from history, but we also deceive ourselves when we selectively take evidence from the past to justify what we have already made up our minds to do.'[19]

A good example of the abuse of the appeasement example occurred in Australia in 2005, when the Australian Foreign Minister Alexander Downer presented the Earle Page Annual Lecture at the University of New England in Armidale. The lecture, written by the Adelaide conservative Christopher Pearson, was delivered at a time when Australia had forces in both Afghanistan and Iraq. The Iraq War, in particular, had become unpopular. The case that it was a grand struggle against a dangerous global threat had collapsed when it became clear that governments had misused intelligence about weapons of mass destruction to justify their intervention against Saddam Hussein. Proponents of war had used the Munich/Hitler analogy. By 2005, however, the gloss was gone. No weapons had been found. American 'liberators' had been exposed as brutally humiliating their captives in an Iraqi prison. Iraq had run an election but was also descending into a morass of sectarian violence and deadly terrorism.

As a consequence, it was more than ever necessary for the 'coalition of the willing' to present the war on terror, in Iraq and elsewhere, as, in Downer's words, a 'great struggle … between freedom and terror and its totalitarian ideology', the descendant of previous great struggles such as that against Hitler in the Second World War. Downer's purpose was also more narrowly partisan: he wanted to contrast the Coalition as a party of duty and principle, prepared to resist tyranny and defend liberty, and the Labor Party, with its record of 'weak leadership' on 'appeasement, isolationism and shirking international treaty obligations'. And Downer wanted to present Labor as a party of weakness in 1938, no less than in 2005.[20]

The principal objection to Downer's understanding of history might simply be that it is wrong, and not in a disinterested way, for it is also designed to advance a partisan cause. As Christopher Waters has shown in his study of Australia and appeasement, the United Australia Party and Country Party in the 1930s were full of staunch advocates of appeasement. All the major Australian leaders – Joseph Lyons, Robert Menzies, Richard Casey, Earle Page and former prime minister and present high commissioner in London, Stanley Melbourne

Bruce – strongly opposed war in 1938 over the Munich crisis. Even some days after Hitler's invasion of Poland in September 1939, Menzies remained unconvinced that it was worth going to war with Germany and hoped for a negotiated peace. All these figures could not have bent any further backwards to see the developing European crisis from a viewpoint sympathetic to Germany's grievances.[21]

These attitudes might have often veered towards cynicism where they were not deliberately dishonest, but they are also comprehensible in view of the circumstances of the time. The desire to avoid another war was intense. Casey, Bruce and Page had all served in the previous one. The Australian government feared Japan, whom it also tried to appease, and worried that a German challenge to the United Kingdom would undermine the British Empire's ability to protect its colonies and dominions in the Far East and Pacific. Labor leader John Curtin – like Lyons, a First World War anti-conscriptionist – and members of his party were not so much appeasers as isolationists, wishing to keep Australia clear of a war in Europe. On Japan, Curtin's views arguably did approach appeasement in the months before Pearl Harbor, but his attitude and approach were hardly distinguishable from those of Menzies. Sensibly, neither wanted a war in the Pacific against Japan if it did not also involve the United States.[22]

Such contexts and nuances are, of course, of no interest to a foreign minister wishing to score points against his opponents. Nor do I doubt for a moment that historians have an uphill struggle in countering the Munich analogy. To win this argument would also mean vanquishing the Churchill cult, an unlikely prospect.

Lessons from history and a usable past

Our only hope in the struggle to prevent the misuse of the past in these ways might be to work to increase historical literacy from the ground up, from cradle to grave – certainly from school through workplace to retirement village. And the most critical capacity that we need to develop is the ability of the decision-makers, and those in the media, think tanks and bureaucracy who most influence them, to draw nuanced historical lessons informed by a sense of context. This will not be an easy task because there is limited taste for knowledge that recognises its own limitations and uncertainties. Too many politicians demand a readily usable past that can be slotted into ready-made categories of their own devising.

The quest for historical literacy will also demand resistance to the injunctions of conservative education ministers for a history curriculum that reflects their own ideology, rather than the best historical scholarship available. It may well require historians to rethink the media through which they work: the highly specialised article in a top-ranked international journal sitting behind a paywall, beloved of university beancounters, may well be less significant than the high-quality school textbook. At the very least, we need to ensure that there are avenues of transmission and communication between the one and the other, as well as between the historical profession and policymakers. We must never cease to be ourselves, but nor do historians have the luxury of being able to shut out a world that they have a deep professional and moral obligation to interpret, as well as to change.

CHAPTER 3

Historians: Bridging the divide with policymakers

James Walter

History is never far removed from the political sphere. Politicians routinely draw on historical analogies to justify a position or argument. Sometimes, they indulge in extensive, competitive debates about Australian history, as in the contentious 'history wars' of the 1980s and 1990s, in which Paul Keating and John Howard were principal players.[1] At other times, a period or philosophy will be rewritten by the politically engaged, or iconic figures reinterpreted – the refiguring of the 1950s, the recent new biographies of Robert Menzies, or the reinterpretation of Australian liberalism (by David Kemp), for example.[2]

The link between mainstream politics and policy formulation depends upon policy professionals – public servants, advisers and consultants. They too, periodically refer to lessons from the past to address problems of the present. Revisiting previous depressions and recessions in formulating successful responses to the Global Financial Crisis (GFC) of 2007–2010, for instance; experience which in turn influenced responses to the 2020 pandemic.[3]

Professional historians also sometimes feel compelled to enter the political fray, deploying their expertise to promote a position about which they feel strongly, embarking on projects intended to influence public consciousness and shift the political register. This chapter deals with historians who are so inclined. But when historians engage in the political sphere – moving from research and analysis to advocacy and influence – their effectiveness depends upon recognition of the distinctive differences in modes of work, institutional constraints and expectations in the political, policy and historical domains.

Political need versus historical inquiry

Harold Lasswell once defined the core question of political science as 'who gets what, when and how?'[4] For politicians, this means, how are such issues to be determined, to my government's advantage? As a result, the question is always framed not only in relation to expressions of public demand, but also by partisan preferences, as other chapters in this collection demonstrate, and the overriding imperative: staying in power. For their policy intermediaries – bureaucrats, advisers and others – the task is to identify how to achieve those ends and implement them once decisions are made. Timelines are short; the need is immediate: to meet promises made in the last election campaign, and to contribute to a commanding position in the next.

Historians, however, ask different questions: who did what, when and why? Their perspective on time is entirely different from that of a politician: rarely contemporary, and long term rather than immediate. The historian is driven by curiosity; the work of a politician or policy adviser is driven by need. The logic of historical inquiry is at odds with the logic of politics and policy.[5] Academic historical projects are often constrained by grant stipulations, and continuous publication expectations are pressing, but historians think in terms of years rather than deadlines of weeks or months. Their professional experience, then, is not well suited to devising research oriented to current policy objectives, even if asked. If invited to operate 'inside the tent', they would encounter alien working conditions, as some, such as James Button and Dennis Glover, testify.[6]

Historians working 'inside the tent'

Despite these obstacles, some do manage to bridge that divide. Feminist historians, such as Kay Daniels, Miriam Dixson, Beverley Kingston and Anne Summers, posed the penetrating questions that some of their peers, such as Elizabeth Reid and Sarah Dowse, simultaneously took forward into governmental roles in the 1970s and 1980s.[7] In the reform period that followed, they learned to adapt the language of feminist reform to the managerial, neoliberal expectations of the time.[8]

Flowing from her pioneering contribution as a feminist historian, Daniels was appointed by Susan Ryan (then Minister for Education) in 1984 as full-time chair of the Committee to Review Australian Studies in Higher Education, which reported in 1987.[9] Her fellow commissioners were an historian, Humphrey McQueen, and a literary scholar with Australian Studies interests, Bruce Bennett. The committee recommended the incorporation of Australian content across the curriculum, not just the development of a specialist field. Australian Studies flourished in the 1980s and 1990s. In that period it influenced curriculum developments, and effected some institutional change, with the establishment of centres at some universities (including a government-funded National Centre at Monash University) and a few, with government support, abroad (at

Harvard, the University of London and Georgetown). By the early 2000s the momentum had flagged.

The careers of professional historians who went on to influential roles in government should be acknowledged. Daniels herself, 'a natural networker', was appointed in 1989 to a senior position in the Department of Communications and the Arts, where she provided intellectual leadership in cultural policy, intellectual property and moral rights, and Indigenous rights.[10] Peter Shergold, an economic historian whose academic career was interrupted by an invitation to serve in government, eventually rose to the top of the Australian Public Service (APS), as Secretary of Prime Minister and Cabinet (PM&C). His talent for bureaucracy was complemented by an historian's insistence on evidence-based argument, enabling him to persuade a reluctant John Howard and his cabinet to support climate emission measures.[11] After leaving the APS, arguably Shergold's work as Coordinator General for Refugee Resettlement in NSW was informed by his earlier experience as an economic historian who had explored settlement patterns.[12] Don Watson, in his remarkable account of working as a speechwriter in Paul Keating's prime ministerial office, has provided perhaps the most extensive testimony of a historian working 'inside the tent'.[13] Inevitably, it provoked an extensive reply from Keating, who objected to Watson's revelations, and disputed his contribution to some of Keating's most influential statements.[14] Yet, despite the subsequent debate over authorship, Watson's research into the tragedy of settler history for Indigenous nations was undoubtedly the fount on which Keating's famous Redfern speech drew.[15]

While these instances provide examples which readers find illuminating, most historians will never be so closely engaged.

For to step inside the tent is a significant diversion from historical research, at which career-oriented professionals may baulk (though, as Watson has demonstrated, it is possible to return).[16] The question for historians, then, is one of how to establish, for political practitioners, the relevance of history as a substantial contribution to contemporary policy and political debate.

Achieving influence from outside the tent

At one level, the work can be educative, and directed to relationship building – such as the Australian Academy of the Humanities' periodic organisation of meetings between politicians and academics, or the Academy of the Social Sciences in Australia's 'The Social Sciences Shape the Nation' project, identifying the contributions of social scientists (including historians) to key social policy initiatives over decades, or the engagement of historians in parliamentary inquiries, such as a recent Senate Committee Inquiry into 'Nationhood, national identity and democracy'.[17] It remains difficult to ascertain how much influence such exercises have on what is subsequently done, but all research on public policy efficacy maintains that relationship building is a core objective.[18]

Investing in relationships

Relationships were integral to a further educational initiative in which, like the earlier Australian Studies exercise, much hope was invested in the 1990s: the Civics Expert Group, and its successor, the Civics Education Group, each led by an historian, Stuart Macintyre and John Hirst respectively. Neither of these worked 'inside the tent'. Instead, Macintyre and Hirst served to link political concern and historical inquiry. Nonetheless, the initial civics group had a secretariat within PM&C, and strong support from then prime minister Paul Keating, with whom Macintyre had established a connection. Concern about a perceived diminution in social cohesion and deficiencies in civic knowledge had been flagged by the Senate Standing Committee for Employment, Education and Training in 1989 and 1992.[19] At the same time Macintyre, who was friendly with a number of Labor politicians, presented an Academy Lecture, 'Rethinking Australian Citizenship'.[20]

In early 1994, Macintyre submitted a short paper to then prime minister Keating arguing that our schools were neglecting civics education. Two months later he was appointed by Keating to chair the Civics Expert Group, with educationists Ken Boston and Susan Pascoe. Macintyre discussed the work of the Civics Expert Group and its report, delivered in December 1994, in a later essay, 'An Expert's Confession'.[21] Before much was achieved in implementing its recommendations, a change to Coalition government in 1996 entailed a new direction, with the group retitled the Civics Education Group, charged with developing curriculum materials, now chaired by John Hirst, and reporting to the Liberal Minister for Education, David Kemp – himself a former academic and, following his political career, a prolific contributor to the history of Australian liberalism.[22] Whereas the earlier report identified means to promote civic awareness, recognition of rights and responsibilities, and institutional knowledge as a foundation for active citizenship, the Civics Education Group presented models of education in Australian democracy, with an emphasis on what were presented as core values – later used by Coalition governments to devise citizenship tests.[23] The outcome was a series of citizenship and civics curriculum materials, and texts of lasting interest, such as Hirst's *Australia's Democracy* and *The Sentimental Nation*.[24] Simultaneously, including citizenship research as a research objective for Australian Research Council grants engendered a brief flourishing of citizenship histories.[25] However, the civics push, as with earlier Australian Studies innovations, proved to be of limited duration – although the question of how citizenship articulates with social cohesion has remained a recurrent concern for governments.[26]

Historians have made a more lasting contribution as expert witnesses in significant political deliberations, such as their participation (along with anthropologists and archaeologists) in the resolution of Indigenous claims to Country. Here, particular outcomes are possible to identify in the success or failure of specific land claims. Further, it is in the field of settler–Indigenous relationships that historians may well have had the most decisive influence on public consciousness, and hence on policy development, as we shall see.

Seizing the moment

Political systems – not only parliaments, parties and civil service agencies, but also the institutionalised ideas generated in a particular historical moment, with lasting effects – are slow to change. The political scientist Alan Davies once talked of the characteristic torpor in Australia's political culture occasionally being disrupted by periods of frenzied reform.[27] Political scientists argue that system equilibrium is the norm, but that this is periodically 'punctuated' by unexpected events or unforeseen consequences of past actions, demanding significant rethinking.[28] Such moments create a 'window' in which new ideas are needed, and reform movements can gain purchase – the conditions for the 'frenzied reform' to which Davies pointed.[29]

We are living in just such an historical moment. For some time, the government-driven neoliberal market reforms of the 1980s and 1990s, in which government is said to have opted for 'steering rather than rowing', have been celebrated as having created the prosperity Australia has enjoyed for decades. Frank Bongiorno explores the fallacies of this heroic narrative in Chapter 2. Yet there has been a growing chorus of dissent, as levels of inequality have increased and casual employment and wage stagnation have undermined faith in the labour market. Further, provision for the welfare of the most disadvantaged has deteriorated; and the promise of privatised monopolies being more agile, cost efficient and responsive to our demands than government bodies, while kept in check by competition and light-touch regulation, has been unrealised.

A decade ago, the GFC was thought by some to augur necessary reform, but neoliberalism appeared so entrenched that politics soon reverted to business as usual – though its critics, including some economists, kept chipping away.[30] Now, however, the COVID-19 pandemic has impelled government action, and economic intervention on such a substantial scale that the relative equilibrium of past decades has been disrupted, opening a window for change *if* proponents of reform can seize the moment. Larry Elliott, a prominent economic columnist in the United Kingdom, argues that the pandemic has made a 20-year-long structural and social crisis so starkly apparent that it may finally put paid to entrenched assumptions, making change imperative: 'if not now, when?'[31] Historians have been quick to respond.

HOW A KNOWLEDGE OF HISTORY MAKES BETTER POLICY

To take one example, Emma Dawson, director of a progressive think tank, and the historian Janet McCalman, commissioned a wide range of contributors from a variety of disciplines (including some politicians) to contribute to *What Happens Next? Reconstructing Australia after COVID-19*, written during the early months of the pandemic.[32] Graeme Davison refers to McCalman's own chapter about the post–Second World War reconstruction project in Chapter 1. The pandemic demanded such a decisive suspension of established conventions that many who had been frustrated when earlier efforts to address the shortcomings of contemporary politics failed to gain purchase, recognised that the moment of disequilibrium presented their opportunity. Though future oriented, their historical impress was strong, with numerous contributors writing from different expert vantages but referring back to, and elaborating upon, the lessons that might be drawn from the transformation of the economy and society achieved in the period of postwar reconstruction. The point was not to suggest that such initiatives could be replicated, but to sketch the varieties of transformative thinking the crises of depression and war had engendered, and to establish that in the face of society-wide catastrophes that threaten us all, such thinking, based on collective action, consensus building and institutional reform, must be revived. Written in a crisp, accessible style, the objective was to reach a wide audience, informing public debate by presenting a positive agenda responsive to public disquiet and uncertainty, that may shift political opinion. We shall see.

Another more immediate-term instance of historians seizing the moment successfully to influence a policy decision was the 2021 campaign, led by journalist Gideon Haigh and Graeme Davison, to secure crucial funding for the National

Archives of Australia (NAA). The NAA had, over many years, been struggling to achieve its mandated objectives as its funding had been incrementally depleted. That it had reached a crisis point was manifest in a review led by former Finance Department secretary, David Tune. Commissioned in 2019, the Tune Review reported in January 2021, and indicated that unless additional funding, estimated at $167.4 million, was provided for digitisation, crucial records would be lost.[33] On releasing the report in March 2021, the government stated that it accepted all of the Tune Review recommendations, but in the ensuing federal budget, no additional funds were provided. One hundred and fifty dismayed researchers, preponderantly historians, immediately rallied to the call from Haigh and Davison to sign an open letter to the government, published in the *Australian*, deploring this failure to deliver. To utilise Haigh's connections to the *Australian*, a broadsheet not favoured by progressives, but widely read by the political class, was strategically canny. Following the letter, a series of articles and presentations by high-profile historians not only in the *Australian*, but also via a range of press, online and radio channels, provided impassioned but accessible, persuasive case studies of what was about to be lost. Meanwhile, less publicly, petitions from genealogical and community history societies, and briefing notes for the prime minister, were initiated. An advocacy coalition was created.[34] Then the Treasurer, Josh Frydenberg, phoned Haigh, met with the director of the NAA, and went on to strongly advocate for additional emergency funding. As a result, the government backflipped, awarding $67.7 million for at risk preservation and digitisation programs, thus averting immediate disaster.[35]

Playing a long game

Most historians hope that their work will reach readers beyond their professional circles. We can learn from instances that have succeeded and have arguably shaped public consciousness and political awareness. These are produced by historians who, rather than entering the policy domain directly, building relationships with contacts in political or policy circles, or 'seizing the moment', instead effect change from below by stimulating public awareness and achieving the crossover into public engagement and debate. They may do so by being so confronting as to deny being ignored, or so innovative and persuasive as to gain a public following, but they typically rely on a cumulative build-up of research in the field in which they appear.

Research into settler–Indigenous relations, by both settler and Indigenous historians, has burgeoned since the 'new history' innovations of the 1970s. Among settler historians, speaking to a non-Indigenous audience, there have been successive waves of publications that have persuaded many Australians to recognise the tragedy of what was experienced by Aboriginal people resisting European incursions on 'the other side of the frontier', and to recognise their resilience.[36] Legal authorities and governments have sometimes responded (as, for instance, in the Mabo decision and legislation that followed), and at other times (as at present) have lagged behind public opinion.[37] One instance of groundbreaking research that confronts us in ways that cannot be denied is Lyndall Ryan's early work on Aboriginal Tasmanians, and recent (continuing) work, with colleagues, mapping the many sites, Australia-wide, where Aboriginal people were massacred. Ryan's first book,

The Aboriginal Tasmanians (1981), documenting the history of Tasmanian Aboriginal people from European colonisation to the present, caused immediate controversy. It not only described the decimation inherent in colonial Aboriginal 'protection', but also challenged the myth that they had not survived, supporting the claims of those who maintained their Indigenous heritage.[38] It was inevitably one of the texts persistently denounced in 'the history wars'.[39] It was sorely misrepresented. Research by others, on massacres in other colonies, had preceded Ryan, and would later substantially amplify her discoveries.[40] Still, Ryan, an exemplar of the long game, persisted. Now, based at the University of Newcastle, she is internationally acclaimed as one of the lead researchers of Colonial Frontier Massacres in Australia 1788–1930, an influential project that has decisively repudiated earlier critics and achieved crossover into the public realm with extensive coverage in the *Guardian* (as the core element in its 'The Killing Times' series), and attention in opinion-leading international media such as *The New Yorker*.[41]

In parallel, we have been encouraged to attend better to how the narratives of settlement, settlers and Indigenous nations are so interwoven that they must jointly be understood. It is limiting to see the settler–colonial state as a unified, oppressive entity without exploring the varied nuances, experiences, and intentions of those comprising the settler population. Historians such as Peter Read and Tim Rowse have been significant contributors to such work over the long term.[42] A standout current instance is the research of Grace Karskens, whose books, *The Colony* (2009) and *People of the River* (2020), drawing extensively on archaeology and history, have been so marvellously evocative and readable that they have garnered literary awards, gaining an audience beyond the academy. In recovering 'the lost worlds of early Australia', Karskens helps us to see how settlers and Indigenous peoples, shaped by different histories and webs of meaning as alien to us now as they were to each other then, became interlinked by circumstance, irrevocably enmeshed in a community of fate.[43]

Another project, led by Mark Finnane at Griffith University, of remarkable innovation that will have enduring influence is The Prosecution Project, which began in 2013.[44] A collaborative enterprise focused on the history of the criminal trial in Australia, it employs, on the one hand, historians in multiple locations familiar with big data collection and, on the other, utilisation of crowd-sourced 'citizen science': volunteers recruited through contacting family and community history societies and state archival volunteer groups. By exploring the conditions under which crime is defined, perpetrated, discovered, investigated, prosecuted, punished or ignored, over time and across space, it will promote understanding of the multiple factors involved in criminal behaviour.

The Prosecution Project aims to digitise and make accessible for future researchers and the wider community the records of criminal proceedings brought against individuals for serious crimes committed in all the Australian jurisdictions from the beginning of European settlement until at least the 1960s.[45] In both its publications addressed to the research community and others directed to general readers, it has already been remarkably productive.[46] It will endure because it not only advances knowledge of precedents, and of the evolution of Australian dimensions of how criminal behaviour is understood and dealt with, but also because of its purposeful resort to continuing citizen engagement and its relevance to family, community and social history. In so doing, it has enhanced general knowledge of the importance of archives and 'become one of those undertakings that draws from as well as contributes to a general community and public understanding of the value of Australia's historical heritage'.[47] Finnane was one of the contributors to the NAA campaign discussed earlier: it is the outreach into community and influence on public awareness of projects such as his that engenders the networks through which such advocacy coalitions can be mobilised.

Lessons from history: The importance of history in creating constituencies for change

Clearly, we can learn from the way in which social and political challenges of the past have been addressed or mishandled. Periodically, crises arise which disturb social equilibrium. Then politicians and their policy advisers may grasp for historical precedents in helping to understand complex problems, or to justify their actions. In such circumstances, community activists too may draw from history in their efforts to articulate a message that will sway decision-makers. Published books and articles may be a ready resource. But there are also opportunities for historians to exercise their expertise in influencing the policy domain, or in mobilising community opinion.

Historians concerned to bridge the divide between their domain and the policy world can find helpful frameworks for doing so, drawn from political and policy studies.[48] These disciplines have developed useful core concepts from which we can learn – network relationships, webs of meaning, punctuated equilibrium, policy windows and advocacy coalitions, for example.

These can, however, be translated into propositions more amenable to historians – the logic to be recognised 'inside the tent', the potential of 'investing in relationships', campaigns to 'seize the moment', and 'playing a long game' to confront and stimulate political awareness and create constituencies for change. The advantage of case studies such as those discussed earlier – indeed, the advantage of the historical approach as a whole – is the demonstration of our capacity to achieve the crossover from expert interchange to community engagement, from disciplinary debate to public mobilisation. On this, political progress depends.

PART II:

LESSONS FROM HISTORY

CHAPTER 4

Making time for history: Climate change and detoxing from progress

Yves Rees

We had 12 years left. Twelve years remaining to avert catastrophic climate change. That was the headline message of the special report of the Intergovernmental Panel on Climate Change (IPCC), released in October 2018. Time was ticking down and there wasn't a minute to waste. Only a dozen short years to keep global warming below 1.5 degrees Celsius. If we failed, the consequences would be horrific: drought, flood, deadly heat, food shortages, poverty – all experienced by hundreds of millions. There'd be resource wars and countless refugees. Earth might become uninhabitable altogether.[1]

By this point, we'd been hearing warnings about climate collapse for decades. Anyone who'd been paying attention knew things were dire. But this report felt different. For the first time, the notoriously circumspect IPCC had given us a hard deadline in the imminent future. Twelve years wasn't our grandchildren's lifetimes; it was us, not too far down the track. And if the IPCC, with its culture of consensus and compromise, was willing to make this alarming call, who knew how bad things really were?

At the time, I was 30 and newly minted as a historian. I'd

set my sights on a career in history while still a teenager and had spent my entire twenties learning the tools of the trade. Now I was finally here, researching the past for a living, only to look up and discover that the world was hurtling towards calamity while I toiled in the archives, breathing in centuries-old dust. In 2030, the deadline given by the IPCC, I'd be only 42 – still in the prime of life. I'd be there to see the climate unravel and had a personal interest in helping stave off nightmare scenarios. But what did my profession have to offer? What use was history to a warming earth?

On a sunny Friday that November, I discussed the 1920s with fellow historians in a cloistered office while school students marched for climate on the streets outside. At that moment, I felt sure I'd chosen the wrong path. When the future was so urgent, surely it was a waste to keep my head stuck in the past. Perhaps history was a trivial indulgence in these times, a form of fiddling while Rome burns. For months, I pondered a career change, trying to imagine myself as a climate scientist or full-time activist.

On closer inspection, however, I realised my mistake. History was far from irrelevant to the climate crisis. In fact, history was everywhere in how we thought and spoke about this existential threat. In the United States, climate activists were calling for a Green New Deal and a Climate Mobilisation – concepts that evoked Roosevelt's New Deal and the mobilisation of the Second World War.[2] The Anthropocene, the name given to our era of human-induced climate change, is itself a historical concept.[3] Then, in early 2019, Extinction Rebellion (XR) burst onto the scene with the message that getting 3.5 percent of the population onside was the magic number for forcing climate action – a figure derived from historical analyses of activist efforts like the suffragettes and the civil rights movement.[4] Later that year, in a speech to US Congress, Greta Thunberg cited the example of Martin Luther King, Jr and the civil rights movement as a model to emulate.[5] The most radical climate activists in the world were placing history at the heart of their message.

History did have relevance, it turned out. But what was its precise function? What exactly did it have to offer in helping us respond to the climate crisis? Most often, it appeared that history was being used as a playbook to provide lessons for how we should act or rules to predict the future. *Faced with a crisis? Try a New Deal – it worked in the 1930s, so is sure to work again. Unsure if activism can impel climate action? Look to the suffrage movement and follow its proven recipe for success.* In other words, this was history as analogy. The unstated assumption was that we can draw meaningful parallels between past and present, because the two are sufficiently alike that the latter can inform the former.

This thinking is seductive but does not hold up to scrutiny, for the simple reason that history teaches us that no two events are ever equivalent. Unlike the social sciences, where generalised models abound, doing history is about drilling into the messy particulars of each time and place. When you go into that detail, you appreciate the specificity of every happening. While the past provides important context, there are no analogies to be drawn or neat lessons to be extracted because nothing is ever replicated. There are always different factors at play – and those factors make all the difference.

To take one example, the suffrage movement cannot provide a playbook for the climate crisis because the two are very different beasts. The former was a campaign for a specific piece of legislative reform – female suffrage – within individual nation-states. The latter, by contrast, requires all-encompassing systemic change at a global level. They emerged in vastly different worlds, a century apart. Both involve activism, to be sure, but that is where the similarities end. As a result, it's doubtful that suffrage campaigns can teach or predict anything about climate activism. Suffrage history may be a source of inspiration, but little else.

But if history doesn't have *lessons* for the climate crisis, how is it relevant? As the months ticked by, and the Savage Summer swallowed vast swathes of Australia, then a zoonotic virus linked to deforestation shut down the world, I read and thought and read some more. What did the study of the past have to do with an alarming present and future? The more I read, the more I began to suspect that the answer to my question lay not in the substance of history – the who, what, when and why – but in the way history makes us think. The answer was about historical consciousness: how we imagine past, present and future to be connected. In short, the answer to my question was about time.

Historians, time and the climate crisis

Historians are time workers. Although we understand history as the study of the past, it's more accurately described as a craft that turns data into story. In essence, historians are storytellers who make narratives about the passage of time. Things happen, and historians posit the relationship between them. These narratives do more than tell us about the past; they also 'build temporal architecture' that structures our thinking and shapes our imagined futures.[6] As historian Samia Khatun puts it, the job of the historian is to 'time travel' along a particular 'temporal index'. Most often, historians travel along that index into the past, but we can also project the same index into the future. Our means of travelling into the past determines 'the particular line of travel [we] can see going forward'.[7] Hence, in the words of Dipesh Chakrabarty, our pasts are 'future in orientation. They help us make the unavoidable journey into the future.'[8] As a result, historians play a crucial role in articulating 'what the lines are along which we imaginatively travel'.[9] The practice of history engineers our understandings of time.

This is relevant to the climate crisis because anthropogenic climate change has been fuelled by a particular understanding of time. During the Anthropocene, 'progress' has been the temporal logic that underpins Western political and economic life. Progress narratives imagine time as a linear pathway, moving from a backward past towards an enlightened future. In a nutshell, progress is the idea of history as a story of perpetual change and improvement. It is time as a straight line, a highway from darkness to light. This meant that the future would always eclipse what had gone before. 'The future would be different from the past, and better, to boot,' historian Reinhart Koselleck explains.[10]

This conception of time influenced how humans acted in the world. From the nineteenth century, a historical imagination structured around progress fuelled both economic growth-manship and imperial expansion: the twin engines of anthropogenic climate change. The logic here was simple. If history was a story of progress, humans must always be doing and making *more*. More production, more knowledge, accelerating extraction. Growth became imperative. As Koselleck puts it, progress required 'an active transformation of this world, not the Hereafter'.[11] Hence the industrial revolution, profiteering, imperial expansion and ceaseless economic development (pursued by communist and capitalist economies alike) appeared the natural way of things. Each was a vehicle that would transport society along the highway towards a glistening future. Any harm caused along the way could be excused as collateral in the service of the ultimate progress of humankind.[12]

Crucially, progress ideology also implied that some people were further advanced than others. Time was a highway but not everyone was at the same point. Some societies were further advanced; others lagged behind – stuck in the 'waiting room of history'.[13] Hence imperialism could be justified as the act of 'advanced' countries like Britain helping more 'backward' societies to catch up by bringing civilisation to their doorstep. In this way, empire became 'ethically thinkable'.[14]

The progress narratives that motored economic growth and imperial expansion were, in large part, invented and popularised by historians. As Priya Satia puts it, the first modern historians 'were not hobbyists on the sidelines, but the very makers of history'.[15] They didn't just document the past; they conceived ideas that changed the future. Progress narratives emerged from Enlightenment thinking that replaced older notions of cyclical history with the idea that history was linear and progressive. Two historians were key here. The first is James Mill, the Scottish historian (and father of philosopher John Stuart Mill) whose 1818 *History of British India* would become the single most influential book among British officials in India. Mill's central thesis was that Britain was tasked with liberating India from barbarity. He posited that 'there was a single route of progress that all societies must travel, leading to the highest pinnacle of human achievement: Western civilisation'.[16] The book was required reading for colonial officials for decades, ensuring that generations of leaders soaked up and enacted these ideas.

One of those officials was Thomas Macaulay, an associate of Mill and a leading figure behind the push to enforce English as the language of education for the Indian elite. After returning from India in 1838, Macaulay reinvented himself as a historian. He embarked on a five-volume *History of England*, published to huge acclaim between 1848 and 1859. In Macaulay's telling, England's past was a story of progress, a tale of a great nation coming into being through ever greater peace, prosperity and liberty. Like Mill, he positioned England as the apex of civilisation, the most advanced nation leading more backward peoples into modernity. Macaulay's *History* was a worldwide bestseller, with the first volume sold out within ten days. His story – and his vision of history as progress – would come to have a profound influence on British thinking.[17] As the historian Catherine Hall puts it, Macaulay's progress narrative 'inspired generations of public schoolboys, historians, politicians, lawmakers and colonial administrators – the governing classes – as well as autodidacts'.[18]

Having begun in history books, the idea of history as progress took on a life of its own. Progress narratives circulated widely in Western culture until they were plain common sense. They operated in simpatico with social Darwinism and provided justification for imperial expansion. Over the nineteenth century and beyond, progress became the taken-for-granted understanding of how time worked. For over two hundred years, it has impacted how we understand the past but has also shaped how we act in the present. It gave a green light to – even demanded – the pursuit of productivity and growth.

Since the 1960s, academic historians, under the influence of postcolonial and poststructural thinking, have largely disavowed progress narratives. Yet this understanding of time continues to be dominant in popular historical consciousness – not to mention political and economic discourse. Take 'development', for instance. The global focus on developing 'underdeveloped' nations is directly indebted to progress narratives that imagined time as a march towards the future, with some societies ahead and others behind.[19] As the anthropologist Anna Tsing puts it, 'we were raised on dreams of modernization and progress' and still today 'their categories and assumptions are with us everywhere.'[20]

These dreams of progress have had nightmarish effects on our Earth. Thanks to the 'celebration of environmental-wreckage-as-progress', we've seen over two hundred years of rampant extraction, exploitation, development and rising carbon emissions – a way of life that has left us, in the 2020s, with what poet Tony Birch calls a 'storm of our own making'.[21] Due to our insistence on being forever bigger and better, our once-bounteous home is now irreparably damaged and fast threatening to become uninhabitable.[22] Australian climate scientist Joëlle Gergis put it bluntly when she wrote in 2020 that 'humanity is facing an existential threat of planetary proportions.'[23] The great irony of an historical imagination structured around progress is that the relentless pursuit of advancement has left us facing the very real threat of our own extinction. 'No jobs on a dead planet' is one slogan of the environmental movement. 'No progress in death' might be another.

This is not to suggest that the history profession caused the climate crisis or is to blame for its human and environmental toll. Such an idea is absurdly reductive and would distract from the very real culpability of political leaders and fossil fuel executives who have allowed the crisis to unfold despite decades of warnings. The point is not that historians are the villains of the piece, but rather that a particular theory of history invented by humans in the recent past helped drive anthropogenic climate change. In other words, the climate crisis is in part a problem of historical consciousness. It's a political problem, an economic problem and an environmental problem, but it's also a problem of time. Progress ideology propelled carbon emissions and its continued influence inhibits meaningful climate action. So long as we continue to believe the story that we're marching through time towards a bigger and better future, we'll struggle to abandon our fantasies of endless growth and undertake the structural transformations necessary to keep global warming below 1.5 degrees.

Lessons from history: Detoxing from progress

If we recognise the climate crisis as a problem of historical consciousness, what does this mean for our efforts to mitigate climate breakdown? First and foremost, this recognition enables us to disrupt the inevitability of progress narratives.[24] At present, with the logic of time-as-progress so entrenched, it's easy to assume this is the natural and inevitable way of things. It's easy to mistake this invented idea for a fact of nature, taken-for-granted and intractable. Like fish oblivious to the water they swim in, we become oblivious to the temporal script that saturates our culture. As Rebecca Solnit puts it, we too readily 'mistake today's peculiarities for eternal verities.'[25] And when that happens, it becomes near impossible to think outside or beyond the progress script. We accept its growth imperatives without question, and so maintain our carbon-intensive existence.

Once we name progress as nothing more than a particular theory of history, it begins to lose its iron grip on our imaginations. It becomes possible to see that progress narratives were made by humans, and so can be unmade by them. Only a few hundred years ago, humans imagined time in other ways, and may well do so again. This is akin to the point made by the late novelist Ursula K. Le Guin when she declared: 'We live in capitalism. Its power seems inescapable – but then, so did the divine right of kings.'[26] Like capitalism, like the divine right of kings, progress narratives are not immutable fact but rather an idea that has arguably reached its use-by date. By recognising this situation, we begin to see that other worlds are possible. Nothing about our theory of history is fixed or inevitable, and it is possible to radically reinvent the temporal scripts we live by.

From here, we might begin to replace progress stories with alternate understandings of time. No longer fooled into thinking that history is inherently linear and progressive, we create space to recover different temporal scripts that will make possible different – more sustainable, more collectivist – futures. As Satia writes, 'what is required is not so much progress as recovery from the imaginary of progress.'[27] We need to detox from progress, you might say.

In practice, this means telling different stories about life on earth. The idea of stories as a weapon against climate breakdown might seem fanciful. However, among leading analysts of the climate crisis, there is widespread agreement that the problems of this moment are bound up in questions of narrative, with new stories regarded as a vital precondition of meaningful change. From cultural critic George Monbiot and ecophilosopher Joanna Macy, to feminist Donna Haraway and philosopher Bruno Latour, to geographer Mike Hulme and economist Kate Raworth, there is consensus that humans apprehend the world through story. For change to happen, the story must first change.[28] 'Stories trap us, stories free us, we live and die by stories,' writes Solnit. In her view, 'the change that counts in revolution takes place first in the imagination'.[29] Even scientists like veteran US environmentalist Gus Speth have acknowledged that meaningful climate action requires a new cultural paradigm. Speth reflected back in 2013 that our environmental crisis can only be addressed via 'a spiritual and cultural transformation. And we scientists don't know how to do that.'[30]

In the effort to displace progress stories with other ideas of time travel, the history profession has a crucial role to play. As society's designated time workers, historians are uniquely equipped to recover, invent and popularise alternative temporal scripts. Samia Khatun, an Australian historian based at the University of London, is one of several voices urging the history profession to rise to this challenge. As she argued in a 2021 interview, 'if the historian invents progress, or institutionalizes progress as the main way of thinking about time, then the historian also has in their hands the power to think of other ways of travelling through time, other ways of imagining hope, and what a better imagined future might look like'. Given we're not used to regarding historians as culture-shapers, this may seem grandiose. Yet, as Khatun explains, as historians, 'we've seen that this is the role that historians played in the past. And so, it's our role to undo it and come up with new pathways forward.'[31]

If historians are to help us detox from progress, what alternative temporal scripts might they deploy in pursuit of a liveable future? The answer is unlikely to be found in the cultures that gave us progress ideology in the first place. As the Black American poet Audre Lorde put it, 'The master's tools cannot dismantle the master's house'.[32] To find more sustainable and humane ways to exist in time, we might look to the colonised peoples whose knowledges were trampled in pursuit of progress. In Australia, this could mean learning from the First Nations cultures that sustained life for tens of thousands of years. These cultures understand time in ways radically different from the settler story of progress. Aboriginal time is generally understood as cyclical and non-linear; it spirals in regenerative loops instead of shooting towards the horizon. This means that multiple times co-exist. According to Tyson Yunkaporta, senior lecturer in Indigenous Knowledges at Deakin University, First Nations peoples 'see past, present and future as one time'.[33] The anthropologist W.E.H. Stanner coined the term 'everywhen' to explain this way of thinking.[34]

By learning from the idea of everywhen, alongside other non-linear temporalities, historians might tell new stories that facilitate a paradigm shift in how we imagine ourselves in time. If we jump off what Yunkaporta calls 'the arrow of time', and instead come to understand time as cyclical, we might lose the pathological compulsion to forever be bigger and better.[35] The idea of throwing out directional history can seem impossible, given its constitutive role in the dominant vision of the world. But at this historical juncture, we arguably have no choice. Progress is a death sentence, and human futures will only be possible if we adopt other ways of being and knowing.[36]

As I wrote this chapter, the IPCC released a new report. Described by UN Secretary-General Antonio Guterres as a 'code red for humanity', the report published in August 2021 warned that the world was likely to heat by more than 1.5 degrees within the next two decades, breaching the ambition of 2015's Paris Climate Accords. Even if we went carbon zero tomorrow, anthropogenic climate change has already caused irreversible damage to the Earth's climate.[37] The question now is not *will things get bad?* but rather *will humanity survive?*

If we are to avoid human extinction, we need to reimagine the way we exist in time. We need to abandon the progress stories that prompt us to burn coal, raze forests, exploit labour and grow GDP, and we need to confront the harm such narratives have caused. We need to refute Macaulay's idea that history is progress, and instead recognise that the passage of time can be understood in many ways. The arrow of time is just a story we've told ourselves, and there are different stories to be told. In short, we need new temporal scripts that will shift the popular imagination so that we might veer off our collision course with calamity. We need climate scientists, we need activists, we need carers and medics and teachers and leaders, but we also need time workers. We need historians.

CHAPTER 5

Urban water policy in a drying continent

Andrea Gaynor, Margaret Cook, Lionel Frost, Jenny Gregory, Ruth Morgan, Martin Shanahan and Peter Spearritt

City people often take water for granted – until there isn't enough of it, or it roars through the city in a flood. Yet as urban populations grow and climate challenges intensify, the provision and management of urban water is likely to become more difficult. It is estimated that by 2050 up to 13.3 million additional people may live in Australia's capital cities, all of whom will expect equal access to clean water and effective sanitation.[1] At the same time, rainfall patterns and quantities are changing in ways that current water infrastructure is not designed for, and for which prevailing water cultures are not prepared. Australia's crisis of water management continues, with restrictions saved for shortages, and flood mitigation addressed largely through engineering rather than planning decisions about where it is safe for people to live. Regulated water usage and recycling remain unpopular and politically unpalatable, potable (i.e. drinkable) water charges generate considerable revenue, and economic and cultural norms retard societal change.

How can history help? The past is never a sure or straightforward guide to the future, but the history of water and Australian urbanisation yields insights that may assist politicians and water managers to find a sustainable approach. For example, our research on water in the five Australian mainland state capitals points to the often short-term and reactive nature of urban water policy and planning. Frequently, the development of solutions has been left until crisis point, and responses have failed to grapple with the inevitability of climatic variation and population growth. Furthermore, decisions made many decades ago have left us with large and somewhat inflexible systems that may require transformation through major investment to deliver integrated water cycle management. Our historical research also suggests that water, which is essential for all life, is rarely best placed in the hands of the market. Political appetite for change, however, will require diverse Australian voters to understand that, like many of the resources we depend upon to maintain our current lifestyles, fresh water is limited. And this means we need to consume less of it.[2]

Past decisions and future choices

All Australian capital cities have been subject to multiple periods of restricted water consumption. Usually these episodes have arisen from population growth, exacerbated by a period of dry conditions that produces conditions understood as a 'crisis'. How a 'crisis' is framed matters because this determines the actors who are summoned to respond to it. In Australia, when urban water supplies have run low, this has rarely been portrayed as a crisis of exceeding environmental constraints, but of inadequate infrastructure and thus supply. While the immediate response has been to restrict water use in order to share remaining supplies, the ultimate solution has been seen to lie in expanding capacity to extract or manufacture more potable water – via dams, rivers, groundwater, or, most recently, desalination. In the case of flooding, the crisis has generally been seen as arising from inadequate provision for floodwater control rather than poor urban planning creating flood vulnerability. This framing has summoned engineers rather than well-informed town planners and local governments. While such solutions have often worked in the short term, they have frequently served to defer problems to the next generation, postponing vulnerability rather than offering true sustainability. As we move further into a period of global climate volatility, in which both extreme rainfall events and periods of drought are expected to increase, the challenge for urban water managers is to proactively plan for enduring, long-term and resilient solutions that encompass the cultural, municipal and technological components of urban water systems.

Forging a new direction will not be easy. The choices that were made at critical points in the creation and development of today's water infrastructure, at both community and individual levels, are prime examples of decisions being subject to what social scientists call 'path dependency'. Path dependence means more than just 'the past matters': it refers to the fact that 'once a country or region has started down a track, the costs of reversal are very high'.[3] Cumulative actions reinforce previous decisions or limit the range of options available for future selection. When considering water network infrastructure, path-dependent development is especially influential because of the highly collective nature of identifying, constructing and sustaining such infrastructure. It is characterised by large set-up (fixed) costs, learning effects (with increased use come higher returns and more effective systems), coordination effects (the system is refined as more people use it) and adaptive expectations (people anticipate future use patterns and adapt towards these expectations). While these effects vary in significance across different contexts, all water infrastructure networks are subject to decisions for which subsequent adoption and replication magnify the initial effect and make action along a different path less likely. Initial choices frequently take advantage of the 'easiest' options of financial cost or location. When these choices focus on short-term gains, or ignore non-financial consequences (such as the environment or social equity), they can have extremely high opportunity costs that are only fully realised many years later.

Take dams and reservoirs, filtration systems, pipelines and sewerage treatment works, for example. The location and construction of these have historically involved high set-up costs. The difficulties in funding the first water storages serving each capital city related directly to the size of these initial costs and disputes over who would pay. Once constructed, these large assets were expensive to change. Desalination plants similarly became locked in, as expandable, modular means of manufacturing potable water. Sewerage networks that dispose of waste by pushing it out to sea with minimal treatment established expectations of 'cheap' disposal.

Past decisions about water supply and sanitation have had far-reaching effects, shaping not only infrastructure networks but also housing. With the advent of deep sewerage, the 'dunny' (lavatory) at the bottom of the backyard joined the bathroom on the back verandah. By the interwar years, piped water and the drive for efficiency in modern housing design enabled the bathroom to move conveniently closer to the bedrooms. Later again, the availability of the odour-free S-bend saw the toilet moved inside as well, though this was a slow process. In 1940s Melbourne, for example, new government houses were still built with the toilet and laundry on the back verandah. In all cities, older rental housing fell far short of the standards of newly built housing. Today, most new houses have two toilets and many have two bathrooms. These conveniences have contributed to a dramatic increase in the per capita consumption of water since the late nineteenth century. In Sydney, for example, water consumption rose from 112 litres per person in 1890, to 488 litres in 1990.[4]

Water availability also shaped conventions and expectations around suburban gardens, which ultimately locked in unsustainable outdoor water consumption patterns. In the nineteenth century and indeed, for much of the twentieth, British cultural norms dominated Australian cities and their suburbs. European trees were prized, familiar flowers and vegetables were grown, and exotic grass lawns were valued for their cool green expanse that kept down dust and provided a soft play surface for children. Initially only the wealthy who had their own water supply from tanks or bores could create and maintain such gardens. Once piped water was available in sufficient quantity and restrictions on its use for garden purposes were lifted, many more householders were able to realise their garden aspirations.[5] Consumption was further elevated by the backyard swimming pools that were only feasible because of abundant and relatively cheap water.

Buying time: Conservation and desalination

Decades of dependency on piped water supply produced deeply ingrained expectations of abundant and convenient water. However, population growth and diminishing opportunities to develop cheap new fresh water supplies have forced authorities to encourage a degree of public water conservation, buying time to 'keep up' with demand. Since the 1970s, user-pays pricing has had an enduring impact on excessive water consumption, especially outdoors – at least among those less able to pay. Campaigns encouraging voluntary water conservation have also had some impact.[6]

The greatest changes, however, have been largely ephemeral. During the urban water crisis created by the Millennium Drought (2001–2009), governments introduced policies and incentives to reduce household and business consumption. Brisbane, with the most wide-reaching policies, offered financial incentives to install water tanks and water-saving appliances, distributed four-minute shower timers to every household, and permitted some garden use of laundry water (enabled by development of safer detergents). Businesses, schools, airports, warehouses – any structures with extensive roof catchment areas – were encouraged to collect rainwater for their own use. As a result, Brisbane reduced per capita consumption to 112 litres per day – lower than in any other capital city. While commendable, however, these policy efforts arguably did little to reduce the path dependency of reliance on large-scale public water supplies. When the overflowing of dams makes the TV news, the public becomes complacent about water use, and standards and habits revert almost to how they were under previous water regimes. Corporatised water utilities facilitate this reversion; given their primary income source is the sale of water to households and businesses, they have a financial interest in scaling back or abolishing water restrictions after periods of high rainfall.

During the long drought, desalination plants were built in most of the capitals between 2006 and 2012. These plants were in some cases technological fixes for governments anxious to show they were doing something about potable water. They were relatively quick to build and integrated readily with existing infrastructure, while energy offset deals were a clever exercise in greenwashing. While Perth and Adelaide have continued to operate their desalination schemes, as rain fell, Sydney's plant was put on standby and Brisbane's was mothballed, along with water harvesting and recycling schemes. If the same amount of money and electrical energy had been invested in water recycling plants, using stormwater and/or wastewater, the environmental achievement would have been impressive.[7] In 2017 the Productivity Commission's National Water Reform Report recommended an integrated approach that included reusing wastewater or stormwater.[8] But these approaches were not mandatory and implementation has been slow. Moving rapidly from an official emphasis on supply to a focus on recycling has been perceived as too politically risky, because voters have come to expect abundant water from sources that they perceive as 'pure' and 'natural'.

According to the logic of path-dependent development, when faced with future challenges to existing networked systems, the tendency will first be towards incremental, low-cost change (such as raising dam walls). If such responses are insufficient, the environmental, economic and social costs of larger and more fundamental change are likely to be high. One key issue is whether the institutions responsible for managing urban water exist within a framework that supports protection of the long-term public interest to provide sustainable water and sanitation.

People and environment versus profits

What does history tell us about the likely risks and opportunities of rearranging the balance of public and private interests in urban water systems? Collective agreement on the importance of protecting water resources has been expressed through legislation establishing catchment control and monitoring. Since the nineteenth century, protecting urban water catchments from private interests such as farming, logging and mining has gone a long way to ensuring the high quality of potable water supplies in Australian cities. In Victoria, for instance, evidence of contamination of Yan Yean's water from timber cutting and farming in the 1860s and 1870s eventually led to the permanent reservation of the catchment for water supplies.[9] As other cities have subsequently found, such an approach is cost effective; in New York in the 1990s, for example, water planners calculated that it was cheaper to buy land to protect water catchments than to build and maintain water treatment plants.[10] Despite Melbourne's leadership in this regard, it is worth noting that resource conflict continues in the Yan Yean catchment, as scientists found in 2019 that the state-owned VicForests had breached its code of practice to limit logging on particular slopes.[11] Meanwhile in the hills to the east of Perth in Western Australia, bauxite mining occurs within reservoir protection zones to which public access is denied.

The ongoing importance of government oversight of

sanitary provision for the public good is illustrated by the flow-on effects of changes introduced to the organisation of water utilities in the 1980s and 1990s. In recent decades, the rise of neoliberalism has led to the corporatisation of urban water in Melbourne (1992), Sydney (1994), Perth (1996), Adelaide (2002) and Brisbane (2010). Corporatisation is essentially a soft form of neoliberal management, in which agencies are fully owned and operated by the state, but have a separate financial and legal status. This ostensibly separates political decision-making from the pursuit of economic efficiency, and managers must account for expenses and revenues as though the utility were an independent company. In some cases, operations have been contracted out to private corporations. According to independent inquiries, both Adelaide's Big Pong of 1997, involving mechanical failures and inadequate monitoring at the Bolivar wastewater treatment plant, and Sydney's 1998 water crisis, which saw public water supply contaminated by cryptosporidium and giardia, were the consequence of newly corporatised agencies favouring cost minimisation over infrastructure maintenance and monitoring.[12]

Closer regulation of urban planning is one proven approach to minimising the human, environmental and economic impacts of urban flooding events. The international hazard scholarship has advocated land use regulation since the 1970s as an effective tool for flood mitigation. The extent and impact of Brisbane's 2011 flood were the consequence of inadequate land use regulations, insufficient flood mapping and continued residential development on the floodplain of the Brisbane River.[13] Similar issues are arising in relation to urban development in areas susceptible to flooding in Western Sydney and the proposal to raise the wall of Warragamba Dam.

These issues involve a conflict of interest between different government roles, as land release and housing development is a historically significant proportion of state government revenue, yet the state is ultimately also responsible for protecting residents from known natural hazards – including flooding. In order to safeguard residents, the incentive to chase revenue – or to engage in patronage relationships with property developers – must be removed, not least as we move further into a climate of increased extreme rainfall events. More broadly, putting profits before people and environments is an unwise approach to urban water management.

If water, then, is inevitably political, what does history suggest about the potential risks and opportunities for democratic management of urban water systems? In a liberal democracy, most Australians have been able to take collective action in demanding improved water infrastructure through voting and a robust free press. Public investment in domesticating water with large-scale water supply and sewerage infrastructure was often piecemeal and reactive, not because of voter resistance to increased charges and cost of connections and fittings, but because of uncertainty about which level of government was responsible. The creation of water boards in Sydney and Melbourne to deliver services across metropolitan areas was one solution. As costs rose due to growing suburban populations pushing usage beyond the capacity of water storages and waste treatment and disposal plants, path-dependent effects made it easier to build new storages and extend old systems, rather than change technology.

In the twenty-first century, the development of sustainable urban water management systems is a 'wicked problem' that defies simple solutions because of multiple, contested causes and interdependencies. In the absence of revolutionary change, solutions will have to be worked out through public dialogue within present political structures, and require active support from the Australian electorate.[14]

In an era of neoliberalism, globalisation, deindustrialisation and technological disruption, political parties of all shades have struggled to develop effective policy solutions to environmental challenges. Rising income inequality, the loss of secure full-time jobs, declining trade union membership and unaffordable housing have impacted Australians unevenly. Voters in outer suburbs, small towns and rural areas are more sensitive to job insecurity and cost of living pressures than those in well-off central and inner cities.[15] Such voters are highly susceptible to narratives that present sustainability as the enemy of growth, or an unaffordable luxury. The challenge for the political class is to lead the electorate to understand the importance of developing water institutions, cultures and infrastructure that will serve us well over the long run. This means not always turning to infrastructure to solve problems, but sustaining the slow process of embedding consideration for water within all of our urban systems, from planning and design to education and the arts. The era of crises followed by infrastructural fixes must end.

Lessons from history: A holistic approach to water

There are some encouraging signs of change. Since the 1990s there has been some implementation of water-sensitive urban design, particularly in new urban developments. This approach integrates the water cycle into urban planning and engineering, resulting in benefits like enhanced public open space and biodiversity, flood mitigation and water conservation, and reuse within the landscape. There is significant potential to roll out such approaches on a wider scale, including retrofitting older suburbs, but a change in organisational culture is required, as well as significant investment. At the pointy end of climate change in a region that has experienced significant rainfall decline since the 1970s, Western Australia's Water Corporation has undertaken a major publicity campaign seeking to educate consumers about the impact of rainfall decline. In 2009 it developed a 50-year plan ('Water forever') that used climate change projections to 2060 and included a 60 per cent increase in wastewater recycling, but only a 25 per cent reduction in annual per capita water use, from 145 KL per person to 110 KL per person. Even though community support for water efficiency and large-scale recycling is high, the main government strategy for eliminating the gap between future water demand and supply is further desalination.[16]

Water has the potential to play a key role in some of the biggest challenges facing our society. Many of these challenges arise from growth, at a range of scales. At a global scale, growth in human consumption of planetary resources is threatening biodiversity and climate. At an urban scale, growth of metropolitan areas is continuing to strain the capacity of existing systems and sources, as well as increasing the complexity and vulnerability of centralised networks. The problem of reliance on endless growth in finite systems cannot be avoided: the question is whether change will be experienced through design or disaster.[17] We know that decoupling economic growth from carbon emissions and other forms of environmental harm will not deliver the biodiversity and climate outcomes we need. We also know that we can no longer pursue the dream of universalising the kind of affluence much of the West has enjoyed for the past seven decades without disastrously accelerating climate and biodiversity harms.

What role might there be for water policy in pursuing a degrowth agenda?[18] While the market has for many years been the dominant mechanism for distributing resources in Australia and other developed countries, water is one of the few areas in which urban residents have accepted the need to reduce consumption during times of crisis in order to ensure that there is enough available for all. If water managers can build on this history of public resource consciousness, along with positive developments associated with new, conservation-oriented ways of dealing with water (such as the best implementations of water-sensitive urban design), this could reduce the fear and uncertainty associated with a transition to degrowth in other areas.

The disruption caused by the COVID-19 pandemic has provided an opportunity for people to reflect on their priorities and the kinds of change they would like to see in society more broadly.[19] While many are suffering from change fatigue and craving a return to business-as-usual, the reality is that life will never be the same, and this disruption perhaps provides an opportunity to work towards new, more sustainable and equitable social norms.

Reflecting, then, on the social history of water in Australian urbanisation, we see several opportunities for learning. There is the pressing need to treat water supply and sanitation holistically, as a set of habits, institutions and infrastructure entangled in wider social and environmental contexts. In the past, responses to urban water issues have been dominated by engineering and infrastructure, rather than tackling the more difficult long-term work of cultural adaptation. This approach has been facilitated by the relatively short-time horizons employed by urban water managers. Infrastructure fixes may solve problems for a matter of decades, but to be truly good ancestors we need to think in terms of centuries, if not millennia. While detailed projections at those time scales are impossible, some of the larger planetary constraints – such as an inability to support indefinite growth at current rates – are obvious. Although path dependency means that change away from our current structures and systems will be difficult, delaying the process of change will only make the job harder. On the positive side, the social history of water provides encouraging evidence that change is achievable: from short-term responses to water scarcity, to the growing implementation of water-sensitive urban design and water recycling. As Australia's Indigenous peoples have always known well, water is life. When settler Australia takes that message on board, we will be closer to achieving the resilience needed to meet the challenges ahead.

CHAPTER 6

War with China: What can history teach us?

Hugh White

Should Australia join the United States in a war against China to prevent China taking the US's place as the dominant power in East Asia? Until a few years ago the question would have seemed merely hypothetical, but not anymore. Senior figures in our government have acknowledged that the escalating strategic rivalry between the US and China could lead to war. Neither side wants war, but both seem willing to accept it rather than abandon their primary objectives. There can be no doubt that if war comes, Washington would expect Australia to fight alongside it. Many in Canberra take it for granted that we would do so, and defence policy has shifted accordingly. Our armed forces are now being designed primarily to contribute to US-led operations in a major maritime war with China in the Western Pacific, with the aim of helping the United States to deter China from challenging the US, or helping to defeat it if deterrence fails. In fact, the risk of war is probably higher than the government realises, because China is harder to deter than they understand.

If war comes, Australians would face a truly momentous choice. Any choice to go to war carries special weight, because the costs and risks that must be weighed against the potential benefits are qualitatively different from those involved in other policy choices. A nation's leaders must decide whether those exceptional costs and risks are justified by the objectives for which the war is fought. That is a big responsibility even for the relatively small wars which Australia has joined in recent decades in Iraq and Afghanistan. But a war with China would be nothing like those. Once fighting began, there would be little chance of avoiding a major war, because the stakes for both sides are very high, and both have large forces ready for battle. This would be the first serious war between two 'great powers' since 1945, and the first ever between nuclear-armed states. It would probably become the biggest and worst war since the Second World War. If it goes nuclear, which is quite probable, it could be the worst war ever. A decision to fight in that war would be as serious as the decisions to fight in 1914 and 1939, which were arguably the most important decisions Australian governments have ever made.

It is important to be clear what the decision would be about. If war comes, it will be sparked by a dispute between the United States and China over something like Taiwan or the South China Sea. But the specific dispute would not be the reason we would go to war with China, any more than we went to war in 1914 over the fate of Belgium or in 1939 over the fate of Poland. On both occasions the decision for war was driven by our concern to help prevent a defeat in Europe which would destroy British power in Asia, which we then relied on for our security. We would go to war with China to preserve the US strategic position in Asia on which we depend for our security. That is not quite the same as saying that we would fight to preserve our alliance with the United States. Many people assume that that would be our primary objective, because the US might abandon its commitments to us if we failed to support it. But Washington's disappointment with us does not threaten our US alliance nearly as gravely as Washington's defeat by China. As long as they have strategic ambitions in Asia, Washington will have good reasons to help defend Australia. What would destroy the alliance would be American defeat and withdrawal from Asia.

Australia would be profoundly affected by a US–China war whether we joined the fighting or not. That might tempt some to think that our decision didn't matter much one way or the other. That obviously overlooks the consequences for those who actually serve, and the possibility that Australia itself could be targeted. But more importantly, it overlooks the possibility that Australia's decisions would influence decisions elsewhere – including in Washington. Recent scholarship has highlighted the remarkable weight given to Australia's attitudes by British policymakers in the crises of 1914 and 1938–39. Douglas Newton has shown how, at a critical moment, Britain's choice for war in 1914 was nudged by Australia's eager support, while David Lee and David Bird have shown the influence of Stanley Bruce and Joseph Lyons on Britain's innermost councils in 1938 and 1939.[1] The possibility that Australia's choices might help to shape the ultimate decisions for war or peace in Asia over the years ahead make it all the more important that we weigh those decisions carefully.

Choices for war are profoundly shaped by historical analogy. Often this is the primary driver of a decision, in part because there is so little else to go on – nothing like the kind of data that can guide decisions on, say, tax policy or health policy. We decide whether to go to war or not largely by looking at what our predecessors did in previous crises. Much depends, then, on which earlier crises we choose to consider, on how well we understand them, and on how closely yesterday's crisis resembles today's. As Australia considers whether to join a US–China war, it is natural and prudent to look for guidance to the two previous occasions when we have faced comparably serious choices: 1914 and 1939. When we do this, we find an acute contrast between the way these two choices are now understood.

Two world wars, two different lessons

Today, no one seriously doubts that we – Australia and its allies in the British Empire – were right to go to war in 1939 against Nazi Germany, nor that we were wrong not to go to war over the Czech crisis of 1938. This was also the seemingly universal view of those who lived and fought through the war. In 1961 the historian A.J.P. Taylor noted how little interest there was in contesting the accepted view of these momentous decisions.[2] The same is true today.[3] The Second World War is seen as a war that had to be fought.[4]

The contrast with 1914 could hardly be starker. No one today seems seriously to doubt that the First World War should not have been fought. Again, today's judgment matches the verdict of those who lived and fought through the war itself. Throughout the troubled decades from 1919 to 1939 there was an almost universal belief that the war had been a ghastly mistake and should never have been fought. Ever since, and despite lively debates about details of the debacle that led to war, especially how much of the blame lay with Berlin, the clear consensus has endured that war came that long-ago summer through the collective folly, weakness and ineptitude of the statesmen involved. The British wartime Prime Minister, Lloyd George, writing soon after the war ended, said the nations of Europe 'slithered over the brink' into a war that none of them intended. *Sleepwalkers*, the title of Christopher Clark's notable recent account of how it all happened, suggests how little those essential judgments have changed.[5]

The intriguing thing about these very different verdicts is that the underlying reason for Britain and the empire going to war was much the same on both occasions. It was to prevent the domination of Europe by a single power that would then be strong enough to threaten Britain itself, and hence Britain's capacity to defend its empire, including Australia. Both times Germany threatened to upset the balance of power between the European Great Powers, on which Britain had relied for centuries to safeguard its security across the Channel and thus allow it to project power around the globe to build and defend its empire. After 1918 this seemed a wholly insufficient reason to go to war. And yet when the same strategic logic drove Britain and its empire to war again in 1939, this seemed entirely justified.

Why the difference? One important reason concerns who did most of the fighting. In the First World War the hardest fighting was done by Britain and France on the Western Front. In the Second World War it was done by the Soviet Union against Germany in Europe, and (as we all too easily forget) by the Chinese against Japan in Asia. That is why, for all its horrors, the Second World War was less horrific for Britain and Australia than the First. But the main reason is of course the nature of the Nazi regime. During the First World War many lurid things were believed about the evils of Prussian militarism, and some of them no doubt were true. But no one would compare them with the truly astonishing evil of Nazi Germany which turned out after the war to be far worse even than most people had imagined. As the liberation of Europe in 1944 and 1945 revealed the reality of life under Nazi rule, it was hard to doubt that this was a challenge that must be defeated.

Not surprisingly, the lessons that have been drawn from 1914 and 1939 are very different – indeed they are diametrically opposed. After the First World War it was universally accepted by national governments that war on that scale must be avoided at almost any cost. It was therefore always better to compromise and accommodate the ambitions of a country that wanted to change the international system in its favour, rather than fight to defend the status quo. The word they used was 'appeasement'. The lesson drawn from 1939, and especially from the failure of the last gesture of appeasement at Munich in 1938, was never to make concessions to any power that seeks to expand its influence in the international system. Accommodation only encourages further demands. An unshakable refusal to compromise, backed by a clear determination to fight if necessary, will probably force the challenger to back off, thus avoiding war. And if they do not back off, then better to fight sooner before the challenger gets any stronger. They will have to be fought sooner or later, before they become too strong to be stopped.

It is not surprising that this stark and simple rejection of the lessons of 1914 should have appealed to people during the six hard years of the Second World War. It is a bit more surprising that it has retained such a strong influence ever since. Today these simple, powerful precepts remain perhaps the most potent element of that vague set of ideas, preconceptions and prejudices that provide the intellectual framework for foreign and strategic policymaking in the Western, and especially the Anglo-American, world. The ideas that we should always be willing to fight rather than compromise, and that the more willing we are to fight, the less likely we are to have to fight, took on the aura of timeless precepts of universal application. As such, they had, and have, obvious appeal. They make difficult policy decisions look easy, and allow leaders and their advisers to look and sound tough.

But the results have not always been happy. The 'lessons of Munich' inspired Britain's debacle in Suez, the US's defeat in Vietnam, their invasion of Iraq in 2003 and many other mistakes.[6] These failures are easy to explain. Lessons of history are inevitably tied to the original circumstances of time and place from which they are drawn, and how well they apply to new situations depends on how far and in what ways the new circumstances resemble the original ones. The lessons drawn from the failure of appeasement in 1939 are specific to the circumstances of that failure, and some of those circumstances were very unusual.

Above all, the shadow of Nazi Germany was unusual and perhaps unique in several critical ways. One was the sheer evil of the Nazi regime to which we have already referred. Another was its unusually stark and clearly stated strategic ambitions. From *Mein Kampf* onwards, Hitler made clear that he planned to do more than build Germany's position as the leading power in Europe by expanding its influence over other countries. He wanted to destroy other countries by seizing and occupying large tracts of territory to provide Lebensraum for the German people. A third was its potential to realise its ambitions on the basis of its formidable national power – economic, demographic, technical and organisational – compared to its neighbours. Against this kind of challenge, the only possible response may well be, as the lessons of Munich suggest, unwavering and uncompromising opposition; if necessary, by fighting a major war.

But neither Nasser's Egypt, nor Ho Chi Minh's North Vietnam nor Saddam Hussein's Iraq were anything like Hitler's Germany. The dangers they posed were nowhere near as serious as was assumed, and the costs and risks of resisting them by force turned out to be much higher than expected, and higher than could be justified to avert those dangers. Even more strikingly, however, the lessons of Munich had relatively little influence on a number of much bigger questions. The postwar architecture hammered out between US president Franklin Roosevelt and Soviet leader Joseph Stalin at Yalta, based on the United Nations, was premised on a spirit of accommodation and compromise. Even more strikingly, so was the West's approach to the one adversary it faced in the postwar decades that was in some ways comparable with Nazi Germany – the Soviet Union. Western leaders sometimes invoked the follies of Munich to advertise and justify hard-line Cold War postures, but their policies were most often guided by a prudent recognition of the need to negotiate understandings with Moscow in order to avert the danger of war.

This was of course all the more imperative as the Soviet capacity for nuclear warfare grew. In the 1950s even the archetypal opponent of appeasement, Winston Churchill, became a fervent advocate of negotiation with Moscow to settle differences in order to avoid nuclear war.[7] In the darkest moment of the Cold War, the Cuban Missile Crisis, President Kennedy was influenced much more by the lessons of 1914 than by those of 1938–39, which prompted him to offer the concessions which defused the crisis.⁸ In any case, the policy of Détente that evolved in the aftermath of that crisis owed a lot more to the lessons of 1914 than those of 1938–39.

It seems clear that, as a new Cold War looms between the United States and China, the lessons of 1939 loom much larger than the lessons of 1914, both in Washington and Canberra. Washington has made it clear that it has no interest in seeking an accommodation with China that would meet any of China's aims to expand its influence in Asia and beyond. Washington's talk of preserving the 'rules-based liberal order' plainly embodies its intention to perpetuate the old status quo of US primacy, and its emphasis on meeting China's military challenge reflects its willingness to go to war with China rather than to compromise that objective. In Canberra, Scott Morrison made clear the influence of Munich on his policy when, launching his government's *Defence Strategic Update* in 2020, he explicitly compared today's strategic circumstances to those of the 1930s and early 1940s.⁹

Is this the right way to think about the problem of China? To be clear, the question is not whether we should try to resist China's ambitions, but how far we should resist them, and at what cost. Should Australia be willing to go to war, whatever the cost may be, to preserve the US-led regional and global order, and block any expansion of Chinese power and influence? Or should we be willing, reluctantly, to accommodate some of China's ambitions by accepting an expansion of its influence, in order to reduce the risks of war? It is not a simple question.

The lessons of Munich do not seem to offer a very helpful guide to answering it. The Chinese Communist Party has many faults and is responsible for much brutality and oppression, but it is not by any stretch comparable to the evil of the Nazi Party. China today is certainly strategically ambitious, but there is no serious reason to fear that – the special case of Taiwan apart, its claim to which the rest of the world acknowledges – it seeks to conquer and absorb others' territory. And although China is set to become the most powerful country on earth, it cannot dominate and subjugate such strong neighbours as India and Russia. Overall, then, the risks that China poses to the regional and global order, though significant, are not like those posed by Nazi Germany, or indeed the Soviet Union.

On the other hand, a war with China may well be as costly as the world wars of the twentieth century, or even more costly, especially if it becomes a nuclear war. That would be an almost unimaginable disaster even if our side won – a victory, as Churchill wrote of the First World War 'bought so dear as to be almost indistinguishable from defeat'.[10] Moreover, there is no reason to assume that we and our allies would win. Indeed, it is hard to see how a major war with China could be 'won' without the kind of full-scale invasion or subjugation of the enemy's country that brought victory in the two world wars. It is somewhat easier to imagine how China could defeat the United States – by imposing such heavy costs that Washington decides to abandon the war, and withdraw from Asia to the Western Hemisphere. That raises the very real possibility that a war with China launched to preserve the US's position in Asia might well end up destroying it, just as the First World War destroyed the empires that went to war to preserve themselves in 1914.

Lessons from history: Setting the limits to accommodation

What, then, do the lessons of 1914 offer as a guide to our policy choices today? In the 1920s and 1930s the majority of those who survived the First World War would have been quite clear about that. They would say that we should avoid war at almost any price, by being willing to go a long way to accommodate China's ambitions by according it a much larger share of influence and authority in the international system. They would have been confident, however, that China's ambitions could be constrained by limits imposed, not by armed force, but by a powerful international institution – the League of Nations – and by what they called 'international public opinion'. They repudiated war as an instrument of policy, but they placed great faith in these alternatives to achieve what war, or the threat of war, had long been relied upon to do. Of course, this did not work. As the historian E.H. Carr wrote just before war broke out in 1939, their misplaced confidence in these constraints, and what he later called 'the almost total neglect of the factor of power' did much to create the crisis which then confronted Britain with no alternative but to go to war again.[11]

We would be wise, then, not to follow their example. Where then to turn? We might begin by noting that the lessons of 1914 and of Munich are both aberrations. They depart from much older traditions of statecraft which had developed over many centuries as the modern European state system had emerged and evolved. Those traditions do not by any means forswear war. Indeed, as the former US Secretary of State Henry Kissinger, one of its foremost contemporary exponents, wrote in the first page of his first book: 'those who forswear war will never have peace'.[12] But the aim is always to achieve the maximum advantages without war, and that entails a willingness to negotiate and accommodate; to appease, in other words. War is not an alternative to accommodation; it is used to set the limits to accommodation and to enforce those limits. This approach prevented any single power dominating Europe for centuries, and after the 1815 Congress of Vienna it prevented any Europe-wide wars for almost a century until 1914. Seen in the light of this tradition, the appeasers' mistake at Munich was not that they accommodated Hitler over Sudetenland, but that they failed to make it absolutely clear that they would go to war to deny him the rest of Czechoslovakia, or any of Poland.

As that example makes clear, the key to this kind of statecraft lies in deciding where to set the limits to accommodation. These are hard decisions to make. As we have seen, one of the attractions of the lessons of Munich as a template for strategic decision-making is its simplicity. But it achieves simplicity by lazily assuming that all ambitious powers are essentially the same and must be treated the same by refusing any accommodation. Taking a more responsible approach requires careful judgments about the current and probable future extent of an adversary's ambitions and power, and nuanced assessments of the implications for our future security. Then we can judge how far we can afford to accommodate them before the costs and risks of doing so exceed the costs and risks of the war we would need to fight to stop them.

Looking back, for example, it is interesting and instructive to think about the alternatives to war in August 1914. Had Britain stood aloof, France and Russia may well have been defeated, leaving Germany the unquestioned leading power in Europe. That appeared an unacceptable outcome to the majority of the cabinet in Whitehall, but a minority argued that Britain could live with it more easily than it could bear the burdens of war, and in the light of events since then they were probably right.[13] After all, the Germany of 1914 was not Nazi Germany. And Australia might well have been better off had the arguments for peace prevailed in Whitehall. Not only would we have been spared the losses we suffered, but Britain would have remained a stronger global power that was better able to defend its Pacific dominions than it proved to be in 1941.

History does not repeat itself, but it does rhyme. As we face the challenge of a rising China we can hear the clear echoes of the choices faced by our predecessors in the last century and the centuries before that. Those echoes tell us that to meet that challenge we need to do a lot more than mouth slogans about Munich. We have to think carefully and realistically about the nature of China's challenge to the old order in Asia, the kind of new order that might be created to accommodate it, the safeguards that would be required to protect our most vital interests in that order, and how that might be achieved at minimum cost and risk. We must also think about how best we can influence our major ally as it addresses the same questions, because its answers will have immense significance for us. All this is a formidable task. Indeed, it is probably the most demanding foreign policy task that Australia has ever faced. But we should not be surprised by that, when we remember that China's rise is the biggest shift in Australia's international setting since Europeans first settled here in 1788.

In meeting that task, it falls to the present generation of political leaders, policymakers, commentators and, ultimately, citizens around the world to navigate one of the biggest, swiftest, most disruptive and most dangerous power transitions in modern history. One might say, too, that it falls to the current generation of historians to contribute to that work by offering a deeper understanding of the choices that were made by earlier generations navigating similar transitions. That is not easy, because the accepted versions of earlier episodes like 1914 and 1938–39 are encrusted with tradition, sentiment and ideology, and few historians have sought to challenge or overturn these accepted versions. Perhaps more will step forward as the nature and seriousness of today's choices, and the need to illuminate them with lessons from the past, become clearer. One key element of such work will be the methodologically vexed but undoubtedly stimulating exploration of counterfactual histories. To assess and learn from the decisions of 1914, we need more nuanced and sophisticated views of how Europe and the British Empire would have fared had Imperial Germany dominated the Continent. To assess and learn from the decisions of 1938 and 1939 we need to better understand what might have happened had different decisions been made. We also need to recognise and meditate on what might have happened had 'our side' not won the last two major power wars. Because we might not win the next one.

CHAPTER 7

Past as prologue: Repairing Australia's trade relationship with China

Philip Chang, Jeffrey Hole and Kieran Brockman

After Australia established diplomatic relations with China on 21 December 1972, the governments of both countries invested heavily to strengthen and broaden their relationship. An amicable political relationship between the two countries enabled the growth of bilateral trade in goods and services, and extended cooperation into other areas, such as culture, defence, and scientific and technological exchanges. The growth in Australia–China trade was further enhanced through China's market-oriented economic reforms, launched in 1978, along with Australia's far-reaching economic reforms initiated in the early 1980s.

While the bilateral relationship ebbed and flowed after 1972, the general trend until recently was a strengthening of Australia's trade relationship with China. Despite some major political differences, both sides prevented these incidents from permanently disrupting trade. The current diplomatic crisis between Australia and China has created a hostile political climate, affecting bilateral trade, investment and other areas of cooperation. This has led to calls by some major business groups and analysts to repair the trade relationship because both economies have benefited tremendously from trade with each other.

What can history tell us about this relationship? We find that two key factors – enlarged trade complementarity and robust political relations between Australia and China – drove the rapid growth of bilateral trade after 1972. However, trade opportunities between the two countries could narrow going forward as China moves towards an innovation-based economy, requiring more knowledge-intensive inputs and technology. If Australia wants to see high rates of future trade growth with China similar to the previous decades, policymakers will not only need to focus on improving the political relationship but also on finding new ways to expand trade complementarity. Australia will also need to develop a bipartisan China policy to provide an effective framework for future engagement based on the long-term national interest rather than short-term political considerations.

Australia and China: Key historical trends of bilateral trade

International trade has been an important contributor to Australia's economic prosperity because it has helped fuel the country's economic growth, create new jobs, and raise living standards. After 1972, trade with China became progressively more vital to the Australian economy. Trade in goods and services with China, as a share of Australia's total bilateral trade, increased from 1 per cent in 1972–73 to nearly 30 per cent in 2019–20; and as a share of Australia's gross domestic product it increased from 0.2 per cent in 1972–73 to nearly

13 per cent in 2019–20. In 2007 China overtook Japan as Australia's largest trading partner.

Australia's trade with China grew steadily between 1972–73 and the early 1990s, but accelerated at a fast pace from the mid-1990s onwards as trade complementarities between the two economies expanded and as the bilateral relationship deepened (Figure 1, page 100). Trade complementarity arises when two countries make natural trading partners, or more precisely, when a country imports goods and services for production or for final consumption from another country that can supply those goods and services at competitive prices.[1] The degree of trade complementarity is influenced by each country's comparative advantage, national economic policies, and stage of economic development.

Australia's goods exports to China as a share of total Australian goods exports increased from 1 per cent in 1972–73 to nearly 40 per cent in 2019–20. Primary products dominated Australia's exports to China but the composition changed to meet China's evolving development needs. Initially, wheat was the dominant export to China in the 1970s. Subsequently, wool became dominant in the 1980s and a large part of the 1990s. Finally, iron ore became the leading export to China in 1997, climbing from 22 per cent of total goods exports to China to 56 per cent in 2019–20.

As a share of total Australian goods imports, Australia's goods imports from China increased from 1 per cent in 1972–73 to 26 per cent in 2019–20. Manufacturing products were the major imports from China but the composition changed as China produced higher value-added manufacturing products. Between 1972 and 2002, textiles, clothing and footwear were the major Australian imports from China. As China became

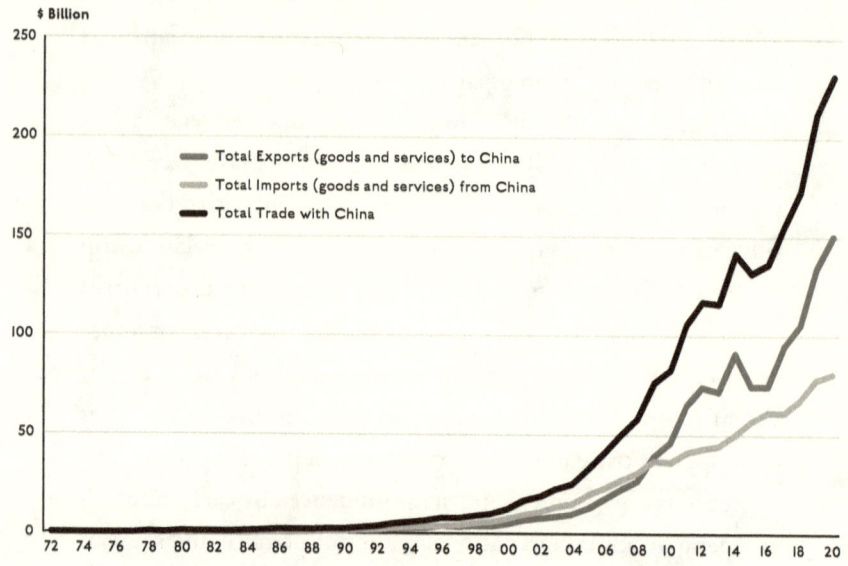

FIGURE 1

Australian exports and imports of goods and services to China, 1972–2020

more efficient at producing higher value-added manufacturing products, electrical machinery, equipment and appliances became the dominant imports in 2003. These accounted for 40 per cent of imports from China in 2019, up from 30 per cent in 2003.[2]

More recently, growing demand for services in China and the broadening of the Australia–China relationship led to rapid growth in Australia's services exports to China. Services exports to China as a share of total Australian services exports increased from almost zero to around 18 per cent in 2019–20, with much of this growth occurring in the last 20 years. Personal travel services and education-related travel services dominated. Exports of personal travel services grew sharply from $257 million in 1998–99 to over $13 billion in 2019–20.

Over the same period, exports of education-related travel services increased from $147 million in 1998–99 to over $10 billion in 2019–20. These two categories accounted for around 80 per cent of Australia's services exports to China in 2019–20.

Economic reforms in China and Australia, 1972–2020

Trade complementarity was one of the key factors that influenced bilateral trade flows between Australia and China in the period 1973–2020. The level of trade complementarity between Australia and China increased progressively as both countries implemented economic reforms, which created new opportunities and markets. In order to understand the nature of the China–Australia trade relationship as it has evolved, we need to understand the key economic reform measures implemented during this period in both China and Australia.

Reform and opening-up in China

In 1978, China was one of the poorest nations in the world, with a GDP of around US$150 billion (2 per cent of world GDP) and a rural poverty rate of 97.5 per cent, where the rural population comprised 82 per cent of the total population.[3] The Chinese government realised that to lift its population out of poverty, it had to restructure the inward-looking command economy, industrialise and urbanise to achieve high, sustained economic growth.

In December 1978, under the leadership of Deng Xiaoping, China launched the reform and opening-up process. It carried out the reforms in a gradual, experimental manner – extending them upon demonstrated success. China initially implemented rural reform in early 1979: collective farms were split into household farms, and farmers and township and village enterprises were allowed to sell their surplus production on the market. Subsequently, the annual average rate of growth in agricultural output accelerated from 2.9 per cent between 1952 and 1978 to 7.7 per cent between 1978 and 1984.[4]

Emboldened by the success of rural reform, China extended reforms to urban areas, particularly to support the development of individual businesses and private enterprises. The Chinese government granted land use rights and access to some inputs in 1981, amended the constitution to allow for the sale of land use rights in 1988, adopted the Corporation Law in 1993, implemented state-owned enterprise reform from the mid-1990s, and incorporated private enterprise and rule of law into the Chinese constitution in 1999. These reforms eased barriers to private sector development, which enabled rapid private sector growth in urban areas and the creation of millions of new jobs. This accelerated urbanisation in China.

China also initiated reforms to boost trade and attract foreign direct investment (FDI). It introduced laws permitting joint ventures with foreign businesses in 1979 and established four special economic zones (SEZs) between 1980 and 1984. These measures allowed China to open up the manufacturing sector to FDI, initially in the SEZs. Through FDI, many domestic manufacturing firms acquired new production technologies and know-how, which laid the foundation for the manufacturing take-off in the early 1990s. China's accession to the World Trade Organization (WTO) in 2001 further opened up new domestic and overseas markets for Chinese and foreign enterprises. In the two decades after joining the

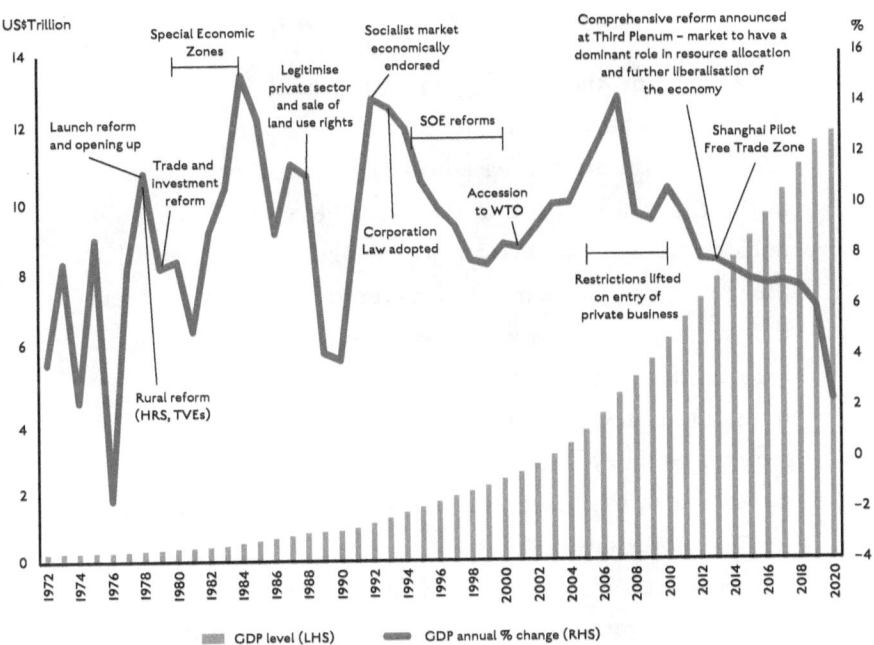

FIGURE 2
Reform and opening-up and China's economic growth, 1978–2020

WTO, the Chinese government eased restrictions on foreign investment in industries, such as civil aviation, energy, financial, infrastructure, resources and transportation (Figure 2).

As a result of reform and opening-up, the Chinese economy grew at an average annual rate of 9.2 per cent between 1978 and 2020, unparalleled in human history (Figure 2). In 2010 China overtook Japan as the second largest economy in the world. Its middle class swelled from 3 per cent in 2000 to over 50 per cent in 2020.[5] The miraculous Chinese economic growth and the rapidly expanding Chinese middle class created a major source of demand for Australian exports of goods and services.

Economic reform in Australia

When reform and opening-up commenced in China, the Australian economy was regarded as highly regulated and protected. Against the backdrop of a period of stagnation in the 1970s, a recession in the early 1980s, and major trade imbalances, a consensus formed among policymakers that the Australian economy had become uncompetitive, and that economic reforms were needed to encourage and enable Australian businesses to exploit the opportunities arising from growth in China and elsewhere.[6] Furthermore, economic reforms would expand access to imported goods and services by Australian businesses and consumers at competitive prices from countries such as China.

Between 1983 and the early 2000s, the Hawke–Keating and Howard governments implemented a variety of economic reforms designed to expose the economy to greater international competition and enable markets to play a greater role in responding to changing economic and trade opportunities. Key reforms included floating the Australian dollar; the dismantling of the quota and tariff system; lifting restrictions on foreign investment; deregulating the financial system; introducing enterprise bargaining; and improving efficiency in state enterprises through structural reform, competition and privatisation.[7] Policies and reforms implemented by subsequent Australian governments further opened up the Australian economy (Figure 3).

The dominant view among policymakers is that economic reform in Australia improved the flexibility and resilience of the Australian economy, and facilitated economic growth (Figure 3). Viewed in an economic context, the reforms implemented by Australia during this period had a positive effect by enlarging

Past as prologue

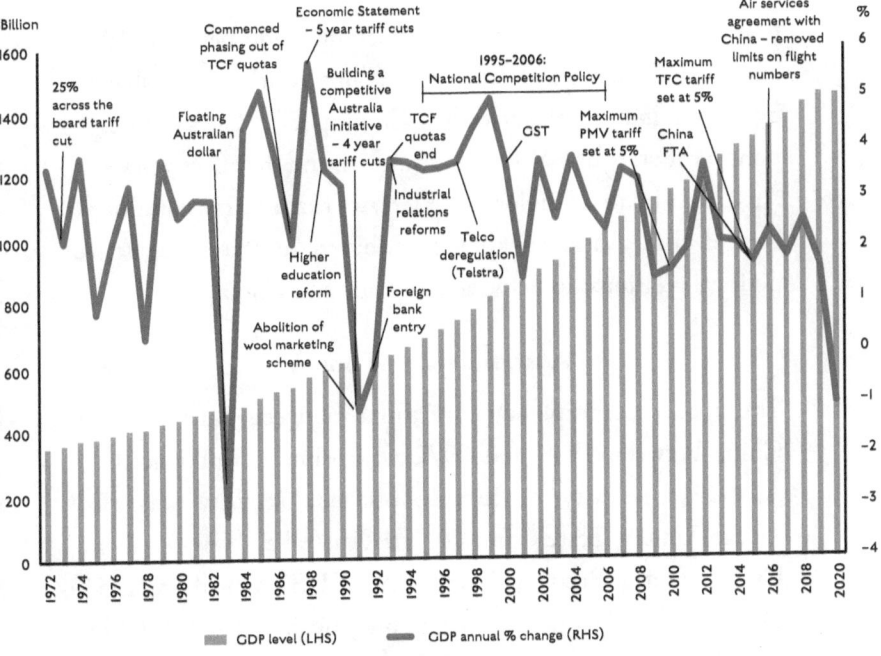

FIGURE 3
Economic reform and Australia's economic growth, 1973–2020

trade complementarity and hence trade flows between Australia and China. Viewed in a broader strategic context, the resulting growth in trade flows has tied the prospects for the Australian economy much more closely to conditions in China.

Australia–China relations: Conditions influencing bilateral trade

The state of Australia–China relations was another important variable that influenced bilateral trade flows. Combined with increased trade complementarity, a favourable political relationship between Australia and China was a key factor that drove the rapid growth of bilateral trade between 1973 and 2016. The state of Australia–China relations was shaped by a combination of Australia's China policy; China's foreign policy; the state of US–China relations; and the effectiveness of Australia's bilateral diplomacy. Here, we examine the conditions behind these variables that contributed to the constructive political relationship between Australia and China.

Australia's China policy

The absence of diplomatic relations between Australia and China between 1949 and 1972 was primarily influenced by Australia's security concerns. Australia's security was tied to the United States through the Australia, New Zealand, United States Security Treaty (ANZUS) signed in 1951. Consequently, Australia's foreign policy position towards China was similar to that of the US, because the Soviet Union and its allies, including China, were seen as a threat to global peace and stability during the Cold War period. By the early 1970s, China was perceived as less of a threat to Australia's security.[8] In December 1972 the Whitlam government ended its diplomatic recognition of the Republic of China (Taiwan) and transferred recognition to the mainland People's Republic of China. This provided the foundations for the expansion of the bilateral relationship between the two countries. The Fraser government further cultivated Australia's relationship with China to counter the Soviet Union's expanded interests in Asia.[9]

From the mid-1980s onwards, security concerns in Australia eased, reflecting reduced global political tensions and the ending of the Cold War. Overall, Australia prioritised economic interests over security interests in its China policy between 1983 and 2016, particularly during the Hawke, Keating,

Howard and Gillard administrations.[10] While the first term of the Rudd government (2007–10) placed greater emphasis on human rights and political differences, it refocused on economic interests during its second term (2013). Similarly, the Abbott government (2013–15) recalibrated Australia's China policy in the second half of its administration towards economic interests and signed the Sino-Australia Free Trade Agreement in June 2015.[11]

China's foreign policy

In the 1980s and 1990s, China's foreign policy focused on peace and development to support the country's modernisation program. In the 2000s, China added 'cooperation' as the third key principle of its foreign policy, which emphasised China's commitment to multilateral organisations. In 2007, President Hu Jintao stated that 'China [would] work to make the international order fairer and more equitable'.[12] In 2013, President Xi Jinping launched the Belt and Road Initiative – a global infrastructure development strategy, which became the cornerstone of China's foreign policy. The five core objectives that have underpinned China's foreign policy for some time have been: to foster domestic economic development, reassure Asian countries of China's peaceful rise, counter efforts to contain China's rise, expand and diversify access to natural resources, and reduce Taiwan's space to engage in international political activities.[13]

United States–China relations

After the US established diplomatic relations with China in 1979, the state of the relationship varied from positive to highly negative. The bilateral relationship between 1979 and

2016 was centred on cooperation and managing differences. The US had two main strategies. The first of these was to engage with China, not only on trade and investment, but also on educational, cultural, scientific and diplomatic exchanges. The second was to balance Chinese military power in Asia, with an increased military or diplomatic pivot towards Asia between 2012 and 2016. The objectives were to encourage China to be a responsible stakeholder in the 'rules-based' international system, and to continue to liberalise its economic and political systems.[14]

Australia's bilateral diplomacy

After establishing diplomatic relations, Australia worked constructively with China to develop the necessary institutional structure to foster bilateral relations and expand trade and cooperation. The Whitlam government opened the Australian Embassy in Beijing in January 1973, which facilitated information gathering and exchange; signed the first China–Australia trade agreement in July 1973, which provided the basis for the bilateral trade and economic relationship; established the joint trade committee (JTC) in 1973, which created a platform for identifying trade opportunities and resolving trade differences; and facilitated the formation of the Australia China Business Cooperation Committee (now known as the Australia China Business Council), which aided bilateral business activities.

In 1978 the Fraser government established the Australia-China Council (ACC), which promoted mutual understanding and fostered people-to-people relations.[15] In 1980 it also renegotiated the China–Australia trade agreement, extending cooperation to other areas, such as culture, defence, development assistance, health, science and technology.[16]

In September 1984 the Hawke government launched the China Action Plan, aimed at increasing bilateral trade and investment. That same year, it established the China-Australia Senior Executive Forum (CASEF), which institutionalised business contacts between the two countries. In 1987 it formed the Joint Ministerial Economic Commission (JMEC), which provided the main platform for ministers from both countries to discuss economic, trade, scientific, technical and educational cooperation, address challenges and resolve differences.

Successive Australian governments built on earlier bilateral initiatives. In 2013, under the Gillard government, Australia and China established the Strategic Economic Dialogue to promote closer economic negotiation, including an annual meeting between the leaders of both countries. Additionally, the frequent high-level ministerial and official visits between 1973 and 2016 were critical in deepening Australia–China bilateral relations, and safeguarding against possible external shocks to the relationship.

Resolving differences through diplomacy

In 1999 Australia's Foreign Minister, Alexander Downer, described Australia's relationship with China as 'a mature and broadly based relationship, a relationship based on mutual respect and mutual advantage. And part of that mature relationship should always be a hard-headed appreciation that China and Australia have both commonalities and differences.'[17] Indeed, there were many differences between Australia and China, such as China's nuclear testing, the China–Soviet dispute, Australia's de-recognition of the Khmer Rouge in Kampuchea, the Tiananmen Square incident, Dalai Lama visits, human rights, Taiwan tension, the South China Sea, Hong Kong protests, and the investigation into the origin of COVID-19. Some differences were tractable, and others were not. Nonetheless, diplomacy was used successfully in tackling some of the major differences. This section highlights three cases to demonstrate the effectiveness of diplomacy, including the framing of issues and approaches to raising issues with China.

The Tiananmen Square incident

The Tiananmen Square incident on 4 June 1989, which involved public demonstrations and a government crackdown, disrupted the Australia–China relationship. On 13 July 1989, the Australian government took concrete actions to express its displeasure over the incident, suspending all ministerial and political visits, defence and police exchanges, as well as bilateral development assistance programs. On the surface, the measures appeared to be a reversal of Australia's China policy, but in fact 'the Australian government demonstrated great flexibility in both rhetoric and conduct, leaving the door open for any new initiative as might be required by changing circumstances'.[18]

On 23 January 1990, the Australian government adjusted one element of the measures announced six months earlier, shifting its total suspension of ministerial visits to consideration of proposed ministerial visits on a case-by-case basis.[19] Following this policy adjustment, in May the Chinese Minister of Metallurgical Industry, Qi Yuanjing, attended the commissioning of the Sino-Australian joint venture at Mount Channar in Western Australia. In September, the Australian Minister for Trade Negotiations, Neal Blewett, attended the third annual session of JMEC in Beijing. Other high-level visits soon followed. On 26 February 1991, the Australian government lifted the remaining restrictions on political and economic contacts with China, with the exception of defence exchanges.

Australian human rights missions to China

After the Tiananmen Square incident, Australia consistently raised human rights issues with China at official meetings. During his visit to Beijing in April 1991, Australia's Foreign Affairs Minister Gareth Evans proposed allowing an Australian human rights delegation to assess the human rights situation in China. In this instance, the Australian government used diplomacy effectively to persuade China to allow the first foreign human rights mission from Australia.

In the lead-up to Evans' visit, the Australian Embassy liaised closely with the Chinese Foreign Ministry and informed senior Chinese officials of Australia's intention. During Evans' meeting with his Chinese counterpart Qian Qichen, the Chinese side had ample time to prepare a well-considered response. Qian responded positively to the request and stressed that the mission would help improve mutual understanding. He suggested that the delegation be called the Delegation of Australian Parliamentarians rather than the Australian Human Rights Delegation. Evans agreed to the name change and was satisfied with the outcome. The first foreign human rights delegation visited China between 14 and 26 July 1991. The second mission visited Beijing, Chengdu, Shanghai and the Xinjiang Uyghur Autonomous Region between 8 and 20 November 1992. The main achievement of the missions was an acknowledgment that 'human rights issues ha[d] a legitimate place on the international agenda'.[20] As a result of Australia's unprecedented human rights mission, China received similar visits from France, Switzerland, Austria, Britain, Canada and the US.[21] If Australia had taken a 'megaphone' approach, these missions might not have eventuated.[22]

The Taiwan Strait crisis and other issues

When the Howard government assumed power in March 1996, a plethora of political issues during the first eight months of the new administration plunged the Australia–China relationship to the lowest level since the Tiananmen Square incident. There were five major issues: Australia's support for the US military response to China's missile tests in the Taiwan Strait in March; Australia's condemnation of China's nuclear test in June; allowing Chen Shui-ban, a leading Taiwanese pro-independence activist, to attend the Asia-Pacific Cities Summit in Brisbane in July; the visit of Primary Industries Minister John Anderson to Taiwan to negotiate the sale of uranium in September; and Prime Minister Howard's meeting with the Dalai Lama in September.[23]

In November 1996, Howard approached China's president, Jiang Zemin, on the sideline of the APEC Summit in Manila. He assured Jiang that Australia's long-standing alliance with the US was for its own security and not directed against China. Howard also reiterated Australia's support for the One China policy, and emphasised focusing on common interests. Howard used diplomacy effectively to resolve misunderstandings and reset the bilateral relationship.

Lessons from history:
We need *both* good relations and expanded trade opportunities to boost prosperity

After diplomatic relations were established in 1972, trade with China became more important for Australia's economic prosperity. The exponential growth of Australian exports to China was driven by both increased trade complementarity and a favourable political relationship between the two countries. However, in 2017 bilateral relations between Australia and China began to deteriorate, as the key factors influencing the bilateral relationship started to change significantly.

In the first place, because of its strong alliance with the United States, Australia's relations with China have been influenced by the changing nature of the US–China relationship. After the ascendency of Donald Trump to the presidency in 2017, the United States' China policy shifted from cooperation and engagement to strategic competition.[24] For instance, the US went down the path of partial disengagement with China by imposing tariffs and restrictions on technology transfer.[25] More recently under President Joe Biden, the US has continued to balance Chinese military power in Asia and the Pacific through mechanisms such as AUKUS (a trilateral security pact between Australia, the UK and the US). For its own part, China's foreign policy has become increasingly assertive, through actions such as the militarisation of the South China Sea and increasing diplomatic pressure on Taiwan.

Partly in response to changes in US policy attitudes towards China, Australia's China policy has focused increasingly on national security over economic interests. This was reflected in the passing of the foreign interference and espionage laws in

June 2018, the exclusion of Huawei from Australia's 5G network in August 2018, the adoption of the foreign relations laws in December 2020, the revival of the Quad (a strategic dialogue between Australia, India, Japan and the US on security and economic issues) in 2017, and the announcement of AUKUS in September 2021.[26] Megaphone diplomacy also seemed to be used more frequently by the Australian government between 2017 and 2020.[27]

A confluence of these factors created a brittleness that affected the Australia–China relationship. Australia's unilateral call for an international inquiry into the origins of COVID-19 in April 2020 then acted as the impetus for a steep downward spiral. Starting in May 2020, China suspended imports of Australian coal, cotton, log timber, lobster and beef; imposed tariffs on Australian barley and wine; and reduced imports of Australian copper ore and concentrates, and sugar. In addition, China suspended ministerial contacts and the China-Australia Strategic Economic Dialogue.

While the total value of Australian exports to China had not been affected in 2019–20 due to record high iron ore export revenue (driven mainly by high iron ore prices), other export commodities subjected to the trade restrictions were affected badly.[28] The risk of a protracted dispute could permanently damage bilateral trade (especially in tourism and education services), as well as business and cultural links.

At present, there is no clear path to resolving this diplomatic rift. Some commentators have suggested that Australia could use back-channel diplomacy by sending a mission comprising Australian business leaders with access to the Chinese leadership to help repair the diplomatic relationship, and/or ease restrictions on some Chinese FDI in Australia.[29]

Debate about resolving the current diplomatic crisis should consider both the context and approaches that have worked in the past, while being mindful of changes in domestic and international conditions, particularly the altered policy stances of the US and China. However, several key lessons for policymakers emerge from examining the history of the Australia–China trade relationship.

First, Australia has previously used diplomacy effectively to address major differences with China. Given that Australia has limited control over the foreign policies of China and the US, if Australia still wants to engage with China in trade and other areas, it would need to use diplomacy in a more intensive and smarter way to tackle differences.

Second, history suggests that a robust political relationship between Australia and China does not guarantee a high rate of future trade growth without increased trade complementarity.[30] Given that China aims to accelerate technological development and innovation, as reflected in its 14th Five-Year Plan (2021–25), trade complementarity between China and Australia could shrink in the near future. If Australia wants to plug into the next phase of China's economic development, it will need to build domestic capabilities to meet emerging Chinese demands.

Finally, it should be remembered that for a large part of the period from 1973 to 2020, Australia's China policy was bipartisan and prioritised economic interests. However, as pointed out earlier, Australia has recently prioritised national security, partly in response to China's increasingly assertive foreign policy within the context of heightened rivalry between China and the US. Additionally, China's economic, technological and military strengths are projected to grow even stronger in the coming years. Given these changing conditions, the challenge for Australia is to clearly define the country's national interest, and craft an astute and bipartisan China policy that advances the national interest. A bipartisan policy would also provide a framework for effective engagement and help minimise domestic political advantage that might undermine the national interest.

CHAPTER 8

Foreign aid: Australia's reputation at stake?

David Lowe

The year 2014 was a momentous one for Australia's foreign aid program. In this year, the Australian government led by Tony Abbott ended the separate standing of the Australian Agency for International Development (AusAID) and integrated it with the Department of Foreign Affairs and Trade (DFAT). Many supporters of the foreign aid program and many connected to its past and recent operations were dismayed. As if to confirm their worst fears, the government announced a substantial reduction in foreign aid funding in December that year. At the beginning of 2014 the foreign aid budget was announced at $5 billion a year and was set to grow; by the end of the year it was to be capped at $4 billion annually and to decline in real terms in coming years.[1]

Behind the focus on spending there ran a rumbling debate on what these changes signalled about Australian values and Australia's reputation overseas. Tim Costello, head of World Vision, declared that the government's decision to reduce spending was 'immoral' and said that Australians needed to question their values as a nation.[2] Yet in the middle of 2014 the DFAT had produced a document, 'Australian Aid: Promoting prosperity, reducing poverty, enhancing stability', that had mentioned national values as fundamental to the foreign aid program. In addition to setting out the aims behind Australia's aid program, it began by declaring that the program reflected 'Australia's values' (and the government's commitment to reducing poverty and lifting standards through sustainable economic growth).[3] Missing from the 32-page document was any explanation of what 'Australia's values' were. In the foreword, Foreign Affairs Minister Julie Bishop pivoted quickly from the fleeting mention of values to a mix of policy adjustments and ambitious goals – of prioritising aid for trade, private sector partnerships and empowering women and girls. Bishop's key message was that foreign aid was about the pursuit of economic diplomacy for shared prosperity. 'Aligning our diplomatic, trade and development efforts will ensure the aid program supports the Government's commitment to put economic diplomacy at the heart of Australia's interactions with the world.'[4]

Bishop's language was a good example of how values and reputation often frame debates about the level and focus of Australia's foreign program, but they are used too fleetingly and inconsistently; and, as in the example provided by Bishop, they can appear tokenistic alongside strings of connected interests and goals. All too often, what the public is presented with are statements that serve the immediate concerns of the government in office. But what if policymakers engaged more fully and consistently with Australians on the connection between foreign aid and Australia's values and its international reputation?

There are indications that the Australian public connects foreign aid to values and reputation, however rubbery these concepts, more than they connect foreign aid to 'harder' ideas such as security. To tease this out further is to think historically, as an international reputation or set of national values implies a longer view. What connections have been drawn between articulations of Australian foreign aid efforts from the 1950s to the 1980s, and what values have been attached to them? The first four decades of Australian foreign aid represent roughly the first half of Australia's official foreign aid efforts to date, and include the Colombo Plan, the establishment of a separate aid agency, the independence of Papua New Guinea (the biggest recipient of Australian aid), and a major public review of the aid program, the Jackson Review, in 1984.

As we shall see, in its *mobilisation* of ideas and the framing of foreign aid debate and policy, the government has shown occasional concern for Australia's international reputation connected to the allocation of foreign aid. However, there remains a communications gap in Australia's foreign aid efforts between values invoked by policymakers and the public's view. Only select aid efforts have strong recognition and appeal with the taxpayer. One well-recognised example, at least to older Australians, is the Colombo Plan that provided opportunities for Asian students to study in Australia from the 1950s to the 1980s. More recently, short-term humanitarian efforts to provide relief in the wake of regional natural disasters have also proven popular.[5] But the foreign aid program as a whole, providing assistance year in, year out, suffers from inadequate understanding and faltering public support.[6] The result, according to a recent history of Australian foreign aid, is that, in addition to falling victim to sudden budget cuts, the aid program is only considered a serious part of Australia's overseas policies by a small number of people. Most changes to the program have come about through incremental bureaucratic measures and the 'court politics' played by those in charge in Canberra.⁷

Frames and values

Any appeal to 'Australian values' is inevitably imprecise. At the broadest level, however, it implies connection to popularly held views. Values do surface regularly in statements of overseas policy. Early in its administration, and 17 years before the competing claims of Tim Costello and Julie Bishop, the Howard government addressed directly the matter of values. In 1997, the first Australian White Paper on Foreign (and Trade) Policy, *In the National Interest*, was produced. In it was a section on 'national values', declaring that Australia's were those of a liberal democracy, which 'include the rule of law, freedom of the press, the accountability of government to an elected parliament, and a commitment to a "fair go"'.⁸ The paper was strong in its commitment to racial equality and eliminating racial discrimination. It also listed human rights as an inseparable part of Australian foreign policy, and it tied foreign aid to both values and Australia's international reputation: 'Australia has a direct interest in an international reputation as a responsible member of the international community, committed to the rule of law, ready to assist in cases of humanitarian need, and a constructive contributor to the economic development of its neighbourhood.'⁹ Values also help explain relationships with others. Most recently, in 2021, Prime Minister Scott Morrison invoked common values underpinning Australia's new trilateral security partnership with the United States and the United Kingdom (AUKUS), claiming that the three nations 'have always believed in a world that favours freedom; that respects human dignity, the rule of law, the independence of sovereign states, and the peaceful fellowship of nations.'[10]

What resonance, if any, do these sorts of values have with what the broader population think? Opinion polls provide one, albeit imperfect, means of assessing this. Until the late 1980s, polling on foreign aid was irregular and the extremely varied framing of questions adds to the difficulty in charting trends with consistency. In their recent history of Australian public opinion and foreign policy Danielle Chubb and Ian McAllister found significant public acceptance of the foreign aid program up to the 1980s. The support was assisted by the greater visibility resulting from the creation of separate government aid agencies from 1974, when the first of a succession of standalone agencies, the Australian Development Assistance Agency, was established. It may be, Chubb and McAllister suggest, that the Cold War also 'muted arguments' against foreign aid. From then on, polling increased but there remain severe limitations in what it reveals. Since 1998 a steady number of Australians (around four in ten) have suggested that levels of aid spending were 'about right', an option that, depending on the level being spent, attracts both proponents and sceptics of foreign aid; but the number wanting less spending has been rising against those who want more. Over the last 30 years, when Australians have been asked how foreign aid should rank in government spending priorities, it has always come a distant last behind domestic areas such as health, education, defence and social welfare.[11]

The language that politicians use to discuss policy significantly shapes public perceptions. Indeed, how the Australian public responds to foreign aid, as Chubb and McAllister argue, 'is a consequence of how political elites choose to draw on the notion of shared national values to mobilise support or opposition for a policy'.[12] How and where political elites engage in such acts of mobilisation are important.

So where can we look for such mobilisations? Logically, we might turn to parliamentary debates, where contest and the task of persuasion are to the fore. A Dutch scholar, Maurits van der Veen, has examined the 'framing' of debates and policy documents on foreign aid in four European countries over a 50-year period. Van der Veen coded the debates in the Netherlands, Italy, Belgium and Norway according to seven broad frames used to justify foreign aid spending: security; power or influence; wealth or economic self-interest; enlightened self-interest; reputation/self-affirmation; obligation/duty; and humanitarianism.[13]

Applying Van der Veen's approach to Australian parliamentary debates (now easily searchable through Historic Hansard) reveals that reputation/self-affirmation was the strongest means by which foreign aid was framed between 1945 and 1980 (predominantly deployed 36 times).[14] Australian politicians drew on all of Van der Veen's frames (security; power or influence; wealth or economic self-interest; enlightened self-interest; reputation/self-affirmation; obligation/duty; and humanitarianism), but there was a big gap between reputation and the next most-used predominant frame, humanitarianism (25 times), followed by enlightened self-interest (22) and power/influence (19).[15]

Let's take just a couple of examples in which reputation has been foregrounded in Australian parliamentary debate on foreign aid. In 1967, Liberal Party member and government Treasurer William ('Billy') McMahon was reputation-minded when defending the level of foreign aid spending against

Foreign aid

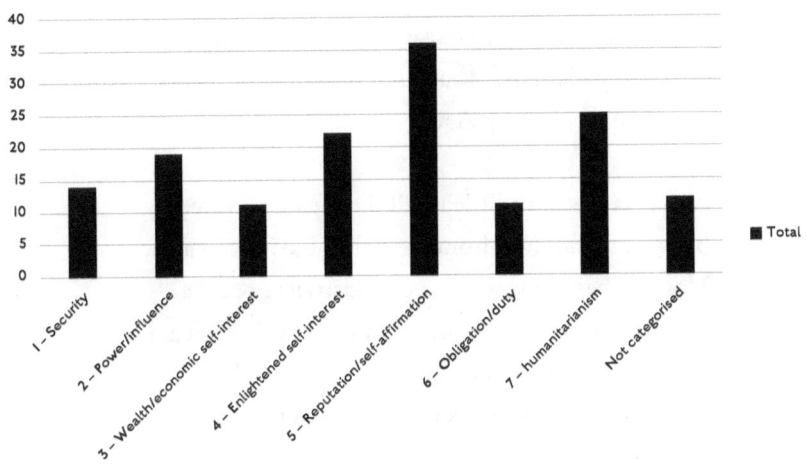

TABLE 1

Australian House of Representatives speeches featuring foreign aid, 1945–80, according to predominant means of framing, using Van der Veen's seven frames.

criticism that it had not reached the UN target of 1 per cent of gross national product. McMahon proudly boasted that Australia's level of foreign aid ranked second only to that provided by France, and that it consisted entirely of grants rather than loans:

> Our record in this field is very good. If there is to be any criticism it must be against the background that we are devoting almost 0.8% of our total national product to assistance for other countries. We are doing this willingly, freely and without any tags attached. No other country gives as freely as does Australia. No other country gives aid without tags.[16]

Five years later, his party colleague Len Reid bemoaned having to continually demand that the government provide more foreign aid to developing Asia:

> Australia has done little to fill the vacuum created by Britain's withdrawal from the South East Asian area. Most of these countries expect Australia to play a more dominant role in the area insofar as foreign aid is concerned. However, we have dismally failed, as little leadership or initiative is being given in this field.[17]

Some frames are more effective than others. A 2018 survey of 4000 Australians found that some frames were likely to elicit stronger support for Australia's foreign aid program. The survey used three broader frames – 'enlightened national self-interest', 'Australia as a global leader' or 'altruism' – to test levels of support for a particular Australian aid initiative. While all three frames helped increase levels of support for aid, the 'enlightened self-interest' category was the strongest; with 'altruism' similar in impact.[18]

But the data swirls around, even in seemingly similar research exercises. Another study found that Australians were likely to support higher levels of foreign aid when they learned that British aid funding was much higher than Australia's – a clear link to reputation.[19] And in another study from 2016, it was moral obligation rather than national interest that people identified as important for determining when Australian governments should provide foreign aid.[20] These findings, for all their variability, are significant in two ways. First, they confirm that Australians connect notions of Australian values and reputation to the foreign aid program; and secondly, this goes to the issue of how to increase public support for the foreign aid program.

What insights do less public, internal reviews of the foreign aid program offer on connections to values and reputation? In Australia, the first such review was small-scale; in 1955, a review was conducted of the Colombo Plan. It concluded that the diplomatic impact of the Colombo Plan, the goodwill generated in parts of Asia, was probably more significant than poverty alleviation. The second review, nearly ten years later, was triggered by External Affairs Minister Paul Hasluck. Writing to Prime Minister Menzies in September 1964, Hasluck commented that: 'The impression I have after having participated since 1951 in Cabinet discussions is that this external aid has grown up as the result of a succession of decisions on a succession of largely unrelated proposals or requests.'[21]

In November 1964 a specially formed interdepartmental committee was created in Canberra to study 'the philosophy and practice of Australia's foreign aid', and to prepare a report with recommendations about the pattern and administration of aid into the future.[22] It covered everything that went by the name of aid, including expenditure in Papua New Guinea, international efforts, such as those under the Colombo Plan, and defence aid materials. It included the most senior public servants, was chaired by Canberra mandarin Sir Arthur Tange, and met 26 times before reporting at the end of March 1965.

The terms of reference also allowed considerable breadth in the purposes of foreign aid. Asked for their views, Australian overseas posts reported back in broad terms, which the committee used to inform six main purposes of Australia's foreign aid. Firstly, the respondents said, foreign aid should demonstrate Australian concern with the development problems of underdeveloped countries. Secondly, it should promote respect and goodwill for Australia, with acceptance or at least sympathetic understanding of Australian policies, of the West, in world and domestic affairs. Thirdly, it should allow entry into influential and governing groups of the recipient countries, thereby facilitating good relations with Australia. Fourthly, it should foster in these countries political systems conducive to good relations with Australia, and creating conditions for sound economic development. Fifthly, it should encourage continued assistance to under-developed countries by our friends and allies, by demonstrating Australia's intention to bear the present share of the load and perhaps more. And finally, it should help pursue Australia's trade interests.[23]

In addition to these, the final report added an extra four: a special commitment to Papua and New Guinea; a commitment to Commonwealth cooperation; commitments to multilateral aid efforts and to the World Bank; and to provide a fair share of humanitarian assistance.[24] These extra points were arguably the strongest connectors to values as they evoked an ongoing commitment to PNG, a reaffirmation of the Commonwealth as a force for good in international affairs and a sense of moral obligation that Australia needed to contribute to the shared task of assisting in development – the notion of the 'fair share' was present in 1965.

Analysing the key policy documents feeding into and including this major review from the perspective of Van der Veen's frames is also suggestive. Consideration of 20 key documents generated by officers of Australia's External Affairs Department (renamed Foreign Affairs in 1970 and then Foreign Affairs and Trade from 1987) for the purpose of the review, reveals that power and influence was the strongest means of framing the benefits flowing from Australian foreign aid (strongly present five times). This was closely followed by reputation (four times). The submissions featured deep thinking about the multidimensional aspects of aid provision and, as most were from overseas posts, also a high degree of reflection on how Australian efforts compared with others' aid programs. All of the seven frames used by Van der Veen were present.[25]

Less confidential but official depictions of Australian foreign aid have followed a similar pattern. In the collection of ministerial and government statements compiled by External Affairs in their monthly bulletin *Current Notes on International Affairs*, the frame of reputation/self-affirmation also loomed largest in relation to foreign aid in 1965 (and indeed in the previous lighter-touch review year ten years earlier). The next most-invoked frame was security in these public statements.[26]

Taking the 1965 review into account alongside the other findings, we might tentatively conclude that while reputation/self-affirmation bridges the two worlds of diplomatic confidential policy papers and public statements, the diplomatic realm is more attentive to power and influence, while public depictions of why foreign aid matters steer more towards security. In one confidential paper from 1972, preparing for the independence of Papua New Guinea, officials declared that the *purpose* of Australian foreign aid was the economic development of recipient countries, but the specific reasons *why* Australia should provide it 'as set out publicly by previous ministers for foreign affairs, have been basically humanitarian'. Purpose and justifications were different things. They then suggested that Australia's *national interest* was also involved, given the 'strategic, economic and trade interest' in promoting development; and concluded by dwelling on the hard-to-measure but important *political value*: 'our record as a sympathetic aid-giver has greatly helped our image as a country which has a real desire to work peacefully with its neighbours'.[27]

In 1984, a major review, the Jackson Report on Australia's Overseas Aid program, tried to cut through such meandering by establishing a 'trilogy' of aid objectives upfront: humanitarian, foreign policy and trade objectives. 'Surprisingly, perhaps', said Foreign Affairs and Trade Minister Gareth Evans afterwards, 'recognition of the need for a clear statement of objectives for Australia's aid was a major step forward', given what he felt had been a lack of realism and a struggle to move beyond declarations of humanitarian good during the previous decade.[28] The language of objectives seemed to signal both a mainstreaming of Australia's foreign aid within a growing Canberra bureaucracy focused on the prosecution of Australia's interests overseas, and a desire to move past unprofitable debates over values underpinning aid.

Lessons from history: Reputation matters

Australian governments have failed to integrate foreign aid as a logical, publicly identifiable component of Australia's overseas policies in ways that might resonate with the public in the same manner as security treaties, alliances, consular work and so on. This might be a legacy of Australia's ambiguous status among 'developed and developing' countries. From the 1950s to the 1980s, Australian politicians and policymakers spent considerable time arguing that Australia was hybrid; part-developed and part-developing, and its commitments to foreign aid needed to be seen in this context. They also struggled to convey how Australia's colonial government of Papua New

Guinea might be folded into broader aims behind foreign aid. How did PNG's dominance in Australia's aid budget before (when it was not foreign aid but colonial or domestic funding) and after independence mesh with the notion of 'our fair share' and appeal to Australian values?

But the missed opportunity by governments to engage more consistently with the Australian public also arises from the mish-mash of aims, purposes and interests that have been publicly served up. Maurits van der Veen suggested that being closely involved in the provision of foreign aid was like working in a restaurant: the reality looks less appealing 'once one scrapes away the veneer of official statements, glossy brochures and rigorously culled anecdotes'.[29]

One of the strongest aims behind foreign aid that is shared by both governments and the Australian public lies in the concern for Australia's reputation. The relativity of aid giving has always mattered. As Billy McMahon made clear in 1967, when Australian governments allocated aid they were conscious of what other governments were spending, and this influenced the scale and sometimes the nature of Australian foreign aid. Those involved in the politics and policy of Australian foreign aid before and after him have always kept a close eye on what others are doing; but they have not spent as much time explaining consistently why foreign aid matters and what is Australian about it.

Policymakers have not made enough of this broadly shared concern for Australia's reputation. The Australian public will respond constructively when invited to think about foreign aid, when given sufficient clarity and opportunity, and foreign aid policy will benefit from more consistently engaged citizens. If Australian governments were to provide greater continuity in connecting aid to values, if they were to embed foreign aid with well-promoted, easily digested histories of Australia in its region and as an international citizen, then the policy benefits might be several. Governments could, working with public expectations, bring more stability to the foreign aid program. Stronger public engagement would render it less easily made a political football, and less likely to experience yo-yo ups and downs in promises versus actual budgets allocated. It could, at last, be elevated as an important aspect of Australia in world affairs, and no longer be the preserve of 'court politics' played out by a select few in Canberra.

CHAPTER 9

An open door? Foreign investment and multinational companies

Simon Ville

Foreign multinational enterprise is a large and powerful institution in most contemporary societies. Yet, for good or bad, these enterprises evoke strong emotions. The privacy intrusions of Facebook or the national security concerns over state-owned foreign firms are contemporary cases in point. In Australia in 2016, foreign firms accounted for over a third of the top 2000 businesses and owned in excess of A$1 trillion of assets.[1] How they exercise their authority remains contentious for government, business and consumers. Government concerns focus on their economic and financial effects, particularly on policy directions and tax yields. More recently, national security considerations have come to the fore when multinationals have been owned or influenced by foreign governments. The impact of multinationals on competition and prices has raised concerns among domestic firms and consumers. On the positive side of the ledger, many countries have viewed multinationals as a vehicle for accelerated economic growth when they bring innovation, employment and new products.

Multinationals have a long history in Australia: at least 200 foreign firms had set up here by 1870, there were an estimated 466 operating in 1914, and around 1360 by 2010. The long sweep of history enables us to examine from hindsight many of the current debates about the nature and impact of multinationals. These include an appreciation of their diversity by origins, sector and organisational form, along with understanding their contribution to innovation and economic growth and their effects on competition in several industries. The history of multinational investment in Australia reveals some surprising patterns and trends; for example, rather than always assuming control of key industries, they sometimes faced stiff competition from local firms and indeed other multinationals. Nor have they all been large global organisations. Governments would do well to recognise these questions of diversity and contestability when designing policies targeting the broad-ranging effects of foreign firms in Australia.

The origins and idea of a multinational enterprise

The term 'multinational enterprise' only originated in the 1960s, coined by US scholars interested in the rapid global growth of large-scale American firms after the Second World War.[2] As one writer recently noted, 'Economists, during the 1960s, fashioned the idea of "multinational enterprise", without realising how long it had existed as a form of business.'[3] However, business historians began to undertake research projects which showed that similar organisations could be traced back at least to the second half of the nineteenth century. Arguably, the multinational dates back a good deal further, with the rise of international trading companies from Europe in the sixteenth and seventeenth centuries, such as the English East India Company. But these companies mostly traded under the protected conditions of a monopoly charter granted by their national government in return for providing political and military influence in regions not formally colonised.[4]

Multinationals are a diverse group of businesses. They are normally defined as firms that control income-generating assets in more than one country; for example, factories for manufacturers, equipment for transport and communications firms, or skilled labour in services. While factories are a clear example, the operation of a modest sales office or servicing centre may also count as income-generating in the absence of local production in the host economy.

A second defining issue is where control of the enterprise lies. This is straightforward in the case of a fully owned foreign subsidiary, but often firms are only partly owned by a foreign entity, and the ownership threshold that is defined as control – commonly known as foreign direct investment – has varied across time. Today, an overseas entity only has to own 10 per cent of the equity of the domestic firm for the latter to be deemed a multinational.[5] A contractual relationship with a local firm in the host country – for example, a licence to manufacture the foreign company's products – presents another grey area. The term 'migrating multinationals' refers to firms that shift their domicility to minimise regulatory barriers or political risks, such as asset seizures by a national government.[6] Nor is *effective* control solely associated with the location of the investment. Some local subsidiaries have a greater say over operations and strategy than do others and this balance of power can shift over time. For instance, many early British multinationals ceded much of their original power to local boards and managers in Australia because of the problems they had in making and enforcing decisions at a time of slow and irregular communications. This began to change from the 1870s with the arrival of the oceanic cable.

History presents further challenges in understanding the multinational. Often, we have insufficient information on investment or effective control to decide unequivocally if a firm was a multinational. Instead, we resort to structural definitions such as where the company's head office was located. This has been the approach to the study of multinationals in Australia before 1914, where investment data and archival evidence are both limited. The historical relationship between two nations also raises questions about a firm's domicility. Were British firms in the Australian colonies before Federation merely extending their activities into other British territories? However, most writers have argued that the interests of these firms were distinct from those of their host nation, particularly after the beginnings of self-government in the Australian colonies from the 1850s.

The historical development of multinational enterprise in Australia

The scholarly study of multinationals in Australia has grown in recent years.[7] The earliest multinationals reached Australian shores in the 1820s, less than 40 years after colonial settlement in 1788.[8] The Australian Agricultural Company (AAC) (1824) and the Van Diemen's Land Company (1825) – the earliest – were land settlement companies. In the following decades, finance companies began to arrive, including commercial banks, mortgage banks, trust companies and insurers. In the wake of the Victorian gold rush, mining companies arrived in huge numbers from the 1850s; many were speculative and few survived long. Among the few successes was the highly adaptive Port Phillip and Colonial Mining Company, based in Clunes in Victoria, which shifted from alluvial to quartz mining, then to specialising in the crushing and treating of quartz for other firms. The company also became an investor in other successful mines.

Most early multinationals operated only in Australia. Contrary to modern conceptions of a multinational that expands overseas from a strong domestic base, they had few operations in their country of origin, Britain, and rarely settled in other host nations. This type of firm was identified as a form of multinational by US business historian Mira Wilkins in the 1980s who termed it the free-standing company. Since they were British-owned and overall strategy resided with British promoters, Wilkins deemed them multinationals.[9]

In the final decades of the nineteenth century, multinationals arrived from a broader range of nations and settled into a more diverse set of industries. In line with Australia's expanding economic and strategic global perspective beyond the boundaries of empire, new firms arrived from North America and Continental Europe, particularly from the United States, Germany and France. The appearance of American enterprises affirms the evidence provided by other historians of a tilt towards closer relations between the two nations.[10] Concepts of economic and social modernity were associated with the developing global leadership of the US and challenged the dominance of imperial Britain.[11]

The challenge to British leadership focused on the new capital-intensive and science-based industries of the second industrial revolution – branded, packaged products; mass-produced light machinery; electrical equipment; industrial chemicals and metals.[12] Firms such as General Electric, Siemens, Kodak, NCR, United Typewriter, Remington and Singer supplied the market for goods such as electrical equipment, typewriters, cameras and sewing machines. They were different in character from firms of the mid-nineteenth century. Many were global manufacturers who would survive well into the twentieth century and some into the twenty-first. General Electric was an emerging modern American multinational. By the First World War, it manufactured in the major markets of Canada, France, England, Japan and Germany. In nations with smaller markets, such as Australia, South Africa and Mexico, it conducted the sale and distribution of its imported products.[13]

General Electric was typical of most foreign manufacturers in Australia before 1914, in limiting its activities to branches that distributed the imports of the company's products manufactured overseas and provided after-sales servicing and repairs. However, in 1905, newly merged Nestlé and Anglo-Swiss Milk Company Australasia acquired production facilities in Australia including farms, creameries and butter factories in Victoria and Queensland.[14] Schweppes was one of the earliest overseas firms to manufacture in Australia, with factories in Sydney from 1877 and Melbourne from 1885.[15]

A very different form of multinational – one rarely identified in the literature – also became evident by the late nineteenth century. By the 1890s wool was increasingly sold in Australia before overseas shipment. Representatives of overseas, primarily European, wool manufacturers began to establish offices in Sydney and Melbourne to participate in the wool auctions. The heterogeneous nature of fine merino wool with many grades and measures of quality encouraged buyers to attend the auctions in person. By the 1920s wool precincts had developed in the main Australian centres and included the modest offices of many overseas wool buyers and brokers, some located inside the city's wool exchange. Forty-two firms had Melbourne offices by 1927, particularly those representing the Flemish textile manufacturers of Roubaix and Tourcoing. Despite their apparently diminutive size, several buyers set up offices across the wool-producing and textile-manufacturing nations. For French wool buyers Masurel Fils, their William Street branch in Melbourne formed part of a global network of buying offices in Sydney, Durban, Port Elizabeth, East London, Buenos Aires and Montevideo. Wool purchased in these centres was then shipped to manufacturing districts in Britain and Continental Europe.[16]

The two world wars impeded the Australian operations of multinationals from enemy nations, particularly Germany. Under the terms of the *Trading with the Enemy Act* (1914) and the *Enemy Contracts Annulment Act* (1915), firms faced being suspended or brought under government control. Van der Eng has estimated that 45 firms were affected, which also included several Australian firms, for trading with the enemy. The diversity of ownership structures complicated the tasks of legislators. Siemens Brothers Dynamo Works, a joint subsidiary of Siemens Brothers & Co. Ltd in the UK and Siemens & Halske AG of Germany, was placed under a controller and continued operating until 1923. Another affected firm, Polack Tyre and Rubber Company in Melbourne, was a subsidiary of B. Polack AG in Germany but was incorporated in London.[17]

In the twentieth century, waves of multinationals arrived from the United States, Europe and Japan.[18] However, the overriding trend has been the further broadening of the geographic origins of multinationals in Australia. Britain's virtual monopoly of the multinational sector in the mid-nineteenth century had begun to diminish by 1914, with 12 other sender nations featuring. In the following century this diversification went much further. By 2010, multinationals based in Australia came from 70 nations spread across the globe (Table 1). The largest share, 30 per cent from the US, was much less than the UK dominance (70 per cent) a century earlier. Other major senders were mostly from Europe, with the exception of Japan. Several firms found their way from smaller and less developed economies – for example, Ethiopia, Pakistan, Jordan, New Caledonia and Bermuda. Diversity by size and industry was again notable.

Many American firms operated in Australia in the 1920s, some for the first time, others to extend their activities from pre-war sales to local production. They were largely market-oriented in their investment strategy, seeing the Australian market as wealthy and growing, with similar tastes to American consumers. Ford had operated a sales office from 1910 to coordinate the marketing and sales of its imports. It produced its first car in Australia, a Model T, in a former wool warehouse in Geelong in 1925, previously owned by British multinational wool broker Dalgety.[19] By the end of 1926 Ford had plants in all mainland states. The same year, General Motors began assembly in Australia and merged in 1931 with Holden's Motor Body Builders Ltd, its supplier of car bodies.[20] Component suppliers followed suit, particularly Goodyear Tyre and Rubber Company in 1927. American firms also led the development of electrical equipment, particularly Standard Telephones and Cables (1928) for telephones and Sunbeam (1934) for household appliances, and they established a strong presence in food and drink, metals, chemicals, pharmaceuticals and oil products.[21]

Continental European manufacturers also began to stake out a presence in consumer industries in Australia between the wars, with Philips from the Netherlands being one of the pioneers in 1933.[22] It produced a wide range of electrical and telephony-related products, including incandescent lamps, radio sets, broadcasting equipment and radio components. A more substantial expansion of European firms in Australia occurred in the 1950s, with the arrival of automotive companies Volvo (1946), Volkswagen (1957), Fiat (1958), Daimler (Mercedes-Benz) (1958) and Renault (1959).[23] There was a further boom in European arrivals towards the end of the century; by 2010 they accounted for around a half of multinationals.

Several Japanese firms had arrived in Australia before Federation, particularly the trading companies Kanematsu and Mitsui. However, it was in the 1960s and 1970s that waves of Japanese multinationals began to arrive, encouraged by the complementary needs of the two economies and the signing of a commerce agreement in 1957. Toyota, NEC, Mitsubishi, Sumitomo, Sony, Fuji and Daikin led widespread investment in the Australian economy across consumer electronics, vehicles, construction and project development, as well as the production, processing and marketing of resources. Building on the knowledge and long experience held by the Japanese trading companies, along with the support of public institutions such as JETRO (Japan External Trade Organization), Japanese multinationals arrived with a good understanding of the Australian market that contributed to the success of many of them.[24]

LESSONS FROM HISTORY

TABLE 1

Multinationals by country of origin, 1820–2010[25]

Country	1820–70	1914	2010
Britain	196 (98)	326 (70)	104 (8)
US		45 (10)	425 (31)
Germany	3 (1)	29 (6)	64 (5)
France		19 (4)	186 (14)
New Zealand		12 (3)	7 (1)
Japan		6 (1)	108 (8)
Sweden		6 (1)	12 (1)
Belgium	1 (1)	6 (1)	7 (1)
Netherlands		3 (1)	46 (3)
Canada		2 (1)	11 (1)
Switzerland		2 (1)	63 (5)
Hong Kong		1 (1)	10 (1)
Austria		1 (1)	2 (1)
China			9 (1)
Czech Republic			11 (1)
Denmark			8 (1)
Finland			27 (2)
Italy			85 (6)
Norway			45 (3)
Spain			37 (3)
Ukraine			6 (1)
UAE			7 (1)
Others		8	80 (6)
Total	**200**	**466**	**1360**

SOURCES For 1910, 1914: Simon Ville and David Merrett, *International Business in Australia before World War One. Shaping a multinational economy*, Palgrave, 2022, chs 4, 5. For 2010: *Foreign Companies in Australia Yearbook 2010*, Commercial Intelligence Service, London, 2010.

NB The eight firms in the Others row/1914 column were all joint ventures.

The effects of multinationals in Australia

The economic, social, political and cultural impact of multinationals on host nations is a highly contested topic. Opponents, for example, have alleged tax evasion practices by firms shifting costs between nations, and anti-competitive strategies made possible by their size and global reach. Supporters, however, point to the new innovations they bring to the host country along with additional employment from local production.

These are not new questions. In Australia tax avoidance and the foreign acquisition of strategic assets have been regularly highlighted and remain important concerns today.[26] Others have argued that multinationals are a challenge to national sovereignty and that foreign values are shaping our belief systems.[27] It has also been argued, though, that the national interest is served by the new investment, ideas and employment which have been brought to Australia via multinational enterprises. Indeed, multinationals have long played an important role in introducing new technology, products and whole industries into Australia. Foreign firms have been responsible for a growing share of patents in Australia in the twentieth century, and their role in the introduction of broad spectrum and general purpose technologies has often been critical in such areas as electricity, motor vehicles, electronics, transport and communications, information technology and medical products. Brash's study of the transfer of American managerial systems to Australia in the 1960s also points to positive outcomes in organisational innovations.[28]

Measuring the effects of multinationals is far from trivial and depends heavily on conditions in the host nation. In less developed host nations where institutions and political power are unstable and infrastructure is weak, multinationals have often acted with disregard for the wellbeing of locals. Indeed, instability or power vacuums could benefit multinationals whose economic interests were assisted by, and in turn justified, imperial policy and the extension of empire. The annexation of Burma through three wars (1823–26, 1852–53 and 1885) was inextricably tied to the interests of British firms operating in the country. Firms such as the Bombay Burmah Trading Company sought access to the valuable resources of the Irrawaddy Valley, including teak and rice. Informal ('residents') and then formal (Federated Malay States) British control of the Malay Peninsula facilitated local rubber production by British traders like Harrisons & Crosfield and Guthries. Dunlop established plantations in Malaya in 1910.[29] American multinationals behaved with similar impunity in the Caribbean and Central and South America. As Mira Wilkins describes, the United States and Nicaragua Company (1903) 'covered more than 10 million acres in northern Nicaragua, and included exclusive mining privileges and the right to build and to operate railroads, telephones, and the telegraph'.[30]

Australia's historical experience of multinationals was quite different and might be termed 'contested multinationality'. Multinationals have had much less freedom of manoeuvre. In the private sector, the settler community was deeply embedded in business and economic activities. There was to be no 'plantation economy' controlled by multinationals, since pastoral and agricultural settlement spread across the country largely in the hands of small family farms.[31] Nor were local industrial and service firms a pushover for their foreign counterparts. In industries such as banking, locals learned to emulate the competitive advantages of British firms.³² Where this was not possible in some of the industries of the second industrial revolution, locals adapted complementary business models, such as to become pharmacy distributors and retailers (Australian Pharmaceutical Industries and Sigma Pharmaceuticals) and vehicle distributors (Tarrant Engineering). Multinationals also faced competition from one another, particularly in periods of changing global leadership. In the late nineteenth century, a changing of the guard occurred as American and German firms challenged British leadership on many fronts. Australia was a significant battlefront – Britain's strong imperial connections were challenged by American and German firms in pursuit of a growing, wealthy market and skilled workforce.

When British and American 'meat packers' arrived towards the end of the nineteenth century, their sphere of influence was constrained by each other, Australian competitors, a strong upstream community of livestock farmers, the state railway systems, and government inquiries. A 1914 royal commission listed 51 'principal' firms in the meat export trade and concluded, 'there is no evidence at present of an attempted restraint or monopoly'.³³ Another battleground among multinationals and local firms was the production of tobacco. In this case, though, the financial resources of the largest multinationals prevailed as the industry consolidated by acquiring local producers. Finally, in 1904 the two remaining giants, Imperial Tobacco from the UK and American Tobacco from the US, formed a holding company, which controlled the local industry.³⁴

Colonial governments had controlled several key areas of network infrastructure and supply chain connections, notably the railways, ports, postal services and utilities, on which businesses relied heavily. In the course of the twentieth century, policymakers sought to balance the benefits of the presence of foreign firms with restricting their freedom to act contrary to the national interest.[35] Until the 1960s, public policy was relatively receptive to foreign firms. However, there was a growing feeling that Australia was missing out on the benefits of multinationals, particularly technology transfer, export opportunities, and the downstream development of the natural resource industries. These concerns spurred policy changes to rein in multinationals and facilitate local participation in joint projects, culminating in the *1972 Foreign Companies (Takeovers) Act*. This was the first peacetime legislation to limit foreign direct investment across all industries. The Foreign Investment Review Board was set up in 1976 to advise the federal government on company acquisitions by foreign firms. Policy swung back to receptiveness from the mid-1980s as part of the Hawke–Keating governments' policies of stimulating economic growth through deregulation.

This brief outline paints a fairly benign picture of the impact of multinationals in a strong host nation like Australia. Yet, multinationals with significant global reach possess a key strategic advantage over national governments because of their ability to shift resources among countries in response to policy or other changes. Although there are limits on the mobility of fixed capital investments, some multinationals have manipulated their intra-firm operations across borders to minimise tax liabilities; this is often referred to as transfer pricing. In recent decades, supra-national governmental efforts to counter this revenue loss have intensified. In 1998, the OECD launched the Harmful Tax Practices project, which identified policies in individual nations likely to abet tax avoidance and encouraged their removal.[36] Despite the progress made by this initiative, some companies continued to pay only small amounts of taxation. In 2013 the OECD renewed its efforts to curtail tax avoidance with the BEPS (Base erosion and profit shifting) project, which now has over 140 jurisdictions participating.[37]

The most recent wave of multinationals arriving in Australia may present the greatest policy challenge. Sinosteel Australia established an office in Perth in 1991 as part of the Channar Mining Joint Venture agreement with Rio Tinto to mine iron ore in the Pilbara. This heralded the expansion of Chinese investment in Australia. Over the following decades, investments followed from other Chinese firms in mining, real estate and services.[38] Overall, Chinese investment has been modest compared with Japan and previous waves from the United States and Britain. China had been liberalising its economy for several decades, encouraging markets and private enterprise. The expansion of trade with China, as previously with Japan, has led to increased investment. However, the main difference with previous waves of multinationals has been the presence of several large State-Owned Enterprises (SOEs). Initially, this raised few concerns. In 2009 China experts Peter Drysdale and Christopher Findlay wrote: 'Anxiety over the growth of foreign investment by China is as unfounded as it was ... over the growth in foreign investment by Japan that accompanied the emergence of Japan as Australia's major economic partner and a major supplier of capital to world markets.'[39]

However, the connection of SOEs, and arguably other Chinese firms, to the ruling Communist Party in an era of Chinese economic and military expansion has raised strategic and security concerns in the last few years. In 2018, Australia was the first country to ban Chinese communications company

Huawei on the grounds of national security because of its alleged connections to the Chinese government. Three years earlier a Chinese-owned firm had been awarded a 99-year lease on the Port of Darwin. Whether this lease should now be revoked remains a source of contention among the political parties on the eve of the 2022 federal election. While not a government-owned firm, the geo-strategic implications of Chinese ownership of the closest major Australian port, located directly southwards from China, are clear. The irony of that company's name – Landbridge Group – may have attracted less notice.

Lessons from history: Balancing the scales of multinational effects

Australia has a long history of hosting foreign firms. Several policy-relevant messages arise from this experience. First, the impact of multinationals is heavily dependent on the nature of the host nation. In Australia, contrary to many natural resource-focused nations, the freedom of action of multinationals is constrained by countervailing forces – the roles of government, the actions of the private sector, and the competition of other multinationals. Secondly, multinational enterprise is a diverse and oft-changing institution, whether viewed by country of origin, industrial sector, organisational structure or size. Most firms are not large global manufacturers. Taken together, these two factors – contestability and diversity – suggest Australia can shape its policies towards multinationals with some latitude, but that those policies must be responsive to change, taking each case on its merits. On this basis, the Foreign Investment Review Board has been a significant advance on broad-based policies of much of the twentieth century, but questions remain about its ability to balance the economic benefits and security implications of new firms under foreign government influence. Australian participation in supranational initiatives in areas like taxation is also vital to counter the influence of the most powerful global corporations. In summary, the lessons of history focus on the need to balance good and bad in understanding the diverse impacts of multinationals and to avoid politicisation of either side of this 'balance sheet'.

CHAPTER 10

Tackling inequality: Lessons from the postwar reconstruction

Andrew Leigh

My grandfather, Roly Stebbins, was born in a tent in 1922. His father was a veteran, who had suffered what we would now call post-traumatic stress disorder while serving in the navy during the First World War. The condition affected him so badly that he lost his job. In 1936, at the age of 14, my grandfather left school and found a job at a holiday resort. The job didn't pay much, but he did extra tasks to earn a few more shillings and sent most of it back to his parents.

When the Second World War broke out, Roly went with his two best friends to enlist. Because they were under-age, the recruiter needed parental permission. The other two boys' parents said yes. Roly's parents said no. His two best mates were killed on the battlefield. If Roly's parents had allowed him to enlist, I might not be writing this chapter.

So brutal were the First and Second World Wars that we can sometimes forget the hardships that came between them. Almost all the gains that had been made in the 'roaring twenties' were wiped out by the Great Depression. Average earnings, in today's dollars, averaged $6.42 per week in 1921. They rose to $7.58 in 1930, before plunging during the crash. By 1937, average earnings were back at $6.42 a week.¹ In 16 years – half a generation – Australian workers got zero real wage gains.

During the interwar period, new forms of entertainment emerged, such as radios and talkie-pictures. Australians thrilled to see Don Bradman on the cricket pitch, and Phar Lap on the racetrack. Max Dupain and Albert Namatjira shook up the art world. But for millions of Australians, this all took place amid a backdrop of relentlessly high unemployment, falling real wages and grinding poverty.

By the end of the Second World War, momentum was growing for a new social compact. Prime Minister John Curtin promised Australians 'Victory in War – Victory for the Peace'. Although Curtin would not live to see a single day of the postwar era, he set in motion many of the coming changes. As the historian Liam Byrne puts it, 'The Curtin government moulded the age. It actively created a new era, transforming our economy, our politics, and our society. It defied the inherited orthodoxies and expanded the bounds of the possible.'²

The Curtin government's slogan was not 'Let's Snap Back to 1939'. For the governments of Curtin and Chifley, victory was about advancing the nation. Their ambition was to build a more prosperous and egalitarian society. It is testament to their vision that they laid the foundations for that work. From our present standpoint, it is especially remarkable that it continued to be implemented by the Menzies government, elected in 1949.

Roly Stebbins was one of the millions who benefited from these changes. He and his wife, Jean, got a cheap plot of land in Seaholme, near Melbourne's Williamstown. With help from mates in the neighbourhood, he built a home – firing bricks in a friend's kiln, and doing nearly all the construction himself.

Roly loved cars, and bought his first in 1949. The man who was born in a tent raised his four children in a solid seaside home.

To a surprising extent, my grandfather's story is the story of the postwar era. Unemployment fell. Home ownership skyrocketed. Car ownership roared ahead. The economy grew, but inequality declined. To anyone who claims that a growing gap between rich and poor is 'the price of progress', the postwar decades are a clear rebuke. It is possible for wages to grow faster on the factory floor than in the corner office. We know it can be done, because that's precisely what happened from the late 1940s onwards.

What spurred on these changes? In part, they were a reflection of the sense among many returned soldiers that too little had changed after the First World War. Despite the horrific loss of life (one in 40 Australian men were killed), the ensuing decades saw high levels of inequality and unemployment. There was little evidence of a 'peace dividend' in the 1920s. Many of the leaders of the 1940s had been shaped by their experiences in the First World War, and wanted to ensure that the benefits of peace were felt by everyone.

A mark of this shift in attitudes can be seen across regional Australia. Many small towns have a memorial – often in the form of an obelisk – listing the local soldiers who died in the First World War. And then they will have public amenities – such as a swimming pool or a set of tennis courts – built in the years following the Second World War. After the first global conflict, Australian towns built symbolic memorials. After the second, Australian towns built amenities that improved the quality of life for their residents.

The nation-building response that followed the Second World War can serve as an example to today's policymakers, at a local, state and national level. After the fighting ceased, there was a determination to invest in human and physical capital, and to create public infrastructure that would tangibly improve the quality of life for everyday people. Postwar reconstruction gave substance to the words so often intoned at remembrance ceremonies: that the dead should not have died in vain. Australia's postwar reconstruction captured the spirit of the age so powerfully that the key reforms endured when a conservative government took office in 1949. In this chapter, I focus on four aspects of reconstruction: jobs, homes, cars and economic inequality.

Jobs

In public policy, a key milestone was the *White Paper on Full Employment*, drafted in 1944 and 1945 by H.C. (Nugget) Coombs and a team of fellow economists in the Ministry of Post-War Reconstruction. It began with an excoriating denunciation of the way that the economy in the interwar years had served Australians:

> Despite the need for more houses, food, equipment and every other type of product, before the war not all those available for work were able to find employment or to feel a sense of security in their future. On the average during the twenty years between 1919 and 1939 more than one-tenth of the men and women desiring work were unemployed.[3]

The *White Paper on Full Employment* didn't mince words. Traditional economists might have called unemployment 'inefficient'. The White Paper said unemployment was 'evil'. Yet it also recognised that work needed to be meaningful. The White Paper praised workplace flexibility. It celebrated technological advances. It rejected 'schemes designed to make work for work's sake'. It might be true that jobs could be created by paying one group of people to dig holes, and another group of people to fill them up again. But the authors of the White Paper recognised that for many people, work is integral to their sense of dignity. This means that if the goal is to raise wellbeing, then jobs must be fulfilling. In effect, the 1945 White Paper rejected what US anthropologist David Graeber recently dubbed 'bullshit jobs'.[4]

In the First World War, Australia supplied hundreds of thousands of men, but relatively little industrial production. By contrast, the Second World War saw a surge in manufacturing employment, as Australian factories produced munitions and equipment for the troops. After fighting ceased, many factories were repurposed to produce consumer goods.[5] This included consumer durables such as fridges and washing machines, as well as cars. In the food manufacturing sector, households that had previously made jam, pickles and biscuits at home now began purchasing them. Canning and bottling technologies allowed families to buy canned meats, vegetables and beverages. The increased uptake of refrigerators expanded the market for frozen foods.

A similar trend occurred with clothing. In the nineteenth century, clothing was typically tailored to the buyer. This might have suited the most affluent. But it meant that working people generally owned only a couple of sets of clothes (sometimes made at home). As an off-the-shelf clothing market developed, it created more opportunities for employment in the clothing and footwear manufacturing sector, as well as in the growing retail market. In the building sector, an increase in residential construction expanded the demand for bricklayers, electricians, plumbers and tilers.

Job creation in the postwar era was not merely a function of consumer demand. Throughout the war, government had played a major role in the economy. After the war, governments looked to grow employment in strategic industries and focused on demand management through control of wages, policies and key lending rates. Union density grew from around one-third of the workforce in the 1930s to almost half the workforce in the 1950s. The size of the federal public service quadrupled between 1939 and 1951.[6]

The Commonwealth Ministry of Post-War Reconstruction (1942–50) coordinated many of these efforts, aided by the fact that full employment was widely recognised as the nation's top policy goal. Not all of the measures adopted would prove themselves in the long run (tariff protection limited the growth of firms that had a comparative advantage on a global scale), but the overall effect was to reshape the labour market. Where work had been scarce in the 1930s, it was plentiful by the late 1940s.

Figure 1, page 154, shows the unemployment rate since Federation, with the years 1945 to 1960 denoted by a shaded area.[7] From a double-digit jobless rate in the interwar period, unemployment dropped to around 2 per cent for the next three decades. From Federation until the outbreak of the Second World War, Australia's unemployment rate only once dipped *below* 3 per cent. From the end of the Second World War until the early 1970s, unemployment only once went *above* 3 per cent. French economists refer to this 30-year postwar period as *Les Trente Glorieuses* ('The Glorious Thirty'). The same could be said of the Australian labour market over these three decades.

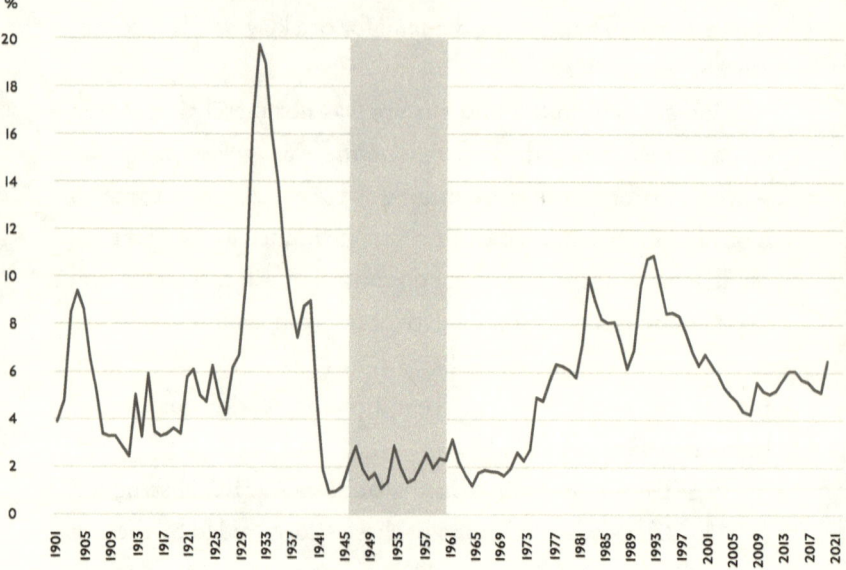

FIGURE 1
Unemployment

This impact flowed through to wages. According to one estimate, real wages grew at just 0.71 per cent per year from 1922 to 1941, but 2.44 per cent a year from 1942 to 1971.[8] Average working hours fell. The 1947 Arbitration Court ruling for a 40-hour week can be readily seen in the average number of hours worked, which fell from around 45 hours per week in the 1930s to 40 hours per week in the 1950s. Paid annual leave increased from one week per year in the 1940s to three weeks per year in the 1960s. Plentiful jobs, rising wages and falling hours led to a sense of shared prosperity. New workplace technologies were increasing productivity, with employees getting a fair share of the benefits.

Homes

Through the Great Depression, reformers had been drawing attention to the inadequacy of the Australian housing stock. For example, Methodist social reformer Oswald Frederick Barnett highlighted the conditions of Melbourne slums, which resulted in the state government establishing a Housing Investigation and Slum Abolition Board. Increasingly, poverty was seen as a result of poor circumstances, rather than individual moral failings. Perhaps the most visible manifestation of these poor circumstances were homeless people, with a tent encampment even springing up on the Sydney Domain during the Great Depression.

Nationally, one report estimated a housing shortfall of 300 000 dwellings.[9] Given the population of the time, this is the equivalent of a one-million house shortage in modern-day Australia.

In 1942, the Australian Parliament's Joint Committee on Social Services linked housing to health and child wellbeing, writing that 'without provision of housing for all on such a scale we cannot hope to establish and maintain the proper standards of public health, child welfare and morality, which are prerequisites to the building up of a healthy, virile and great people'.[10] Inadequate housing was regarded as a constraint on population growth, on the grounds that people would be reluctant to have children – or would limit family size – in response to overcrowding. Poor housing was seen as a disease risk, and even as a factor that might lead to a decline in moral standards (though in this case the causal connection was perhaps more dubious).

This era featured major planning exhibitions, aimed to educate and excite the public about developments in urban design and architecture.[11] In 1944, the Commonwealth Ministry of Post-War Reconstruction sponsored a major exhibition in Sydney that showcased a 'modern urban development', featuring a community centre, schools and shops. Many of the streets were cul-de-sacs, intended to reduce through-traffic and encourage families to socialise on their front lawns. Architectural models showed the latest home designs, using new building materials and featuring spacious living areas. The exhibition travelled to Newcastle, Brisbane, Adelaide and Perth. A similar exhibition in Melbourne subsequently toured through regional Victoria and Tasmania. Sparked by urban exhibitions in the United Kingdom and the United States, these events were a conduit through which modernist design ideas were transmitted to the public and helped inspire investment in housing.

Between 1945 and 1949, 200 000 homes were built. Some of these were the product of the first Commonwealth-State Housing Agreement, which constructed new dwellings for rental, many on the outskirts of major cities. But many of the new homes were owned outright, leading to an unprecedented increase in the home ownership rate.

Figure 2 charts the home ownership rate since the start of the twentieth century, with the earliest reliable estimate being for 1911.[12] From 1911 to 1947, just over half of Australians owned their homes. Then, over a seven-year period – from 1947 to 1954 – the home ownership rate shot up by a remarkable 10 percentage points. Home ownership continued to rise in the ensuing decade, peaking at a remarkable 73 per cent in 1966. Not only was this historically high by Australian standards, but it exceeds the home ownership rate in the United Kingdom,

Tackling inequality

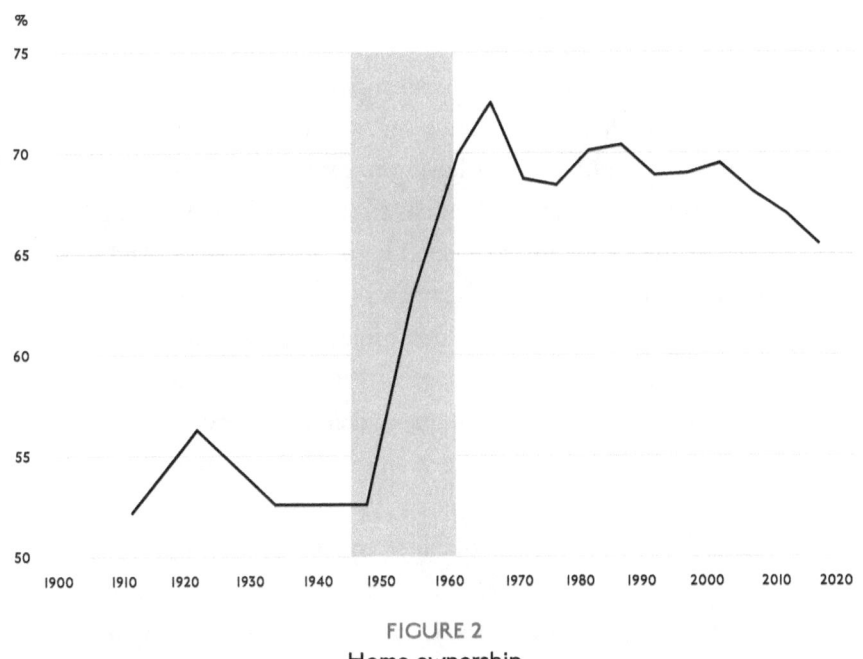

FIGURE 2
Home ownership

Canada and the United States at any point in the twentieth century.[13] Since then, the home ownership rate has declined, falling to 66 per cent in the 2016 census.

The quality of Australian homes also improved in the early 1940s and early 1950s. When my grandfather was born in 1922, living in a tent was not all that remarkable, even for the family of a naval veteran. Even a generation later, living under canvas was not unheard of. In 1947, 15 450 Australian households lived in tents.[14] Just seven years later, this number had halved. From 1947 to 1954, there was also a marked drop in the share of people who lived in homes made from stone, iron or tin; and a substantial rise in the number of homes with outer walls made from brick, concrete or fibro cement.

Cars

For many Australians, car ownership represented a vast increase in wellbeing. Owning a car meant not having to walk to work in the rain and not having to carry groceries home by hand. It made it easier for families to see loved ones who lived in places that were not connected by public transport. And it enabled people to take a holiday away from home (sometimes sleeping in the car). When the first Holden sedans rolled off the assembly line in Fishermans Bend in 1948, they cost about two years' wages for a minimum wage worker. By the mid-1960s, a new Holden cost one year's work on the minimum wage.

Figure 3 charts the growth in Australian car ownership.[15] National figures are only available from 1922, so to produce the longest possible time series, I extend this back to 1910 using figures for New South Wales. Cars are typically shared within a household, but because average household size falls from five people to three people over this period, it risks distorting the trends. Accordingly, I present vehicle ownership both as cars per person, and as cars per household.

These estimates show that at the end of the Second World War, there were just 0.07 vehicles per person in Australia. By 1955, this had doubled to 0.15 vehicles per person. By 1970, it had doubled again to 0.31 vehicles per person. Today, there are 0.57 vehicles per person in Australia; a figure that has remained steady since 2014.

On a household basis, car ownership was 0.28 vehicles per household in 1945, 0.57 in 1955, and 1.09 in 1970. Assuming that few households owned multiple vehicles in the 1940s and 1950s, the household results suggest that car ownership passed 50 per cent in 1954. In the modern era, multiple car ownership is commonplace, with an average of 1.7 cars per household.

Tackling inequality

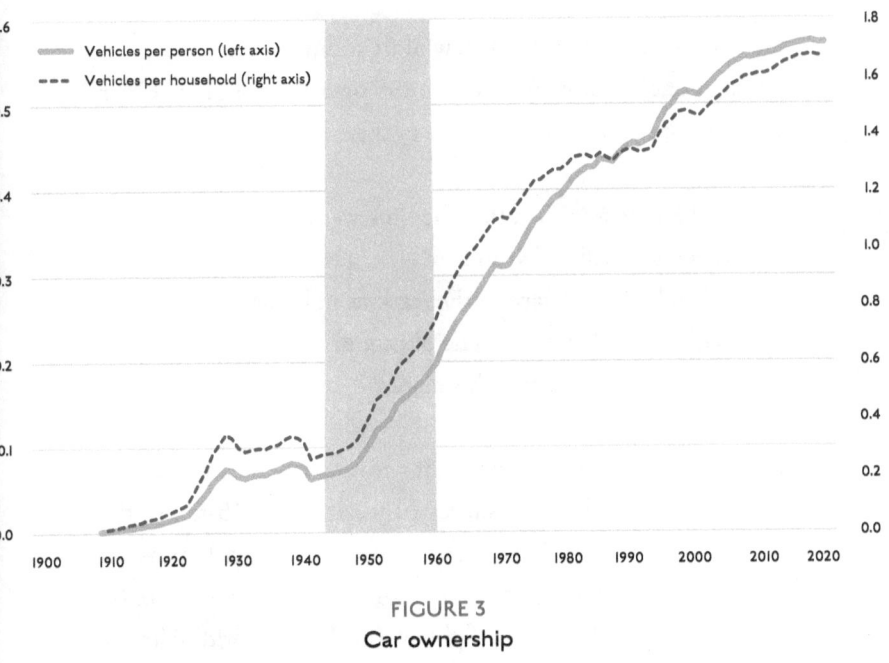

FIGURE 3
Car ownership

A different source of data – the population census – also provides some insights on this question. The 1966 census was the first to ask Australians whether their household owned a car. Fully 76 per cent of households reported having at least one vehicle, with 23 per cent reporting owning multiple vehicles. Car ownership had gone from just over one-quarter of households at the end of the Second World War to three-quarters of households a generation later.

Inequality

Australia has always prided itself in a distinctively egalitarian ethos. You're more likely to be called 'mate' than 'madam' or 'sir'. We don't have private areas on our beaches. Many of us sit in the front seat of taxis, while few of us stand up when our prime minister enters the room. In his 1895 poem 'Since Then', Henry Lawson captured this masculine egalitarianism:

> And I almost wished that the time were come
> When less will be left to Fate –
> When boys will start on the track from home
> With equal chances, and no old chum
> Have more or less than his mate.[16]

Yet despite this, levels of inequality around the time of the First World War were high. A survey of wealth in 1915 found that the richest 1 per cent held over one-third of the nation's assets: a greater level of inequality than in the United States in 2020.[17] Many soldiers who left to fight in the First World War had formerly been unemployed.[18]

To gain an accurate picture of inequality across the twentieth century, it is insufficient to rely on surveys. The Australian Bureau of Statistics only began asking about incomes on a regular basis in the late 1960s, so surveys provide a patchy picture of income distribution in the 1940s and 1950s.

The alternative is to use taxation statistics, which are published annually, and can be analysed using external control totals for population and personal income. In Figure 4, I present two data series.[19] The first is the income share of the top 1 per cent of adults, which can be calculated at a federal level back to 1921, and back to 1912 using Victorian taxation statistics (NSW did not publish the relevant figures for this period). The second series is the Gini coefficient of male incomes – an index which ranges from zero (perfect equality) to one (complete inequality).[20] From 1942 onwards, a majority

Tackling inequality

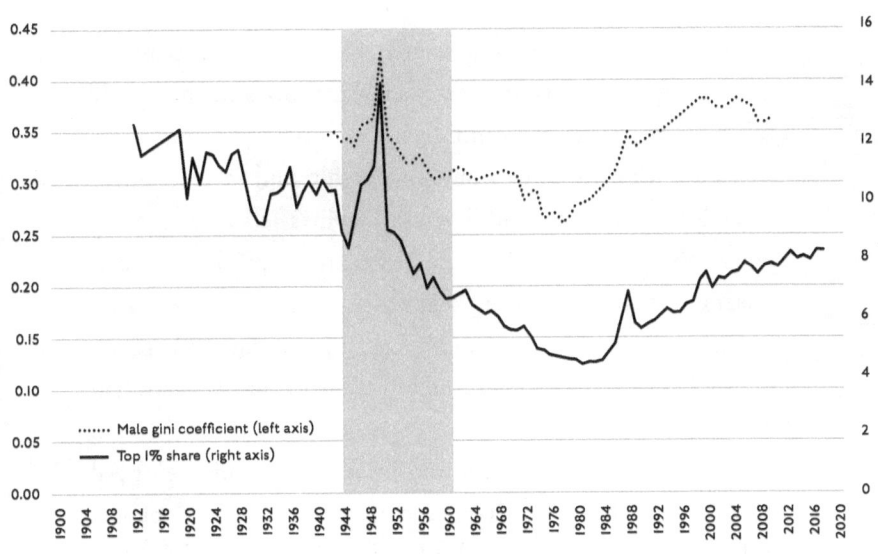

FIGURE 4
Inequality

of adult men paid tax, so taxation data – combined with census records where available – make it possible to estimate the Gini coefficient for men. While men constitute less than half the population, they report most of the income earned by households, so it turns out that the male Gini coefficient tracks the household income Gini coefficient quite closely in contexts where both can be estimated.

An immediately striking fact about inequality in the postwar era is the huge spike in the 1950–51 tax year, which was driven by the Korean War wool boom. Setting this aside, both male income inequality and the top 1 per cent share fell steadily. From 1945 to 1980 (the low point for Australian inequality across the twentieth century), the top 1 per cent share dropped from 8 per cent to 5 per cent, and the Gini coefficient of male incomes dropped from 0.34 to 0.28. To put this change in perspective, the reduction in inequality is equivalent to the modern-day inequality gap between Australia and the highly egalitarian countries of Scandinavia.

In addition to rising home ownership and increasing car ownership, increasing middle-class incomes led to increasing ownership of appliances. By the 1960s, the typical Australian household had a vacuum cleaner, washing machine, radio and television. In that era, most British, German and Italian households lacked a refrigerator, but 97 per cent of Australian homes had one.[21]

Another metric can be found in William Rubinstein's 'All Time Australian 200 Rich List', which identifies those people whose wealth exceeded a fixed cut-off (0.17 per cent of national income) from 1788 onwards.[22] Rubinstein focuses on wealth at the time of death, but if we consider those who were in their last two decades of life, then there was an average of 22 all-time Australian rich people in any given year. However, these people are not evenly spread across the centuries. In the 1820s and 1880s, there are an excess of all-time rich listers. But from 1940 to 1980, there were precisely zero members of the all-time rich list living in Australia. For these four decades, Australia became a mogul-free nation.

The equalising era would not have occurred without the Second World War. As historian Walter Scheidel notes, the history of inequality is of long periods of rising or stable inequality, punctuated by sudden compressions. Those levelling episodes have typically been due to four causes: warfare, revolution, state collapse and plague. 'All of us who prize greater economic equality', Scheidel notes, 'would do well to remember that with the rarest of exceptions, it was only ever brought forth in sorrow.'[23] In the 1940s and beyond, the impetus for egalitarianism was warfare. In the 2020s and beyond, might the plague of COVID-19 inspire a more equal era?

Lessons from history: Striding boldly forward, not snapping back

At the end of the Second World War, my grandfather Roly Stebbins was 23 years old. For today's 23-year-olds, what should the federal government's priorities be?

As a federal member of parliament, one of the joys of my job is the chance to speak with a wide variety of Australians in their early twenties. From these conversations, clear themes emerge. Young Australians want their nation to play a leadership role in reducing our carbon emissions, and encouraging other countries to do the same. No advanced nation is more affected by dangerous climate change than Australia, and our abundant wind and solar resources make this an opportunity to create jobs and boost the productivity of the economy.

In the world of work, someone who is just hitting the labour market today may not retire until the 2060s, 2070s or 2080s. By then, many of today's jobs will not exist, and a plethora of new jobs will have been created. We don't know what those jobs will be (a generation ago, who would have predicted the growth of data scientists and speech pathologists?), but we do know that they will require more education than the jobs of today. In the past generation, automation has supplanted the jobs of many 'routine' workers, who perform repetitive tasks in factories and offices. Over the next generation, it may take over the work of many manual workers.[24] The best bet is to have a broad base of skills, and the ability to continue to learn. Getting that right means improving the quality and quantity of education.

Young Australians are as passionate about fairness as any cohort in society today, and keen to link up with the world (an enthusiasm that has only grown with the closure of our international border). They tend to be less racially prejudiced, and more open to the gains from immigration and ethnic diversity.[25] An ambitious federal government today would be pursuing a strategy of 'engaged egalitarianism' – seeking the productivity gains from migration, trade and foreign investment, while ensuring that the costs of engagement do not fall unfairly on any segment of society. This approach would be quite different from the high tariff barriers of the postwar decades, reflecting the widespread recognition that trade not only provides a greater variety of affordable products and services, but also gives a dose of competitive pressure to local firms. Managing our relationship with China has become more complex under President Xi, as the country has become more powerful, militarised and authoritarian. But China has never been a democracy, and it ought not be beyond the wit of the Australian government to work together on shared challenges such as climate change and economic development in the Pacific, while standing firm for liberal democratic values.[26]

Finally, there is a strong yearning to build a healthier civic community.[27] Over the past two generations, Australians have become less likely to join community groups, play organised sports, volunteer their time, donate to charity or engage in the political process. A reconnected Australia would draw on the strengths of successful groups such as Pub Choir (which brings strangers together to sing a three-part harmony in a Brisbane pub), parkrun (which organises hundreds of free running events every Saturday morning), and Puddle Jumpers (a fast-growing Adelaide charity that provides camps for children who don't live with their birth parents). A more connected nation will not only be happier, but more productive too.[28]

In the early days of the COVID-19 crisis, it was common to hear members of the federal government talking about their hope that Australia would 'snap back' to its pre-crisis state. But a philosophy of 'back to 2019' exhibits what might be called the soft bigotry of low ambitions. Australia needs a step forward, not a snap back. The success of the postwar reformers in tackling the challenges of their era should inspire us in addressing the opportunities of our age.

CHAPTER II

Electricity problems? Call a historian. Learning from the history of electricity reform in Australia

Jeffrey Hole

Electricity has been an important enabler of economic and social development around the world over the past 150 years. But as we are now acutely aware, its generation through burning fossil fuels has also had a major detrimental impact on the environment. A key challenge facing all nations, including Australia, is finding ways to ensure that electricity continues to support economic and social development, while reducing its adverse environmental effects.

Australia's energy and climate policy is at a crossroads. In the lead-up to the November 2021 United Nations Climate Change Conference in Glasgow, the Australian government announced a commitment to reduce emissions of greenhouse gases to net zero by 2050. It also released a long-term strategy that attempted to explain how this target is to be achieved. This strategy is just the latest, however, in a series of proposals to deal with climate change. Over more than a decade, plans have been proposed, implemented, unwound or rejected. The

Gillard government introduced a carbon tax in 2012, but it was abolished in 2014 after the Liberal-National Coalition, led by Tony Abbott, came to power. In 2018, the Commonwealth proposed, then withdrew, the National Energy Guarantee, a policy intended to reduce emissions and ensure energy reliability. The latest strategy provides funding to develop new energy technologies but it lacks interim targets or new policies for reducing emissions from the electricity sector. State governments have stepped into the national policy void and introduced a wide variety of targets and policies to achieve them.[1] Political battles over climate and energy policy in the last decade have contributed to the downfall of prime ministers and opposition leaders on both sides of politics, leading to the lament that the last decade has been a period of policy 'drift'.[2]

Commentary on reforming the national electricity market seldom considers that Australia has previously experienced periods of major change in the electricity industry. The present makeup of the industry looks very different from its composition prior to 1998, when the national electricity market was introduced. Understanding the role of government in previous transformations offers key lessons for politicians, policy advisers and the community about what needs to be done to break through the current impasse on national energy and climate policy. It highlights that previous transformations were characterised by bipartisan agreement on policy priorities, and the extensive use of royal commissions and public inquiries to help build a consensus for change.

Previous transformations in Australia's electricity supply industry

Today, the electricity industry is a complex system of institutions and physical infrastructure networks connecting electricity markets along the east-coast states of Queensland, New South Wales (NSW), the Australian Capital Territory (ACT), Victoria, South Australia and Tasmania. Separate systems operate in Western Australia and the Northern Territory. The industry comprises many public and private enterprises involved in one or more of the many activities required to produce and sell electricity to end users. These activities (often called the 'supply-chain') include: electricity generation; transmission over high-voltage powerlines; distribution through lower-voltage local poles and wires; and retail services (comprising bulk power purchasing on behalf of customers, and billing and marketing). Today, each supply-chain activity is subject to complex rules and oversight by national and state regulators, all working to achieve the aim of promoting 'efficient investment in, and operation and use of, electricity services for the long-term interests of consumers with respect to price, quality, safety, and reliability and security'.[3]

This complex industry structure is a product of several major transformations over the last century. While the pattern of development across Australia has varied, reflecting local conditions and events, several broad reform phases can be identified.

Electricity in Australia: The early years

The period from roughly 1880 to 1914 saw local experimentation in the use of electricity in Australia. It was also a time when electricity and gas competed to provide lighting. Some of the earliest uses of electricity in Australia were for street lighting but over time, electricity expanded to include industry and transport in the form of tramways.[4]

In the very early years of the industry, the role of state governments was limited to that of consumers of electricity for lighting government buildings. The early suppliers were local government authorities or private enterprises. Whereas private firms initially dominated in cities like Adelaide and Brisbane, a mix of the two supplied Melbourne and Sydney.[5] Most of these early electricity networks were very small due to the expense of laying wires to transmit electricity, the limited number of customers, and uncertainty about rights to develop electricity supplies.

The state steps up: Electricity is seen as vital to economic development

State governments gradually came to appreciate the enormous potential of electricity, which is reflected in a long period of policy evolution. Drawing on British precedent, state governments initially introduced regulation that was intended to clarify the right to supply electricity, prevent wasteful duplication, and increase safety and reliability. Such legislation was first passed in South Australia (1891) and other states followed. Victoria's *Electric Light and Power Act 1896*, for instance, required new private electricity undertakings to obtain, what was in effect a franchise. It also gave electricity operations run by local government authorities the right to acquire private undertakings 'at valuation' after 30 years.[6] At a time when capital for private electricity undertakings was scarce, such legislation made investing in electricity supply riskier because of the limited duration of franchises and the prospect of council takeovers.

The First World War enhanced appreciation of the importance of electricity for economic and rural development, and defence. As a result, state governments sought to accelerate the coordinated development of electricity supplies. Tasmania and Victoria were the first states to establish state-owned electricity businesses to supply electricity. In 1919, for example, Victoria appointed several electricity commissioners to advise the government on the development of the industry. In 1921 this arrangement was formalised as the State Electricity Commission of Victoria, with one of Australia's most successful wartime commanders, Sir John Monash, appointed as inaugural chairman. In the following decades, other state governments established state enterprises to produce electricity. Initially, these enterprises operated at the early stage in the supply chain, producing bulk supplies of cheap electricity for resale by private and municipal undertakings.

Between 1918 and the late 1930s, state governments took a more active role in encouraging the development of the electricity industry. Sometimes, as in the case of Queensland, the state provided grants to encourage towns to establish electricity supplies.[7] In Victoria, convinced that municipal and private sector control was inefficient and wasteful, the government empowered the State Electricity Commission to take over municipal and private undertakings.[8]

During the 1920s and 1930s, industry and household demand (for those who could afford it) started to take off. Public and private electricity businesses expanded capacity rapidly in an attempt to keep pace with this growing demand. In this period, technological improvements allowed electricity suppliers to generate increasing quantities of electricity and transmit power economically over long distances. In 1924, the first electricity was transmitted to Melbourne from the Latrobe Valley, via a 145 kilometre long high voltage transmission line.[9] Over time, state governments concluded that large-scale production and transmission of electricity supply was the most economical and reliable method of organising production. They began to undertake long-term planning and provision of such services.

The pace and pattern of these developments occurred at different times in each state, in response to local factors. The fact that Victoria's State Electricity Commission was a pioneer in this process reflected the Victorian government's desire to reduce its dependence on unreliable black coal imports from NSW. The State Electricity Commission was tasked with developing abundant brown coal resources that were discovered in the Latrobe Valley.[10] However in South Australia, a private company led the development of the electricity sector in the period up to the Second World War, by virtue of having access to private sources of capital and technical capabilities that were in short supply in South Australia.[11]

Postwar growth:
The extension of the state enterprise model

After the Second World War, Commonwealth and state government involvement in the electricity sector increased. Initially, the war had the effect of interrupting the rapid expansion of the electricity sector. Restrictions on the import of capital goods, together with labour shortages, had resulted in a tightening of supply and a significant backlog in the number of towns and properties that were unable to access 'essential' electricity supplies. The supply situation was so serious that some states implemented rationing well after the end of the war. The dire supply situation, compounded by national security concerns, led the Commonwealth and state governments to prioritise rapid expansion of the electricity sector. In 1949, for example, the Commonwealth commenced construction of the massive Snowy-Hydro Electric Scheme to supply electricity to NSW and Victoria. The demand for electricity continued to grow after the war, due to a combination of strong population growth, the expansion of manufacturing and unprecedented household adoption of electrical appliances for lighting, heating and cooking.

During the postwar period, all state governments established new state enterprises or expanded the role of existing ones. While the scope differed in each state, all encouraged their enterprises to invest in additional generation capacity and expand their networks. In some jurisdictions, state enterprises were encouraged to take over municipal and private undertakings involved in electricity distribution and retail. New state electricity commissions were established in Western

Electricity problems?

Australia (1946), South Australia (1946) and NSW (1950) to go with those established earlier in Tasmania and Victoria.[12]

The state electricity enterprises that operated in Australia from the early 1950s were arguably well adapted to meeting government priorities of encouraging growth in business and household demand for electricity, and state-wide electrification. They possessed a high degree of autonomy, and, apart from NSW and Queensland, were involved right across the supply-chain: from long-term planning, construction and operation of increasingly large power stations, to the operation of coal mines (or contracting with coal suppliers), construction and operation of long-distance transmission infrastructure, construction and operation of distribution networks, and connecting/disconnecting and billing customers (although some local authorities retained responsibility for supplying consumers using bulk electricity supplies purchased from state enterprises). In NSW and Queensland, regional bodies and local councils were responsible for distribution and retail functions. State enterprises were also responsible for regulating electrical safety, which included licensing appliances and electrical workers, and some were also involved in retailing electrical products.

While there were setbacks and mistakes, by the 1970s, state enterprises were seen by policymakers to have successfully delivered the priorities of meeting rapid growth in demand, and state-wide electrification. A history of the State Electricity Commission of Victoria, for example, proudly reported that in the 30 years to 1966–67, the supplier had succeeded in electrifying the entire state, while ensuring that prices rose by only 43 per cent, compared to a rise in the Consumer Price Index of around 270 per cent.[13]

Changing times:
The decline of the state enterprise model

By the late 1980s the state enterprise model had reached its limits, in the view of some governments. With electricity supplies now available state-wide, and demand growth having slowed, government priorities shifted to the cost of supply. Governments became increasingly concerned about overcapacity and inefficiency, especially after a projected resources boom failed to materialise in the early 1980s. Adding to these concerns were large cost-over runs on major projects, overstaffing and high levels of industrial unrest. State government finances were also being squeezed by a combination of high levels of government debt and associated interest payments, inflationary pressures, and lower revenues as a result of cuts in Commonwealth government grants. Community criticism of state enterprise was also growing due to concerns about the environmental and amenity effects of unbridled expansion, as illustrated by the opposition to a proposed hydro-electric development on the Gordon River in south-west Tasmania. State enterprises were also criticised for focusing on increasing the consumption of electricity and neglecting energy conservation. Concerns about climate change were building, especially after the 1988 Toronto conference on the changing atmosphere.

In response, state governments attempted to rein in the autonomy of state enterprises. Some were required to invest in demand management and energy efficiency, and to pay greater attention to the environmental and social impacts of their decisions. However, the main priority for the states was improving the financial performance of electricity enterprises.

State governments introduced measures during the 1980s

that were designed to make state enterprises more commercially focused. Given labels like commercialisation and corporatisation, they included legislative changes to set out government expectations of state enterprises, introduce new corporate reporting requirements (including performance targets), and clarify ministerial powers to intervene. Some states initiated major public inquiries into the performance of state enterprises, leading in certain cases to the deferral or cancellation of planned investments in new power stations. A 1986 inquiry into the Electricity Commission of NSW found that there was a major problem of oversupply, resulting in unnecessary costs for users.[14] In several jurisdictions, plans to build large new power stations were scrapped or postponed.

State electricity enterprises responded with major efficiency measures. In 1989 the State Electricity Commission of Victoria, for example, announced that it would reduce its workforce by 20 per cent over three years; eventually it achieved a 50 per cent reduction over the following four years.[15] Other state enterprises introduced similar reductions. These had huge ramifications for affected workers and local communities that had grown around energy production, such as the Latrobe Valley in Victoria.

During the 1990s, the Commonwealth government sought to accelerate the pace of reform in the electricity sector. This was prompted by the desire to improve the competitiveness of the manufacturing sector by reducing the cost of state government–provided inputs, such as electricity. In 1990 it commissioned the Industry Commission to undertake a review of the electricity and gas sectors.[16] This review made a public case for major structural reforms designed to create an interconnected and competitive national wholesale market for electricity, with the remaining monopoly transmission and distribution functions to be separated out and subjected to 'light-handed' regulation. The inquiry report estimated that implementing electricity reform would produce very large gains to businesses and households.[17]

Following the Industry Commission report, the Commonwealth commissioned a review of competition policy, which supported the introduction of competition into areas dominated by government enterprises, including the electricity sector.[18] Armed with these reviews, state governments came to the view (sometimes independently, as in the case of Victoria under the Kennett government, and sometimes with the encouragement of Commonwealth financial incentives) that further gains could be achieved by restructuring state enterprises and creating a national market for the supply of electricity. The reforms that created the present market structure were subsequently agreed through the Council of Australian Governments. They were incorporated in National Competition Policy agreements signed by the Commonwealth and state governments in 1995.

Establishment of the national electricity market

The reforms that resulted in the creation of the national electricity market have been extensively discussed elsewhere.[19] Essentially, the Commonwealth and states agreed to establish a national electricity grid, along with a national wholesale electricity market to form what is now known as the National Electricity Market. To enable the development of competition in electricity generation and the retailing of electricity to consumers, state electricity enterprises were also broken up.

Those in Victoria and South Australia were also privatised. New regulatory institutions were established to determine the rules governing the operation of the national market, to regulate and enforce these rules and to operate the national wholesale market. These reforms produced the national electricity market that exists today, which involves all states and territories, except Western Australia and the Northern Territory.

In a radical departure from the past, the new national market would no longer use a model of centralised planning based on forecasts by state enterprises of future demand growth. This model had been introduced in Victoria after the First World War and gradually adopted elsewhere. The role of centralised planner was replaced by a wholesale market. The market would provide a price signal in the form of movements in spot and future prices for electricity, indicating the need to expand or reduce capacity. Effectively, it was considered that a market comprising many buyers and sellers could perform at least as well as a centralised planner, if not better. The new system would transfer the financial (and political) risks arising from forecasting errors from consumers onto market participants.[20]

The wholesale market was expected to resolve one of the central problems facing the electricity sector: managing demand and supply uncertainty. Undertaking long-term planning in the electricity sector had been eloquently described by Cecil Edwards in a history of the State Electricity Commission of Victoria as:

> the art of steering between the rocks of 'too little, too late' and 'too much, too soon'. The first brings down on an electric supply system the wrath of the consumer

who cannot get or use the power when they want it; the second exposes the undertaking to charges of wasteful expenditure and the risk of having to raise tariffs to meet the fixed costs of plant not fully used.[21]

In the postwar period, state enterprises faced rapid demand growth and were encouraged to lean towards erring on the side of 'too much, too soon'. Faced with a surplus, state enterprises could stimulate sales through marketing or the sale of appliances. Governments could also offer subsidies to large electricity users (like aluminium smelters). But as demand growth slowed and pressures to reduce energy consumption mounted, the costs of adopting a strategy of 'too much, too soon' became unacceptable.

Future challenges for the electricity industry

After more than 20 years of experience, a consensus among policymakers emerged that the national market had not performed as intended. Electricity price rises in Australia prompted numerous public inquiries by the Australian Competition and Consumer Commission and others.[22] The rapid adoption of intermittent renewables has highlighted reliability risks, especially in unfavourable weather.[23] Poor marketing practices in the retail sector undermined trust in electricity companies.[24] Governments also found that they were unable to avoid political risks: they are still blamed by the public when electricity prices rise or supply is threatened. The factors explaining disappointment with the results of the electricity market are complex and relate to issues of market design, the behaviour of market participants, and government policy failures. Irrespective of the causes, disappointment has led to further Commonwealth and state government interventions in an effort to cut emissions, reduce prices and maintain reliability.

Recent government interventions include renewable energy targets, financial incentives for various forms of private investment in renewable energy generation, and regulatory changes (such as the reintroduction of retail price controls and increases in reliability standards). There has also been a reassessment of the role of government in planning for future investment in the electricity industry.

Governments are again undertaking centralised planning, in an effort to stimulate and guide new investment in additional generation and transmission system capacity, and to ensure that the electricity supply is reliable as aging, coal-fired generators close down. The main body responsible for operating the national market (the Australian Energy Markets Operator) now publishes long-term (20-year) plans, identifying prospective locations for renewable developments, future network constraints and opportunities to expand the transmission network.[25] State governments are also undertaking long-term planning to support the investment in new renewable generation capacity and transmission network upgrades, including in collaboration with the market operator.[26]

In addition to policy changes, technological developments are also driving changes in the electricity industry. For example, new technologies are breaking down the traditional separation between consumers and producers of electricity. This includes the increasing uptake by households of rooftop solar power and batteries, which result in greater two-way flows of electricity on the network. New methods of automation are also allowing greater control of electricity use and supply to take advantage of fluctuations in electricity prices during the day. New uses for electricity are also emerging, such as electric vehicles and hydrogen production. These developments, along with the challenge of reducing emissions, are some of the factors driving demands for a new round of reform in the electricity industry.

Lessons from history: We need to build political and policy consensus for reform

The history of electricity reform in Australia offers many lessons for policymakers dealing with the present-day priorities of lowering emissions, reducing electricity prices and ensuring reliability. Two lessons relating to the role of government policy stand out as especially significant. Firstly, as former Prime Minister John Howard has observed, major economic reform in Australia is only possible with bipartisan agreement or through a strong prime minister able to expend political capital.[27] Indeed, the history of electricity reform serves as an important reminder that bipartisan agreement about policy priorities is crucial. After the Second World War, for example, there was bipartisan agreement within the states on the need to quickly expand access to the 'essential service' of cheap and reliable electricity. State electricity enterprises were not the only possible vehicle for achieving this aim, but the model was progressively adopted by governments of varying political hues after Victoria and Tasmania took an early lead. A change in government priorities in the 1980s to emphasise economic efficiency and competitiveness then led to bipartisan agreement to fundamentally restructure state enterprises.

While there is now a bipartisan commitment to achieving a target of net zero emissions by 2050, differences exist on the need for interim targets and the policies needed to achieve them. Interim targets are important because achieving net zero by 2050 will be extremely challenging, given that coal and gas account for about 70 per cent of electricity generation and that transmission systems are currently configured around existing centres for power generation, such as the Latrobe Valley in Victoria and the Hunter Valley in NSW. The Australian government, has however, chosen to retain the interim target set under the Paris Agreement of a 26–28 per cent emissions reduction on 2005 levels by 2030.

Respected bodies such as the Organisation for Economic Cooperation and Development have called for Australia to develop more ambitious interim targets and policies to achieve them.[28] There are several reasons why this is a priority. First, the present strategy effectively defers much of the effort needed to achieve net zero by 2050, thereby shifting more of the burden onto future governments and taxpayers. Second, resisting adoption of more ambitious interim emissions reduction targets and national policies such as carbon taxes or tighter limits on emissions also increases risks that international investors and governments will impose pressure on Australia to bring forward carbon emission reductions, through some combination of international financial markets imposing a 'climate risk premium' on lending to carbon-intensive industries, and international actions such as the imposition by other nations of carbon taxes on Australian exports. Third, an absence of interim emissions reduction targets and supporting policies also means the practice of each state developing its own, probably more costly, approaches will also continue. Despite this, the lack of a consensus on interim targets and policies to achieve emissions reductions in the electricity sector represents a major obstacle to further reform.

LESSONS FROM HISTORY

A second lesson from history is that royal commissions and public inquiries played an important role in building consensus about the need for, and direction of reform of Australia's electricity sector. In Victoria, for example, between 1908 and 1918 the government sought and published formal advice on electricity supply on at least five separate occasions; commissioned experts in 1908, 1911 and 1912 were interspersed by a royal commission in 1911, and followed by an advisory committee in 1918. This advice was debated in parliament and influenced the decision to establish the State Electricity Commission of Victoria in 1921.[29] In 1991 the Industry Commission finalised its report recommending development of a national electricity market, leading eventually to the commencement of the wholesale market in 1998.

More recently, national inquiries by the Australian Competition and Consumer Commission, among others, into the electricity sector have led to important changes in the regulatory and institutional framework, such as the reintroduction of retail price controls and changes to the rules governing the operation of the national market. These recent inquiries have largely taken the Australian government's energy and climate policy objectives as a given. Perhaps it is time for a consensus-building inquiry which would examine interim targets and future policies to achieve decarbonisation of Australia's electricity industry, as well as the roles of the Australian and state governments in orchestrating this transition.

In conclusion, the history of electricity reform in Australia provides valuable lessons for policymakers about the importance of consensus building on the need for, and direction of reform, and about the role of royal commissions and public inquiries in helping to achieve consensus. Understanding the history of reform in the electricity sector doesn't provide the recipe to address the decade of drift that has afflicted climate and energy policy in Australia, but it does identify some of the key ingredients.

CHAPTER 12

Governing during economic crisis: The importance of memory

Joan Beaumont

In the early months of the COVID-19 pandemic, Prime Minister Scott Morrison addressed the House of Representatives:

> We know who we are as people, and the legacy and inspiration that has been given to us from those who have come before us and shown us the way through challenges and tests just like this. So we summon the spirit of the Anzacs, of our Great Depression generation, of those who built the Snowy. Of those who won the great peace of World War II and defended Australia. That is our legacy that we draw on at this time.[1]

Morrison was not alone in invoking the memory of the Great Depression during the pandemic; in public life the comparison between the two crises was very commonly made. This is not to say that the policy responses of 2020–21 were explicitly shaped by the memories of the Great Depression. Many of the lessons of the Depression years had been taken on board decades earlier. Rather, today's politicians had learned that in times of crisis, public support for government intervention of an unprecedented kind could be legitimised by the memory of a past national crisis.

Facing a threat that again seemed existential, the Australian public needed to hear a narrative of past struggle – a resort to a cultural reference point that was almost instantly recognisable – if it were to find the resilience and cohesion to survive as their forebears had.

It is nearly a century since the Great Depression, but it is still recognised as the greatest economic catastrophe to afflict the world. The crisis was deeply complex – it was a series of crises within crises, generating an ever more disastrous cumulative effect – and it played out differently in various countries. Australia was hit particularly savagely. Thanks to its reliance on the export of a few primary commodities and high levels of public indebtedness, the Australian economy was especially vulnerable to external shocks. By 1932, perhaps a third, or even more, of the Australian workforce was unemployed, while many thousands of Australians lost their businesses, farms, savings and homes. Government budgets were slashed and the nation itself faced insolvency.[2]

Inevitably, the Great Depression placed immense strain on Australia's political and social institutions and exposed yawning policy gaps. In the decades that followed, many of these would be consciously addressed. But, in time, the direct impact of the Depression on policymaking would become more tenuous. New macroeconomic theories evolved, new generations of policymakers came to power and the Australian economy adjusted to the challenges of globalisation in the late twentieth century. Yet, if the link between policymaking and the Great Depression weakened, its memory continued to infuse public discourse in times of crisis. As the response to the COVID-19 pandemic in 2020 and 2021 showed, the Great Depression remained a powerful collective memory, in that its very name invoked an instantly recognisable image of economic and human catastrophe that might be repeated if the new crisis were not met with an extraordinary policy response.

Trapped by orthodoxy: Government responses to the Great Depression, 1929–32

The challenges posed by the Great Depression were initially well beyond the capacity of Australia's policy instruments and institutional capacity to resolve. It was not simply that the federal government had more limited power to impose its agenda on the states than it does today, but Canberra's capacity to formulate and manage national economic policy was rudimentary.[3] The role of the Commonwealth Treasury, which was staffed at the senior level by accountants, was confined to supervising the collection of government revenue and expenditure, and managing loans issues. It did this in conjunction with the Commonwealth Bank, which then scarcely functioned as a central bank. Professional economists were only just emerging as an external source of policy advice to governments, and politicians had limited exposure to Keynesian and monetarist theories, both of which were in their infancy. Even more importantly, there was little history of state intervention to regulate the economy.

The most significant policy gap in the Depression years was the lack of a social welfare safety net. Prior to 1929, the federal government offered a range of pensions: old age and invalid pensions (introduced in 1908); maternity allowances (1912); and a generous suite of 'Repatriation' benefits granted to the returned soldiers of the First World War and the families who had lost breadwinners. But there was almost no provision for the relief of the unemployed. Only Queensland had a system of contributory unemployment insurance, introduced by the reforming Labor government of Edward (Ted) Theodore in 1923. Across the nation, the primary responsibility for giving aid to the unemployed and other destitute Australians resided with charities, churches and municipal authorities.

This reliance on voluntarism was soon anachronistic. With unemployment soaring in 1929–30, it was clear that charities often staffed by well-meaning, if sometimes controlling, middle-class matrons, could not cope, even with some government funding. All state governments thus introduced, from 1930 on, systems of 'sustenance' (aka 'susso') whereby the unemployed were given rations of food and other basic commodities. The regulations were often contentious, the dole was subject to means testing, and officials tended to view the unemployed as work-shy and inclined to fraud, rather than as victims of global economic forces. Still the 'susso', together with a plethora of community fundraising and voluntary relief programs, held starvation at bay. Meanwhile, modest government-funded relief programs (mostly constructing public infrastructure or rural development) offered many unemployed Australians some work, albeit part-time and often on sub-award wage rates. Importantly, most of these initiatives were funded and managed at the state or local level, rather than the federal.

This was partly because of a second major policy constraint that the Great Depression exposed: the limits on the ability of the federal government to control monetary policy. The director of the Commonwealth Bank, the Scottish-Australian Sir Robert Gibson, was implacably opposed to deficit financing and committed to 'sound finance'. So, too, were the conservative (Nationalist) majority in the Senate, the rest of the Australian banking sector and the City of London, which was scathing about Australians' financial acumen and their ability to service their already massive debts. Throughout 1930 and 1931, Gibson consistently blocked the expansion of the money supply that many on the left of the Labor government of J.H. (Jim) Scullin, including Theodore (now treasurer), believed to be necessary to stimulate the economy and reduce unemployment.

Devaluation of the currency, another policy option which could have assisted recovery by making Australian exports more competitive, was also resisted by Gibson and many others in the private banking sector that largely controlled currency exchange. Even when, in late 1929, Australia effectively abandoned the gold standard, which required convertibility of the currency into gold, many of the private banks remained committed to maintaining the Australian pound as close to parity with the pound sterling as possible.

In effect, the Commonwealth Bank had a veto over monetary policy. After a divisive 'battle of plans' in early to mid-1931, when the NSW Labor premier, Jack Lang, outraged conservatives by refusing to pay interest on his state's debts, policies of deflation were adopted, to varying degrees, across the nation. Budgets were balanced, and salaries and interest rates cut, in an effort to spread the burden of the Depression equitably across society. With its radical wing in uproar, the ALP split, as it had over military conscription in 1916–17. The United Australia Party, a hybrid of non-Labor forces that came to power in early 1932 under a Labor defector and former Tasmanian premier, Joseph (Joe) Lyons, waited for the international economy to recover – as, indeed, it started to do, slowly and spasmodically, from 1932 on. Only the outbreak of the Second World War, however, brought full employment, in 1941.

Yet, if the advocates of deflation won the day in 1931, politicians across the political spectrum knew that policy reform was necessary, especially in social welfare and banking. The Lyons government from 1932 to 1939 lacked policy innovation – it was memorably called by Paul Hasluck, then official historian of the Second World War, 'an emergency government that outlived the emergency' – but even conservatives accepted the need for an established system of unemployment relief.[4] The attempts to introduce a contributory national insurance scheme in the late 1930s, however, unravelled in the face of opposition from a formidable array of medical practitioners, communists, grassroots organisations and those who thought the priority in government expenditure should be defence, given the threatening international environment.

After the depression: Social welfare and financial reform

When war finally came, and the ALP subsequently returned to power in October 1941, major reform in social welfare policy was possible.[5] The memory of the Great Depression was still raw for Australia's Labor leaders, John Curtin (prime minister, 1941–45) and Ben Chifley (treasurer, 1941–45; minister for post-war reconstruction, 1942–45; prime minister 1945–49). 'I cannot forget,' Chifley said in November 1946, 'how miserable those hundreds of thousands of men must have felt when they went back each night to their families after tramping the streets all day in search of work.'[6] But other influences also worked to create a climate for reform. For one thing, Australia's leaders, like those in the United Kingdom, knew that they had to offer their citizens the hope of a better postwar world if they were to demand the sacrifices required by war mobilisation. Furthermore, the signing of the Atlantic Charter by the Allied Powers in 1941 committed them to global economic co-operation, the advancement of social welfare, and the pursuit of a world free of want and fear. Finally, the comparatively orderly conversion of the Australian economy to a total war footing in the early 1940s appeared to confirm that governments could intervene in the economy to a greater degree than before with desirable social and economic effects.[7]

Thus, from 1943 on, Australian delegates to major international conferences sought to have a commitment to full employment enshrined in the multinational agreements that the war spawned. In 1945, the team of the External Affairs Minister, Dr H.V. Evatt, lobbied successfully for the United Nations Charter (article 55) to include the aim of promoting 'higher standards of living, full employment and conditions of economic and social progress'. At home, the Chifley government, fearful of a postwar slump, introduced the *Unemployment and Sickness Benefits Act 1945* and progressively built the foundations of a fully-fledged welfare state. Inevitably, such reform had its critics, among them the then leader of the Liberal opposition, Robert Menzies, who thought the recipients of welfare should make contributions rather than be mendicant on the state. But by the late 1940s, there was a bipartisan consensus that the Australian state had an obligation to support those who were unable to work, be it through sickness, accident or economic change.

It is a principle that has lasted to this day. This is not to say, of course, that the dole has been an arena free of ideological contest. Far from it. As in the Depression years, governments across the decades have debated the levels of support, the degree to which eligibility for the dole should be means tested, and the obligations, if any, of the unemployed to work for their benefits. Still, for all the disputation, no one contests the need for the Australian state to provide a social safety net of sorts. This was a policy issue 'resolved' by the Great Depression.

The question as to who controls monetary policy was also progressively worked through in the decades after the Depression. Once again, Lyons was not inclined to take the initiative, but such was the distrust of the banks, who had foreclosed on property owners and tightened credit in the early 1930s, that Lyons established in 1936 a royal commission on banking, and monetary and exchange systems. This recommended that there should be a mechanism to ensure close and cordial relationships between the federal government, the Loan Council (which had been established by state and Commonwealth governments in 1923 to coordinate federal and state debt raising) and the Commonwealth Bank. While the bank must retain its independence, the government should have primacy in the event of any irreconcilable difference of opinion about monetary policy.[8] Addressing two other issues that had proved contentious in the previous decade, the royal commission also recommended that the Commonwealth Bank should hold the surplus foreign exchange reserves of the private banks, and that these banks should be obliged to keep deposits with the central bank up to any percentage approved by the federal treasurer.

Again, little happened until a decade later. In 1945, the Chifley government passed legislation that confirmed the obligation of the Commonwealth Bank to give effect to government policy. Chifley, alas, then overreached himself. When, in August 1947, the High Court struck down the requirement in the 1945 banking legislation for state and local government authorities to conduct their business with the Commonwealth Bank, on the grounds that this infringed the constitutionally guaranteed freedom of interstate trade, Chifley attempted to nationalise the banks. Public ownership, he insisted, would ensure banking was conducted in the national interest. It was a rash move that proved to be 'a compelling case study in how not to do public policy'.[9] The High Court again ruled in favour of the banks. So, too, did the Privy Council in London. With the banks pouring their resources into a hysterical anti-socialist campaign, and the majority of the population opposing nationalisation, Chifley's government fell in the December 1949 election.

The principle of government primacy in monetary policy endured, however. In 1959, the Reserve Bank of Australia was created, separating the previous trading and savings bank functions of the Commonwealth Bank from its role as a central bank. The independence of the Reserve Bank from the political process in the operation of monetary policy was again affirmed, but once more the legislation enshrined that if there was an irreconcilable difference between the bank and the government, the politicians would prevail – on the condition that they present to parliament the reasons for their disagreement with the Reserve Bank.[10] This provision has never been invoked. Disagreements between governments and the Reserve Bank triggered some discussion about invoking clause 11 in later decades, but in the event, one side or the other backed off.[11]

A post-depression generation brings new policy directions

It is difficult to determine with any precision when the influence of the Great Depression on social and financial policy ceased to be explicit and direct, but its influence faded with generational change and new macroeconomic thinking. By the 1980s, Australia's national leaders were essentially a post-Depression generation with few, if any, personal memories of the crisis. Malcolm Fraser was born in 1930; Bob Hawke in 1929; John Howard in 1939; and Paul Keating in 1944. With the passage of time, too, the Australian population's experience of mass unemployment receded into the emotional distance. Although the rates of unemployment would rise in the last quarter of the twentieth century – and, at their worst, would be more than 10 per cent – they never came near the stratospheric numbers of 1932.[12]

Moreover, policy formulation is never mono-causal. Even in the cases cited above, multiple influences were at work, making the Depression only one of the factors shaping change. From the 1930s on, economic and financial policy was shaped by new macroeconomic theories: Keynesian economics, and as these proved unable to cope with the stagnation of the 1970s, monetarism and neoliberal market-oriented economics. The transformation of Australian economic policy in the latter part of the twentieth century was not driven by any 'lessons' of the Great Depression but by a need to make Australia more competitive in an increasingly globalised environment. This inspired the slashing of tariff protection for the manufacturing sector, a shibboleth of all parties in the 1930s, and the deregulation of the economy (including the floating of the

Australian dollar in 1983); the easing of restrictions on the entry of foreign banks into the domestic retail banking sector; the corporatisation of public enterprises, banking and the transport sector; and the reform of the highly centralised labour market. These reforms were accompanied by a hardening of rhetoric towards the unemployed, as job security was eroded by offshore competition, automation and the pursuit of ever greater efficiency.

Yet, if the direct connection between the Depression and policy innovation weakened over the twentieth century, we should not discount the continuing symbolic power of that massive economic and social crisis. Even as Australians ceased to have any direct experience of the Depression, it persisted as a powerful historical narrative in Australian political life. Many Australians remembered this crisis through the stories, images and behaviours they grew up with – what we might call 'post-memory'.[13] They recalled their parents or grandparents being risk-averse, hoarding their savings in the bank rather than spending them on luxuries, and being timid about financial exposure. They remembered, too, tales of shanty towns on Australia's riverbanks or town outskirts, long queues of desperate men waiting for work or the dole, and single men hawking pathetically small bags of low-value items from door to door in the city and country. But the details of this post-memory are hazy, and the Depression has never competed in the national imagination with the mass slaughter, destruction and genocide of the wars that preceded and followed it. While the centenary of the First World War produced a torrent of publications and an orgy of commemorative activities, anyone looking to find memorials to the relief works of the Great Depression will be disappointed. No one has proposed that we invest the same amount of taxpayers' money in recording the names of the countless thousands thrown into unemployment, bankruptcy and poverty during the 1920s and the 1930s as we have in digitising the files of Australia's defence personnel. None of the anniversaries of key events of 1929 to 1932 appear on the national commemorative calendar.

The power of the Great Depression in collective memory

But for all this, the Great Depression has remained in the Australian public discourse as an enduring site of collective memory. The term 'site of memory', popularised late in the last century by the French scholar Pierre Nora, is commonly assumed to relate only to physical sites, such as Gallipoli and the Western Front, or material objects, such as the cenotaphs, obelisks and statues of 'diggers' that populate public spaces in almost every Australian town. But 'sites of memory' can also include, to quote Nora, 'the products of reflection, such as the concept of a historical generation … or the "region" as an object of memory, or certain "divisions" in the way the French perceive their national territory'.[14] In Australia's case, the Anzac legend is the pre-eminent example of such a site of memory, but the 'Great Depression', too, has become enshrined as a cultural point of reference: a time of unprecedented social distress and policy failure during which Australians manifested a remarkable capacity to survive, thanks to community and personal resilience.

The power of this collective memory became strikingly apparent during the COVID-19 pandemic crisis which afflicted Australia from 2020 on. When the social and economic implications of this global health catastrophe began to be evident, the federal government moved quickly to install systems of financial support that would have been unthinkable in the early 1930s. Through the JobKeeper payment, the federal government ensured that Australians continued to receive income while the businesses that employed them lost their revenue stream. Through JobSeeker, it increased the payments to those already on unemployment and sickness benefits. Beyond this, businesses were allowed to trade when insolvent, while the banking sector, despised during the Great Depression as rapacious 'Money Power', provided many borrowers with mortgage 'holidays' and deferral of loan repayments.

All of these schemes had their limitations, of course. JobKeeper and the increase in payments under JobSeeker lasted only until March 2021. Minimal provision was made for casual workers, for those on temporary working visas and for international students (often one and the same). In early 2021, the banks started to require homeowners to repay their loans, and tenants became vulnerable as rental moratoriums ended.[15] But still, there were none of the haunting scenes of the Depression when families defaulting on rental payments were thrown into the street, and the rain, together with their furniture. Moreover, as lockdowns continued during 2021 in the face of the more infectious Delta variant, the federal government renewed its financial support to individuals and industries that faced significant losses of income and revenue. These responses of government to the COVID-19 pandemic might have been incomplete and politicised but they attested to a radically different understanding of the role of the state from that of 1929.

This response, it should be said, had an economic as

much as a humanitarian logic. It had long been recognised, by Keynesians and monetarists alike, that stimulus packages were a far sounder response to recession than the deflation of 1930–32 which had only deepened the economic crisis. A collapse of property values, if there were widespread foreclosures on mortgages and rental evictions, would prolong the economic damage of the pandemic. But the responses to the COVID-19 crisis were also invested with legitimacy by the reference to the collective site of memory, the Great Depression.

In federal parliament the COVID-19 pandemic was routinely compared with the Great Depression. A digital search of debates in the House of Representatives and Senate reveals 179 explicit references to 'the Great Depression' between 1 March 2020 and 1 September 2021. The 'Spanish flu', in contrast, appears only 39 times in this same period, even though this pandemic, which killed between 12 000 and 15 000 Australians after the First World War, provides the more obvious historical comparisons with COVID-19. Time and again, the contemporary pandemic was invoked by Members of Parliament in apocalyptic terms: 'the worst recession since the Great Depression'; 'the worst economic shock that we've had in essentially 100 years since the Great Depression'; 'the greatest global depression that we've seen since the Great Depression'; 'the biggest jobs crisis since the Great Depression'; and 'the biggest problem in the labour market since the Great Depression'.

These comparisons between the Depression and the pandemic rarely involved specific facts and evidence, but detail was not needed. The very words 'Great Depression' evoked across all political parties a sense of another existential global crisis over which governments had little control, and for which there was no predictable end. It represented a level of economic disruption, social distress, poverty and unemployment that was politically intolerable. Moreover, the Depression, as a site of memory, embodied values, qualities and behaviours that governments need Australians to emulate in the new pandemic crisis: notably, endurance, resilience and communal support. A Liberal senator from Western Australia, Ben Small, said on 4 August 2021, 'We have, however, shown great resilience and adaptability in the face of the biggest health crisis since the Spanish flu pandemic and, arguably, the biggest economic calamity since the Great Depression'.[16] Josh Frydenberg, the federal treasurer, meanwhile, told parliament on 6 October 2020, 'The Great Depression and two world wars did not bring Australia to its knees, and neither will COVID-19'.[17]

Commentary about the pandemic outside parliament also slipped into ready comparisons with the Great Depression. Articles in the press featured images of dole queues in the 1930s as well as more recent photographs of empty seats at desolate outdoor dining venues. Unemployment rates of both crises were juxtaposed, to the advantage of the pandemic which failed to fulfil the most gloomy prophecies.[18] Government responses to the pandemic were also compared with those of the Great Depression, as well as to the funding of the Second World War through Victory loans. Anything less than a 'gargantuan stimulus', an article in *The Conversation* argued, 'runs the risk of a debt-default deflationary spiral of the kind seen in the Great Depression, when the ability of households and businesses to pay their debts decreased with deflation and the resulting defaults led to further deflation'.[19]

Lessons from history:
The Great Depression as a cultural anchor

Whether such comparisons between the Great Depression and the COVID-19 pandemic were valid or accurate is not of any real consequence. The significance of this invocation of the Great Depression lies in the function it served. Australia's leaders realised that the Great Depression provided the imaginative context within which the policy responses to the pandemic could be positioned and legitimised. The Great Depression was the greatest economic crisis in Australian history, and so, too, was COVID-19 a 'once-in a century' crisis. Radical policy options, which required phenomenal levels of government indebtedness and intervention in the economy, were thus justified. This reminds us that policymaking is not a simple exercise in rational or statistical analysis. Rather, memories of the past that remain dominant in the political culture, and which attest to societal values that have an enduring relevance, make policy innovation possible.

CHAPTER 13

We need to hear the voices of refugees: Citizen engagement for reforming refugee policy

Niro Kandasamy

The story of the so-called Biloela family from Queensland is familiar to many people. The fate of Priya, Nades, Kopika and Tharnicaa Murugappan has become emblematic of the punitive refugee policy of successive governments since 2001. Less well known is the role that refugee advocates like Aran Mylvaganam, founder of the Tamil Refugee Council, are playing in the campaign for refugees like the Murugappan family to remain in Australia.[1] Mylvaganam himself is a former refugee. He arrived in Australia in 1997 when he was 13 years old as an unaccompanied minor and was sent to Villawood Immigration Detention Centre, where he remained for three months. If policymakers are to design a more humane and responsive refugee policy, history suggests that they need to listen better to former refugees and refugee advocates like Mylvaganam. Mylvaganam repeatedly draws on his personal experience in his advocacy work, reminding both policymakers and the general public that refugees must be part of the process of formulating refugee policy reforms.

The Commonwealth government currently makes no provision for citizens of refugee backgrounds to be actively involved in policies that directly affect their families and others in their countries of origin. This failure to consult people with on-the-ground experience partly explains Australia's harsh approach to refugees, an approach that attracts international ire and condemnation. In seeking more humane and effective policies with better outcomes for both refugees and Australian society, policymakers can draw inspiration from efforts to settle earlier waves of refugees. Those efforts reveal that structures that encourage consultation from those with direct experience as refugees in both the host country and after arrival in Australia lead to policies that effectively respond to refugees' experiences of conflict, displacement and trauma. The angst of the Biloela family and thousands of others languishing in detention can be avoided. Involving citizens in policymaking is arguably one of the most important signs of a healthy democracy.

From the late 1970s to the early 1980s, the Commonwealth government responded to Tamils seeking permanent protection after the outbreak of the Sri Lankan civil war. The government had clear pragmatic processes to guide its engagement with its Tamil citizens. It did not readily accept narratives about Tamil persecution. Instead, the Australian government supported official versions which played down the atrocities against Tamils. In its consideration of options for refugee resettlement, the government put an emphasis on developing services that were suited to the particular needs of Tamil refugees, including establishing direct lines of communication between immigration officers and Tamil community leaders. This was possible because the government called on the knowledge of Tamils who had already arrived in Australia. In seeking to reform our desperately inadequate refugee resettlement services, today's policymakers can draw inspiration from the actions of the Fraser and Hawke governments in the late 1970s and early 1980s. Taking a look at past responses to refugees, we find contexts for radically different ways of responding to the current refugee protection crisis.

Australia responds to the outbreak of conflict in Sri Lanka

In order to understand the circumstances that informed these earlier practices, we need to cast our eyes even further back, and examine the situation that led thousands of Tamils to flee Sri Lanka and seek asylum in Australia. After Sri Lanka gained independence from British colonial rule in 1948, successive Sinhala-Buddhist governments universally rejected the political aspirations and self-determination of Tamils. Anti-Tamil measures have tainted the island since. In 1949, the *Ceylon Citizenship Act* excluded Indian Tamils from Sri Lankan citizenship, and in 1956, the *Official Language Act* made Sinhalese the official language of the country, thereby excluding more than 20 per cent of the Tamil population, which did not speak Sinhalese. These exclusionary measures paved the way for the mass Tamil refugee exodus with the onset of war in the early 1980s.

By the 1970s, government aggression against Tamils had reached new heights. In July 1977, the general election was the first to be held under the new constitution of Sri Lanka, which had been enacted a month earlier. The new constitution, however, did not result in better political representation for the Tamils, who had overwhelmingly voted for the Tamil United Liberation Front (TULF) to advocate for a separate Tamil state in the north and east of the island. Less than a month after the elections, a Tamil massacre engulfed the island, sparked when Sinhala policemen attacked Tamils in the north. It was the third anti-Tamil pogrom since Sri Lanka had gained independence, and resulted in the looting of Tamil homes and shops, displacing around 75 000 Tamils, and killing 300. In 1979, the Sri Lankan president J.R. Jayewardene introduced the *Prevention of Terrorism Act*. The new law was used to justify the widespread abduction and torture of individuals, particularly of ethnic Tamils suspected of being involved with Tamil militant groups.[2]

In 1978 the Australian-based Ceylon Tamil Association (CTA) was established by local members of the Tamil community, in response to mounting political conflict in Sri Lanka and the increased marginalisation of ethnic Tamils. In June 1981, the Jaffna Public Library, the epicentre of Tamil history and culture, was burned by Sri Lankan state-sponsored mobs. This act of violence marked a watershed moment in the conflict, and foreshadowed the exodus of Tamils from Sri Lanka throughout the 1980s. In July 1983, Sinhala mobs backed by the government destroyed, looted and burned Tamil-owned business and homes. Armed with electoral rolls, Sinhala mobs targeted Tamils across the island. They were raped, burned and hacked to death, causing 2000 deaths. Known as 'Black July', this anti-Tamil pogrom forced thousands more Tamils into refugee camps in Sri Lanka and neighbouring India. Against this violence and the beginning of the war, the only possible response for many Tamils was to search for better lives elsewhere.

Initially, host countries showed clear sympathy towards the plight of Tamil refugees. Prime Minister Malcolm Fraser and his Labor successor Bob Hawke struck an admirable 'balance between humanitarian concerns, domestic political considerations and foreign policy'.³ The CTA, together with members of the Tamil community, lobbied government to allow more Tamils to resettle in Australia. These advocates met with Australian politicians and exposed the widespread nature of attacks against Tamils, hammering the point that Tamil persecution was a state-sponsored project.⁴ Their advocacy proved not to be in vain, as the politicians in turn pressured the government to act on the matter.

Shortly after the anti-Tamil riots in July 1983, the recently elected Hawke Labor government processed Tamil people's applications inside Sri Lanka under the Special Humanitarian Program (SHP). This program allowed those who were not eligible for normal migration entry or family reunion to be considered for entry into Australia. The specific implementation of the SHP for the Sri Lankan situation was a direct outcome of discussions between policymakers and Tamil refugee advocates. Significantly, it is the only instance of Tamil perspectives being taken into serious consideration by the Australian government on Tamil refugee matters.

Inclusive refugee policymaking

The CTA, like other ethno-specific organisations, has been crucial to addressing the immediate resettlement needs of refugees. By tackling gaps in government-run services, the CTA provided newly arrived Tamil refugees with furniture, translation services, access to housing, and other critical supports. With the escalation of violence in Sri Lanka, the association expanded its activities to include lobbying bureaucrats in the Immigration Department. After the riots of 1983 (which the Sri Lankan government downplayed, with President Jayewardene offering no sympathy to Tamils), the CTA led a transformative period of engagement between the government and Tamils in Australia.

The 1983 riots were not the first catalyst for Tamils to directly engage with policymakers in Australia. In June 1981, when government-backed Sinhala mobs had burned Jaffna Public Library, a Tamil community petition was delivered to Commonwealth parliament, explaining the devastating effects as the mobs went on a rampage: 'killing innocent people, [and] set[ting] ablaze shops, homes and public library with historic Tamil documents, Tamil bookshops, newspaper offices and printery, presumably in an attempt to destroy Tamil identity and culture.'[5] The burning of the library also sparked the first Tamil protest in Australia; at the Australian Labor Party conference in Melbourne, dozens of Tamils distributed leaflets about the political conflict. Crucially, the Tamils established working relationships with politicians, many of whom then went on to raise the political conflict in Commonwealth parliament. Working from a good understanding of each politician's interests enabled Tamil representatives to shift from challenging the misinformation of the Sri Lankan government to framing solutions alongside Australian policymakers. Community representatives sought not merely to be consulted about policy, but to communicate to the government the best options for Tamils suffering persecution.

Why was connecting with politicians significant? For the CTA, it enabled them to connect with politicians through direct meetings, which in turn was an important precondition for their involvement in developing adequate policy responses to Tamils fleeing persecution. As one of the association's founding members observed, meetings with key federal politicians such as Stewart West, Minister for Immigration and Ethnic Affairs, were formative for the implementation of the SHP in Sri Lanka in 1983. Upon hearing about the burning of Jaffna Public Library, West arranged a meeting with Bob Hawke to discuss urgent policy responses to allow Tamils to seek asylum in Australia. The significance of the initial meeting with West was not lost on the CTA founding member, who explained, 'immediately they gave something called Special Humanitarian Program'.[6]

This meeting between the government and the Tamil community transformed refugee policy responses to Tamils in the early 1980s. West instructed his department to allow those who were not eligible for normal migration entry or family reunion to be considered under the SHP. Moreover, images of the looting, burning and mass displacement of the Tamils following the riots of 1983 fuelled the humanitarian concerns of politicians across political lines. Alan Missen, Liberal Party senator for Victoria and chairman of the Australian Parliamentary Group of Amnesty International, visited Sri Lanka in 1984. Described as a 'small "L" Liberal' by his parliamentary colleagues, Missen returned home 'most concerned that the terrible breaches of human rights of 1983 could well be repeated'.[7] A year later, Missen returned to Sri Lanka, describing 'exhaustion on both sides' and discounting the short, three-month ceasefire as a solution.[8] After speaking to government officials and Tamil representatives, Missen left Sri Lanka convinced that the breaches of human rights against Tamils that had occurred in July 1983 would be repeated. While acknowledging the longer histories underpinning Tamil persecution and migration, historian Anna Arabindan-Kesson reflects that the 1983 anti-Tamil pogrom led to a series of beginnings and endings.[9] For Tamils in Australia, it marked the beginning of a new global awareness of the Tamil refugee plight that strengthened their refugee advocacy work:

> That is the very first time that the truth started coming out. Before that, Sri Lankans were bluffing it, saying that it was a terrorist problem. But this is a different terror incident which was given much support. It changed the whole pattern of the situation from Sri Lanka.[10]

Community input clearly functioned as a necessary part of the government's resettlement program for Tamils arriving in Australia through the SHP or other migration programs, including family reunification visas. The government's broad definition of a family member also enabled Tamils in Australia to sponsor relatives. These government decisions reflected widespread Tamil concerns about the deteriorating conflict: 'everyone had the feeling that we are being attacked because each and every person had one of their family members affected there.'[11]

The SHP was all the more imperative for opening new communication channels for Tamils to strengthen their involvement in future government refugee responses. Shortly after the program was implemented, the CTA organised a special committee to interact with immigration authorities on a regular basis to discuss resettlement approaches, needs and supports for Tamils seeking asylum. The respect and trust that had been established between the Tamil community and the government made this new initiative possible. But the interactions were not always harmonious. One point of contention arose from the fact that the SHP was not specific to Tamils. As the CTA founding member explained, 'they didn't say Tamils because of the Sinhalese objections'.[12] Representatives of the Sinhalese and Burgher (European and Sri Lankan heritage) communities objected to Australia giving favourable treatment to Tamils over the other ethnic groups. This caused enormous problems for the government as it sought to balance refugee protection without inflaming intra-community tensions.

Balancing diplomatic and refugee interests

Not surprisingly, concerns expressed by the Sinhalese and Burgher communities echoed homeland anxieties – indeed their biggest fear was that giving Tamils special migration consideration would transport the inter-ethnic conflict to Australian streets. On 8 August 1983, Dr Quintus de Zylva, a member of the Sri Lankan Burgher community in Melbourne, wrote to Prime Minister Bob Hawke about 'violence amongst Sri Lankan people [who had] recently [arrived]' in Australia.[13] De Zylva claimed to represent concerns held by the majority of the Sri Lankan community and argued that an intake of Tamil refugees would disrupt the 'balance of migrants', particularly in Melbourne, where there were significant Sinhalese, Burgher and Tamil communities.[14] He went a step further and complained that the development of separate Tamil and Sinhalese organisations had increased intra-community tensions, which would intensify if Tamils were allowed entry into Australia. These fears were repeated by Dennis Pereira, the Sri Lankan high commissioner, who explained to the Department of Foreign Affairs that the Tamils in Australia were donating money to the Middle East region where military equipment was being purchased to support Tamil militant groups in Sri Lanka.[15] In response to these aspersions on the Tamil community, the Immigration Department provided a steady stream of letters from Tamil citizens protesting against persecution in their homeland. The CTA objected vigorously and countered that the Sinhalese and Burgher communities were abusing the government's special consideration for war-affected Tamils in order to enter Australia for economic reasons.[16]

But the concerns of the Australian government went much further than managing community tensions. In a rapidly changing geo-political context, the government also aimed to strengthen relations with its Indian Ocean Sri Lankan neighbour. Australia was becoming increasingly aware of the need to bolster this relationship, to secure its position in the Asia-Pacific region politically, militarily and economically. For this reason, the Department of Foreign Affairs chose not to criticise the Sri Lankan government for persecuting Tamils because it wanted to avoid being seen as supporting Tamils over other ethnic groups in Sri Lanka. The department stated that the SHP 'does not justify considering Tamils as having a prima facie case for refugee status or accepting [sic] under Special Humanitarian Program simply on the basis of their ethnic origin. Moreover, refugee status can only be considered once the applicant has left his [or her] country of origin.'[17]

In the end, the SHP in Sri Lanka lasted until 1988. During the first two years 720 people in total were accepted, with smaller numbers approved in the remaining years.[18] It is unclear how many of these refugees were Tamil, as the government navigated a thin line between managing intra-community tensions and pursuing its own diplomatic concerns. Despite Australian officials frequently contacting their colleagues in Sri Lanka for 'situation reports' that clearly highlighted Tamil persecution and which should have justified their refugee status, Tamils who arrived during the 1980s were resettled not as refugees, but as migrants.[19] In response, the Sri Lankan government and its officials repeatedly downplayed the violence, claiming the human rights abuses were acts of interrogation rather than orchestrated government policy.

In the face of official denials from the Sri Lankan government, Tamil diaspora organisations became crucial conduits of information about abuses for host countries. In the years after the riots, Tamils arrived in Australia not only as humanitarian entrants, but as part of skilled and family reunification programs, among other migration streams. But it was far from clear how distinctions between migration streams were made in resettling Tamils. While there were genuine displays of concern in parliament about the limitations of the migration program for Tamils seeking asylum, citizen engagement in the late 1970s and early 1980s was a new expression of community consultation.[20] Given the effectiveness of these interactions between the Australian government and the local Tamil community, it is disappointing that this engagement with Tamils did not continue. Today, Tamil refugee advocates find themselves in a situation of complete alienation from refugee policymaking. And although the war in Sri Lanka may have ended in 2009, the continuous arrival of Tamils seeking asylum indicates that the protection crisis is not going to end. Significantly, then, the lack of Tamil community engagement in refugee policymaking risks perpetuating poorly constructed and internationally criticised refugee responses.

Tailoring policy to the needs of the Tamil community

As intermediaries between government and refugees, Tamil refugee advocates did more than fill the gaps in government welfare service provisions. They connected newly arrived Tamils to mainstream services and local knowledges in culturally appropriate ways – a critical set of skills, which government services did not have. This meant that newly arrived Tamils received material support, as well as information about cultural centres, Tamil language schools, Hindu temples, Tamil mass at churches, and social events. In other words, the success of ethno-specific organisations in meeting the immediate and long-term resettlement needs of Tamils suggests that involving citizens in government decision-making has immense benefits. The CTA founding member I interviewed illustrated this point when he recalled immediate supports that were provided to newly arrived Tamils as they resettled in the new land: 'We managed to get things like furniture, beds, and all that and we used to take them in small trucks and deliver them free because it is very hard for them to start their life at that time after losing everything when they came here.'[21]

These organisations were especially crucial at a time when the Hawke government (1983–91) was considering shifting from ethno-specific resettlement delivery models to mainstream agencies. Yet, the government also understood the critical role played by ethnic communities in resettling new arrivals. The broader agenda of the Hawke government, however, was to locate multiculturalism within a national framework, with the 'National Agenda for a Multicultural Australia. Sharing Our Future' in 1989 calling on newly arrived migrants to integrate into Australia. The increasingly nationalist strains of multiculturalism shifted further from the approach outlined in the report *Migrant Services and Programs*, commissioned by the Fraser government in 1978. This report had promoted 'liberal multiculturalism', which recognised that successful resettlement of migrants was a complex, long-term process: 'its end point is the acceptance by and the feeling of belonging to the receiving society'.[22]

The results of this community-centred refugee response have extended well beyond the first generation. Since the 1980s, for example, cultural and religious institutions like the Tamil Language School and Hindu temple have played a vital role in helping the next generation build a sense of belonging in their new home. These Tamil spaces were crucial for young people who had experienced disrupted education due to the war. A young Tamil explained that connecting with other Tamils helped to establish a feeling of belonging:

> Because I went to Tamil school I had met other people so I was able to hang around with them. I didn't have proper education for two years, so from Year 8 to Year 10 I didn't have it. So, I had to catch up in Year 10. Through Tamil school I was able to make some good friends who were also studying at the same high school.[23]

Even though interviewees left Sri Lanka at a young age and did not return, they were raised in settings that daily referenced an imagined Tamil homeland – ideologically, materially and emotionally. The distribution of Tamil community resources in the early 1980s was driven to a large extent by the government, including Tamil concerns in refugee policymaking: the power of migrant communities, trusting relationships with government officials, and recognising the long-term benefits of inclusive decision-making for contributing to successful resettlement. These community-driven supports demonstrate the value of citizens as being critical to humanitarian resettlement efforts in the host country. Involving citizens extends beyond changing policy, it has the transformative power to prioritise community-centred approaches to resettlement and demonstrate what it means to accept refugees based on the experiences and truths shared by those war-affected diaspora communities.

Lessons from history: Listen to former refugees

Today, it is almost impossible for Tamil refugee advocates to support newly arrived Tamils as a result of policies that prevent refugees from accessing basic welfare supports. International experts reject Australia's refugee policy as an effective model for addressing the current global refugee protection crisis. The experience of Tamils fleeing Sri Lanka at the outbreak of the civil war and arriving in Australia shows that listening and engaging with war-affected communities is crucial to developing sound refugee policy. Put simply, such inclusive policymaking helps to address refugee protection crises; in this case, viewing Tamils not as problems, but as part of diaspora communities with longer histories of migration. By focusing on these historical agents, we can bring into focus experiences of war that might otherwise be undermined or erased.

When it comes to refugee policymaking, governments must ensure that they include war-affected communities in their refugee responses. Governments must take this local, on-the-ground knowledge seriously. This will not always be entirely successful, as indeed was the case with Tamils. The Australian government did not officially recognise that Tamils were being persecuted in Sri Lanka. Instead, it went to pains to avoid being seen as supporting Tamils by reassuring the Sri Lankan government that it was not giving Tamils special consideration for resettlement. Ultimately, the number of arrivals was small under the SHP.

At the same time, the government worked directly with its Tamil citizens to enact its humanitarian concerns while enabling the community to deliver critical resettlement supports to newly arrived Tamils. In order to respond to complex and longlasting crises, governments need to develop refugee policy in conversation with refugees themselves and their communities. It is simply not possible to construct refugee policies without working with the people who are directly affected by the crisis in their homeland. Community views challenge the dominant narratives of the government, but it is precisely these perspectives that need to be considered.

CHAPTER 14

The 'Muslim Problem' in Australia: The role of political leadership

Mahsheed Ansari

The recent withdrawal of American and coalition forces from Afghanistan marked the end of the longest war in Australian history (2001–21).[1] To the roughly 600 000 Muslims in Australia, the war in Afghanistan was a poor foreign policy choice borne of the misconceived 'War on Terror'.[2] Indeed, in the aftermath of the 9/11 attacks, Muslim Australians have endured a domestic 'era of terror'.[3] While the opportunities provided by a multicultural and liberal Australia have generally seen Muslim Australians thrive, since 9/11 they have become one of the country's most targeted and vilified groups.[4] Muslim communities have endured repeated mosque attacks and verbal and physical abuse in public spaces such as buses, trains, streets and suburban shopping centres. They are frequent targets of right-wing extremism.[5]

Politicians have much to answer for. Scholars have demonstrated a strong correlation between anti-Muslim rhetoric in political discourse and Islamophobic attacks.[6] In the run-up to several elections since 9/11, politicians have, not coincidentally, drawn attention to the 'imminent threat' of terrorism, with waves of new laws and domestic security measures. Australia has passed over 60 pieces of anti-terrorism legislation since 9/11. According to the sociologist Scott Poynting, the 'Howard Government alone between September 2001 and its departure from office in 2007, enacted 48 new anti-terror laws: one new law on average every 6.7 weeks'.[7]

Many of us will remember when One Nation leader Pauline Hanson walked into the Senate chamber wearing a black burqa in August 2017. The stunt was designed to ridicule Muslims and underline her call for the traditional garment to be banned. The sensationalising of the 'Muslim problem' by bigoted and self-serving politicians has given legitimacy to pockets of ultra-nationalists and White supremacists, and led to organised violent crimes against Muslims.[8]

When an Australian man resident in New Zealand, Brenton Tarrant, slaughtered 51 worshippers at two mosques in Christchurch, Muslim Australians and New Zealanders felt trauma, fear and concern for their safety.[9] To add to the scale of the atrocity, the terrorist broadcast the murders in the Al Noor and Linwood mosques in Christchurch live on social media. Yet in the aftermath of the attacks, Australian Senator Fraser Anning blamed New Zealand's immigration policy for allowing Muslims into the country.[10] Anning also raised Muslim immigration to Australia as a key issue, calling for its ban in his first speech on 14 August 2018, wherein he evoked and praised the 'White Australia' policy in the hope of prompting its return. His comments were widely condemned by Prime Minister Scott Morrison, opposition leader Bill Shorten and most MPs. However, in November the same year, several politicians, including Morrison and Home Affairs Minister Peter Dutton, blamed the Muslim community for the Islamic State–inspired terrorist attack in Bourke Street, Melbourne, in which one man was killed and two injured. They criticised

Muslim communities in Australia for not doing enough to stop extremism, 'making excuses' and ignoring potential risks.[11]

Peter Dutton linked the attack to the government's re-evaluation of Australian citizenship. He said it is 'much harder' to deal with Australian citizens radicalised in Australia than a visa holder, who can be deported, signalling he would make an announcement in 'due course'.[12] Two years earlier, Dutton suggested that it had been a mistake to settle so many Muslim Lebanese in Australia in the 1970s. Despite objections from the United Nations, he gave preference to Christian Syrians and Iraqis for refugee status in 2015 by classifying them as 'persecuted minorities'.[13] After the Bourke Street attack, terrorism experts dismissed the notion that Muslim leaders needed to do more to counter terrorism, as the man was known to intelligence agencies and had been classified as low risk. Despite appeals from Muslim community leaders about the destructive political debates that conflate Islam and terrorism, this political discourse routinely appears, usually in the lead-up to elections, with lasting repercussions for the Muslim community.

The roots of the anti-Islamic attitudes that are so prevalent today can be traced back to colonial Australia, with the introduction of policies that dehumanised non-White and non-European minorities. The experiences of Muslims, from the Afghan cameleers and Malay pearl divers of the nineteenth and early twentieth centuries, to the more recent post–Second World War migration, reveal a pattern of religious and racial discrimination. It is also possible, however, to discern exceptions to this discriminatory attitude to immigration and cultural difference in Australian history. Immigration reform after the Second World War was driven by changing geo-political circumstances and shifting community attitudes, but crucially, it was also championed by progressive politicians. History shows that strong leadership at the political level is vital to counter the appeals to division and bigotry that are sadly not uncommon today.

The 'Muslim problem' in Australian history

The so-called 'Muslim problem' in present-day Australia has many precedents in our history. During the nineteenth century, non-Europeans were free to arrive and settle, but they were not always permitted to own land or given equal status in social, commercial and official dealings. Muslim migrants, such as South Asian cameleers, began arriving after the mid-century gold rushes. They lived on the outskirts of settlements, building their tin houses and mosques in outback fringe locations. The explorers Robert O'Hara Burke and William Wills employed cameleers on their trek from Melbourne to the Gulf of Carpentaria in 1860, before perishing on the return leg.[14] The 'Afghans', 'Ghans', 'Hindoos' or 'Syrians', as migrants from places including Kashmir, Punjab, pre-Partition Pakistan, Egypt and Turkey were collectively categorised, were frequent targets of racism and discrimination.[15] Also known as 'Mohammadans' or 'Mohomets', (though some were of Hindu and Sikh faiths), they were eyed with suspicion for their lack of Christian belief.[16] The writer Hanifa Deen has argued that the 'Afghan problem' in the late nineteenth century generated the kind of anxious discussion and consternation that is evoked in relation to asylum seekers and refugees in contemporary Australia.[17]

The beliefs that underpinned the desire for a White Australia came from the ugly mix of certitudes and anxieties that permeated the newly 'settled' Australian colonies, and were later present in the Commonwealth of Australia.[18] Colonisation and exploitation were justified by the assertion of racial, religious, cultural and civilisational superiority of the coloniser over the colonised.[19] These assertions of racial superiority were boosted by the distorting quasi-science of social Darwinism, which premised a hierarchy of races, in which the Anglo-Saxon races sat at the apex. The self-serving beliefs that literary critic Edward Said later described as 'Orientalism' also allowed the coloniser/occident to represent himself (and this was a male-dominated system of power) as culturally and biologically superior to the colonised/oriental.[20]

Anxieties about immigration and race increased during the 1890s, as economic depression gripped the south-eastern parts of the continent. Sentiments such as 'Australia for the white man' were increasingly heard, and reflected in colonial government policies that targeted non-Anglo communities. This racial ideology culminated in the *Immigration Restriction Act 1901*, which was the first piece of legislation passed by the new Commonwealth parliament. The act delineated Australia as a 'White nation', not explicitly, but through its invidious stipulation that potential migrants could be asked to take a 'dictation test' in any European language. Britain's Secretary of State for the Colonies, Joseph Chamberlain, had successfully lobbied the Commonwealth government to introduce the dictation test instead of the explicit policy of exclusion preferred by the Labor party, as a means of appeasing non-White members of the empire.[21] If applicants failed the test, they could be refused entry to Australia. The *Immigration Restriction Act* became a principal pillar of the tenuous Australian 'national identity', which was British, Christian and openly hostile towards non-White peoples.

With the introduction of the White Australia policy came a further hardening of attitudes towards non-Anglo populations. The first settled Muslim community – the cameleers – was subjected to punitive conditions. Camel drivers were required to apply for special certificates to cross state boundaries, and pay licence and registration fees to continue the work they had always done.[22] In 1907, the Macassar Trepang fishermen were banned by South Australian authorities from entering the country. So-called Malay pearl divers (a group that actually included Singaporeans and Indonesians) were granted an exemption from the *Immigration Restriction Act*, but deported decades later when they sought to unionise in an effort to improve working conditions.[23] Among these divers was Samsudin bin Katib, who was deported to Sumatra in 1948, despite having served with distinction in the Navy during the Second World War. In her book *Ali Abdul v. the King*, Hanifa Deen describes the plight of Ali Abdul, a greengrocer from Sydney who was unlawfully convicted of being an illegal immigrant after failing the dictation test in 1931.[24]

Resistance to White Australia

Australia is a diverse migrant nation, despite the dominance of Europeans in the continent's very recent history. Research is increasingly revealing the close contact, trade and cultural exchange between the First Australians and their neighbours.[25] Indigenous people engaged in trade since at least the 1700s with Macassar Muslim traders for trepang sea slugs. One wonders how things might have been if Australia had not embarked on a racially restrictive path in 1901, which limited the free flow of people and trade; how it would have affected Australia's regional leadership in South-East Asian markets as well as our political culture.

The experiences of non-White people, whether they were Indigenous, Muslim or from some other discriminated-against minority, drop in and out of the Australian historical record. A smattering of accounts have survived of daily interactions, cultural exchanges and marriages between Asian Muslim cameleers, hawkers and pearl divers and their European and Aboriginal counterparts.[26]

A handful of Anglo-Australians, including the philanthropist and humanitarian Caroline Chisholm (1808–77), sought to protect the civic rights of migrants. They acted with goodwill, generally aiming to improve the inadequate conditions and welfare of the poor and needy. Although most philanthropical works and services were focused on the early colonial settlers and convicts, there is evidence of provision for other races as well. The construction of shelter sheds in goldmines, which had been proposed by Chisholm, proceeded from 1855, and protected 'Chinese and possibly Aboriginal or other dark-skinned Asians'.[27] There is little evidence of other assistance, apart from mutual exchange of benefits from those who worked with cameleers or were in the sea slug business. Most efforts at advocacy were overridden by the racism of European Australians, who barely tolerated non-White people as lowly workers and little else.

The British government put increasing pressure on Australia about its racially discriminatory immigration policy over the course of the twentieth century. Australian voices who spoke for disaffected minorities, including Afghans, Indians and Malays, became louder too. For example, a group of white eyewitnesses provided court testimony to support the Sydney greengrocer Ali Abdul, who was threatened with deportation. He later won his appeal, since he had migrated legally to Australia before 1901, and was able to call on the testimony of friends and acquaintances from over the decades, and the help of goodwilled lawyers.[28] Similarly, the political activist Elizabeth Marshall (1879–1964) and her husband lobbied the Immigration Minister Arthur Calwell and other members of parliament to support the Malay pearl diver and Second World War special forces commando, Samsudin bin Katib, in an appeal after his application for naturalisation was rejected. Katib, a highly skilled pearl diver, had been deported after the war. He was targeted as a trouble-maker, having organised divers against the 'Master Pearlers' who had been accustomed to dealing with cheap, tractable indentured labour.[29] The advocacy of the Marshalls was successful, and Katib was allowed to return to Australia in 1949.[30]

Some Muslim immigrants succeeded in circumventing the White Australia policy, among them the Punjabi Fatteh Mohammed Dean and the Kashmiri Fatteh Gulab Deen. The Punjabi Dean was successful in bringing his young bride to Australia after Federation. She would later return to India with her baby sons, all bearing 'Exemption from Dictation Test' certificates, which would later allow them to re-enter Australia legally. Dean was a 'city Muslim', in contrast to most of his contemporaries who were in the camel trade. He succeeded in his integration strategy as a 'suit-and-tie' Muslim – a successful businessman who was able to prosper despite the obstacles to coloured people in this era.[31]

The end of White Australia

In 1945, Australia became a founding member of the United Nations. The Foreign Minister, H.V. Evatt, was elected president of the UN General Assembly in 1948, the same year that the Universal Declaration of Human Rights was adopted.[32] From the late 1950s, with Britain's turn away from its former empire towards Europe, Australian geo-political strategy began a slow reorientation to Asia. These developments compelled Australian policymakers to adjust to an increasingly globalised world that was less tolerant of nations with racially discriminatory practices. Australia could no longer afford to overtly discriminate against nations with whom it sought economic and strategic cooperation.

In 1958, the notorious 'dictation test' was abolished.[33] Further, in 1966, Australian Immigration Minister Hubert Opperman 'secured legislation ... that allowed for increased migration of skilled non-European migrants', and gave them the right to citizenship after living in Australia for five years.[34] As chairman of the Immigration Advisory Council, Sir Keith Wilson pointed out in the House of Representatives on 24 March 1966, 'from now on there will not be in any of our laws or in any of our regulations anything that discriminates against migrants on the grounds of colour or race.'[35] Thus, even prior to the Whitlam government's official renouncement in 1973, substantial steps had been taken towards dismantling the White Australia policy. Moreover, large migrant communities from eastern, southern and central Europe and parts of Asia became an increasing presence in Australian society between 1945 and 1972.

A significant step in Australian engagement with its Asian neighbours occurred with the introduction of an innovative educational scheme nested within a bigger cooperative development venture, the Colombo Plan, in 1951.[36] Australia's scholarships provided under the Colombo Plan were aimed at strengthening relationships with Asia and soon became a useful form of advertising for Australia as an education destination.[37] It led to Australia's successful international engagement in the region.[38] In this era new opportunities opened for Muslim tertiary students who arrived in Australia as early as the 1950s and 1960s from Malaya, Singapore, Indonesia, Pakistan and India.[39] Australia attracted foreign students from Iran, Afghanistan and Egypt as well.[40] The vast proportion of these were private international students, whose presence ensured the establishment of societies and associations, which had a lasting impact on social and political relations between Australia and its regional neighbours.[41]

After the White Australia policy was officially abandoned in 1973, bipartisan support emerged for a policy of multiculturalism to replace the old policies of assimilation and integration into a white majority culture.[42] The political changes in Australian public policy since the 1950s and seismic shift to multicultural policy since the 1970s altered the nature of migration to Australia.[43] With greater cultural acceptance of non-Europeans, the increased migration of Asian and other non-Anglo and white Muslims was now possible. Young Muslims from various parts of the world came to study in Australian universities, and the new era also encouraged general migration of non-Europeans with some assisted programs to Muslim migrants.[44] By the 1970s and 1980s, Turkish and Lebanese Muslim migrants were joined by Albanians, Yugoslavians and Cypriots.[45]

Muslim Australians thrived in multicultural Australia. There were greater opportunities for education and employment for the children of the settled Muslim migrant workers. Other positive examples of a working multicultural policy included the establishment of Islamic associations and the development of city mosques in Melbourne and Sydney. The personal attendance of the Labor opposition leader, Gough Whitlam, at the inauguration of Preston mosque in 1976 underlined the sense of a new era for migrants and Muslims.[46] It also demonstrated that minority communities could thrive socially and politically if their social and political rights, and freedom to practise their faith were ensured.

Lessons from history: The need for political leadership

Australia is no longer the institutionally racist society of the first two-thirds of the twentieth century. But there is no doubt that the War on Terror has undone many of the gains made during the era of multiculturalism. Once again, Muslim Australians have become targets of fear, hatred and politically motivated scapegoating. As the historian Regina Ganter suggests, the War on Terror had the effect of compressing various non-European ethnic communities into one body of 'Muslims'.[47] The populist conservatism that thrives in sections of contemporary Australia seeks to drive wedges of fear and suspicion between Muslims and other Australians for political gain. It risks further inciting those on the far right who are fuelled by racial and religious hatred and motivated towards terror.

Australia's geo-political and economic interests are best suited to multiculturalism and a multifaith philosophy. Mutual respect between Muslim and other Australians, rooted in genuine appreciation for the identity and individuality of all humans irrespective of their race and creed, is not just morally right, but also conducive to the success and growth of a progressive liberal nation-state. As writer Hanifa Deen describes:

> History teaches us many lessons: what to be proud of and what to shun. Some people worry that the old gravitational pull from the days of White Australia will reassert itself again – but I am more optimistic, for Australia is not a racist society today. I also know, however, that escaping a racist past doesn't happen overnight; there are lessons to be learnt from looking at the way we once were.[48]

Leaders who seek to leave a 'positive mark' on Australia, with bold, game-changing policies like 'multiculturalism', and increased political and cultural integration with Asia must reject the xenophobic and Islamophobic discourse that loiters around parliament and the wider community. The history of the 'Muslim experience' in Australia shows that politicians must not be seduced by populist waves of racist bigotry, as tempting as these may be when seeking to harness electoral support. Eventually such populist temptations wither away in the face of policies based on reason and geo-political reality. Bold leaders can be the champions of true multiculturalism and find a new definition of 'we are one but we are many'.

CHAPTER 15

Why soldiers commit war crimes – and what we can do about it

Mia Martin Hobbs

In 2020, the Inspector-General of the Australian Defence Force (IGADF) released the Afghanistan Inquiry into Australian Defence Force (ADF) Special Forces atrocities in Afghanistan (hereafter IGADF Report). The report resulted in a flurry of analysis debating how and why Australian soldiers could have committed war crimes. Some commentators focused on 'high operational tempos' that increased soldiers' dependence on their teams. Others emphasised how operational independence among 'elite' forces allowed 'charismatic leaders' to influence teams with a 'warrior hero' culture.[1] A common thread was that counterinsurgency warfare made it difficult to differentiate allies, civilians and enemies among the local population.[2]

While these factors are important, analyses focusing on unit problems tend to treat culture as a static and internal problem, rather than an ongoing practice influenced by broader society. Similarly, the stress on counterinsurgency warfare negates the fact that similar crimes are also well documented in trench warfare and in occupations in conventional wars.[3] For policymakers, military leaders and the general public, a deeper understanding of the nature of war crimes is crucial if we want to prevent them from happening again.

War crimes reflect social prejudices. They are shaped around wartime laws and policies, and are facilitated by cultural veneration of the military. Historical comparisons between general infantry forces in Vietnam and special forces in Afghanistan show that atrocities have at least as much to do with broader social, political and cultural fabrics as they do with tempo, leadership and internal culture. Far from an aberration, military leaders, policymakers and civilians should recognise that atrocities are a likely outcome of warfare. As we shall see, by proactively tackling troop prejudices, anticipating the manipulation of policies in the field, and encouraging civilian engagement with the realities of warfare, we can reduce the likelihood of war crimes in the future.

War crimes:
The social influence

Military recruits are commonly trained to dehumanise the race or ethnicity of their enemy forces. This dehumanisation facilitates combat and strengthens the collective identity among soldiers. By portraying an enemy group as fundamentally different – less valuable, less human – the group establishes unity within the 'Self' and justifies violence towards the 'Other'.[4] American and Australian Vietnam veterans, for instance, remembered their training as 'bastardisation', where 'the loathing was hammered in'. They were 'taught to hate the gooks, to see them as less than human. You can't kill a Vietnamese, but it's easy to blow away a gook or a slope.'[5]

Troop racism is often an intensified version of prejudices apparent in broader societies. After 9/11, for example, Islamophobia in Australia became more pronounced, with overt discrimination, suspicion and violence towards Muslims.[6] Suspicion of Afghans flows through the IGADF Report into Australian war crimes in Afghanistan: 'local nationals were presumed to be hostile', and Special Forces aimed to '"clear" the battlefield of people believed to be insurgents, regardless of the Law of Armed Conflict'. This suggests that the soldiers viewed the entire population on 'the battlefield' – that is, Afghans living on their own lands – as the enemy. Racism in the larger Australian military allowed atrocities to continue unchecked: ADF officers responded to Afghan complaints about Special Forces conduct with 'a presumption, not founded in evidence, to discount local national complaints as insurgent propaganda or motivated by a desire for compensation'.[7]

Similarly, militaries from patriarchal societies find misogyny among their ranks, manifesting in both institutional violence and war crimes.[8] Historian Christian Appy found that in US basic training for Vietnam, 'the model of male sexuality offered as a military ideal in boot camp was directly linked to violence ... Drill instructors repeatedly described war as a substitute for sex or as another form of sex.'[9] Sexualised descriptions of warfare are prolific in Vietnam War memoirs: 'killing is sexual. Death too ... Someone once asked me to describe up-close combat in a nutshell. How about this? Pure pussy.'[10] These links between masculinity, sex, violence and military authority produced atrocities. Journalists and scholars reported that the rape and murder of women was so widespread in Vietnam that soldiers coined the term 'double veteran' to glorify perpetrators.[11] In a war where combat soldiers felt vulnerable to guerrilla attacks, mines and booby traps, rape was frequently used to assert control, reinforcing soldiers' sense of masculinity and authority.

Underlying gendered and racialised atrocities is a psychological drive to conquer through violence. Australia, like other Western nations involved in the War on Terror, saw a resurgence of white male supremacy in the twenty-first century.[12] Indeed, the agendas of neo-colonial 'West versus the rest' foreign policies 'supercharged' white male supremacist movements.[13] This resurgence is particularly apparent in the military, with groups of deployed soldiers bearing white supremacist symbols, including the Nazi and Confederate flags, Ku Klux Klan hoods and the Crusader's Cross.[14] White male supremacy helps to explain atrocities that intentionally degrade victims: torture, rape and war pornography. For soldiers who see themselves as 'crusaders' fighting a war for 'civilisation' against 'barbarism', racialised and gendered violence are logical steps in maintaining racial and gender hierarchies.[15] Political scientist Laleh Khalili notes that in the War on Terror, torture practices were frequently shaped around religious humiliation and emasculation, based on 'an orientalist understanding of what is considered honourable or shameful in "Muslim culture"'.[16] Similarly, the common tendency for soldiers to document their atrocities reflects a desire to exert total control over the Other.[17] Finally, degrading war crimes are often collective practices. Perpetrators enact and share power with one another, reinforcing values and establishing loyalty within the group.

War crimes and military policy

Soldiers who commit atrocities are responding to military policies: Laws of Armed Conflict (LOAC, international law) and Rules of Engagement (RoE, country-specific policies). Some soldiers who commit war crimes interpret RoE in contradiction to LOAC. Some deliberately exploit RoE to violate LOAC. In both situations, crimes are shaped by the policies set out to prevent them.

There is strong evidence to suggest that military frameworks prevent soldiers from recognising violations of international law. Veterans used techno-strategic language to describe torture during interrogations, corpse desecration, forced displacement and small-group civilian killings in free-fire zones, indicating that they learned these crimes as lawful tactics.[18] For example, in both Vietnam and Afghanistan, Australian soldiers desecrated corpses. One Vietnam veteran remembered:

> I blew up bodies ... It saved time digging a hole. They used to call it an engineer's burial. I was well aware of the psych ops angle of it because they'd always try and take their dead away with them. If you understand the Asian mind, you know they all want to go to the happy hunting ground in one piece and have a proper burial.
> So, by blowing the body to shithouse, it will piss off the ones that are still alive.[19]

The veteran's choice of words here – 'they used to call it' – indicates this was not an isolated incident. Another veteran remembered a 'policy of dumping VC [Viet Cong] bodies in town market squares or dragging them behind Armoured Personnel Carriers, in sight of the village children, both methods supposedly meant to draw out further VC sympathisers'.[20] Similarly, the ABC's 'Afghan Files' revealed that in 2013, an SAS corporal severed hands from the bodies of three Afghan insurgents. When questioned, the corporal explained that it was 'a tactical necessity' to collect fingerprints.[21]

Vietnam veterans were also trained to think that mistreating and killing civilians was lawful under certain circumstances. The US-led pacification strategy to isolate rural civilians from revolutionary forces involved the forced displacement of civilians. To secure the Australian base at Nui Dat, the nearby villages of Long Tan and Long Phuoc were destroyed and the villagers resettled by 'clearing patrols':

> we'd put up huts and then we'd go into a village and say, 'right, we are going to shift you into this lovely beaut place you're going to live in'. And you'd take them out of there, take everybody out. Then you'd burn them [the villagers' huts]. And then you start to hear screaming. And then they'd all come out, because some of them were Viet Cong.[22]

Once the area was 'cleared', it was designated a 'free-fire' or 'restricted' zone, which soldiers were instructed to treat as 'enemy territory'. Free-fire zones are not a legal instrument of war. Nor is displacing civilians and destroying their property.[23] Yet through these policies, soldiers justified mass killings and total destruction. 'I flew infantry on helicopters', one US veteran recalled, 'and we did search-and-destroy missions. We would fly into a village, enemy village, and we would kill everything and every pig and chicken and water buffalo and burn down every hooch in the place, just because it's enemy territory.'[24]

Killings in free-fire zones are the kinds of acts commonly referred to as 'fog of war' incidents. Recent investigations into Australian war crimes deliberately avoided all 'fog of war' accounts, because ambiguity around intention made them nearly impossible to prosecute.[25] Yet examining more ambiguous actions reveals that military policies can produce atrocities. Social anthropologist Heonik Kwon argues that displacement and 'free-fire' policies led directly to massacres. While Australian and American military understood that any Vietnamese in 'free-fire' zones were the enemy, displaced civilians monitored the situation in their homes carefully, petitioning local authorities for visitation rights and travelling back and forth to tend to family farms. 'Safe' villages attracted returning civilians, but could be quickly recategorised as 'free-fire' zones by military command without the villagers' knowledge. In the case of the 1968 My Lai massacre, the villagers 'considered the US soldiers in [nearby] My Khe to be friends'.[26]

Soldiers also exploited ambiguity around 'fog of war' incidents to commit atrocities. US Vietnam veterans described a policy whereby Vietnamese were deemed enemy forces if they ran away. Soldiers would shoot near civilians to 'test' them, and kill them when they jumped or fled: 'they were killed for being frightened. And of course they were frightened, because they knew they might be killed.'[27] Similarly in Afghanistan, the IGADF Report alleges that soldiers developed an expansive interpretation of RoE around 'spotters' and 'squirters' – people suspected of relaying information to the Taliban, or believed to be running to or from a weapons cache – to justify killing. In doing so, they instilled fear among the local population, giving Afghans good cause to flee and allowing soldiers to claim further killings of 'squirters'.[28] Military lawyers were aware of these 'sanctioned massacres', and tried to limit soldiers' ability to kill by changing the RoE, but soldiers 'just got more creative in how they wrote up the incidents.'[29]

Civilian murder is a direct result of 'body count' or 'kill count' measures of victory, where military success is equated to the number of enemy killed. In both Vietnam and Afghanistan, soldiers competed to outscore other patrols in the count and deliberately planted 'throwdowns' (weapons or equipment) on dead bodies to document them as legal killings. The My Lai massacre, for instance – in which over 500 civilians were slaughtered, with many tortured and raped – was initially reported by the US military as a 'fierce fire fight', in which US soldiers killed 128 'enemy', justified by the recent 'free-fire zone' designation and three planted weapons.[30] In Afghanistan, the IGADF Report concluded that Australians' frequent use of 'throwdowns' originated as a 'strategy of avoiding scrutiny' when a killed Afghan 'turned out not to be armed'. It then morphed into a deliberate practice to conceal calculated murder, with soldiers allegedly carrying a backpack with materials to plant on non-combatants.[31] The practice was widespread enough that soldiers 'use[d] to joke about how the same serial number [of a gun] was in every single photo of a dead Afghani [sic]'.[32]

The torture and murder of prisoners also demonstrates deliberate subversion of Laws of Armed Conflict. Sociologist Samantha Crompvoets found 'corroborated accounts' that Australian Special Forces in Afghanistan would detain men and boys in guesthouses in villages and torture them, depriving them of food, water and medicine, 'do anything at all they wanted to', and then kill them.[33] These practices were justified as 'interrogation', an institutional as well as individual defence by Western forces in the War on Terror.[34] A common justification for the murder of prisoners is 'medical termination'.[35] An Australian Vietnam veteran described killing a wounded enemy in his memoir, and when later challenged claimed it was a 'mercy killing'.[36] More recently in Iraq, US Navy SEAL medics admitted that they killed a captured militant by doing 'medical scenarios on him until he died'.[37] UK and US soldiers confirmed no one they fought with ever wanted to save a wounded enemy combatant.[38]

Culture, national myths and war crimes

The occurrence of these atrocities contradicts a widespread belief that combat soldiers exhibit an unwillingness to kill.[39] Many civilians want to believe that soldiers can fight effectively, honourably and unwillingly out of duty. This belief allows civilians to revere soldiers who do the nation's 'dirty work'. Underpinning this admiration is a view that international law is abstract and idealistic, and that soldiers have their own 'moral code' grounded in the realities of warfare.[40] 'War is a messy business', according to the former Australian War Memorial Director Brendan Nelson, who 'question[s] whether the national interest is in trying to tear down our heroes'. A petition to 'stop the witch hunt' against alleged war criminal Ben Roberts-Smith described how Special Forces 'deploy to the hottest hot spots ... [to] do a job that the vast majority of people cannot do', and claims that 'you want men like this defending the country'.[41] Our cultural approach to war tacitly approves ultraviolence while avoiding any discussion of what it actually entails, entrenching the idea that combat and killing impart special knowledge and setting soldiers beyond civilian judgment. Ironically, the belief that 'good' soldiers use violence unwillingly promotes the idea that killing is the key to military legitimacy.

Military veneration produces soldiers who are attracted to service because it allows for 'state sanctioned violence'.[42] In post-Vietnam 'professional' Western militaries, violence is linked to status: the most elite soldier is one whose work 'outside the wire' is dangerous and taboo.[43] In 2018, the Chief of the Australian Defence Force, Angus Campbell, had to issue a ban on 'death symbols' among deployed troops who expressed their military identity with 'violent, murderous and vigilante symbolism'.[44] Fascination with violence manifests in atrocities that perform brutality: stomping, beating, or 'crushing the life' out of people; collecting body parts as 'trophies' of military prowess; 'blooding' new soldiers with the murder of a prisoner to achieve their 'first kill'.[45] Blooding establishes killing as a rite of passage for a military elite, binding perpetrators into a code of silence. Crimes that perform brutality reinforce military veneration and fascination with violence: Australian perpetrators were 'equated with being good and effective soldiers'.[46]

National narratives that celebrate 'good' soldiers as the pinnacle of national identity also shield perpetrators of war crimes. In Australia, a central theme of the Anzac legend is that Australian soldiers are innately superior to those of our allies. This narrative is frequently deployed to deflect allegations of Australian atrocities. During an admission of Australian war crimes in Afghanistan, one soldier added that 'whatever *we* do … I can tell you the Brits and the US are far, far worse'.[47] Another theme is the idea that Australian soldiers are so good at warfare – so formidable, yet honourable – that other groups recognise and respect them.[48] Media coverage of Australian war crimes in Afghanistan emphasised that Australians were 'feared red beards fighting a fierce but just campaign', idolising soldiers even as they reported alleged atrocities.[49] The term 'red beards' is actually used by Afghans as a pejorative for special forces across Western militaries, because of their mistreatment of civilians.[50] In this reverent cultural context, war crimes allegations in Australia just don't seem to stick. Afghans have repeatedly accused Australian soldiers of atrocities throughout the 20-year War on Terror, but although 'many atrocities have been documented in the media', they 'seem to disappear shortly after they surface'.[51] Cultural mythologisation of Australian warfare allows soldiers to get away with murder.

Lessons from history: Acknowledging the past and deradicalising present-day forces to prevent future atrocities

Soldier atrocities reflect the social and cultural fabric of their home nation, and crimes are shaped by military policies intended to prevent them. These factors are often interlinked; the process of the blooding of a soldier (cultural) requires both the dehumanisation of the local population (social) and the exploitation of RoE to cover it up (policies).

What can we do about war crimes? The first step is acknowledging that they have happened throughout history, and that they are happening now. Ongoing impunity suggests that these actions are not only considered justified in the context of war, but morally acceptable. Civilians and journalists should critically evaluate how the historical narratives they deploy around Australian warfighting erase wrongdoing and perpetuate fascination with violence.

The military also needs to learn from the devastating results of dehumanising enemies in past conflicts. They need to urgently implement de-radicalisation in recruitment and training processes. This must go beyond ineffective cultural sensitivity training.[52] Prospective defence members should be screened and soldiers continuously evaluated for prejudices.

These prejudices must be taken seriously, with the connection between prejudice and atrocity made explicit to soldiers. More broadly, Australians ought to question foreign policies that reflect and encourage racism in our communities, which will inevitably be reflected in our institutions.

To avoid future atrocities, military leaders must anticipate that strategies and tactics will be subverted in the field to commit crimes. They should explore 'fog of war' incidents to understand how military policies can produce atrocities, drawing lessons from war crime allegations. Leaders should pay attention to how psychological operations against 'the enemy' engender brutality against 'the people'.

The history of war crimes shows us that atrocities are a likely outcome of warfare. The IGADF Report claimed that 'few would have imagined some of our elite soldiers would engage in the conduct that has been described'.[53] Yet for anyone who had paid attention to the unfolding War on Terror, the allegations came as no surprise. If preventative actions seem beyond the scope of possibility, we must question whether our military can serve its purpose. The IGADF Report acknowledged that in Uruzgan province, where Australians were based with the mission of 'improving the conditions of the Afghan people', ADF operations were counterproductive: 'it is plain that [raids] were a terrifying experience for villagers'.[54] Violent counterinsurgencies engender deep resentments, undermining local authorities who cooperate with occupying forces and weakening resistance to insurgent movements. Long-contested territory in the War on Terror, Uruzgan was among the first provinces to fall to the Taliban in August 2021.[55] The 'fear and terror' our soldiers instilled in the local population surely played a role.[56]

CHAPTER 16

How can we fight the far right?

Evan Smith

Since 2015, the threat of the far right in Australia has grown, as both a political phenomenon and as a proponent of violence.[1] In April 2021, two members of the National Socialist Network (NSN) in South Australia were arrested for terrorism offences, while the next month, the NSN's leader, Thomas Sewell, was arrested for alleged armed robbery in Victoria.[2] In 2020, an 18-year-old in New South Wales was charged with terrorism-related offences.[3] Alongside these arrests, the extreme right accelerationist group Sonnenkrieg Division was the first proscribed right-wing extremist group in Australia since new legislation was brought in after 9/11.[4] At the same time, the Director-General of the Australian Security Intelligence Organisation (ASIO) stated that security services had been increasingly attuned to right-wing extremism, with 'ideological extremism' now comprising 40 per cent of ASIO's counter-terrorism caseload.[5] As well as these responses from the police and security services, investigative journalists in Australia and the United States have documented the networks of the extreme far right in Australia and its links to overseas groups.[6]

In electoral politics, Pauline Hanson's One Nation Party

had four senators elected in 2016. One of those senators, Malcolm Roberts, was ruled ineligible to sit in parliament the following year, before being re-elected in 2019. In addition, former Labor leader Mark Latham became a member of the New South Wales Legislative Council in 2019 for One Nation. Other (now former) federal politicians, such as George Christensen, Craig Kelly and Fraser Anning, also sought to exploit the space to the right of the Liberal/National Party and courted support from the far right.

Between the electoral sphere and the extremist element, the far right has also attempted to gain a presence on the streets. Since 2015, a range of far-right groups has emerged in Australia, principally in protest against Islam. These groups are inspired by similar movements in Europe, such as the English Defence League, Germany's PEGIDA and Generation Identity, which started in France and has spread across most of Western Europe. A combination of in-fighting among those involved in these groups, arrests for various offences and counter-protests against them, led a number of people to move into more clandestine forms of far-right organising. But others have been galvanised by the anti-lockdown protests during the COVID-19 pandemic and, as journalists and activists have shown, far-right personalities have been prominent in the anti-lockdown movement across Australia.[7] This was the case in the anti-lockdown demonstrations in Melbourne in September 2021 and in the 'Canberra Convoy' in February 2022.[8]

There has been much deliberation about how to respond to the far-right threat in Australia. Labor's Shadow Minister for Home Affairs, Kristina Keneally, has recently called for greater action by the state in dealing with the far right, including proscription, increased funding for counter-extremist programs and actions to counter far-right extremism on social media.[9] She also stated that we 'need our national leaders to be consistent in naming and condemning right-wing extremist views'.[10]

Keneally's urge for Canberra to crack down on right-wing extremism comes after equivocation from the Coalition government over the issue. There has been a propensity for government members, such as the Defence (and former Home Affairs) Minister Peter Dutton and (former) Senator Concetta Fierravanti-Wells, to speak about far-right political violence only in the context of also mentioning Islamic and 'left-wing' terrorism.[11] In the aftermath of the far-right storming of the US Capitol on 6 January 2021, the former Australian Deputy Prime Minister, Michael McCormack, drew a comparison between this and the Black Lives Matter rallies across the world the previous year, characterising both as 'unfortunate events'.[12]

The call for greater state intervention to address the challenge posed by the far right, particularly extreme right political violence, is problematic. First, the tools that the state can use against extreme right-wing groups likely to be involved in political violence, such as proscription and prosecution for terrorist-related offences, are ones that have been predominantly forged during the 'War on Terror' against jihadist groups. They may not be as effective against right-wing extremism.[13] Secondly, calls for a government crackdown seek to address the most violent forms of right-wing politics in Australia. They do not address the other forms the far-right threat takes in Australia, such as political parties, street campaigns and the use of social media to spread their messages. Historically, the state's approach to far-right activism on the streets has been to treat it as a public order issue, but this has often involved heavy policing of counter-protests against far-right marches and public gatherings.[14] Thirdly, the far and extreme right in all their forms are driven by many of the same racist and settler colonialist ideas that underpin the institutions of the state and mainstream Australian politics. This can be seen in the widespread endorsement of the restrictive border control system and the racial discrimination and violence experienced by minorities in this country.[15] A broader fight against racism *in all its forms* is needed for combating the far right, otherwise it allows the mainstream to portray racism as 'other', rather than something embedded within Australian society more generally.

People making policy decisions need to be aware that the far right can be more effectively fought if the wider issue of racism in society is also addressed. It requires the mobilisation of different sections of society to confront the racism of the mainstream political parties (such as the bipartisan support for strict border controls), the institutions of the state (such as the police or the welfare system) and the racial discrimination experienced in 'everyday life', such as in the workplace or on the streets. A lesson for policymakers from past episodes is that when there are efforts to combat racism on a broader scale, popular movements against fascism and the far right can have more of an impact. In Australia, anti-fascist activism has had more success when it has mobilised people from various sections of society, such as the trade unions, community groups, students and the left, and has combined this with campaigns for Aboriginal rights, against apartheid, against police racism and for refugee rights.

Anti-fascism here and abroad in the 1930s

In the 1930s, Australians felt the threat of fascism and war both domestically and internationally. In early 1931, a right-wing paramilitary group known as the New Guard formed to protect Australia from communism, militant trade unionism and Jack Lang's Labor government in New South Wales.[16] According to historian Keith Amos, by the end of the year, it was estimated that membership of the New Guard had reached at least 50 000, with around 36 000 in the greater Sydney area.[17]

In response to the rise of the New Guard, there was both organised and unorganised opposition. Both the Australian Labor party and the Communist party of Australia had their members form workers' defence groups. The Australian Labor Army (ALA), formed from the NSW Labor Party and the Workers Defence Corp (WDC), was established by the Communist Party of Australia (CPA), with support from the NSW Labor Council.[18] The WDC had originally been created to protect striking workers in 1929 and was revived in 1931 to combat the New Guard.[19] While these groups did mobilise on occasion to protect public meetings and confront the right-wing agitators, historian Andrew Moore argues that, in general, 'the paramilitary response of the labour militias to the New Guard was truncated'.[20] At the same time, there were also street fights between the New Guard and communists, particularly as the New Guard targeted meetings of the communist-aligned Unemployed Workers Movement (UWM) – although Moore also contends that these pitched battles were not as frequent as previous historians had stated.[21]

While left-wing opposition to the New Guard may have been tempered, it is nonetheless significant, because it was tied to other campaigns that reached into the community. The New Guard was seen as a symptom of capitalism in crisis during the Great Depression. The communists, as well as left-leaning sections of the labour movement, linked the fight against the right-wing paramilitary group to actions defending trade union activity and the unemployed. Starting in 1930, the UWM was highly active throughout the Depression years, claiming 68 000 members in the eastern states by 1934.[22] Targeted by the New Guard for its activism in support of the unemployed (such as anti-eviction actions), the UWM became intrinsically connected to the defence of the working class against embryonic fascism in Australia.[23] As activist historian Alex North wrote in *Jacobin* in 2020, the 'UWM may have lacked wealthy sponsors and the support of field marshals – but it could call on the power of organized labor, employed and unemployed, as well as deep community support'.[24]

The threat of the New Guard dissipated after the dismissal of Jack Lang as NSW premier in May 1932. The changing situation overseas, however (including the rise of Nazi Germany, the Japanese invasion of Manchuria and Italian colonialism in Africa), saw the mobilisation of the left, primarily the Communist party, against fascism. The prospect of another world war loomed. In 1933, the CPA was instrumental in setting up the Movement Against War and Fascism (originally the Council Against War), which saw militarism and fascism as twin threats to the world, 'waging war against the working class at the same time that it prepared for war abroad'.[25] Fighting both militarism and fascism also meant fighting colonialism and imperialism. This included solidarity with Ethiopians during the Italian–Abyssinian War in 1935, support for Indian independence from Britain and campaigning for Aboriginal rights in Australia.[26] Historian Padraic Gibson has shown that the Communist party and its fellow travellers in the labour movement argued that the struggle against fascism and militarism abroad could not be conducted without simultaneously fighting racism in Australia. This primarily meant combating the discrimination and violence experienced by Indigenous people.[27]

At the same time, fascism was being confronted in Australia's Italian communities. The Fascist government in Italy had placed significant emphasis on building support for the Mussolini regime among the Italian diaspora around the world, including in Australia. Anti-fascist activists among the Italian communities in Melbourne and Sydney agitated against this, publishing several anti-fascist journals and organising anti-fascist clubs within these communities.[28] But it was in North Queensland where Italian anti-fascists made their presence felt most emphatically.

During the interwar period, especially in the areas where sugar cane was grown, North Queensland was known as the 'Red North', due to the militant trade union movement and the influence of the CPA.[29] Within the North Queensland Italian community, particularly around Innisfail and Ingham, there were a number of communists and anarchists who interacted with the Communist party in order to combat fascism.[30] In the early to mid-1930s, there were several instances of Italian anti-fascists physically intimidating fascists who came to the region. Over the next few years, anti-fascists also mobilised in solidarity with Republican Spain and the burgeoning anti-war movement.[31] Like the Communist Party's fight against the New Guard in the early 1930s and subsequent campaigns against militarism and fascism, the Italian anti-fascists linked their local anti-fascism to events happening abroad and embedded their anti-fascist activities within other struggles, such as trade union actions concerning workplace issues.

Anti-fascism in the 'decade of dissent'

In the first decades after the Second World War, the far right in Australia was marginalised and mentioned infrequently in the media – and only then as a tabloid spectacle. Its anti-Semitism was monitored by the Jewish community, as well as by the Communist party and the Returned Services League.[32] As left-wing radicalism grew during the 1960s, the far right attempted to intervene, seeking to publicly confront the movements against the Vietnam War and apartheid in South Africa in particular. The National Socialist Party of Australia (NSPA) mobilised its small membership, holding counter-demonstrations and physically intimidating anti-war and anti-apartheid protesters. The party also caused property damage to Jewish and left-wing shops. Police were forced to intervene on occasion to prevent violent altercations between left-wing protesters and the far right.

By the early 1970s, the leadership of the NSPA was primarily located in Canberra and Melbourne, with the national organiser and national secretary of the party being the husband-and-wife team of Cass and Katrina Young. Residing in Melbourne, the Youngs sought to enhance the profile of the party by running in the 1970 Senate election. They gained just 0.13 per cent of the vote.[33] But Melbourne was also a significant hub of radicalism in the early 1970s. The city hosted the first national Vietnam Moratorium March in May 1970, and student protest movements developed on several university campuses, including Monash and La Trobe.[34]

Between 1971 and 1972, there were several protests against the National Socialists in Australia, bringing together various Marxists from the anti-war movement and militants within the Jewish community. David Harcourt and Philip Mendes give the example of the crowd of socialist and Jewish activists who coalesced on the bank of the Yarra River in January 1971 to protest against a planned NSPA march; when the neo-Nazis did not show, some of the activists descended on the NSPA headquarters in North Carlton, only to be prevented from entering the property by police.[35] Skirmishes between neo-Nazis and various movements on the left occurred over the next year and a half. NSPA members attempted to disrupt events and demonstrations, such as an address by Gough Whitlam in Sydney in March 1971 and the Vietnam Moratorium March in June of the same year.[36] These confrontations culminated in conflict at the NSPA's annual congress in Melbourne in June 1972, with an anti-Nazi demonstration held in the City Square and around 100 protesters later going to the Young's house. Unlike the protest action surrounding the NSPA headquarters nearly 18 months earlier, the police were seemingly not present to stop the house being vandalised.[37]

The protest action at the NSPA's annual congress in 1972 was taken by two unlikely allies, the Maoist Worker Student Alliance (WSA) and the Radical Zionist Alliance (RZA), a student group established to combat anti-Zionism within the new left in Australia.[38] While the two groups had diametrically opposed views of the Israel-Palestine conflict, both opposed the Vietnam War, apartheid in South Africa and the National Socialist Party of Australia. In a reflection on the history of the Australian Jewish Left, David Zyngier, a member of the RZA, explained to journalist Mika Benesh how the two groups came together for this anti-fascist action:

> This was less about antisemitism and more about anti-fascism. That's my strong gut feeling about it. The view was, Nazis are fascists and fascists need to be defeated. While from a Jewish perspective of course we were concerned about the antisemitism, and I'm not trying to say that this wasn't an issue for the non-Jewish left, but this was seen as part of the broader struggle against imperialism and fascism.[39]

For those opposing the far right in the early 1970s, opposition to fascism and anti-Semitism was often combined with opposition to US imperialism in Vietnam and apartheid in South Africa. In the case of the WSA and the RZA, these different groups mobilised together against neo-Nazism when other issues, particularly the Israel–Palestine conflict, kept them very separate and in conflict with each other.

Taking the far right more seriously

The NSPA faded away over the next few years and was succeeded by two competing strands of the extreme right. On one side was the National Front of Australia (NFA), which was linked to the National Front in Britain and endorsed the creation of a white Commonwealth. On the other side were the 'radical nationalists', who began as National Resistance in 1977 and through several different mutations, eventually became National Action (NA) in 1982. The NFA gained considerable media attention when it was launched in 1978, but soon faded away.[40] But National Action (and its Western Australian breakaway group, the Australian Nationalist Movement (ANM)) became a much more concerning threat, as it was involved in campaigns of racial violence and harassment throughout the 1980s and into the 1990s.

Prior to the 1980s, far-right activists in Australia were often dismissed as cranks and were predominantly a low priority for the authorities (with attention paid more to the potential clashes between the far right and the far left). But during the years of Labor government under Bob Hawke and Paul Keating, the government, the police and security services took the threat of the far-right agitators more seriously, as instigators of political violence and disseminators of racist propaganda. ASIO assessed 'the threat of violence from NA and ANM to be low' before 1988, despite 'the firebombing of a vehicle owned by an anti-apartheid campaigner and damage to the home of the then Minister for Immigration and Ethnic Affairs, Mr Hurford'.[41] But between 1988 and 1991, the Australian government and ASIO realised the far right's capability for extreme violence. Several NA and ANM members in New South Wales and Western Australia were subsequently jailed for acts of violence.[42]

One reason for the increased recognition of the far-right threat by government was that numerous organisations, such as anti-racist, church and migrant groups highlighted the racism that ethnic minorities in Australia faced from the far right, as well as the intimidation of anti-racist campaigners.[43] The Hawke and Keating governments promoted multiculturalism and non-racism at the official level, creating an environment where popular opposition to the far right could be vocalised and mobilised. But it should be acknowledged that despite this government commitment to multiculturalism, racism still existed within Australian society, including within institutions of the state. As the anthropologist Ghassan Hage has written, in the Hawke–Keating years, there seemed to exist two perceptions of 'race relations' in Australia: 'Multiculturalism is working well and belongs to one (mainstream) reality, and racist violence is occurring in another (marginal) reality. Multiculturalism is in one valley and racist violence in another ... And the two are not supposed to be related in any way.'[44]

Several scholars have pointed to varieties of anti-fascism, such as militant, liberal or moderate and state or legal anti-fascism.[45] While militant and liberal anti-fascism are often grassroots initiatives against fascism, state or legal anti-fascism is the way in which the police, government and security services have targeted fascism or the extreme right. In the late 1980s and the early 1990s, the latter approach gained ground in response to the threat of NA and the ANM. Alongside increased policing of these groups, another response by the state was an inquiry into racial violence by the Human Rights and Equal Opportunity Commission. The inquiry's 1991 report identified the far right as a particular problem, stating:

> 15. The activities of extremist groups, which have become more violent in recent years, constitute a small but significant part of the problem of racist violence in Australia.
>
> 16. The activities of extremist groups, some of which have resulted in prosecutions, show a close connection between racist propaganda and racist violence.

> 17. In assessing the extent of organised racist violence, it is important to acknowledge the role of long standing racist organisations which do not perpetrate violence themselves, but nevertheless provide the impetus for others. These organisations essentially incite and maintain prejudice.[46]

The report recommended a number of legal reforms to stop racist violence, intimidation and harassment. Crucially, it also recommended other reforms take place within government agencies to counter racial discrimination and to encourage fairer reporting in the media. How far any of these recommendations were implemented is arguable. For example, one of the recommendations was legislation against racial vilification and harassment, amending the *Racial Discrimination Act 1975*. The Keating government eventually passed the *Racial Hatred Act* in 1995, but after wrangling in the Senate, the legislation only provided civil provisions, rather than criminal sanctions.[47]

There were also campaigns against the far right from below, which brought together both militant and moderate activists against National Action. Historian Vashti Jane Fox has discussed the history of anti-fascism in Melbourne against NA and showed how groups such as Community Action Against Racism (CAAR) and Brunswick Against the Nazis (BAN) mobilised support from 'broader unions and community groups' against planned street activities by National Action.[48] When National Action attempted to conduct a White Pride march in Brunswick in 1994, BAN gained support from several groups, with Fox writing:

> Endorsements flowed in from the Authority and Services branch of the Australian Services Union, members of the Public Sector Union at the Brunswick CES, Martin Kingham, State Secretary of the CFMEU, and John Cummins, State Secretary of the BLF. The Chinese Student Community, the Kurdish Association of Victoria and the Australian Jewish Union of Students all threw their support behind the action, as well as the Student Unions of RMIT, La Trobe and VUT (Footscray).[49]

This anti-fascist mobilisation helped discourage National Action from organising in public. It demonstrated that there was widespread popular opposition to the far right, which could unite activists from a variety of community and political groups.

Combating Hansonism in the late 1990s

Extreme right organisations such as National Action and the Australian Nationalist Movement went into decline in the 1990s. This was partly because a number of NA and ANM members had been arrested and jailed, and partly a result of popular opposition on the streets and within mainstream political discourse. But a right-wing populist party led by Queensland politician Pauline Hanson made attempts to tap into a 'backlash' against Asian immigration and multiculturalism in the 1980s and 1990s, often couching its pitch in terms of economic hardship and the Australians 'left behind' by mainstream politics.[50] Hanson was originally a Liberal candidate for the seat of Oxley in the 1996 federal election. After being disendorsed for making racist comments about Indigenous people, she entered parliament as an independent. Hanson capitalised on the publicity generated by her xenophobic comments in parliament and in the media. She formed One Nation in 1997, which won 11 seats at the Queensland state elections in 1998, and obtained 8.4 per cent of the vote at the 1998 federal election.[51]

Hanson and One Nation were different from the fascist and extreme right parties, but there was (and remains) a concern about the blurring of the lines between the right-wing populism of One Nation and the extreme right.[52] Some of the left-wing groups that were involved in anti-fascist actions against National Action argued that similar confrontational tactics, such as pickets and hectoring of public meetings, could be used against One Nation. For example, the Trotskyist group Socialist Alternative wrote in 1998:

> we also need to directly confront Hanson and other racists whenever they appear. The rally in Perth where thousands pelted fruit at Hanson, the Geelong demonstration that prevented the Hansonites from holding their meeting, the Hobart protest at which Hanson was driven off – these have succeeded in putting the racists on the backfoot.[53]

But the historian Sean Scalmer has argued that while these '[c]ontestational gatherings disrupted the public spectacle of Hansonism', they also allowed Hanson to portray herself as the victim of an intolerant left and generated more media attention around these highly charged events.[54] For Scalmer, the more successful anti-Hanson actions came in the form of 'autonomous, disruptive gatherings', such as 'marches, rallies, street theatre, and, in one case, the occupation of Prime Minister John Howard's Sydney office'.[55] These types of protest often brought together a wider variety of people coming out against racism and in support of multiculturalism, including trade unions, school students, local politicians, community groups and church representatives, alongside a more 'welcoming reception within the media'.[56] For Scalmer, this broad coalition helped voters around the country reject One Nation as a political force in the late 1990s and early 2000s. Even the conservative right that orbited around the Liberal Party vocally opposed One Nation at this time, with future Prime Minister Tony Abbott calling Hanson and her party the 'feral right'.[57] Arguably, however, Liberal opposition to Hansonism was largely about stemming any bleeding of voters from the Coalition to One Nation, rather than political conviction. As political scientist Rae Wear argued, John Howard 'embrace[d] many of One Nation's themes and elevate[d] the version of Anglo-Australian identity that Pauline Hanson and her party defended'. The Coalition under Howard also made 'policy commitments consistent with One Nation's demands', such as the strict treatment of refugees and asylum seekers, the portrayal of Islam as a threat during the 'War on Terror' years and the abolition of the Aboriginal and Torres Strait Islander Commission (ATSIC).[58]

Lessons from history: Collective action beats intolerance

The far right in Australia has often remained small and on the fringes of political life. But it has, on occasions, attempted to break through, either as an electoral or extra-parliamentary force – often involving violence, harassment and intimidation.

In the present day, the presence of the extreme right, alongside the blurring of the lines between the far and mainstream right (both here in Australia and overseas), is a major cause for concern. The solution offered by politicians and sections of the media focuses on policing and legal measures, including increased monitoring of the far right by the security services, the banning of extreme right groups and stronger penalties for stirring up racial hatred (such as proposed laws to ban the swastika in Victoria and New South Wales).

However, focusing on state-based legal and policing solutions to the threat of far-right groups overlooks the political and social landscape from which they emerge. It isolates combating the far right from the wider struggles against racism in Australian society. At several points in Australian history, activists have cooperated to fight the far right, bringing together different sections of society and linking the battle against the far right to similar battles overseas. From the coalition of trade unionists, communists, unemployed workers and members of the ALP against the New Guard in the early 1930s, to the joining together of community groups, church leaders, local politicians, trade unions and school students against Pauline Hanson in the late 1990s, the fight against the far right has worked effectively when various sections of the population collectively challenged racism, fascism and white supremacy, in all their forms. For policymakers and the wider public, these examples from history can be the inspiration for similar fights against the far right today.

CHAPTER 17

The genie is out of the bottle: Self-determination and First Nations peoples of Australia

Laura Rademaker and Ian Anderson

You might have heard that Indigenous self-determination is over. That it failed. Perhaps rumour reached you that it was a lost cause to begin with; a policy with good intentions, but poor outcomes. Or maybe you have doubts that it was ever properly tried, that Indigenous people were ever given a chance to manage their own affairs. 'Self-determination', by this view, was an empty promise. The term is associated with the policy agenda introduced by the Whitlam government in 1973. Under the banner of 'self-determination', Gough Whitlam held a royal commission into Aboriginal Land Rights (the Woodward Commission), set up a federal Department of Aboriginal Affairs, affirmed First Nations' cultures and funded Indigenous corporations. Whether this actually amounted to 'self-determination' as First Nations peoples themselves (or the United Nations, for that matter) hoped for is debatable. Either way, many scholars and activists consider the 1970s and 1980s a high point for self-determination in Australia.[1]

After that, supposedly, things fell apart. In the decades that followed, government commitment to the language and ideals of self-determination faltered and even withered away altogether. In the early years of the twenty-first century, some thinkers pointed to continuing socioeconomic inequalities between Indigenous and non-Indigenous Australians to argue that self-determination had failed.[2] Governments should try a new approach, they said. For some conservatives, expressions of self-determination through national forms of Indigenous representation contradicted their ideals of the equality of citizens and, they said, divided the nation. In 2005, therefore, the Howard government dismantled the Aboriginal and Torres Strait Islander Commission (ATSIC), which the Hawke government had set up to provide a nationwide elected Indigenous structure of governance and representation.[3] Next, the Howard government's 2007 Northern Territory Emergency Response ('the Intervention') wound back many of the self-governing freedoms of remote communities (while also boosting funding for Indigenous organisations on the ground). Linguist and anthropologist Peter Sutton's 2009 *The Politics of Suffering* along with Guugu Yimirhirr lawyer and activist Noel Pearson's various writings called for a new policy consensus, arguing that self-determination had been unsuccessful.[4] Meanwhile, thinkers and activists on the left also argued the policy had failed, but for the opposite reason; true self-determination had never properly been attempted.[5] Both sides believed self-determination was over.

But we are not so convinced that self-determination, either as policy framework or political vision, is done with. This is partly because we think self-determination can be understood in a broader, more holistic way. There are different ways to think about self-determination. Some emphasise governance (with self-determination existing on a spectrum from mere consultation to full self-governance), others emphasise cultural rights and identity. We focus here on self-determination as the policy framework introduced in the 1970s. But we also see it as an ongoing Indigenous project that preceded and outlives that policy.[6] Self-determination includes cultural resurgence – language and the arts – and the work of historical truth-telling as well as First Nations' political interventions, and none of these shows signs of decline. Although the state might constrain a First Nations polity, First Nations people themselves are drawing on their political networks, visions and capacities right now.[7] So although governments' commitment to self-determination has waned, First Nations peoples have found other ways to seize control of the policy agenda.

One way that First Nations people took control was through their own organisations. Looking to history, we see that the policy changes of the 1970s prepared the ground for the growth of an Indigenous organisational and institutional sector that now has a life of its own. While governments have created contexts that have variously hindered or supported Indigenous self-determination, whatever the policy context, the self-determination 'genie' is out of the bottle. First Nations' self-determination is not waiting for governments. First Nations people are not only asking governments to work with them, they are resetting the terms of engagement so that governments cannot work without them.

The origins of the Indigenous sector

The Indigenous community-controlled sector is made up of an array of non-profit organisations based in Indigenous communities, governed by boards made up of Indigenous people and serving the interests of Indigenous communities. Although

Whitlam often gets the credit, it was not his invention. It began with the initiatives of First Nations peoples. Aboriginal people in places like Redfern looked to the example of the Black Panther Party in the United States, which was running urban survival programs such as medical clinics for Black communities.[8] Inspired, the Aboriginal Legal Service opened a shopfront offering legal representation in Redfern in 1970 after activists began recording incidents of police violence.[9] The Aboriginal Medical Service (AMS) came the following year. In 1972, the Murawing Preschool and Childcare Service opened as a breakfast program run out of the AMS, with Aboriginal women in full control from 1973. Around the same time, the Aboriginal Housing Company also began operation in inner Sydney.[10] A group of these same community organisers from Redfern set up the Aboriginal Tent Embassy in early 1972. Legal academic Larissa Behrendt (Eualeyai Kamillaroi) argued that the Embassy's commitment to building Aboriginal-controlled institutions – the AMS, the Aboriginal Legal Service, Aboriginal community-controlled childcare and the Black Theatre – ensured its enduring legacy.[11]

So the Whitlam government's 1973 commitment to self-determination was in *response* to the calls of First Nations people; self-determination began as an Indigenous project not a government agenda.[12] The Black Theatre (established in 1972) actually announced Whitlam's successful election during the interval of its performance of 'Basically Black' in December 1972.[13] They came first. Whitlam's new Department of Aboriginal Affairs had an enormous budget and Aboriginal organisations such as those in Redfern suddenly received generous funding with minimal government oversight, at first.[14] But even in the 1970s, the Indigenous sector's visions quickly diverged from those of governments. Governments were mostly interested in achieving socioeconomic parity with the non-Indigenous population, but the Indigenous sector understood itself as something more; it was to be a means of achieving self-determination. It therefore expected full Indigenous control of its funding, governance and activities.[15] For these activists, government funding for Indigenous organisations was not charity or dependence; it was their due, owed by settler governments to Indigenous people as compensation for injustice and dispossession.[16] Governments, meanwhile, considered this 'taxpayers' money' and required detailed reporting.[17] As with other sectors, the proper relationship between the Indigenous sector and the governments that hold the purse strings has been contested almost from the beginning.

Indigenous activists in the 1970s also saw government funding for their organisations as an important way to secure their political voice, channelled through these organisations.[18] Gary Foley (Gumbainggir), for instance, explained that the AMS considered itself 'in the context of the political struggle because we're simply an extension of that struggle, working … to ease the plight of the people we are politically working for'.[19] Key bureaucrats in the Whitlam government, H.C. Coombs and Barrie Dexter, likewise intended Indigenous organisations to become a means by which First Nations people could voice and achieve their political aspirations (as these organisations had already been doing). That is, they were to have a representative function. And this was considered appropriate: they were locally based and drew on existing partnerships and networks. For the Whitlam government, the blossoming sector was an organic expression of an Indigenous polity.[20]

This community-controlled sector evolved over the

decades from a tiny cluster of organisations powered by a few volunteers and minimal grants to a professionalised enterprise commanding billions of dollars. Commonwealth health expenditure on Aboriginal community organisations, for instance, swelled from just over a million dollars in 1973 to $13 million by 1983, and to $54 million in 1993.[21] In the 1970s, there were limited institutional structures that could be used to express self-determination: a handful of community-controlled services and a couple of land councils. Today, health remains the largest segment of the community-controlled sector, but the sector also extends to legal, education and family violence prevention services, along with multiple Aboriginal statutory land rights and native title organisations and Indigenous regional governance structures. The organisations in the sector are mainly government-funded services, with governance drawn from communities. Although funded by the state, they draw money from various levels of government so are not entirely dependent on any. Many are represented by the national peak body, the Coalition of Peaks. There is also a growing Indigenous business sector, but at this stage it does not have sectoral representation and is not connected to the Coalition of Peaks.

Things have changed since the 1970s. But many of the changes for Australian Indigenous people can be attributed, in part, to the successes of the Indigenous organisational sector. There is a growing highly educated professional class within the Indigenous community. We now have numerous Indigenous parliamentarians across Australia. The community-controlled sector has enabled First Nations people to challenge institutions, forge pathways into universities, create culturally safe spaces in schools and workplaces and to take up ranks in the professions and academies. At the local level, Indigenous community organisations have become key instruments of authority and have enabled communities both to build their own services and develop their own skills and capacities.[22]

The Coalition of Peaks and Closing the Gap refresh

In the early 2000s, as both sides of the political spectrum were decrying the death of self-determination, a coalition of grassroots Indigenous and non-Indigenous organisations coalesced into a new campaign. They wanted to 'Close the Gap'. At first it was a community-driven movement. It sprung up as many across the political spectrum were searching for new policy consensuses in Indigenous affairs. Close the Gap, led by the Australian Human Rights Commission (renamed the Human Rights and Equal Opportunity Commission – HREOC – in 2008) and the Aboriginal and Torres Strait Islander Social Justice Commissioner, Tom Calma (Kungarakan Iwaidja), brought a human rights approach to questions of health equity. It campaigned for governments to develop clear Indigenous policy targets that would 'close gaps' between Indigenous and non-Indigenous Australians.[23]

Yet as governments became involved, the Indigenous organisational sector was shut out of the movement. In 2007 and 2008, the Council of Australian Governments (COAG) settled a series of agreements referred to as 'Closing the Gap'. These included Indigenous policy targets for: life expectancy; infant mortality; early childhood education in remote communities; reading, writing and numeracy achievements; retention rates to Year 12; and employment outcomes. They also included national partnership funding agreements across sectors related to these targets. These were negotiated among governments rather than the organisations that originally campaigned for this approach; Indigenous organisations were consulted but had no seat at the negotiation table. Each year in parliament since 2009, the prime minister has tabled an annual *Closing the Gap Report* (to which HREOC has responded annually with its counter reports, *Close the Gap*). The outcomes have been disappointing.

Self-determination, meanwhile, seemed to be at a low ebb. In May 2017, the authors of the Uluru Statement called for 'a First Nations Voice' to achieve 'justice and self-determination'.[24] But the Turnbull government dismissed the Statement as soon as it had been delivered. Like other conservative governments, it was suspicious of national articulations of Indigenous self-determination through representation, preferring instead to work with local Indigenous organisations. In the meantime, governments had begun developing a 'Closing the Gap Refresh' and in October 2018 a newly formed Coalition of Aboriginal Peak Organisations intervened in the Refresh process. According to the Coalition of Peaks, this intervention was an 'act of self-determination'.[25] The Coalition wrote to the prime minister, premiers and chief ministers, insisting that Indigenous communities must be represented in these negotiations:

> We write concerning the Closing the Gap Refresh, a joint initiative of the Council of Australian Governments (COAG), to ask that you not endorse any revised approach at COAG without the necessary input and support from Indigenous communities; and that you put in place a mechanism for those representing Indigenous communities to be able to negotiate and reach agreement

on the new Closing the Gap framework and for a
continued role in its implementation.[26]

At this stage, the Coalition of Peaks was an alliance of 13 organisations across the health, legal, family violence prevention and land rights/native title sectors (it now comprises over 50 peak and member organisations). They had been consulted, individually, through the processes for setting priorities and targets. They had not, however, been included in drafting policy documents or the COAG decision-making process. Their intervention was to insist that governments go beyond consultation to shared decision-making with 'those representing Indigenous communities'.[27] Indigenous organisations put governments in a position where they could not refuse Indigenous involvement.

The negotiations resulted in the first intergovernmental agreement in which non-government Indigenous stakeholders were also signatories. Having non-government partners at the table interrupted the usual Commonwealth/State and Territory dynamics. The Indigenous involvement also produced a markedly different agreement. The final National Agreement on Closing the Gap included a significantly stronger focus on Indigenous-led data and evaluation processes; building and strengthening structures that empower Aboriginal and Torres Strait Islander people to share decision-making authority with governments to accelerate policy and place-based progress; a stronger and defined role for the Aboriginal community-controlled sector; and a clearer policy objective in the reform of government systems. The Coalition of Peaks was particularly concerned about improving the quality of Indigenous access, control and use of data. It also ensured that independent First

Nations–led reviews will be carried out following independent reviews by the Productivity Commission. The idea was to create a mechanism whereby governments could be held accountable to First Nations peoples.[28] They flipped older models of accountability upside down.

Of course, the Coalition of Peaks was imperfect and limited in its representation of Indigenous communities.[29] Not all its peak organisations agreed on all policy priorities and targets, nor were its positions representative of the full diversity of Indigenous political interests. Significantly, it is not a democratically elected representative body and most of its member organisations remain dependent on government sources of funding. Its capacity to challenge governments, therefore, was necessarily limited. It is not the Voice to Parliament envisaged by the authors of the Uluru Statement.[30] Leading constitutional lawyer Megan Davis (a Cobble Cobble woman) expressed concern, therefore, that First Nations peoples are framed simply as the 'Indigenous sector', along with the 'business sector' or 'education sector'. First Nations political claims lie in their distinct peoplehood because, whereas peoples and nations might be self-determining, sectors have only 'interests'.[31] There is a real risk, therefore, that understanding First Nations peoples primarily as a sector inadvertently diminishes the strength of their unique claims.[32]

But unlike other 'sectors', we think Indigenous organisations can be understood as constituting an Indigenous order of government for the way that they both serve and represent distinct peoples (rather than a mere interest group). If government is understood as a process rather than simply a structure, the Indigenous sector can claim to represent Indigenous people in some way.[33] Most importantly, in the absence of a body that might speak to parliaments or governments (and in light of government actions to dismantle such bodies as ATSIC or thwart their establishment, as in the Voice) the Coalition of Peaks had a vital representative function. Interestingly, many Indigenous leaders in the community-controlled sector of today had been involved in ATSIC, including Pat Turner (Arrente Gurdanji) herself, the convenor of the Coalition of Peaks. The efforts of the Coalition of Peaks, therefore, in part grew out of the formative experience of ATSIC. Through the Coalition of Peaks, First Nations peoples found alternative and innovative avenues to build forms of representation and engage in decision-making.

According to historian Tim Rowse, the ongoing difficulties faced by the Indigenous sector in claiming legitimately to represent Indigenous people date right back to flaws and contradictions (reflecting internal differences) in the Whitlam government's agenda for self-determination in the 1970s. The Whitlam government encouraged Indigenous political expression and self-government through the Indigenous sector, acknowledging these organisations had a representative role, while also pursuing 'parliamentary' or democratically elected forms of representation.[34] The relationship between these two forms of representation and their role in achieving self-determination has been unresolved ever since. This tension was evident within ATSIC as it sought to fulfil both forms of representation: its function as an elected body and its program-delivery role (a dual function that left it vulnerable to charges of misuse of funds).[35] And it continues today in discussions around the role of the community-controlled sector and its relationship to the anticipated Voice to Parliament.

Lessons from history: 'Work with us'

Government commitment to a vision of self-determination for First Nations people might be at a low ebb. But that does not mean self-determination has failed. As Wiradjuri scholar Robynne Quiggin has argued, Indigenous Australia is self-determining and calls on governments to catch up with its agenda: 'The most consistent call from Indigenous Australia since the abandonment of self-determination policy is – "listen to us". Consistent with the fact that we continue to be self-determining despite government policy, we say "Listen to us", "work with us so that we can set our own course".'[36]

When Whitlam heeded Indigenous calls for self-determination and identified the emerging Indigenous community-controlled sector as central to achieving that vision, his government set in motion a form of self-determination that cannot be contained. Indeed, the Indigenous sector has been described as the defining legacy of the Whitlam self-determination policy; its successes as well as its limitations were set in motion through the policies of that era.[37]

Since the 1970s, and through the energy, experiences and empowerment of the Indigenous sector, new generations of First Nations leaders have emerged across the community, academy, public sector and business world.[38] The Indigenous professional class is booming, growing in size by some 75 per cent from 1996 to 2006 and gaining on the professionalisation of the general population.[39] First Nations people are exercising increasing control of their own affairs in the domains of land rights, health, education and environmental management through Indigenous organisations, as well as self-government through local Aboriginal councils.[40] Building on experiences in this sector, First Nations people within government bureaucracies and peak bodies are meanwhile also advancing Indigenous interests, despite the absence of a democratically elected representative voice, and becoming ever more assertive.[41] Policymakers can no longer simply consult First Nations people; they must work with them.

The example of the Coalition of Peaks is testimony to the resilience and permanence of diverse forms of Indigenous representation. We do not know yet what the long-term effects of the National Agreement will be, and there is much the Coalition of Peaks was unable to achieve due to governments' resistance. Still, its ability to insert itself into inter-government negotiations shows how Indigenous non-government actors can exploit the possibilities of liberal governmentality to benefit the communities they serve. First Nations people created an infrastructure that, in light of the failure of governments to commit to constitutional change, provided a form of Indigenous representation at the highest of levels as the constitutional discussion rolled on. This, we suggest, is a kind of Indigenous self-determination, particularly in the absence of other more fully representative options.

The example of the Coalition of Peaks shows how self-determination can be realised in different political forms, in different political structures, in ways that respond to the circumstances of Indigenous Australia and harness its creativity and political will. It also shows how, once institutions are established (in this case the Indigenous community-controlled sector), they create pathways that are not readily unwound, no matter the policies and views of subsequent governments.

The genie is out of the bottle

Governments might provide conditions that either hinder or support self-determination. But whatever they do, the self-determination genie is well and truly out of the bottle.

CHAPTER 18

Pipelines and catalysts: Lessons from the history of women in corporate leadership

Claire E.F. Wright

> The full utilisation of women in leadership and building the talent pipelines into leadership for all our organisations is one of the most effective, efficient and equitable ways in which we can actually create an environment in which Australia can prosper.
>
> Sam Mostyn, President of Chief Executive Women.[1]

In 2019, former competition watchdog chairman Graeme Samuel alleged that an 'impenetrable' club of women was keeping other women out of the boardroom. His comments aroused a frustrated response. As a member of the group that still dominates corporate leadership, Samuel's conjecture about gate-keeping was considered to be tone-deaf to the real problem.[2] Although in recent times the number of board seats held by women has increased, it is still only around one-third of the total.[3] Women make up less than 10 per cent of CEOs and around 25 per cent of executives. Depressingly, in 2020–21 there was only one female CEO appointed to an ASX300 firm (compared to 22 male appointments).[4] Women are less likely to hold influential board positions such as the chair or the head of various committees.[5] If women do happen to reach these career milestones, they then face a pay gap that exceeds that of the general workforce.[6]

While the gross under-representation of women in the boardroom remains of pressing concern, the response to Samuel's provocation – largely by the wealthy white women in corporate leadership roles – skated over a valid and important issue. Men might dominate Australian corporate leadership, but the small number of women who *do* occupy board seats are in exclusive company.[7] While their entry into boardrooms is an important step along the road to equality, Australia's corporate women comprise an elite and homogenous group, if not an outright 'club'.

Increasing the representation of women in corporate leadership has been subject to industry, public and policy action over the past two decades. Women occupying positions of influence – including in corporations, politics, sport and media – normalises and creates space for women's empowerment, which can be transformative through improvements in health, education and social protection.[8] For corporations, increasing the number of women in leadership has been associated with greater equality throughout the organisation, with declining gender pay gaps and improving their appointment to management roles. By injecting new knowledge and skills and disrupting the sometimes siloed decision-making of all-male environments, women in leadership have been found to deliver better company performance, adherence to environmental standards and corporate social responsibility (CSR) objectives.

It also signals a public commitment to equality and modernity that can attract substantial investment capital.[9]

In recognition of the importance of women in leadership, most countries, including Australia, have adopted all or some of the recommendations of the United Nations' *Sustainable Development Goal 5: Achieve gender equality and empower all women and girls*. The Australian federal government requires large firms to implement policies to achieve gender equality; the Australian Securities Exchange (ASX) mandates reporting of gender diversity figures; and the primary professional body, the Australian Institute of Company Directors (AICD) reports on, and sets targets for the number of women on top company boards. In 2018, the federal Minister for Women, Kelly O'Dwyer, argued that increasing women in leadership was a key priority, and was crucial for 'stronger advice and solutions, more rapid innovation, and more productive stakeholder relationships'.[10]

Although this targeted action has increased the number of Australian women in corporate leadership, the challenge for policymakers and the corporate sector lies with sustainable improvements in corporate diversity. Rather than simply increasing the number of female board members – which can be seen, justifiably, as tokenistic window dressing – we need to ensure that women occupy positions of similar influence and pay across the suite of leadership roles. Intersectional improvements are also needed, with recruitment of women with a broader range of professional and personal characteristics. History has important lessons for those who seek to make change. The experiences of female board members in the past suggest we need to build pathways for improving access and diversity. Specifically, in order to achieve real reform we need to address blockages in the 'pipeline' to the boardroom (that is, structural career barriers) and shore up the 'catalysts' (or external and regulatory pressures) that force change on staid institutions.

Diversity in Australia's corporate elite

The primary responsibility of a board of directors is to oversee and approve the strategic direction of a firm. Company boards emerged in the eighteenth century in response to the potential 'negligence and profusion', as Enlightenment philosopher Adam Smith famously described it, of joint stock companies. Independent, non-executive directors became crucial for mediating between the competing interests of salaried managers (who may wish to direct resources to themselves, or may be insufficiently vigilant with others' money) and shareholders (who own the firm but are too dispersed to control management directly).[11] Throughout the twentieth and early twenty-first centuries, the expansion of large, publicly traded firms has given greater weight to the role of board members. Advocates argue that their knowledge, skills and contacts facilitate good decision-making and mitigate against unexpected events.[12] But there are also downsides. Corporate boards require a unique blend of skills, as well as solidarity and teamwork, which can favour those (men) who have traditionally accrued professional qualifications and whose demeanour aligns or is perceived to align with that of existing members.[13]

Australia's company directors have overwhelmingly been older, white, professional men residing in affluent suburbs in Australia's key capital cities. In the early twentieth century, directors had expertise in shipping and trade, or were trained in professions such as law, accounting, engineering and banking. From the 1980s onwards, an assemblage of business disciplines like management, finance and marketing has become commonplace. Professionals had a long pathway to board roles, beginning with entry level positions, either in large companies or prominent external consulting firms. They progressed to highly paid executive roles, before 'retiring' or transitioning to a second career as a non-executive director. The lifelong accrual of wealth among this Anglicised corporate elite has meant that most board members have lived in wealthy suburbs in Sydney (Vaucluse, Potts Point, Rose Bay, Double Bay and so on) and Melbourne (almost exclusively in Toorak). Directors have also adhered to the group's social expectations, with membership of upper middle-class sports (golf, yacht, turf, racing) and members' clubs (the Australia, Melbourne or Commonwealth). The requirement of directors to provide advice, improve decision-making, and work as a team has contributed to very narrow appointment procedures and, as a result, a homogenous group.[14]

Australia's corporate elite has become more, rather than less, homogenous over time. In the absence of external disruptions, new appointments have largely adhered to the status quo in regard to age, ethnicity, geography, class and social activities.[15] A more stringent regulatory environment since the 1980s has also deepened the dominance of professionals in the elite. Several high-profile corporate collapses following the stock market crash of October 1987 prompted new legal structures, banking prudential regulations and professional standards of conduct in the operation and assessment of large firms. At the same time, microeconomic reform encouraged the implementation of new management techniques to improve efficiency and adapt to new markets. Deregulation of the banking sector increased the complexity of corporate finance, and shareholder activism amplified scrutiny of company disclosure. These new external accountabilities created greater need for professionals in leadership.[16] The board member 'profession' has also increasingly controlled the entry of new members, establishing training, accreditation and a new professional association, the AICD (Australian Institute of Company Directors). There is now a very rigid career pathway for entry to top company boards – including training and work in a traditional profession like law, and then re-training as a company director later in life.[17] While these regulatory changes have protected shareholders and consumers, they have had the unintended consequence of narrowing the profile of company leaders. Women have, however, been the exception, with targeted government and industry action making meaningful improvements in their representation on corporate boards.

Australia's female board members

Prior to the 1980s, women were not formally represented in Australian corporate leadership. Although women had been admitted to Australian universities since the late nineteenth century, their paid work largely adhered to the female mission to 'nurture and civilise', in nursing, teaching, social work or clerical assistance.[18] Structural barriers in the form of unequal pay and social pressure to give up work upon marriage made it very difficult for women to combine work and family, or be promoted to management roles.[19] The lack of women on the 'executive track' meant there were none who could reasonably be appointed to company boards. An additional pathway for women in corporate leadership, which was important elsewhere, was family firms. In Australia, in the small number of large dynastic firms, female family members were excluded from leadership appointments. Although a substantial proportion of women were able to influence the corporate sector informally through family and marriage, they were blocked from official decision-making roles.[20]

From the 1980s, women began to access top company board positions, with a ten-fold increase in their numbers between 1986 and 1997, and a doubling of this number every decade since. The pace has quickened since 2010, and in recent years around one-third of board positions in Australia's top companies have been held by women.[21] Women have also come to occupy central positions in the corporate community. Since 1997, more women have held multiple top board positions compared to men, and have been more likely to sit on the board of prominent or well-connected companies.[22]

Why such a swift and radical change? The foundations were provided a generation earlier by advances in women's empowerment in the 1970s and 1980s. Advocacy by the second wave feminist Women's Movement, and policy reform by the short-lived but progressive Whitlam Labor government (1972–75) targeted improvements in education and workplace participation for girls and women, the removal of barriers to employment for married women, and increased childcare funding to enable women to manage work and family responsibilities, (see Chapter 19 for more detail). As a result, women's participation in tertiary education increased, and their career choices diversified beyond teaching, nursing and social work to include accounting, law, engineering and business. In the 1980s and 1990s, legislative and policy changes promoted a range of equal opportunity and affirmative action measures, including the Commonwealth *Sex Discrimination Act* (1984), which legally prevented unequal pay between men and women. Policies to improve the number of women on public sector boards and in political leadership – first introduced by the Hawke federal Labor government in the early 1980s – set later expectations for women in corporate leadership.[23]

The success of corporate women today is often down to career pipelines that were laid as far back as the 1970s. For example, Ilana Atlas is currently in her sixties, and has been a prominent non-executive director since 2010. Atlas had a 35-year pipeline for her non-executive director roles, training in law in the 1970s, and in the 1980s, at the age of 30, being made a partner in corporate law firm Mallesons Stephen Jaques. After 15 years in leadership at the firm, Atlas moved to Westpac, where she spent ten years as an executive. Atlas's stellar career provided the foundation for non-executive directorships; it gave her access to contacts, knowledge and experience that smoothed her career transition. One of Atlas's first major non-executive directorships was at Suncorp Bank, an appointment facilitated by her executive experience in banking, and contact with board members in her legal work.[24] Similarly, Sam Mostyn trained in law in the 1980s. She worked for several corporate law firms and as an adviser to government ministers throughout the 1990s, before becoming an executive in communications and insurance. Mostyn transitioned to non-executive directorships at a similar time to Atlas, in 2010, with two decades of corporate experience providing the foundation for her new career.[25] For Atlas, Mostyn, and indeed most contemporary Australian female board members, structural change from the 1970s – including access to tertiary education in corporate professions, equal(ish) pay, promotion mechanisms, and the ability to combine work and childrearing – laid the foundation for their board appointments decades later.

If cultural and political changes from the 1970s built the 'pipeline' for women in leadership, external regulatory pressures in more recent years have provided the catalyst for their board appointments. From the 2000s, the societal focus of women's empowerment shifted from improving their access to work, to specifically increasing success in leadership. Building on earlier federal government policies to increase the number of women in elected office, the gender imbalance of corporate leadership became a focus. Shareholder activism, public sector inquiries and engagement from the Australian Human Rights Commission (AHRC) increased scrutiny of women in corporate leadership and threatened direct government intervention. This culminated in 2012, when the federal Labor government, led by Julia Gillard, implemented the *Workplace Gender Equality Act*, which required firms with more than 500 employees to implement a strategy to address numerous issues, including workplace gender composition, the gender pay gap, flexible work arrangements, and sex-based harassment and discrimination.[26]

To discourage government intervention, the Australian Stock Exchange (ASX) and the AICD allied to increase the number of women in leadership through self-regulation. In 2010, the ASX revised its *Corporate Governance Principles and Recommendations* to encourage firms to monitor, disclose and establish policies to improve the number of women in executive and board positions. This has operated on a 'comply or explain' basis, with firms able to establish their own goals and timelines, and justify their appointment processes if they fail to meet targets.[27] The AICD, as the peak professional body for company directors, administers accreditation, organises networking events and produces publications for members. It complements the regulator, the ASX, by monitoring the number of women on boards in 'real time'. In 2015 the AICD went beyond the vague ASX procedures to set a voluntary target of 30 per cent women on the top 200 boards by December 2018 (this was achieved partway through 2019).[28] While the target was nonbinding, it was highly publicised, with success or failure seen by media and the public to reflect the sector's commitment to equality.[29] The AICD has also funded scholarships for women seeking to train as board members, in addition to a mentoring program that matches male allies with aspiring corporate women. Several other professional groups – such as Women on Boards (established 2001) and Chief Executive Women (established 1985) – have lobbied government and regulators, and facilitated networks among women directors in Australia.[30] These regulatory actions have been an effective catalyst for the appointment of women like Atlas and Mostyn, who were the beneficiaries of structural change in the 1970s and 1980s, and already a fair way along the corporate career pipeline by the late 2000s.

While these regulatory pressures have been successful at promoting some women to leadership positions, enduring inequalities at earlier points in the career pipeline have contributed to the central tension outlined in my introduction: the enduring dominance of men in corporate leadership, alongside the accumulation of power by a small number of highly privileged corporate women. Relatively few women have the necessary executive experience, with unconscious bias regarding ability, efficiency or inherent 'leadership qualities' contributing to gender-based pay disparities and barriers to promotion.[31]

There are also structural difficulties, with most Australian women still taking on the lion's share of childrearing, and yet facing inadequate support and career stigma when they do so (see Chapter 19). For example, Nicola Wakefield Evans has reflected that she expected to be held back from promotion in her career as a lawyer due to having school-aged children and a husband who also worked in the corporate sector.[32] Diane Smith-Gander has similarly argued that the lack of access to longer term childcare has been the 'biggest impediment' to women's promotion. As she reflects:

> When you know that you have got to perform better than a man to get promoted, that you are likely to get 17 or 18 per cent less pay for doing the same job and you have very limited childcare available and the price of it is so high, that doesn't add up to a value proposition for someone who has two children.[33]

Those women who have become corporate leaders are thus the small number of privileged women who are able to overcome these career barriers. The second wave Women's Movement largely highlighted issues faced by straight, white women.[34] Although feminism has come a long way since the 1970s, the long-term pipeline for corporate leadership means more recent advances have not yet produced change in the boardroom. Women have accessed board positions by conforming to the increasingly homogenous standards of a wealthy, conservative and Anglo-male elite. For example, Diane Smith-Gander told profiler Anne Davies that her corporate leadership opportunities have come from a 'deliberate strategy of hanging out where the boys hang out', namely the North Cottesloe

Surf Lifesaving Club in Perth.[35] Corporate women have been inducted into the same narrow set of professions as corporate men – particularly investment banking, law, accounting and business – and have been members of the key professional body, the AICD. Male 'champions of change' have provided a bridge between women and the corporate community. David Gonski, for instance, has been outspoken in his support of women in leadership, mentoring many successful female board members in recent years.[36] While these developments are very welcome, only women with a very narrow set of personal and professional characteristics have access to these initiatives. Conscious and unconscious bias in the corporate labour market – based on ethnicity, sexuality, class, disability, profession or even place of residence – means that most women don't get to the point where they can benefit from the sector's new-found openness to women in leadership.

Lessons from history: Widening the pipeline

History tells us that increasing the number of women in the boardroom requires a mix of cultural and regulatory changes. Corporate leadership is, at heart, a vocation, calling on a unique combination of personal and professional skills. A career as a corporate leader is often the work of a lifetime, and involves a long and complicated career trajectory. In the case of female board members, addressing structural barriers in women's work and promotion has been crucial. The second wave Women's Movement improved entry to the career pipeline for some, which then positioned them perfectly to benefit from recent pressure regarding the appointment of women to top company boards. In contrast, women from non-White ethnic backgrounds, from outside the middle class, members of the LGBTQIA+ community, or those with disability face substantial barriers to the corporate labour market, and the opportunity to become leaders decades down the track.

In addition to removing these structural barriers to the corporate world, external and regulatory pressure are vital. If left alone, most organisations, including boards of directors, will maintain and replicate the status quo. That's the reason why Australia's board members have become – with the exception of gender – more homogenous over time. Pressure from shareholders, government and the public has largely focused on women, and has been very successful in supporting their access to the boardroom. Addressing both the 'pipeline' and the 'catalyst' has created meaningful change in the appointment of female board members, and a similar approach can and should be used to expand women's access to leadership.

Only the application of external pressure to the corporate sector will see more women land prized executive roles, such as that of CEO. Longer term work at removing blockages in the career pipeline will lead eventually to women from a broader range of backgrounds being able to enter the boardroom. These are important next steps in developing a more innovative and adaptive corporate sector.

CHAPTER 19

Beyond productivity: Working mothers and childcare policy

Carla Pascoe Leahy

> We were talking about going back to work after 12 months, and I got a bit gutsy, and I said, 'I don't feel right, leaving a child at 12 months to go back to a full-time job' ... And she said, 'Well, if I didn't go back to work, my career would really suffer ... It looks really bad on your resume'. And I looked at her straight in the eye ... and I said, 'Well, my résumé must look like shit'.[1]

The women's liberation movement of the 1970s successfully fought to decouple maternity from femininity by focusing on the non-maternal aspects of women's lives.[2] A growing sense that adult womanhood comprises more than solely motherhood, and a rising conviction that women have the right to choose whether they wish to become mothers, has led to the rise of autonomous, or post-patriarchal motherhood.[3] This significant cultural shift in Australia over the last 50 years has sparked a realisation that it is not solely gender inequality that mothers face. Contemporary Australian mothers experience a double discrimination based upon not only their gender but also their caring roles.

Since the 1970s a range of government policies has attempted to ameliorate this discrimination. The 1972 *Child Care Act* provided subsidised childcare services, followed by an expansion of childcare services in the 1980s. Overt workforce discrimination against women became illegal in the mid-1980s. Mothers have been entitled to unpaid maternity leave since 1979; this was extended to paid leave for mothers in 2011 and for partners in 2013. And yet there is plenty of evidence that policies concerning maternal workforce participation and early childhood education and care have not done enough. As Kristen's quote which opens this chapter illustrates, Australian mothers still feel torn between caring for their children and engaging in paid work – and insufficiently supported to do either.

How and why have government policies fallen short since 1972? How have mothers negotiated care and work at different points in time? Drawing on interviews with multiple generations of Australian mothers, this chapter explains the ways in which their experiences of, and opinions on, work and care have changed over the past half-century.[4] As we will see, mothers' reasons for engaging with government schemes are often different from the objectives of maternal and family policies as outlined by governments. Policymakers need to better understand mothers' experiences if they are to develop policies that serve women's needs as mothers and workers.

The 1970s: A gender revolution begins

Before the women's liberation movement, there was minimal Commonwealth support for working mothers.[5] Although workforce participation rates among migrant and working-class mothers were high, the cultural ideal of the postwar years was that of the stay-at-home mother.[6] Amid calls for reform in the lead-up to the 1972 election, the McMahon Coalition government passed the *Child Care Act*, which subsidised childcare services in recognition of the increasing workforce participation of women. Following its election in 1972, the Whitlam government increased funding for childcare and drew up the blueprint for a Children's Commission, which was expansive in that children's services would not have been tied solely to maternal workforce participation. Instead, it aimed to create services that also focused on the needs of children, families and communities.[7] However, the Whitlam government was dismissed in 1975 before the legislation could be enacted. The subsequent Fraser government largely took the view that the care of children was the responsibility of family and the market rather than the state, with conservative politicians expressing consternation at the impacts of working mothers on children. As part of a broader objective of reducing spending on social services, childcare subsidies were restricted to those families deemed 'needy'.

Beyond debates in Canberra, these policy changes of the 1970s were occurring in a cultural climate in which the concept of mothers engaging in paid work was still considered controversial. Some early adopters experimented with radical new arrangements. Sally was a teacher who grew up in a regional, Lebanese-Australian family. She and her husband split the day into two halves after their first child was born in 1978, with father and mother sharing paid work and caring responsibilities evenly. Sally said:

> because I was the primary breadwinner I went back when the child was just over six weeks old ... I was half-time teaching and he was with the baby in the mornings. I'd come home, breasts engorged and ready to feed and then he'd go off and do his classes in the afternoons and evenings.[8]

Nevertheless, Sally felt conflicted about whether she should be with her baby full-time, and recalls that attitudes towards the desirability of mothers engaging in paid work and children attending childcare were still very divided.

Miroslava was raised in an inner-urban area by Macedonian-born parents and had her first child in 1975. She remembers that most mothers in her working-class neighbourhood were forced by financial imperatives to return to work in their low-paid factory jobs and place their children into childcare. Consequently, she says that 'they still say to this day no grandchild of mine is going into childcare because I know what it was like when I had to put mine in'.[9]

Others outside the safety net of heterosexual marriage sometimes had fewer options. Sybil was from a Welsh-Australian, middle-class background. After separating from her husband, she found that financial considerations as a single mother forced her to return to a daytime teaching job. Her own children were at school by then, so she relied on the assistance of grandmothers and friends to manage the gaps between their school hours and her working hours.[10]

1980s: Legislative reform

Childcare services continued to expand under Labor governments in the 1980s and were mainly community-based and not-for-profit. The Commonwealth saw its role as encompassing the planning and building of non-profit childcare services to ensure equitable access across Australian communities.[11] Legislation such as the *Sex Discrimination Act 1984* and the *Affirmative Action (Equal Opportunity in Education) Act 1986* was passed with the intention of facilitating female employment. But Australian mothers continued to face obstacles to workforce participation, particularly a shortage of childcare that met their needs and desires. As sociologists Jan Harper and Lyn Richards discovered: 'neither the mother at home, nor the "working mother" feels clear societal approval'.[12] As gender norms shifted, stay-at-home mothers felt some pressure to work, and working mothers felt some condemnation that they were not constantly with their children.

Hazel was from a middle-class, Anglo-Australian family and had her first child in 1989. Her progressive employer offered paid maternity leave and provided on-site childcare, which facilitated her transition into working motherhood. Although Hazel felt judged by others for working when her child was young, she realised that the maintenance of her pre-maternal career was important for her emotional wellbeing. She explained,

> I realised very early on, you know that your world contracts ... even though it was a juggle I was quite glad to go back to work ... Somebody once said to me 'happy

mother, happy child,' when I was worrying about going back to work. [But] my mother-in-law, in particular, was very, very critical of that.[13]

Some mothers waited until their children were at school and then took up flexible work. Genevieve grew up in a Catholic, Anglo-Australian family. She left her job in advertising when her first child was born in 1989 because she felt that 'mothering was a valuable role' and 'a job that deserved respect and equal status'. However, she also felt that in her progressive, inner-city neighbourhood in the 1980s, some people judged women for 'only' staying at home and praised the importance of childcare. She recalls, 'that harping of "Children love it! They're so stimulated! They'd be bored at home!"' Once Genevieve's children were at school, she and a friend started a business that allowed them flexible hours to fit around their children's school time, which was a pattern of combining care work with paid work that suited her.[14]

In regional areas, choices were particularly circumscribed for working mothers. Carol was a teacher who had six children, with the youngest born in 1984. She went back to work for financial reasons when her youngest was 18 months old. Doing emergency teaching two or three days a week, Carol would have little advance notice of the days she was going to work and there were very limited options for childcare in her regional town. Fortunately, a nearby friend offered to help mind her children. She expressed how hard it was for her to leave her youngest child to go to work and how reassuring it was to know he was being cared for by a trusted, close friend.[15]

The 1990s: Transitional decade

The 1990s were a period of transformation in gender norms. The Parental Leave Test Case that came before the Industrial Relations Commission in 1990 extended application of the maternity leave clause to fathers, in order to provide them with up to 12 months' unpaid leave following the birth of their child. However, paternal take-up was very slow. The Inquiry into Equal Opportunity and Equal Status for Women in Australia found that a lack of childcare places combined with inflexible workplaces contributed to a persistent gender imbalance in both pay and workforce participation.[16] In 1991, Labor began the commercialisation of childcare by extending subsidies and tax benefits to for-profit childcare providers and abolishing capital assistance to the non-profit sector. The Howard government continued this marketisation of childcare but declined to introduce paid maternal leave. Simultaneously, high tax rates on the second earner in families encouraged mothers to remain in unpaid care in the home.

The Australian gender order was in flux in the 1990s, with views decidedly mixed on whether mothers should engage in paid work and whether children should be in childcare.[17] Caitlyn was raised in a large Irish-Australian family. Living in a small regional town when she became a mother, she felt that she was judged for returning to paid work in 1992 when her firstborn was 15 months old. However, she believed that the choice was vital to her emotional wellbeing. It allowed her 'to get my identity back. Get my sanity back. Feel useful.' In Caitlyn's community, 'Childcare back then seemed like a dirty word.'[18]

Katherine was born into a highly religious, Dutch-Australian family. She had her first child in 1993 and realised when her baby was three months old that her partner's part-time salary would not cover their expenses. She reluctantly went back to paid employment and discovered that although she needed childcare urgently, the waiting lists for local centres were months long. Instead, she found a local woman in her urban neighbourhood who offered family daycare. As her children developed close relationships with this care provider, Katherine felt increasingly comfortable with her decision. She explained the importance for her 'of them going to one woman, who may not have been perfect in every way, but she was *their* person, you know; it wasn't an institution. I felt very comfortable with that.'[19]

Working and caring in the twenty-first century

At the dawn of the new millennium, Australian mothers increasingly engaged in paid work outside the home, but they continued to struggle amid an inconsistent policy environment that sent mixed messages.[20] In a new tax-benefit arrangement introduced in 2000, the Howard government granted working parents the right to 50 hours of childcare subsidy per week for each child, while non-salaried parents could claim 24 hours.[21] Subsequently, however, a 2007 Human Rights Commission report confirmed what interviews also indicate, that 'parents often preferred their children to be cared for by someone they knew, such as grandparents or friends, rather than in formal centres.'[22] Interviews conducted in 2005–2007 found that recently arrived migrant women preferred to rely upon fathers and grandparents to care for their children.[23] Time-use surveys revealed that mothers managed the difficult juggle of work and care by reducing their own leisure time, so that the burden of inadequate policy supports fell upon them rather than employers or children.[24]

Kristen was raised in the UK and Australia in an Anglo-Australian family by a deaf mother. She had the first of her three children in 2009 and decided not to return to paid employment until her youngest was in kindergarten. In her middle-class suburb of professional women where work is the 'new religion', this decision left her feeling misunderstood by other mothers and hence socially isolated. She recalled that, 'Philosophically, for me, motherhood was easy – and I think in that regard, I was quite different from a lot of my friends … who just thought about a career, and then motherhood.'[25] Motherhood was challenging and disruptive for Kristen's friends who had based their sense of identity upon their careers.

Between 2007 and 2013 Labor governments reformed early childhood education and care with the intention of building workforce participation and therefore productivity. In 2011, government-funded maternity leave was introduced for the primary carer followed by the introduction of Dad and Partner Pay in 2013. In 2018, a new childcare subsidy was implemented that requires parental work or an activity that improves work skills. Sociologist Deborah Brennan argues that this contradicts international trends to provide free or low-cost services focused on children's needs not parental work.[26] Recent Australian policies leave mothers who have chosen to prioritise what they perceive as their children's best interests over career progression, feeling alienated from the maternal norm promoted by government policy. This was the case for Kristen, whose experiences opened this chapter.

Despite decades of campaigning for parental leave and subsidised childcare, and the general overturning of prejudices against mothers of preschool-aged children working, we have not yet realised a working mother's paradise. Many contemporary mothers report feeling mixed emotions and considerable strain in trying to combine care work and paid work. Rowena decided to work part-time after having children. She had watched her own mother battle with working full-time and feeling constantly guilty and stretched. She clarified that 'I don't want to put myself through that because … if I'm lucky enough to have kids, I want to focus on, you know, having them and nothing else really matters as much. Like, people think they're indispensable at work but everybody's replaceable.'[27]

Ariana has an Anglo-Australian background and was raised by a single mother. She has a partner and three children and works full-time. Ariana described being a working mum as:

> really … difficult … on so many levels and for so many different reasons … You do care about your job. But you also care about having a family. You shouldn't have to choose which one you care more about but it's like people expect you to … I'm really careful not to tell too many stories about my kids … at work.[28]

Ariana told me that she feels guilty and sad when her children tell her they don't want to go to childcare, but that she doesn't want to be a permanent stay-at-home mum and she doesn't see how she can work less than full-time in her role. She concluded that she feels 'this need, this yearning, to maybe get better balance and not go to work five days a week because I feel like I should be with my kids more but I don't quite know how I'm going to do it.'[29]

Grasping towards solutions

The patterns of behaviour that we revert to under conditions of crisis tell us much about our most deep-seated gender values around care and work. In this regard, the COVID-19 pandemic has illuminated tensions between maternal care work and paid work. The closure of schools to all but the children of 'essential' workers has revealed starkly gendered patterns in home-schooling. Overwhelmingly, mothers have taken on a greater proportion of the increased care and education of children in the home.[30] Yet, alongside the public health orders requiring parents and children to work and study from home if they can, there has been no accompanying government mandate that employers reduce the normal working hours of parents conducting remote learning. The result has been that in most households, an additional load of teaching and supervising children is added to a mother's customary workload. Building on sociologist Arlie Hochschild's influential work on the 'second shift' that mothers undertake, we might call this a 'pandemic shift' that mothers are required to squeeze into their day.[31]

COVID-19 has also been profoundly revealing of what we value – and therefore remunerate – and what we do not. When the federal government temporarily made all childcare free early in the pandemic, we glimpsed the possibility that this could be a permanent reform. But the subsequent removal of this extra support for working parents clearly communicates that this is not something that the government is willing to prioritise, when so much care is otherwise performed unpaid by mothers.[32]

Alongside free early childhood education and care, what other kinds of policy changes do mothers want? A reconsideration of the roles of fathers and partners – as well as grandparents and other family members – is a useful place to begin.

Looking back upon the history of Australian mothering since the mid-twentieth century, it is clear that progress in gender-equitable parenting has not been linear. Some parents in the 1970s were inspired by the women's liberation movement to try radical new ideas to share the care of children beyond the sole responsibility of a stay-at-home mother.[33] But since then, the gender revolution in care seems to have largely stalled. Many contemporary Australian women are confident *before* they become mothers that they will divide care work and paid work equally with their partner. But after the birth of a child, they find that taxation systems and social structures work against equal parenting.[34]

With such a stubbornly entrenched social issue, where cultural attitudes have partially shifted but practices lag behind, social policy has enormous potential to effect change. But to do so, base assumptions about ultimate policy objectives need to be expanded, as does our understanding of the potential beneficiaries of family policy. This chapter started with the question: how have Australian mothers interacted with family policies? We could equally ask this of fathers/partners and children. I asked my six-year-old what she thought about the history of mothers working and she said:

> In the olden days, all the dads went to work and all the mums stayed at home. But that was really unfair on the dads, who didn't get to spend much time with their kids.

Now dads can spend more time with their kids and that makes them feel happy, and their kids like it too.

Note her assumption here: that all parents *want* to spend more time with their children if they have the opportunity and the means. Following this line of thought, what would family policy look like if its objectives were more than simply increasing maternal workforce participation?

Many contemporary fathers and children report wishing that they could spend more family time together.[35] Perhaps, therefore, the objectives of family policy could be widened to encompass promoting maternal, paternal and child mental wellbeing, by making it possible for all parents to spend more time with their children if they desire. Or to restate what sociologist Bettina Cass contended as far back as the 1990s: the problem is not the ways in which women's lives intertwine with care roles, but rather men's seeming independence from care responsibilities.[36] Social policies that extend the paid parental leave of both partners – in line with similar schemes that have been highly successful in Sweden – would have multiple benefits, including increasing maternal workforce participation, heightening paternal involvement in parenting, and enhancing parental and child wellbeing.[37] These kinds of reforms would provide positive outcomes to families that extend beyond the narrowly economic.

Lessons from history:
We need a more holistic approach to childcare

In the last few decades, government policies have gradually offered more support to working mothers, particularly through childcare subsidies and parental leave. But government statements about the benefits are narrowly focused on female workforce participation and economic productivity. Media accounts have been dominated by discussions of the affordability, availability and flexibility of childcare. These are not the only factors that motivate mothers to participate in such schemes, nor influence their decisions about work and care. Public debates remain mired in the rational and the economic, while mothers describe their decision-making as motivated also by emotions and relationships.

Despite the diversity of circumstances and views among Australian mothers, there are consistent threads in their stories. Most mothers want some continuity with their pre-maternal identity, want to feel a sense of contribution to their society, want to be able to enjoy their relationships with their children, and want them to be looked after by people they trust. They do not want to feel that they have to make 'either/or' decisions about work and childcare. Mothers' motivations are as much about wellbeing as they are about money and career.

Family policy can only be partly successful when governments fail to comprehend the reasons why mothers choose to use various supports. Workforce participation and economic productivity are reasonable objectives of government policy, but they are not sufficient unto themselves. If we ignore the equally important objectives of parental and child wellbeing, we will continue to see rates of perinatal depression and anxiety rise. Increasing numbers of Australian women will ask the reasonable question: why choose motherhood when your society fails to adequately support that choice? One of the key lessons of recent history is that family policy can only be truly successful if it understands and responds to the broader needs of all members of the Australian family – mothers, partners and children – and the communities in which they live.

CHAPTER 20

Too much talk, not enough action? Federal government responses to domestic violence

Ann Curthoys, Catherine Kevin and Zora Simic

On 9 March 2021, Anne Summer, livestreamed her International Women's Day keynote speech. Are 'we as a country', she asked 'succeeding in reducing domestic and family violence against women'? Pointing to evidence which showed no discernible reduction since the inauguration of the *National Plan to Reduce Violence against Women and their Children 2010–2022*, her short answer was 'No. We are not.' To explain the failure of the National Plan to achieve its core objective – 'a significant and sustained reduction in violence against women and children' – Summers offered two interlinked explanations: 'political failure and bureaucratic ineptitude, manifested in the absence of any indicators to measure progress'. She also hoped that 'someone is working on a history of the National Plan because we need to know, in granular detail, how it went awry'.[1]

A week later, thousands of women protested across the country against sexism and gendered violence, including in Parliament House. Soon after these #March4Justice rallies, the federal government's Women's Safety Taskforce announced a National Summit on Women's Safety to be launched with an online national survey to discuss the next 12-year National Plan.

In swift response, people from across the domestic and family violence sector expressed cynicism about another 'talk-fest' at a time of unprecedented pressure on frontline services, pressure due in large part to the 'shadow pandemic': the upsurge in domestic violence under conditions of isolation and lockdown.[2] The domestic violence crisis of which so many spoke seemed intractable. Even as overall rates of violence have fallen, rates of domestic, family and sexual violence have not. Indeed, national surveys show that since 2014, there have been increases in women being hospitalised and people seeking homelessness services as a result of family and domestic violence.[3]

Due to pandemic restrictions, the National Summit on Women's Safety was held virtually on 6–7 September 2021, with Prime Minister Scott Morrison delivering an opening keynote address in which he described the number of women killed by their former or current partners as a 'national shame'.[4] While over 400 people participated in the Summit and in roundtables in preceding days, scepticism about the federal government's commitment to eradicating gender-based violence continued. The exclusive nature of the invitation-only Summit and its narrow remit were widely criticised, including by the LGBTQIA+ community and by Aboriginal and Torres Strait Islander women who called for a separate National Plan. With no major announcements made at the Summit, Delia Donovan, CEO of Domestic Violence NSW, declared it a 'missed opportunity'. 'Without action', she wrote, 'a plan is just that – a plan.'[5]

How can history help us understand domestic violence? How can historical knowledge and perspectives contribute to the development of policies and strategies that significantly reduce domestic violence and mitigate its effects? One of the ways an historical understanding can help is to know how and why we have the policies we do and what alternatives have been considered. When, how and why did domestic violence become a matter of government concern? What ideas are embedded in current policies, and what other ideas have there been? How valuable have past 'talk-fests' been in the development and implementation of policies? Here we focus on discussion at the national level, looking at significant national conferences, summits and forums and the ideas, knowledge, strategies and policies that arose from them.

National conference on domestic violence, 11–15 November 1985

We start with the first government-initiated national conference devoted to the question of domestic violence, held in November 1985. The attorney-general, Lionel Bowen, requested that the Australian Institute for Criminology in Canberra host such a conference as a basis for providing the government with advice. At this point, there had been 12 years of feminist activism on the issue, beginning with the establishment of the first women's refuges from violence in Sydney in 1974. One by one, state governments had responded and established agencies to formulate policy and provide services, but the federal government had played little role. An important factor in the Hawke Labor government's new interest in the topic was its decision, in the wake of the world conference in Nairobi in July 1985 that concluded the UN Decade for Women, to develop a plan of action for advancing the status of Australian women. The government recognised that any such plan would need to include policies concerning domestic violence.[6]

Organisers of the inaugural national conference on the issue intended that it would provide the government with the information it needed to develop adequate criminal justice and welfare policies, including provision of resources for 'ethnic groups and Aborigines' about whom knowledge was relatively scarce.[7] They wanted an 'action conference'; one that would gather and present current research, bring individual voices into conversation with this research, and encourage small group discussion wherever possible. The planning of these discussions was presented as both an acknowledgment of the 'personal nature' of the issue and a way of working towards 'attitudinal realignment', which was understood as integral to any change. The audience included staff from women's refuges, police, employees of Commonwealth departments, as well as victim/survivors. Over five days, more than 300 participants listened to the testimonies of survivors and support workers, representatives of various church and migrant community organisations, and the findings of academic researchers in disciplines including psychology, history and sociology.

Even at this early stage, there was a sense that the government needed to convert talk into action. In his opening address, Bowen spoke of 'inquiry after inquiry' and said he was encouraged by the prospect of this much-needed national overview. Bowen's address criticised the legal mechanisms available to women, especially in family law, and called on the police to see their responses to victims as crucial and not be discouraged by poor sentencing outcomes.[8] It quickly became clear that developing consensus on the best way forward would not be easy. Even the term 'domestic violence' itself was under dispute. The very first presentation, by refuge worker Dawn Rowan, began with a critique, referring to 'Criminal assault of women in their homes (euphemistically called domestic violence)'.⁹ Vivien Johnson reminded the conference that the women's refuge movement had carved out the terrain, including the replacement of the term 'wife bashing' with the 'spurious neutrality of "domestic violence"', which distanced the issue and avoided the critique of marriage contained in 'wife bashing'.¹⁰ The work of women's refuges as sites of data collection and deepening understanding of the issue was central to the first phase of the conference, in which 39 out of the 45 papers were presented by women. Feminist perspectives were well represented, with the patriarchal family as a site of violence against women and children featuring in many of the presentations. Feminist contributors wanted to have domestic violence considered and treated as a crime and saw long-term solutions as dependent on the achievement of gender equity. A paper by Judith Allen, then a postgraduate history student, contributed an historical perspective and helped inaugurate historical studies of domestic violence in Australia.¹¹

The move towards a national strategy on domestic violence, 1986–96

The Hawke Labor government's decision to develop a plan of action concerning the status of Australian women was followed by a flurry of discussions, consultations and reports, many of them commissioned by the Office for the Status of Women (OSW). Some of these investigations addressed domestic violence, such as a report in 1986 on Aboriginal women's issues written by Phyllis Daylight and Mary Johnstone, which drew attention to concerns that domestic violence in Aboriginal communities was increasing, and that alcohol played an important role.[12] In a major report entitled *Setting the Agenda* in 1987, the OSW observed that during the extensive consultation process, 'Violence against women and children emerged as a priority'.[13] This report laid the groundwork for the Commonwealth government's promised action plan, entitled *National Agenda for Women* and adopted in February 1988. The *National Agenda* represented a milestone in the development of national domestic violence policy, announcing that the government's aim was to 'see an Australia which was free from violence in the home'. In pursuit of this aim it would introduce strategies to reduce the incidence of domestic violence, change community attitudes, further develop support services, and improve police responses.[14]

Also drawing attention to domestic violence was a growing national government concern with violence in Australian society generally in the wake of two mass firearms killings in Melbourne in 1986 and 1987. In October 1988 the government established a National Committee on Violence in which gender issues were included in its terms of reference. At the committee's invitation, the Australian Institute of Criminology commissioned a series of reports and convened two major conferences, in 1989 and 1993, to gather expert opinion on violence in Australia, the second of which paid serious attention to domestic violence and the competing theoretical approaches to explaining it.[15] These were published in 1995 as the edited collection *Australian Violence: Contemporary Perspectives*. In a prescient preface to the book arising from the second conference, Sandra Egger commented:

> The deconstruction of masculinity, the examination of the interactions between gender and other powerful forms of

oppression such as class and race, and the examination of the role of masculinity in the different forms of violence in different social relationships (including male to male violence) represent potentially useful avenues of inquiry in our search for explanations.[16]

There were several other important national initiatives at this time. In 1991, a coordinating body called the Secretariat of National Aboriginal and Islander Child Care Agencies produced a handbook by Maryanne Sam entitled *Through Black Eyes: A Handbook of Family Violence in Aboriginal and Torres Strait Islander Communities* (1991). It began with Maureen Watson's evocative poem 'Don't Bash the Loving out of Me'.

In her introduction, Sam wrote, that 'it has become important to talk about family violence, to open all the closed doors, to change the attitudes and dispel the myths that have for so long kept many of our people in the dark and alone'.[17] The handbook outlined many of the issues surrounding Aboriginal family violence and proved popular, leading to a second edition in 1992.

The National Committee on Violence delivered its final report in February 1990, recommending the development of uniform national legislation and improved training of police officers.[18] Soon after, the government committed $1.34 million to establish a committee to deal specifically with violence against women. The new National Committee on Violence Against Women was asked to initiate research, coordinate education programs, provide a forum for consideration of policy and legal issues, and above all to develop the first national strategy on violence against women, which would coordinate the work of federal and state governments.[19]

It was clear that the problem was larger than even experienced feminists had realised. As part of Women's Liberation, Anne Summers had been a co-founder of Elsie, Australia's first feminist refuge. Later she became a 'femocrat', initially as the head of the OSW during the Hawke Labor government and subsequently as an adviser to Paul Keating, who became prime minister in December 1991. In that role – despite her experience at Elsie almost 20 years earlier, and the emergence of violence against women and children as a priority for the OSW in the late 1980s – she was 'staggered' that in focus groups 'almost every woman' mentioned violence. 'I had no idea violence against women was so pervasive', she later wrote, 'and I did not have a clue how to respond to it.'[20]

In October 1992, the Labor government launched a *National Strategy on Violence Against Women* and presented it in December to a meeting of all the state premiers. It aimed to focus state and federal governments on similar goals and continue the task of encouraging research and engaging with experts.[21] It was far reaching, announcing that 'This National Strategy has been prepared within the context of a changing society; the ongoing development of relations between Commonwealth and State/Territory Governments; an evolving national identity; and constitutional reform.' It was also ambitious, announcing its intention 'to provide direction to governments to seriously and systematically address violence against women and measure their progress towards the ultimate goal of eliminating violence against women in Australia'. The strategy was strongly influenced by feminist approaches, attributing domestic violence to male attitudes and power over women, and recommending policies aimed at gender equality and women's economic independence.[22] In her autobiography, Anne

Summers describes the strategy as a 'dry' document, which was at odds with the passion women brought to the issue.[23] Perhaps it was, but almost 20 years later, people working in the field on domestic violence were still telling researchers of its value and regretting that more had not become of it.[24]

The *National Strategy on Violence Against Women* lasted for only three years, for Labor would lose office in March 1996. It saw some action, such as the production of national guidelines for training people working in the area, which continued to be used for years after, and a *Stop Violence Against Women* community awareness campaign in 1993.[25] Public awareness and government accountability were heightened in December 1993 by the UN General Assembly's adoption of the Declaration on the Elimination of All Forms of Violence Against Women, a declaration in which Australian representatives had been closely involved. Significantly, in May 1994 the Australian Bureau of Statistics published the first Australian National Crime Statistics on domestic violence.[26] Yet the mood in Canberra was shifting. The year 1994 was the UN International Year of the Family, which produced in Australia fierce debates over what a family was, and which brought into prominence the rise of new right conservatives keen to keep families together, whatever the circumstances. It was also the time when an angry, anti-feminist 'men's rights' movement was emerging, which explained men's violence as a product of their unequal treatment in the family law system and argued that women were just as violent as men.[27]

'De-gendering' domestic violence in the Howard era

Feminist influence on government policy on a range of issues including domestic violence plummeted when a socially conservative Coalition government led by John Howard came to power in March 1996.[28] Openly anti-feminist, it cut many services to women, slashed the funding of the OSW by 40 per cent, and abandoned concern with many 'women's policy' issues.[29] The new government was concerned with maintaining strong families, and was aware that domestic violence undermined family life and placed a heavy strain on police, courts and health systems.[30] The result was not an abandonment of involvement in domestic violence but rather a reconceptualising of it, 'de-gendering' it to align with the conservative government's espousal of family values.[31]

In September 1996, only six months after the new government came to power, the OSW mounted yet another national conference on domestic violence with the task of developing a new government policy. A year later, on 7 November 1997, Howard convened a National Domestic Violence Summit in conjunction with the annual meeting of state premiers, at which the new policy was launched.[32] Howard commented that,

> Domestic violence not only has traumatic personal consequences but also inflicts enormous social and economic costs on the whole community. Many women do not seek help from crisis services, and it is time we addressed their needs. We have all come together today to find new approaches which work so that Australian

families can live free of the fear of violence ... We must acknowledge that domestic violence is not a private matter, but a serious issue for our whole society.³³

The government described its new program, called *Partnerships Against Domestic Violence* and supported by all Australian heads of government, as 'a major part of the Government's strategy for strengthening families, preventing family breakdown and creating healthy and safe communities'.³⁴ It left considerable responsibility to the states but did emphasise the importance of a cross-fertilisation of knowledge and provided Commonwealth funding for a range of programs.³⁵ Despite its distinctively different language and approach, the new policy continued many of the features of the old, in supporting specific groups and funding public education on the issue. Important initiatives funded under the Partnerships program included a clearinghouse for domestic and family violence research and data at the University of New South Wales, a national study of the annual cost of domestic violence, and a focus on Indigenous family violence.³⁶ After six years in operation, it was replaced by the Women's Safety Agenda in 2005, which continued many of the Partnership program initiatives.

Framing domestic violence since 2007

Another change of government, this time from Coalition to Labor in November 2007, brought another change in direction, one that was reminiscent of the changes made by Labor in the late 1980s and early 1990s. In a speech on 17 September 2008, the new Labor Prime Minister, Kevin Rudd, made it clear that the new government saw domestic violence as a gender issue.

'Violence against women', he said, 'is difficult to talk about … it is degrading and damaging to experience.' He asked how it could be that half a million Australian women experience violence from their partners and emphasised the need to turn this terrible statistic around. 'Because each of these statistics is a human face. And it is my gender – it is our gender – Australian men – that are responsible.'[37] Reintroducing the language of 'violence against women' that Coalition governments had removed, Rudd announced the creation of a new body to develop a new plan for action to reduce violence against women and children.[38] After extensive consultation, in March 2009 the Council to Reduce Violence against Women and their Children released its national 12-year plan for 2010–22. It was supported by all state governments, and after a very close election in August 2010 and with Julia Gillard as prime minister, an updated version was finally released in early 2011.[39] In launching it, the Minister for the Status of Women, Kate Ellis, presented the plan as innovative in seeking to 'focus so strongly on prevention', to 'look to the long term – building respectful relationships and working to increase gender equality to prevent violence from occurring in the first place' and 'to focus on holding perpetrators accountable and encourage behaviour change for the future.'[40]

Feminist framings of domestic violence were again at the foreground, but with a greater focus on community-specific responses. This plan, which is due to expire in 2022, has a strong emphasis on prevention, on holding perpetrators to account, special provision for Indigenous families, and national support services. The plan was divided into four three-year segments, each of which was carried out, despite a change back to Coalition government in 2013. It is noteworthy that where the Howard government had overturned the Keating government's plan and replaced it with an entirely new one, the Coalition governments from 2013 onwards have not done so. In the last ten years, domestic violence has gained more public attention than ever before, especially with the appointment in 2015 of bereaved survivor of domestic violence Rosie Batty as Australian of the Year. On 24 September that year, Prime Minister Malcolm Turnbull described domestic violence as 'a national disgrace' and called for it to become 'UnAustralian' to disrespect women.[41] His successor from August 2018, Scott Morrison, in introducing the fourth and final stage of the National Action Plan, pledged an extra $328 million to combat domestic violence, and commented that the government would target 'the negative attitudes that lead to violence'. He went on to say that a 'culture of disrespect towards women is a precursor to violence, and anyone who doesn't see that is kidding themselves.'[42] As the closing date of the government's National Action Plan came into view, the Coalition government felt it incumbent on it to produce a new plan. Hence the 2021 Summit with which we began. It is indicative of how the conversation around domestic violence has changed since the Howard years that the keynote speakers for the Summit included June Oscar, Aboriginal and Torres Strait Islander Social Justice Commissioner, Kate Jenkins, Sex Discrimination Commissioner, and Julie Inman Grant, eSafety Commissioner, as well as Prime Minister Scott Morrison.

Lessons from history: We need talk *and* action

So, what do we make of this brief history of federal government policy on domestic violence since 1985? How might it help those involved in the struggle to reduce domestic violence and support its victims?

First, we find it significant that both sides of parliament now assume that Australia must have a national plan to address problems of domestic and family violence and violence against women generally. When Paul Keating launched the first such plan in 1992, the *National Strategy on Violence Against Women*, it was something new. Even five years earlier, it was unclear to many whether the national government should be concerned with domestic violence at all. Domestic violence has been a highly political matter, and Labor and Liberal-National Coalition governments have developed different policies, but beyond these political differences we can see a shared concern with the persistence and destructiveness of domestic violence for women and their children. A lesson from history, then, is that bipartisan support for crucial issues is possible, and that it can be sustained and built on by those in the sector, as well as by policymakers.

Second, the connections between feminism and the task of challenging domestic violence have been strong and yet troubled. Key debates over the causes of domestic violence, the role of gender power differentials and gender dynamics, and the question of criminalisation of domestic violence and its effects in marginalised communities, have been going for a long time and remain unresolved. The call made by Sandra Egger in 1995 for an intersectional analysis, which takes into account the operations of gender, race and class remains as important as ever. While the needs of Aboriginal women and their families have been recognised in feminist and other public discussions for some time, it has taken longer for governments to properly address the very important question of how best to tackle domestic and family violence in Aboriginal communities, a process that needs to be led by Aboriginal people. Given this history, we suggest that governments support the recent call made by leading Aboriginal women for their own dedicated National Plan.

Third, understanding the emotional dimensions of domestic violence has come to the forefront, stimulated by Jess Hill's insightful book, *See What You Made Me Do: Power, Control, and Domestic Abuse* (2019). The domestic violence sector had sought a public education campaign on emotional abuse as a form of domestic violence during the Howard years, but a proposed campaign in 2003 was cancelled when 'senior figures did not like the advertising message'.[43] Perhaps it will help those grappling with the issues raised by the notion of coercive control to know that domestic service providers have been conscious of this issue for a long time.

Finally, there is the question of talk and action. The history we've outlined here indicates their strong relationship. The foundational 1992 strategy, for example, emerged from the conferences, consultations and research preceding it. While the political complexion and commitment of any government in power has an enormous effect, so too has the accumulation of knowledge and experience in the domestic violence sector since it emerged in the 1970s. Sharing of ideas and information has been effective in the past.

The impatience of service providers with the 2021 Summit we see as not so much a protest against talk *per se*, but rather, in a context where service providers are stretched to the limit, against talk which simply repeats what we already know, ignores rather than builds on past experience, and does not have a practical effect. Sadly, this is what appears to be the case in the 2021 National Summit on Women's Safety. The final delegates' statement reiterated meaningful commitments which have been made many times before: to primary prevention; to long-term government investment by all levels of governments; to Aboriginal and Torres Strait Islander peoples leading their own responses; to improving the criminal justice system; to recognising lived and diverse experiences; and to gender equality, among other priorities.[44] Ultimately, however, the outcome from the 2021 Summit was simply a plan to make a plan. Given the existing National Plan lacks proper indicators to measure its progress, the onus is on present and future governments to properly substantiate and resource their oft-proclaimed commitment to ending violence against women and children.

CHAPTER 21

The neglected north: Developing Northern Australia from the south since 1901

Lyndon Megarrity

In 1909, Australian poet Mabel Forrest urged her fellow Australians to:

> Arm the empty North that drowses by its tide-washed
>   sandy slopes;
> There is iron in the ranges, there is silver in the stopes,
> There is wealth undreamed – your birthright – in the
>   country's scattered parts,
> There is grit and honest courage in your people's loyal
>   hearts.[1]

Forrest's 'pioneer' sentiments now seem old-fashioned. Nevertheless, the economic progress of the less-populated northern half of Australia remains a national project that shows no signs of completion any time soon. Since Federation, the Commonwealth has created policies and programs designed to develop Northern Australia and to alleviate isolation for its residents.[2] Over several generations, especially since the Second World War, the Commonwealth has made a major contribution to improving life in the tropics. Despite these gains, the political fear that the north is not living up to its full potential remains visceral, and claims that the north is neglected continue to be vehemently expressed by state and national MPs.

Historically, Commonwealth politicians and officials have tended to regard the north primarily as a distant, economic frontier. This traditional mindset continues to influence contemporary policymakers and, as we will see, such frontier sentimentality gets in the way of developing effective policies that enhance the quality of life for all Northern Australians. Policymakers must also understand that imagining Northern Australia as a broad geographical zone is not always helpful in understanding the nature of local and regional communities within the tropics.

Northern development policy, 1901–60

Northern Australia has no official geographical status. It will be defined here as those parts of Queensland, the Northern Territory (NT) and Western Australia (WA) which are located north of the Tropic of Capricorn, although policymakers have often included areas far below the Tropic line as part of the remote north. Over the last 120 years, this concept of Northern Australia as a super-region encompassing all Australian territory north of Capricorn has gone in and out of fashion.

Pastoralism was the dominant industry in much of inland Northern Australia by 1901, although as the twentieth century progressed, large-scale mining became increasingly significant. Sugar was also profitably produced along the North Queensland coast, which had higher rainfalls and more fertile soil than elsewhere above the Tropic of Capricorn. The transport of sugar, mining and pastoral products to the coast resulted in population growth in Townsville, Darwin and other regional ports, but the north was otherwise sparsely populated by Europeans in the early twentieth century. Roughly 115 000 non-Indigenous people lived north of the Tropic of Capricorn in 1901, and of these, up to a quarter were non-Europeans. Inland from the populous areas of the coast, Northern Australia had a substantial Indigenous population, many living in Christian missions or working within primary industries such as pastoralism. Historian Russell McGregor has estimated that at the turn of the twentieth century, the Indigenous population was 'probably ... declining but still numbered over 100,000 across the north'.[3] Because Australian elites were focused on developing and maintaining a European-dominated Australia, Aboriginal and Torres Strait Islander people tended to be disregarded in discussions of Northern development policy.

Northern Australia's low population troubled many white Australians in the first half of the twentieth century, a time when the notion of a White Australia predominantly settled by British migrants was at its height. The north of the continent was often regarded as dangerously 'empty' because its European population was limited. If the region was not developed by Australians, it was argued, Asian countries would be tempted to invade and destroy 'White Australia' forever. Aside from fears of invasion by foreign powers, many northern boosters were perturbed by the notion of an untamed northern frontier not realising its commercial potential.

In part, a shortage of federal funds and the expense of providing infrastructure over a vast region discouraged Commonwealth action on northern development for several decades. Political reasons also led to northern neglect. There were only a handful of northern electorates, and most voters lived well south of the Tropic of Capricorn. With few leading politicians having much experience or genuine interest in Northern Australia, fear of the 'Empty North' tended to be abstract rather than real. Consequently, before the Second World War, the Commonwealth's two major northern policy initiatives were marked by fine parliamentary speeches but lukewarm commitment to the north itself. The federal government purchased the Northern Territory from South Australia and established an administration in 1911, but starved it of funds that might have created improved infrastructure and amenities. Further, while the Commonwealth-funded Australian Institute of Tropical Medicine (established in 1910) conducted research which helped to disprove popular perceptions that whites could not physically and mentally thrive in the tropics, by the 1930s the institute was closed, and government funding was transferred to the School of Public Health and Tropical Medicine at Sydney University.

The Second World War was a turning point in the history of Commonwealth engagement with Northern Australia. Because the Commonwealth from 1942 became the only Australian government allowed to collect income tax (a temporary wartime measure that has remained in place) federal powers were expanded. This encouraged northern people to seek Commonwealth support for local projects, using the renewed fear of Asian invasion during the Pacific War as a bargaining chip.

Queensland politicians, such as Premier Ned Hanlon (1946–52), were especially vocal on the importance of developing the postwar north. Indeed, the economic and political clout of North Queensland's urban centres had grown as northern sugar, mining and beef production accelerated in the postwar years. Ironically, infrastructure such as roads and bridges was, in some years, an insufficient match for the elements, with rains cutting off a number of northern towns for extended periods. Crippling droughts and the lack of substantial dams in some areas increased the business uncertainty of primary producers. However, the Chifley Labor government was unmoved by the Queensland government's push for more Commonwealth funding for northern development.

In contrast to his caution over northern proposals, Prime Minister Ben Chifley initiated the ambitious Snowy Mountains scheme in 1949. Completed 25 years later, the scheme diverted water inland from the eastward-flowing Snowy River, allowing the redirected water to be used for hydroelectricity and irrigation in parts of New South Wales and Victoria. The Snowy River scheme proposal had been discussed in state and federal circles for several years. By contrast, northern infrastructure projects were distant from Canberra and the overall return on federal investment was unclear.

Liberal-Country Party Prime Minister Robert Menzies (1949–66) placed Northern Australia very low on his agenda. Yet the Korean War and Asian militarism drew renewed attention to Australia's vulnerable north. The public imagined that if Australians did not develop the north, other nations would. The increasing exploitation of northern minerals, such as uranium and iron ore, during the Menzies era added to the sense that the north needed to be both defended and populated as a national priority. Further, the development of Northern Australia was viewed by many politicians as a potential nation-building exercise, inspired largely by the hugely popular Snowy Mountains scheme. Projects like the 'Snowy' and projected northern proposals appealed to traditional European notions of taming the wilderness, defined concisely by Menzies' National Development Minister W.H. Spooner as the 'achievement of man's age-old dream of making nature serve his purposes'.[4]

The politics of northern development, 1960–75

The Menzies government responded to electoral pressures regarding northern neglect by supporting a limited, but significant, number of large projects. It provided a major loan to the Queensland government to help finance a reconstruction of the Mount Isa to Townsville Railway; it invested heavily in beef roads for northern producers; and it also agreed in 1964 to build a large army base in Townsville. But these achievements remained overshadowed by persistent claims by the media and the federal opposition that the north was not living up to its full potential.

The urbane Gough Whitlam emerged as an unlikely advocate for northern development. As deputy opposition leader (1960–67) and opposition leader (1967–72) he saw an opportunity to increase Labor's vote in development-oriented Queensland by portraying himself as the neglected north's champion in Canberra. It also provided him with an opportunity to show his party and the electorate that he had the vision to be prime minister.

Crucially, Whitlam believed that securing votes in the north, especially in Queensland, could assist in the revival of federal Labor's fortunes. The modest increase in the number of electorates in Queensland during the postwar years gave credence to the rising politician's conviction. Before 1949, there were only two Queensland House of Representatives electorates situated above the Tropic of Capricorn: Kennedy and Herbert. Another electorate, Capricornia, was partly above and partly below the Tropic of Capricorn. Population growth along the north coast and an enlargement of the parliament subsequently led to the creation in 1949 of two new federal divisions in northern Queensland – Leichhardt (Far North Queensland) and Dawson (centred on Mackay and surrounding districts). The people of north-west Western Australia and the Northern Territory, on the other hand, had only one Lower House seat each in federal parliament during the twentieth century. Indeed, from 1901 until relatively recently (2008), north-west Western Australia was part of the gigantic but sparsely populated federal electorate of Kalgoorlie, covering most of the geographical area of the state.

In his parliamentary speeches and on the campaign trail in the 1960s, Whitlam argued that Northern Australia's mineral and agricultural wealth held the key to Australia's future economic prosperity. The north's consequent national importance justified federal investment in schemes like the proposed retention of the Snowy Mountains Authority to develop northern water resources. Whitlam insisted that only the Commonwealth had the resources necessary to complete an ambitious northern infrastructure program of dam-building, road construction and power generation.

Whitlam's national vision for Northern Australia was not overly original. He drew upon ideas canvassed in the postwar years by a broad range of individuals and groups, including newspaper journalists; academics, such as Douglas Copland; North Queensland lobby groups, such as the People the North Committee; and even William Hudson, the head of the Snowy

Mountains Hydro-Electric Authority. What Whitlam added to the political debate was his tremendous confidence in the capacity and righteousness of Commonwealth action. Where Menzies and his ministry were often keen to dismiss northern matters as the responsibility of the states concerned, namely WA and Queensland, Whitlam, in theory, saw no impediments to Commonwealth authority. Section 96 of the Constitution, as Whitlam keenly pointed out, gave the Commonwealth the ability to give money to the states for any purpose it saw fit.

The high point of Whitlam's commitment to Northern Australia came in 1966, when he helped Labor candidate Rex Patterson win the by-election for the Mackay-centred Queensland federal seat of Dawson. A well-respected expert on sugar, Patterson had recently resigned from the Commonwealth public service over government inaction on northern policy. Concentrating on the theme of northern development, Whitlam tirelessly campaigned alongside Patterson who won what had been considered a safe Country Party seat with a swing of 12 per cent. Probably connected to the shock of the Patterson win, the Holt government and its Liberal-Country Party successors subsequently increased federal support for the Ord River irrigation project in north-west Australia. Completed in 1972, the Ord River Dam gave the Coalition a spectacular northern project for which it could claim some credit.

By the late 1960s and early 1970s, however, the Australian national media and most Commonwealth parliamentarians had lost enthusiasm for Northern Australia as a political issue. Whitlam himself turned more and more to foreign affairs policy to boost his personal profile as opposition leader. Northern development remained part of the federal Labor program, however, and when he became prime minister in

1972, Whitlam appointed Rex Patterson as Australia's first Minister for Northern Development.

Patterson's ministerial freedom was severely undermined because the ministers for Transport, Minerals and Energy and other portfolios enjoyed nationwide jurisdiction and had no incentive to hand over regional responsibilities to a Northern minister. Nonetheless, he did secure bilateral agreements with Asian countries to purchase Queensland sugar. The Whitlam government also provided several million dollars to facilitate the building of northern dams and beef roads. However, the outcomes were modest in comparison to Whitlam's frontier vision of a vast new Snowy Mountains scheme to develop the tropics. In any event, doubts were emerging about the wisdom of focusing on nation-building dams. The Ord irrigation scheme in the north-west, for example, had proven to be relatively unprofitable.

One reason for the decline in attention to northern matters was that circumstances had changed. The gradual dismantling of the White Australia policy between 1966 and 1973 meant that stirring up fears of Asian invasion was no longer an appropriate or relevant way of drawing attention to the north, but nothing as compelling had yet taken its place. Further, the notion that commercial development of the so-called Empty North was a moral right and duty was now being questioned by the general community, with the desire to save natural attractions such as the Great Barrier Reef from environmental damage posing a challenge to would-be developers.

The increasing freedoms and rights granted to Indigenous groups in the 1960s and 1970s were also changing public perceptions about the nature of development in the north. Significantly, legislation passed in 1962 gave Indigenous people the right to vote in Commonwealth elections, and by 1965, Aboriginal people and Torres Strait Islanders were entitled to vote in state elections in each of the six states. Around the same time, Indigenous people were officially encouraged to leave missions and reserves and live an independent life, often in regional towns and cities. Suddenly, politicians were compelled to respond to Indigenous people in the north as activists and electors; partly as a result, Indigenous land rights became a lively political issue, especially in the Northern Territory.

The advent of land rights legislation under Whitlam and his successor, Liberal Prime Minister Malcolm Fraser, served to challenge the popular assumption that northern development was an unqualified good that did not need to take into account Indigenous wishes. As a result of a Commonwealth Act of Parliament in 1976, the return of traditional lands in the NT to Aboriginal people began to occur: the clash this caused with mainstream developers with more commercial attitudes to land use was a key issue influencing debates about the future of northern development. After the Mabo High Court decision in 1992, the right of traditional owners to native title was enacted by governments across Australia. Negotiations between native title owners and developers, especially mining companies, have become part of the cultural and political process of northern development.

Another reason Northern Australia faded as a policy concern during and after the Whitlam years was because the north was and is too fragmented to be the focus of a single overarching suite of development policies. Of the three political regions resting under the Northern Australia umbrella, the northern parts of Queensland are by far the most developed, thanks to a series of medium-sized cities across the coast.

North-West Australia, North Queensland and the NT (self-governing from 1978) are sufficiently distant from one another to have their own social, political and economic traditions based on state and territory boundaries.

Northern neglect:
The suburban frontier of Northern Australia

While better sealed roads, greater access to commercial flights, the internet and other improvements and innovations have alleviated much of the physical isolation of living in the north since the 1970s, there remains in Northern Australia a sense of psychological isolation from the main centres of political and financial power. The cyclical calls for northern dams, big mining projects and business opportunities give a level of media attention to the north it does not usually receive. Conveniently forgetting the suburban nature of most of the northern population, the perennial idea of the north as a frontier needing people and development continues to have passing appeal to armchair ruralists in the south.

Since the Whitlam era, the notion that the north has been marked by national neglect has also been pursued by a range of northern-based politicians, including Bob Katter Junior. Subsequently, the Liberal-National Coalition saw benefit in highlighting the 'neglected north' narrative as a major political theme in the lead-up to the 2013 federal election.[5] Notably, the Coalition attracted the media's interest by promoting the concept of the 'Northern food bowl'. This would be created by harnessing Northern Australia's rainfalls through new dams and agricultural development, allowing northern producers to feed the growing Asian populations to the north. The northern food bowl idea was not new. For decades, its advocates had argued that strategic water projects were a fail-safe recipe for agricultural wealth. However, the aridity of the climate, the limited fertility of the soil and the north's unpredictable rainfall patterns have discouraged both government and private investment.

Nevertheless, the Coalition in 2013 presented the northern food bowl as a viable proposition. As Whitlam had found in a previous generation, Northern Australia gave Liberal opposition leader Tony Abbott a talking point in the media, as he attempted to position himself as the alternative prime minister. Abbott's promotion of Northern Australia allowed him to talk about grand themes at a time when the Australian media's focus on Labor issues tended to be on its internal divisions rather than its policies.

Like the ALP in the 1960s, the Coalition in 2013 saw electoral advantage in selling the north as a wilderness for the nation to tame, stating that

> Northern Australia ... is often regarded as Australia's 'last frontier'. No longer will Northern Australia be seen as the last frontier: it is in fact, the next frontier ... it remains underutilised relative to the rest of the country, despite its natural, geographic and strategic assets.[6]

The Coalition won the 2013 election. While the northern food bowl thought bubble quickly burst, the new government subsequently released a white paper on developing Northern Australia, which indicated that the Coalition continued to view the north through a narrow economic prism. The 2015 White Paper envisaged that the Commonwealth's role was to facilitate, but not drive, commercial development. It also asserted that the successful economic development of Northern Australia required rapid population growth. The Coalition hoped to see the region grow from 1.3 million people in 2015 to 4–5 million by 2060.

The history of northern cities such as Townsville and Darwin over the last three decades suggests that if the Northern Australia White Paper's proposed population surge goes ahead, the social and cultural problems surrounding development will frequently be sidelined by developers and various layers of government. The aspects of a northern district which make it unique and valued by residents are all too often deemed expendable by economic decision-makers. Mirroring patterns of civic development across the nation, many heritage buildings have been destroyed and the landscapes of northern coastal towns now feature high-rise buildings and motels that fail to blend in with the environment. It remains to be seen whether the Coalition's uncritical support of high population and economic growth in the north can be carefully balanced with other popularly supported northern goals, such as environmental sustainability and tourism.

Following the White Paper, the Coalition's progress on fulfilling its northern vision has been relatively slow, often marked more by announcements of funding than the completion of roads and special northern projects.[7] Designed to provide financial assistance for major development projects which could create jobs and infrastructure in the north, the Coalition's $5 billion Northern Australia Infrastructure Facility (NAIF) initiative was panned by Labor as the 'no actual infrastructure fund': only $218.4 million had been spent by October 2020.[8] Nevertheless, by mid-2021, NAIF had committed $2.9 billion to support a 'wide range of industries' such as 'agriculture, aquaculture, energy and resources'.[9] Tellingly, while regional universities are benefiting from Commonwealth NAIF loans for new major buildings, the study of history, literature and other humanities subjects at the same institutions has been allowed to decline sharply since the 1990s. Neither is there much Commonwealth interest in arts and media infrastructure, which is mostly dominated by southern organisations.

Port Darwin, sovereignty and Australian history

For all the renewed policy focus on Northern Australia, Commonwealth officials still seemed to be taken by surprise by an incident involving the Northern Territory, Australian sovereignty and diplomatic relationships with two major powers: China and the United States.[10] In 2015, the NT government agreed to give the Chinese-owned Landbridge company a 99-year lease over key port facilities at the Port of Darwin. The deal gave the revenue-hungry NT administration $506 million and the potential to win political kudos, indirectly, from the expansion of economic activity at the port. Ideologically committed to 'small government' and privatisation, the Coalition government in Canberra expressed its approval. The federal Minister for Northern Australia, Josh Frydenberg, described the Port of Darwin deal as a 'vote of confidence in the Northern Territory', which displayed 'foreign investor confidence in the economic opportunities available in Australia's north'.[11]

Doubts, however, soon emerged about the wisdom of allowing foreign investors with potential links to the Chinese government to have long-term commercial access to the strategic northern Port of Darwin. Ironically, the Port of Darwin lease deal emerged a few short years after the ALP government under Julia Gillard and then US president Barack Obama set in place a long-term joint defence initiative, involving the training of US marines (together with Australian defence force personnel) each year in the Top End of Australia. That the joint training program was located in Northern Australia was not surprising; it was symbolic of policy concerns given expression in the Defence White Paper of 2013: 'An effective, visible force posture in northern Australia and our northern and western approaches is necessary to demonstrate our capacity and our will to defend our sovereign territory.'[12]

Yet subsequently, the NT government leased the Port of Darwin to a Chinese company in 2015 with what appears to have been extremely limited Commonwealth oversight. The US government was not told of the sale before the public announcement. It is possible that the Australian authorities viewed leasing the Port of Darwin as just one more of a string of expedient privatisations by state/territory governments; but the US Obama administration expressed disappointment that its Australian allies had not kept it informed of a decision involving China, the US's major geo-political rival in the Asia-Pacific.

The Port of Darwin lease was one of many Chinese investment projects in Australia in recent years which have attracted local media, political and public attention.[13] Such commercial undertakings have created an atmosphere of uncertainty about the Chinese government's intentions within Australia's broader region. Major Chinese investments in Australia have been taking place within the context of heavy involvement of state-owned enterprises in Chinese overseas mining investments and territorial disputes in the South China Sea, along with an accelerated Chinese economic presence in the Pacific.

Arguably, a factor which contributed to the Commonwealth's policy confusion over the Port of Darwin controversy was the fact that since 1901, Northern Australia has tended to be on the periphery of Commonwealth concerns. It is assumed by the media, citizens and officials that the nation's important events and decisions generally take place in the south-east corner of the country. Therefore, it can be difficult for policymakers to respond comprehensively to Northern Australian issues and events when they suddenly become the focus of media interest. It follows that potentially serious issues of sovereignty and diplomacy in the north may continue to create awkward moments for the Commonwealth well into the future.

Lessons from history: Responding to local and regional diversity

As with Australia–Asia relations, the north is regularly 'discovered' by politicians and journalists, and the image of an 'Empty North' seems a necessary political narrative for each generation of 'pioneer' visionaries wanting to place their stamp on Australia's northern frontier. Almost as regularly as a hot, debilitating northern summer, Northern Australia becomes a big news item as publicity gets generated for a variety of schemes, such as ambitious dams, large mines and agricultural ventures. Just as regularly, Northern Australia disappears from the political agenda, as journalists and politicians get bored with it, and only so much ever gets delivered out of all the promises and rhetoric.

The reason politicians and journalists move on very quickly from the Northern Australia issue is that the north remains for most Australians as remote from their lives as it was in Chifley's time. Furthermore, the notion of Northern Australia as a super-region is more a convenient policy fiction than a fact: it is a currently fashionable label predominantly applied to economic and construction projects of local and regional significance in specific areas of the north.

What, then, can policymakers learn from the history of Commonwealth engagement with the north? First and foremost, federal and local politicians need to acknowledge the strengths and limitations of the age-old, grand Northern Australia vision. While the super-region concept is applicable to areas such as defence and the protection of national borders, the claims of northern neglect have a great deal in common with those in other regional and local areas across Australia. Therefore, a strong national commitment to improving amenities, basic infrastructure and quality of life across the continent in regional and local communities would ultimately be of more benefit to the north than the quick fix of mega-projects.

Second, the working definition of 'northern development' needs to be broader than that which has traditionally guided Commonwealth policy. Sometimes the best northern development may involve *minimising* development: we need, for example, to preserve areas of natural beauty such as tropical rainforests and islands so that future generations can appreciate and be enriched by them.

Furthermore, it should be remembered that capitalist concepts of northern development do not necessarily appeal to Aboriginal people living on traditional lands in remote areas who are reluctant to move because of family ties. The current Australian economic system advantages those who live in major and regional cities or are willing to move to them for work. How can remote Indigenous groups benefit from northern development while retaining their links to Country? Northern Institute researcher Rolf Gerritsen has argued that 'traditional Aboriginal skills in land and fire management could be augmented by roles in biosecurity and biodiversity protection to create a natural resource management ... economy' across 'remote Australia'.[14] In any case, it is clear that a northern development framework which incorporates consultation with rural, remote and urban Indigenous people will result in more democratic and targeted policy outcomes.

Finally, policymakers need to question the hidden assumption that Northern Australia is a wilderness that needs to be tamed through economic development and population growth. Such policy assumptions serve to devalue the wider aspirations of people who live in the tropics. Our national understanding of the north must encompass more than economic development, it must also incorporate civics, culture and the environment. Commonwealth and state investment in social and cultural infrastructure in the north is needed to create intellectual and creative opportunities for the next generation of northern residents, and to build on the strengths, talents and initiative of local communities. Such a flowering of new ideas and energy would surely benefit the nation as a whole.

CHAPTER 22

How to fix our federation

Carolyn Holbrook

Federation – the moment in 1901 when Australia became a nation – does not loom large in the public imagination. In all the debate about changing Australia Day, you rarely hear people suggest 1 January, the date that the Commonwealth of Australia was created, as an alternative to 26 January. Research done in the lead-up to the centenary of Federation found that 43 per cent of people were unable to explain what the federation meant.[1]

Yet, if nearly half the population did not understand their federal system of government before the COVID-19 pandemic, they would be hard-pressed to maintain their ignorance now.[2] While previous national crises have boosted the Commonwealth, the pandemic has reminded us that the states still possess significant power in our federal system. Indeed, state governments have achieved a prominence they have rarely enjoyed since the earliest years of the federation. 'Gladys' (now former premier), 'Dan' and 'Annastacia', in particular, have become national figures and the subjects, variously, of idolatry and derision. Western Australia's Mark McGowan has enjoyed the most conspicuous political success. The 'rockstar' premier has charmed the Western Australian public with a mix of humour and competence that even inspired a fan-girling comedian to write a country music song about her 'knight in shinin' armour['s] ... hard, hard, hard border'.[3]

The heightened profile of our federal structure as a result of the pandemic offers an opportunity to revisit the urgent matter of its reform. There is a consensus among politicians and experts that the federation is 'broken' and in need of 'a massive overhaul'.[4] The main problem with the federation is fiscal; the way that money is raised and spent. Ideally in a federal system, each level of government raises the revenue necessary to fulfil its functions, as defined by the Constitution. This enhances the incentive to govern efficiently and removes the capacity to blame other levels of government for inadequate services or high taxation.[5] The Australian federation is far from this ideal. We have one of the highest levels of so-called 'vertical fiscal imbalance' in the world. While the Commonwealth raises about 80 per cent of tax revenue, the states spend nearly half the outlay of the entire government sector. It is this imbalance that is responsible for disputes over GST allocation each year, and the lack of accountability and blame-shifting about issues such as funding for schools and hospitals.

The federation, like the Constitution itself, has proved notoriously difficult to reform. Only eight of 44 referendums have succeeded since Federation, and most of those successes have related to technical and procedural issues. Whether from caution, ignorance, or our innate suspicion of the political class, when in doubt, we vote 'No'. Australians' inclination to vote down any proposed change is so great that politicians have pretty much given up holding referendums. The last successful ones were passed back in 1977, and the most recent were the failed republic and constitutional preamble referendums in 1999. In 2013, Tony Abbott trumpeted a federal reform process, which was subsequently quietly shelved when Malcolm Turnbull succeeded him as prime minister in 2015. Scott Morrison's National Cabinet was more of a PR exercise than a meaningful reform. The federation is stuck; unfit for purpose, but unable to be reformed. What is to be done?

Before we can prescribe a solution, we need to diagnose the problem. Apathy lies at the heart of our failure to fix the federation. Australians just don't care enough about the federation – or any aspect of our democratic system, for that matter – to inform themselves about the details of reform proposals. As we shall see, this is a problem with deep historical roots. If policymakers want to fix the federation, first they must make Australians care.

The first Commonwealth Day

Our lack of attachment to the federation can be traced to the decision to establish the new Commonwealth on 1 January 1901. Joseph Chamberlain, the British secretary of state for the colonies, is responsible for the fact that Australia's birthday falls on New Year's Day. Chamberlain was 'captivated of the fitness' of 1 January 1901, the first day of a new century. Edmund Barton, who would soon become Australia's first prime minister, agreed that it 'was a picturesque and appropriate date'.[6] But there were sceptics. The South Australian premier, Frederick Holder, worried that 'the national idea would run a risk of being lost sight of' if federation coincided with New Year's Day. He lobbied for the Queen's proclamation of the Commonwealth to be gazetted on 1 October 1900, so that anniversary could be celebrated as 'Proclamation Day'.[7] Holder received the backing of the New South Wales, Victorian and

Queensland premiers, though Western Australia's John Forrest and Tasmania's Neil Lewis favoured 1 January.[8] The alternative proposal was conveyed by the South Australian governor to the colonial secretary, but nothing came of it.[9]

While Sydney hosted the official ceremony on 1 January 1901, Federation was celebrated enthusiastically in cities and towns around the new nation. Reports of the first 'Commonwealth Day' noted the confluence of the birth of the nation with the dawn of a new century. The date was portentous; it conferred a sense of progress and destiny, which echoed the idealism of the federationists. As the new Commonwealth marked its six-month anniversary on 1 July 1901, Prime Minister Edmund Barton was excited about the prospect of celebrating the one-year milestone in style. Reflecting with satisfaction on the government's achievements to date, Barton predicted that the celebration would 'be on a scale to be remembered'. The *Age* observed 'an evident determination to make 1st January as great a day in Australia as is 4th July in America'.[10]

But Barton's enthusiasm in July 1901 would be belied by his subsequent inaction. By December, newspapers had begun to note the lack of planning for the Commonwealth's first anniversary. Barton countered that he had been preoccupied with 'Commonwealth business' and had been given no opportunity to make arrangements.[11] He also noted that the nation was faced with 'a certain embarrassment of choice' in selecting a date for the anniversary: 'The 1st of January is the anniversary of the actual inauguration, but there are other days, which, like certain sites for the Federal Capital, have equal claims to choice.'[12] Barton listed the alternatives as 1 July – by which he meant 9 July, the anniversary of the date on which Queen Victoria assented to the Constitution bill; 1 May – by which he meant 9 May, the anniversary of the date on which the Commonwealth parliament first sat; and 30 September – actually 19 September – the anniversary of the date on which Queen Victoria's proclamation of the *Constitution Act* appeared in the London *Gazette*. Barton expected that one of those dates would be chosen, but he showed no inclination to do the choosing.

Apart from exchanges of official telegrams, there was no effort to mark the first anniversary of Federation. It was clear that the date of Commonwealth Day worked against its observation. The *Daily Telegraph* reported that Sydneysiders had enjoyed an 'ideal holiday' for the first anniversary of the Commonwealth. The pleasant weather encouraged harbourside picnickers, and crowds thronged to the Randwick races and the Highland Games at the Sydney Cricket Ground. Others kept an eye on the scoreboards about town, posting news of the Ashes test being played in Melbourne. The theatres did big business in the evening. Despite the *Daily Telegraph*'s headline proclaiming 1 January to be 'Commonwealth Day', no formal activities were planned to commemorate the first anniversary of the Commonwealth, and the occasion passed like any other New Year's Day.[13]

The Sydney *Australian Star* anointed 1 January as 'Australia Day: The Birthday of Federation: The First Anniversary'. Its report recalled the inauguration of the Commonwealth as 'a period of abandoned joyousness to Australian people', when 'Sydney was transformed into a wonderland'.[14] Yet, despite the significance of the occasion, the paper thought it was 'rather notable that there has been no effort to more immediately identify the day with its true significance to Australians'.[15] The Sydney *Evening News* cut to the chase when it declared that 1 January was 'out of the running' for a Federal holiday because it fell on New Year's Day. This sentiment was echoed by the *Sydney Morning Herald*, which thought that 1 January 'could hardly be diverted from its present use to form a federal festival'.[16]

The attorney-general, Alfred Deakin, was convinced that 1 January should be observed as Commonwealth Day.[17] But Deakin's parliamentary colleagues were less certain. The postmaster general, Senator Drake, observed that 'a great number of persons desire on New Year's Day to go to sea-side resorts, and that it would not be a convenient day to adopt as Commonwealth Day. It would have no special significance.'[18] Senator Symon favoured 9 July: 'It would be an excellent time of the year, certainly much better than the 1st of January, for the commemoration of a great historical event.'[19] Senator Stewart, however, could not 'understand this rushing up and down the calendar for a day on which to celebrate the proclamation of the establishment of the Commonwealth … We cannot, without stultifying ourselves, depart from the 1st of January.'[20] Senator Glassey agreed that to substitute 1 January for any 'other day would rob the celebration of its charm and effect in the minds of a great number of people'.[21]

The Department of Home Affairs faced similar equivocation when it proposed to build a monument in Corowa to commemorate the 1893 conference at which the idea of an elected constitutional convention originated. Labor members evinced the same unsentimental attitude that had characterised their attitude to Federation itself. The Member for Yarra, Frank Tudor, told parliament that such an expenditure could not be justified given the 'dire distress which exists in the Commonwealth'.[22] Some members thought Corowa was no more worthy of commemoration than other places associated with the federal movement. The Free Trade Member for Wentworth, William McMillan, mocked the parochialism that pervaded federal politics when he proposed that the monument 'should take the form of a wooden Colossus, with one leg planted in Corowa and the other on the other side of the [Murray] river. That would be a very fair settlement of the difficulty ...'[23] Needless to say, the proposal did not advance any further.

Federation gets forgotten

The press continued to question the prime minister about commemoration plans as the second anniversary of Federation approached. Barton made clear his reluctance to fix an alternative anniversary to New Year's Day on the basis that there were already too many public holidays, and to declare another one 'would seriously hamper business'.[24] Nor did Barton propose to take any special steps to mark the milestone: 'If the people feel inclined to celebrate the anniversary, they can do so without the Government taking the initiative.'[25]

The depleted prime minister used the post-Christmas period to enjoy some respite at his home in suburban Sydney, while the governor-general, Lord Tennyson, passed a quiet holiday at Marble Hill, South Australia. 'In the absence of the Governor General', noted the *Age*, 'no official functions were held.'[26] The only official recognition of the second anniversary in Melbourne – the temporary seat of the national parliament – was the flying of the Royal Standard and the Union Jack on the flagstaffs at each end of Parliament House in Spring Street. In a telegram to Barton, Tennyson referred to the early trials of the Commonwealth, principally the dissatisfaction of the smaller states at the loss of customs revenue: 'With patience we will overcome, I have no doubt, all the difficulties necessarily arising at first in our new-born constitution', he wrote.[27] Barton was equally frank in reply: 'I share your confidence that, like other federations, we shall overcome these early difficulties which arise from the necessary assimilation of conditions hitherto widely diverse.'[28]

The general air of apathy about the new Commonwealth was remarked upon by a columnist in Victoria's *Numurkah Leader*, who contrasted the indifference of 1903 with the enthusiasm of 1901:

> He would have been a bold man indeed who in 1901 would have ventured to predict that in two short years the patriotic fervor (we had almost said fever) and imperialistic rejoicings with which the inauguration of the Commonwealth was celebrated would have been practically non-existent.[29]

The Launceston *Examiner* contrasted the general indifference to 1 January with attitudes to 4 July in the United States.[30] The lack of interest could be explained by the widespread hostility towards Federation, the paper claimed; if the referendum were held again, the population would vote 'No'. People had been promised that the costs of government would diminish, only to find it had increased. Such increases were not inherent in the federal system, but due to the 'absence of administrative ability of our rulers'. The prime minister was 'content to sit at the feet and obey the mandates of the Labor Party, and Mr Kingston's administration of the Customs duties has been so overbearing that he is in a continual state of turmoil with the importers'.

If this 'federal extravagance' could be checked, the 'federal spirit' would rise, the paper claimed.[31]

After those sparing and fitful attempts to establish 1 January as Commonwealth Day in the first two years after Federation, discussion of the anniversary disappeared from the parliamentary record. There was no effort to establish the alternatives mooted by Barton as the Commonwealth anniversary. In November 1910, the attorney-general, Billy Hughes, was asked in parliament whether the government had taken any steps towards celebrating the tenth anniversary of the Commonwealth. Hughes replied in the negative.[32] When he was questioned again a few weeks later, Hughes' reply echoed the apathy that had characterised the issue from the start: a celebration had 'not been considered by the Government, but Ministers are willing to consider it, and will be glad to receive any suggestions which the honorable member may have to offer', he said.[33] No action was taken, and the occasion passed without official acknowledgment.

As politicians argued and equivocated about the Federation anniversary, the Australian Natives' Association led a campaign to establish 26 January – the anniversary of the date that the First Fleet arrived in Sydney Cove in 1788 – as the national day. By 1935, Australia Day was celebrated over a long weekend in all the states and territories. Australia Day became more prominent in the period following the bicentenary in 1988, and also more controversial. Meanwhile, Commonwealth Day, the date on which Australia became a nation, was completely forgotten. 1 January reverted to what it had always been: New Year's Day.

The disappearance of Commonwealth Day from the national calendar has had wide-reaching consequences that are still with us today. There is, as historian John Hirst observed, a 'strange gap' between the magnitude of Australia's democratic achievement and our lack of regard for it.[34] By failing to commemorate Federation, our political leaders did not place the keystone in the arch of our civic history. We lost the opportunity to develop a strong attachment to our Constitution and democratic system of government; the kind of attachment that might prompt us to engage with matters of federation reform.

Lessons from Anzac commemoration

It is not too late to ignite public interest in Australian democracy. The success of recent governments in promoting popular attachment to the Anzac legend provides a useful case study in how national mythologies can be bolstered by determined political leadership. The Anzac legend provided Australia with the genesis mythology that Federation failed to do. According to the legend, the nation was born on the shores of Gallipoli during the First World War. The popularity of the Anzac legend has ebbed and flowed since 1915.[35] It flourished initially as a symbol of the Anzacs' fighting skills and their distinctively Australian characteristics – laconic humour, independence of thought and irreverence towards authority. By the late 1950s, the Anzac legend was losing favour as social values changed. As represented in the famous play by Alan Seymour *The One Day of the Year*, the Anzac legend came to be associated with chauvinism, bigotry and an excessive fondness for beer. The Vietnam War and second wave feminism exacerbated the growing impression that Anzac commemoration was indistinguishable from the glorification of war.

The Anzac legend defied predictions of its imminent demise. During the 1970s and 1980s, an historical interest in the First World War began percolating among descendants of the soldiers, social historians and filmmakers. This kinder and gentler version placed less emphasis on the outdated values of the diggers, and more on their mateship and suffering. By the late 1980s, astute politicians sensed that the tide of public sentiment had turned. Prime Minister Bob Hawke accompanied a group of elderly diggers to Gallipoli for the 75th anniversary of the landing in 1990. The success of this trip ushered in the era of political patronage of Anzac commemoration, wherein the prime minister has been elevated to the position of 'commemorator-in-chief'.[36]

While government did not initiate the Anzac revival, it has dedicated massive funding and resources, lubricated by generous applications of rhetoric. Australia far outspent *all* other nations in commemorating the centenary of the First World War, with a budget of more than $550 million.[37] Government profligacy has continued beyond the centenary. The Coalition allocated $498 million in the 2019 budget to the Australian War Memorial for the creation of major new exhibition spaces related to the Iraq and Afghanistan wars.

Lessons from history:
Move over Anzac, we need a democratic legend

There is a lesson for policymakers wanting to reform the federation from the government's billion-dollar Anzac bonanza. Government cannot conjure sentiment where none exists, nor dam a wellspring of popular feeling – witness Paul Keating's failed attempt in the 1990s to reorient the Anzac legend from

Gallipoli to the Pacific. But the vast financial, institutional and rhetorical resources of the state *did* transform the grassroots revival of interest in the First World War during the 1970s and 1980s into Anzac 2.0, the most potent and pervasive mythology of Australian nationhood. Based on the example of Anzac, it seems likely that, with concerted effort, government could rouse us from our civic indolence with a large-scale and cleverly crafted public education campaign.

There are more lessons to be taken from Anzac. As I have argued in previous work, the popularity of the Anzac legend derives from its capacity to evoke emotion. Anzac commemoration is an *experience* with many of the characteristics of religious ritual – it is not a rational engagement with the history of the First World War.[38] Sceptics will counter that the mythmaker has poorer materials with which to work in the Federation story, that students find the violence and tragedy of the First World War fascinating but are uninspired by the greybeards of Federation.[39] And yet, research also suggests that young Australians are eager for more knowledge to enable them to participate in and contribute to civic society.[40] They need to be shown how their concerns relate to reform of the Constitution.

Our political leaders must build a new civic mythology around the history and concept of Australian democracy. There is enough celebratory grist in our civic history to please even a conservative education minister seeking to renew the culture wars. Australia pioneered government-provided ballot papers and was early to give the vote and right to stand for parliament to (non-Indigenous) women. Unlike other Western democracies, we have preferential voting and make voting compulsory. We vote on Saturdays, not on weekdays like in the United Kingdom and the United States. Australia avoids the election gaming and voter suppression of the United States because our electoral system is overseen by non-partisan bureaucrats.

In the face of the assault on democracy in the United States by Donald Trump and his supporters, culminating in the storming of the Capitol Building on 6 January 2021, the value of Australia's prosaic democratic rituals has been underlined. A government that wants genuinely to reform the federation needs to finish the work of the founders by sponsoring a mythology of Australian democracy that excites and motivates the Australian public. Government must then think imaginatively about how the often-technical issues raised by Australian federalism can be refracted through the democratic legend, in order to engage and motivate Australians. In her advocacy for federation reform, the constitutional lawyer Cheryl Saunders has argued that it must follow the fault lines of democratic representation. Reform must start, not with bureaucrats and bureaucratic processes, but with 'the people who give legitimacy to the government and in turn are owed accountability'.[41] It must demonstrate how reform will benefit citizens through better services in health, education, aged care and other vital areas.

In failing to ensure that a civic tradition was tamped into the Australian imagination, the founders did the nation a disservice. They designed a state-of-the-art constitutional house, then forgot to leave the keys. But in carping at Joseph Chamberlain's failure to troubleshoot 1 January and Barton's lassitude, we also should remember that they bequeathed a dynamic constitutional structure that they expected future generations to maintain. How can we better fulfil that expectation? Imagine a national government that stops channelling hundreds of millions of dollars into the already bloated Anzac industry but invests instead in building a mythology of Australian democracy. The first Commonwealth elections were held on 29–30 March 1901. Picture a government that picked one of those dates as the new Australia Day and symbolised its commitment to democratic renewal by crowning a new national icon – the democracy sausage, served with onions, tomato sauce and a generous squirt of laconic humour.

CONCLUSION
The history of the future

Carolyn Holbrook, Lyndon Megarrity
and David Lowe

Historians are experienced time travellers. They have shown that we orient ourselves in the world by building narratives that frame meaning, that paint human endeavours on vibrant canvases, that suggest bigger stories in which we come and go. They also remind us that what might, at first glance, appear to be unquestionable interpretive themes, such as 'progress' or 'development', are in fact highly specific to circumstances and often overshadow other important concepts and behaviours we are prone to forget. To not question these apparently immovable paradigms is to invite only narrow possibilities for change. And to not question also risks what some in this collection have reminded us are the dangers of 'path dependency'. It is easier and usually cheaper in the short term to continue down paths that are well marked, despite the social, economic and emotional costs that may already be evident to thoughtful observers.

The power of good historical writing is something we believe in firmly and hold dear. Yet, right now, this is not enough. Globally, nationally and locally, 'wicked problems' defy solution: environmental degradation, the decline of neoliberalism without a clear public policy model to take its place, the frequently tenuous link between public policy and the values of citizens, the dangerous pursuit of endless economic growth on a planet of finite resources, to name just a few of our contemporary crises. The question needs to be asked: what can historians do to help society understand and address the challenges of the here and now?

The contributors to *Lessons from History* have responded in different ways. They include early, mid-career and senior historians with a healthy diversity of personal backgrounds, opinions and approaches to the discipline of history. Nevertheless, several recurring themes emerge. One is the importance of history as a means of ensuring that officials are accountable to the people they serve. The use, misuse, or inadequate use of history by politicians is something that concerns contributors. Being unscrupulous with history, or claiming that no precedent exists for current circumstances, are short cuts open to politicians wanting to be less accountable.

A growing sense of necessary activism – for historians to mobilise better than previously, in order to address more squarely the challenges of our time – is present, either directly or indirectly, in most of the works here. Authors make recommendations that go both to current policy settings and the process of policy debate and formation. Recommending policy has not been a traditional part of the academic historian's toolkit, but the chapters here show that it can be added, and in ways that promote the public good.

How historians engage better with the policy process is a work in progress – and we hope that this book is evidence of progress. Historians should go further and down new roads connected to policy. British historian Alix Green has argued that historians need to relax their protection of their disciplinary boundaries, and find ways to engage in 'collective puzzling' with policymakers.[1] Can this occur more systematically than policymakers joining academic workshops or guest historians appearing at departmental briefings? This book does not offer a definitive answer to the question of whether historians are better to recommend to, or partner with, policymakers, but it seeks to keep the question to the fore in how we work.

Indeed, at its most basic, the chapters here demonstrate the virtues of writing to be read by a wider public. Writing rigorous work for publication in specialist outlets is a focus which historians can retain, but they can also work on distillations and summaries of their research that reach an interested public. Is there time to do both? The overwhelmingly positive responses we had when we approached contributors to this book suggests that academics are determined to make the time. Given the state we are in, with some of the biggest policy challenges we have ever faced in front of us, and with the humanities subject to undermining efforts by recent governments around the world, perhaps it was not surprising that the contributors here relished the chance to join.

Making time, and facilitating opportunities for exchanges and/or collaborations between historians and policymakers goes both ways. The decline in policy capacity in the public service in recent decades has been well documented, as has the increasing and expensive reliance on consultancy firms for policy advice. Government needs to rebuild its inhouse capacity for long-term policy development and optimise mechanisms through which the public service draws on the academy. Instead of starving the tertiary sector of funding and forcing universities to seek money in ways that distort their civic purpose, government could resource them adequately. Imagine the benefits if government worked collaboratively with universities, rather than acted punitively, to encourage academics to more explicitly link their research to the public good.

Despite the rise of disciplines that cater more directly to contemporary tastes, history has endured, because thinking about the past is a fundamental and profound exercise. *Lessons from History* adds to a chorus of literature demonstrating our failure to deal with a range of formidable problems. As some of the fundamental assumptions of the Western way of life come under question, so must the sources of knowledge that have justified and sustained them. We urge policymakers to turn to history, not least for its versatility, its embrace of uncertainty and its fundamental humanity. Like a soft but insistent bass, history thrums the rhythm of human experience. Now, in the midst of a global pandemic and climate crisis, historians must play their role in writing the history of the future. And policymakers must listen.

Acknowledgments

As we put the finishing touches to this manuscript, there is war in Europe, and freakishly high flood levels have again devastated parts of Queensland and New South Wales. Dozens of people continue to die from COVID-19 each week in Australia, but the pandemic has slipped from the headlines. The sense of crisis and policy paralysis that motivated us to compile this volume shows no signs of abating.

Lessons from History extends the work of Australian Policy and History; a network that connects historians with politicians, policymakers, journalists and the wider public. The book arose partly from a conference and workshops sponsored by Australian Policy and History and the Contemporary Histories Research Group at Deakin University in 2019–21. We thank Deakin University for continuing to support historical research that informs and enriches.

The editors would like to thank all our contributors for their hard work and enthusiasm for the project. We could not have done it without you! We would also like to acknowledge the great support of the NewSouth Publishing team, especially Elspeth Menzies and Paul O'Beirne. Thank you to our copy editor Briony Neilson for working so closely with us to get the manuscript in tip-top shape.

Carolyn Holbrook thanks her colleagues in the Contemporary Histories Research Group at Deakin University, as well as Anthony Forsyth, Catherine Forsyth and Sarah Forsyth. Thank you also to Jodie Hamilton and Kerry Humphries for the invaluable wi-fi hot-spotting in Lennox Head during

Acknowledgments

the final stages of copyediting. Lyndon Megarrity would like to thank L.P. Megarrity, R.G. Megarrity, Rod Sullivan and Frank Bongiorno. David Lowe thanks his colleagues in the Contemporary Histories Research Group at Deakin, and Andrea Shimmen, Ben Lowe and Tristan Lowe.

Stuart Macintyre was planning to contribute a chapter to this volume, but had to withdraw due to the ill-health that took his life in November 2021. Stuart was the emblematic 'citizen historian'. His historical writing was deeply rooted in questions about the contemporary world, and how we could make it better. We dedicate this volume to Stuart's memory.

Notes

Introduction: Seeing the world *with* the past. A call to historians and policymakers

1   Stephen Stoll, *Ramp Hollow: The Ordeal of Appalachia*, Hill and Wang, New York, 2017, p. 31.
2   Frank Bongiorno, 'The Citizen Historian, Stuart Macintyre, 1947–2021', *Inside Story*, 1 December 2021, <www.insidestory.org.au/the-citizen-historian/>, accessed 14 December 2021.

1   Writing the history of the future

1   Francis Bacon, 'Of Studies', in his *Essays* (1597), Everyman edition, Dent and Sons, London, 1906, p. 151.
2   Jo Guldi and David Armitage, *The History Manifesto*, Cambridge University Press, Cambridge, 2014, p. 13.
3   Deborah Cohen and Peter Mandler, 'AHR Exchange: *The History Manifesto*: A critique', *American Historical Review*, vol. 120, no. 2, 2015, pp. 530–42; Marc Parry, 'Historians attack the data and ethics of colleagues' manifesto', *The Chronicle of Higher Education*, 17 April 2015. For a range of responses to *The History Manifesto*, see <www.cambridge.org/core/services/aop-file-manager/file/5788a54071ffd65665313b7a/The-History-Manifesto-Media.pdf>, accessed 14 January 2022.
4   Karen Barlow, 'Scott Morrison defends minister Greg Hunt and Pfizer deal, but keeps key details in doubt', *Canberra Times*, 9 September 2021.
5   George Santayana, *The Life of Reason: The Phases of Human Progress*, Charles Scribner's Sons, New York, 1955.
6   Lucy Delap, Simon Szreter and Paul Warde, 'History & Policy: A decade of bridge-building in the United Kingdom', *Scandia*, vol. 80, no. 1, 2014, pp. 97–118.
7   Michael Howard, *The Lessons of History*, Oxford University Press, Oxford, 1989, pp. 5, 195.
8   Eric Hobsbawm, *The Age of Extremes: The short twentieth century*, Abacus, London 1994, p. 585.
9   Eric Hobsbawm, 'Looking Forwards: History and the future', (1981), in his *On History*, Weidenfelt and Nicholson, London, 1997, pp. 37–55.
10 Richard Neustadt and Ernest May, *Thinking in Time: The uses of history for decision-makers*, Free Press, New York, 1986.
11 Peter Hall, *Great Planning Disasters*, Penguin, Harmondsworth, 1980.
12 Graeme Davison, 'History on the Witness Stand: Interrogating the past', in Iain McCalman and Ann McGrath (eds), *Proof and Truth: The humanist as expert*, Australian Academy of the Humanities, Canberra, 2003, pp. 53–67.

13. Peter Berger and Thomas Luckmann, *The Social Construction of Reality*, Doubleday, New York, 1967, p. 5.
14. Tom Griffiths, 'History, Fiction and Truth-telling', Address to History Teachers' Association of Victoria Conference, July 2018, p. 13. I am grateful to Tom Griffiths for permission to quote from this unpublished address.
15. Richard Evans, *In Defence of History*, Granta Books, London, 1997, pp. 224–52.
16. See <www.honesthistory.net.au/wp>, accessed 14 January 2022.
17. Bain Attwood, *Telling the Truth about Aboriginal History*, Allen & Unwin, Sydney, 2005; Henry Reynolds, *Truth-Telling: History, sovereignty and the Uluru Statement*, NewSouth, Sydney, 2021.
18. First Nations National Constitutional Convention & Central Land Council (Australia), *Uluru: Statement from the Heart*, 2017, <www.nla.gov.au/nla.obj-484035616>, accessed 14 February 2022.
19. Henry Reynolds, *The Law of the Land*, Penguin Books, Melbourne, 1987, pp. 81–103.
20. Graeme Davison, *The Use and Abuse of Australian History*, Allen & Unwin, Sydney, 2000, pp. 221–37.
21. Hugh Stretton, *Selected Writings*, edited by Graeme Davison, LaTrobe University/Black Inc., Melbourne, 2018, pp. ix–xxvii. See also Graeme Davison, *City Dreamers: The urban imagination in Australia*, NewSouth, Sydney, 2016, pp. 195–216.
22. Stretton, Application for Rhodes Scholarship 1945 in Rhodes Scholarship Selection Committee Papers, University of Melbourne Archives.
23. Hugh Stretton, 'A Use for History', in Stretton, *Selected Writings*, pp. 211–14.
24. Hugh Stretton, *Political Essays*, Georgian House, Melbourne, 1987, p. 251.
25. Hugh Stretton, *Capitalism, Socialism and the Environment*, Cambridge University Press, Cambridge, 1976, p. 15.
26. Griffiths, 'History, Fiction and Truth-telling', p. 16.
27. Lawrence Wright, *The Plague Year: America in the time of Covid*, Allen Lane, London, 2021, pp. 49–51, 55–56; and see Markel et al., *The Influenza Encyclopedia*, <www.influenzaarchive.org/about.html>, accessed 14 February 2022.
28. Howard Markel, 'History Won't Help Us Now', *Atlantic*, 19 August 2021, <www.theatlantic.com/ideas/archive/2021/08/1918-influenza-pandemic-history-coronavirus/619801/>, accessed 14 February 2022.
29. Emma Dawson and Janet McCalman (eds), *What Next? Reconstructing Australia after COVID-19*, Melbourne University Press, Melbourne, 2020, p. 19.
30. Another stimulating example, which came too late for me to consider here, is Hilary Cooper and Simon Szreter, *After the Virus: Lessons from the past for a better future*, Cambridge University Press, Cambridge, 2021.

2 Learning the right lessons? Two policy stories

1. Stuart Macintyre, 'The Writing of Australian History', in D.H. Borchardt (ed.), *Australians: A guide to sources*, Fairfax, Syme & Weldon Associates, Sydney, 1987, p. 8.
2. R.M. Crawford, *'A Bit of a Rebel': The life and work of George Arnold Wood*, Sydney University Press, Sydney, 1975; Andrew G. Bonnell, 'Stephen Roberts as a Commentator on Fascism and the Road to War in Europe', *History Australia*, vol. 11, no. 3, 2014, pp. 9–30.
3. Laura Tingle, 'Political Amnesia: How we forgot how to govern', *Quarterly Essay*, no. 60, 2015.
4. Geoffrey Blainey, *The Causes of War*, Macmillan, London, 1973, chapter 2.
5. Paul Kelly, *The End of Certainty: The story of the 1980s*, Allen & Unwin, Sydney, 1992, chapter 1.
6. John Rickard, *H.B. Higgins: The rebel as judge*, George Allen & Unwin, Sydney, 1984, pp. 186–87.
7. Frank Bongiorno, 'Whatever Happened to Free Trade Liberalism?', in Paul Strangio and Nick Dyrenfurth (eds), *Confusion: The making of the Australian two-party political system*, Melbourne University Press, Melbourne, 2009, pp. 249–74.
8. Ian W. McLean, *Why Australia Prospered: The shifting sources of economic growth*, Princeton University Press, Princeton and Oxford, 2013, chapters 3–6.
9. N.G. Butlin, A. Barnard and J.J. Pincus, *Government and Capitalism: Public and private choice in twentieth-century Australia*, George Allen & Unwin, Sydney, 1982, chapter 4; David Merrett and Simon Ville, 'Tariffs, Subsidies, and Profits: A re-assessment of structural change in Australia 1901–39', *Australian Economic History Review*, vol. 51, no. 1, 2011, pp. 46–70; Francis G. Castles, *The Working Class and Welfare: Reflections on the political development of the welfare state in Australia and New Zealand, 1890–1980*, Allen & Unwin in association with Port Nicholson Press, Wellington and Sydney, 1985.
10. McLean, *Why Australia Prospered*, p. 151; C.B. Schedvin, *Australia and the Great Depression: A study of economic development and policy in the 1920s and 1930s*, Sydney University Press, Sydney, 1970, pp. 141–45.
11. George Megalogenis, *The Longest Decade*, Scribe, Melbourne, 2006; Paul Kelly, *The March of Patriots: The struggle for modern Australia*, Melbourne University Press, Melbourne, 2009.
12. James Walter and Carolyn Holbrook, 'Policy Narratives in Historical Transition: A case study in contemporary history', *Australian Historical Studies*, vol. 49, no. 2, 2018, p. 234.
13. Frank Bongiorno, *The Eighties: The decade that transformed Australia*, Black Inc., Melbourne, 2015.
14. Kevin Rudd, 'The Global Financial Crisis', *Monthly*, February 2009, <www.themonthly.com.au/issue/2009/february/1319602475/kevin-rudd/global-financial-crisis/>, accessed 14 January 2022.

15 Kerry O'Brien, *Keating*, Allen & Unwin, Sydney, 2015, p. 318.
16 McLean, *Why Australia Prospered*, p. 223.
17 Margaret Macmillan, *Dangerous Games: The uses and abuses of history*, Modern Library, New York, 2009, p. 159.
18 Macmillan, *Dangerous Games*, pp. 162–63.
19 Macmillan, *Dangerous Games*, p. 164.
20 Alexander Downer, 'Earle Page Politics Speech', Earle Page College, University of New England, Armidale, 17 May 2005, <www.australianpolitics.com/2005/05/17/alexander-downer-earle-page-politics-speech.html>, accessed 14 January 2022.
21 Christopher Waters, *Australia and Appeasement: Imperial foreign policy and the origins of World War II*, I.B. Taurus, London and New York, 2012, pp. 2, 80, 130.
22 John Edwards, *John Curtin's War*, vol. 1, Viking, Melbourne, 2017, pp. 132–35, 246–49.

3 Historians: Bridging the divide with policymakers

1 Stuart Macintyre and Anna Clark, *The History Wars*, Melbourne University Press, Melbourne, 2003.
2 John Howard, *The Menzies Era: The years that shaped modern Australia*, HarperCollins, Sydney, 2014; David Kemp, *A Liberal State: How Australians chose liberalism over socialism, 1926–1966*, Melbourne University Press, Melbourne, 2020.
3 Steven Kennedy, 'Australia's Response to the Global Financial Crisis', Australian Government/The Treasury, Canberra, 24 June 2009, <www.treasury.gov.au/speech/australias-response-to-the-global-financial-crisis>, accessed 14 January 2022; Steven Kennedy, Secretary to the Treasury, 'Emerging from the Crisis: Recovery and reform', Address to the Australian Business Economists, Canberra: Australian Government/The Treasury, 18 May 2021 <www.treasury.gov.au/speech/address-australian-business-economists>, accessed 14 January 2022.
4 Harold Lasswell, *Who Gets What, When, How?*, Whittlesey House, New York, 1936.
5 Matthew Laing, *Scientists and Policy Influence: A literature review*, CRC for Water Sensitive Cities, Melbourne, 2015, pp. 47–48.
6 James Button, *Speechless: A year in my father's business*, Melbourne University Press, Melbourne, 2012; Dennis Glover, *An Economy is Not a Society: Winners and losers in the new Australia*, Black Inc., Melbourne, 2015.
7 Miriam Dixson, *The Real Matilda: Woman and identity in Australia 1788–1975*, Penguin, Melbourne, 1976; Kay Daniels and Mary Murnane, *Uphill All the Way: A documentary history of women in Australia*, University of Queensland Press, Brisbane, 1980; Anne Summers, *Damned Whores and God's Police*, Penguin, Melbourne, 1975; Beverley Kingston, *My Wife, My Daughter and Poor Mary Ann*, Thomas Nelson, Melbourne, 1975.

8   Marian Sawer, *Femocrats and Ecorats: Women's policy machinery in Australia, Canada and New Zealand*, Geneva: UNRISD Occasional Paper, No. 6, United Nations, 1996.
9   Committee to Review Australian Studies in Tertiary Education, *Windows onto Worlds: Studying Australia at tertiary level*, AGPS, Canberra, 1987.
10 Jill Roe, 'Kay Daniels: 1941–2001', *Australian Historical Studies*, vol. 33, no. 119, 2002, pp. 186–89.
11 Peter Shergold, *Report of the Task Group on Emissions Trading*, Australian Government, Prime Ministerial Task Group on Emissions Trading, Canberra, 2007.
12 See Carolyn Holbrook, 'Redesigning Collaborative Governance for Refugee Resettlement Services', *Australian Journal of Political Science*, vol. 55, no. 1, 2020, pp. 86–97; Doug Dingwall, 'Peter Shergold's Refugee Role Takes Him Back to Beginnings', *Canberra Times*, 19 October 2020, <www.canberratimes.com.au/story/6917108/peter-shergolds-refugee-role-takes-him-back-to-beginnings/>, accessed 14 January 2022.
13 Don Watson, *Recollections of a Bleeding Heart: A portrait of Paul Keating PM*, Random House, Sydney, 2002.
14 Kerry O'Brien, *Keating*, Allen & Unwin, Sydney, 2016, pp. 540–41; and see Paul Ryder and Jonathan Foye, 'Whose Speech Is It Anyway? Ownership, authorship, and the Redfern Address', *M/C Journal*, vol. 20, no. 5, 2017, <www.doi.org/10.5204/mcj.1228>.
15 Research such as that manifest in Don Watson, *Caledonia Australis: Scottish Highlanders on the frontier of Australia*, Collins, Sydney, 1984.
16 Watson remains a prolific contributor to public debate, much of his work drawing historical lessons; see his *The Bush: Travels in the heart of Australia*, Hamish Hamilton, Melbourne, 2014.
17 Academy of Social Sciences in Australia (ASSA), *The Social Sciences Shape the Nation*, ASSA, Canberra, 2017; Senate Legal and Constitutional Affairs Reference Committee, 'Nationhood, National Identity and Democracy', public round table conducted 7 February 2020, <www.parlinfo.aph.gov.au/parlInfo/search/display/display.w3p;query=Id%3A"committees%2Fcommsen%2F30c8ad35-bd2a-4ec8-a3ea-04f3f2859396%2F0000>, accessed 14 January 2022.
18 See Laing, *Scientists and Policy Influence*, p. 41.
19 Cited in Stuart Macintyre, 'An Expert's Confession', *Australian Quarterly*, Spring, 1995.
20 Stuart Macintyre, *Rethinking Australian Citizenship*, Academy of the Social Sciences in Australia, Canberra, 1992.
21 See Civics Expert Group, *Whereas the People: Civics and Citizenship Education*, AGPS, Canberra, 1994; Macintyre, 'An Expert's Confession'.
22 Kemp's *A Liberal State* is the fourth volume in his intended five-volume history.
23 See Gordon Crane, 'The Civics Push', *Education Links*, no. 56–57, 1998, pp. 13–16.

24 John Hirst, *Australia's Democracy: A short history*, Allen & Unwin, Sydney, 2002; John Hirst, *The Sentimental Nation: The making of the Australian Commonwealth*, Oxford University Press, Melbourne, 2000.
25 For instance, Brian Galligan and John Chesterman, *Defining Australian Citizenship*, Melbourne University Publishing, Melbourne, 1999; John Chesterman, *Citizens Without Rights: Aborigines and Australian citizenship*, Cambridge University Press, Melbourne, 1997; James Walter and Margaret MacLeod, *The Citizens' Bargain*, UNSW Press, Sydney, 2002.
26 Senate Legal and Constitutional Affairs Reference Committee, 'Nationhood, National Identity and Democracy'.
27 See James Walter, 'Bureaucracy and Democracy in the American Century: A.F. Davies on administration and "The Knowledgeable Society"', *Australian Journal of Public Administration*, vol. 58, no. 1, 1999, pp. 23–32.
28 On punctuated equilibrium, see J.L. True, Bryan D. Jones and Frank R. Baumgartner, 'Punctuated-Equilibrium Theory', in Paul Sabatier (ed.), *Theories of the Policy Process* (2nd ed.), Westview Press, Boulder, CO, 2006, pp. 155–87.
29 On policy windows, see John Kingdon, *Agendas, Alternatives, and Public Policies* (2nd ed.), HarperCollins, New York, 1995.
30 Ross Gittins, 'The Era of Neoliberalism is Ending and Reversing', blogpost, 19 July 2017, <www.rossgittins.com/2017/07/the-era-of-neoliberalism-is-ending-and.html>, accessed 14 January 2022.
31 Larry Elliott, 'The Pandemic-Induced Global Slump is Just Part of a 20-year Financial Crisis', *Guardian Australia*, 26 August 2021, <www.theguardian.com/commentisfree/2021/aug/25/pandemic-global-slump-20-year-financial-crisis>, accessed 14 January 2022.
32 Emma Dawson and Janet McCalman, *What Happens Next? Reconstructing Australia after COVID-19*, Melbourne University Press, Melbourne, 2020.
33 See <www.naa.gov.au/about-us/tune-review#scope-of-review>, accessed 14 January 2022.
34 On advocacy coalitions, see Paul Sabatier and Christopher Weible, 'Advocacy Coalition Frameworks', in Sabatier (ed.), *Theories of the Policy Process*.
35 Senator the Hon Michaelia Cash, '$67.7 Million to boost National Archives', Media release, Australian Government, Attorney-General's Department, 1 July 2021, <www.ministers.ag.gov.au/media-centre/67-million-boost-national-archives-01-07-2021>, accessed 18 February 2022.
36 Henry Reynolds, *The Other Side of the Frontier: Aboriginal resistance to the European invasion of Australia*, Penguin, Melbourne, 1982, has been notably influential. Originally published in 1981 by James Cook University.
37 Richard H. Bartlett, *The Mabo Decision and the Full Text of the Decision in Mabo and Others v. State of Queensland*, Butterworths, Sydney, 1993. Murray Goot and Tim Rowse, *Divided Nation? Indigenous Affairs and the imagined public*, Melbourne University Publishing, Melbourne, 2007.
38 Lyndall Ryan, *The Aboriginal Tasmanians*, University of Queensland Press, Brisbane, 1981.

39 See, for example, Keith Windschuttle *The Fabrication of Aboriginal History, Vol. One, Van Diemen's Land 1803–1847*, Macleay Press, Sydney, 2002, chapter 5.
40 Paul Daley summarises key works: 'As the toll of Australia's frontier brutality keeps climbing, truth telling is long overdue', *Guardian Australia*, 4 March 2019, <www.theguardian.com/australia-news/2019/mar/04/as-the-toll-of-australias-frontier-brutality-keeps-climbing-truth-telling-is-long-overdue>, accessed 14 January 2022.
41 See the Colonial Frontier Massacres in Australia 1788–1930 website, <www.c21ch.newcastle.edu.au/colonialmassacres/introduction.php>, accessed 14 January 2022; *Guardian Australia*, 18 November 2019, <www.theguardian.com/australia-news/ng-interactive/2019/mar/04/massacre-map-australia-the-killing-times-frontier-wars>, accessed 14 January 2022; Ceridwen Dovey, 'The Mapping of Massacres', *The New Yorker*, 6 December 2017, <www.newyorker.com/culture/culture-desk/mapping-massacres>, accessed 14 January 2022.
42 For instance, Peter Read, *Haunted Earth*, UNSW Press, Sydney, 2003; Tim Rowse, *Indigenous and other Australians since 1901*, UNSW Press, Sydney, 2017.
43 Grace Karskens, *Colony: A history of early Sydney*, Allen & Unwin, Sydney, 2009; Grace Karskens, *People of the River: Lost worlds of early Australia*, Allen & Unwin, Sydney, 2020. On policy action and 'webs of meaning', that is, social facts constituted by the meaning actors give to them, see Mark Bevir and R.A.W. Rhodes, 'Interpretation and Its Others', *Australian Journal of Political Science*, vol. 40, no. 2, 2005, pp. 169–87.
44 See <www.prosecutionproject.griffith.edu.au/about/the-research-project/>, accessed 14 January 2022.
45 Mark Finnane, 'What Counts? Essays from the Prosecution Project', *Australian Historical Studies*, vol. 51, no. 3, 2020, pp. 245–49.
46 See <www.prosecutionproject.griffith.edu.au/publications/>, accessed 14 January 2022.
47 Finnane, 'What Counts?', p. 246.
48 See Laing, *Scientists and Policy Influence*.

4 Making time for history: Climate change and detoxing from progress

1 Intergovernmental Panel on Climate Change, *Special Report: Global Warming of 1.5°C*, 2018, <www.ipcc.ch/2018/10/08/summary-for-policymakers-of-ipcc-special-report-on-global-warming-of-1-5c-approved-by-governments/>, accessed 11 August 2021.
2 Lisa Freidman, 'What is the Green New Deal?', *New York Times*, 21 February 2019; Emma Foehringer Merchant, 'Should We Respond to Climate Change Like We Did for WWII?', *New Republic*, 12 May 2016.
3 Cameron Muir, Kirsten Wehner and Jenny Newell (eds), *Living with the Anthropocene*, NewSouth, Sydney, 2020.

4   Extinction Rebellion Australia, <www.ausrebellion.earth/what-is-xr>, accessed 11 August 2021; Erica Chenoweth and Maria J. Stephan, *Why Civil Resistance Works*, Columbia University Press, New York, 2011.
5   Greta Thunberg, 'I have a dream that the time for fairytales is over', *Independent*, 20 September 2019, <www.independent.co.uk/voices/greta-thunberg-congress-speech-climate-change-crisis-dream-a9112151.html>, accessed 11 August 2021.
6   Paul Kramer, 'Bringing in the Externalities: Historians, time work and history's boundaries', *History Australia*, vol. 17, no. 2, 2020, p. 293.
7   Samia Khatun in 'What You Look For is What You Find', Archive Fever podcast, 2021, <www.archivefeverpod.com/s3ep08>, accessed 11 August 2021.
8   Dipesh Chakrabarty, *Provincializing Europe*, Princeton University Press, Princeton, 2000, p. 250.
9   Khatun, 'What You Look For is What You Find'.
10 Reinhart Koselleck, *Futures Past*, Columbia University Press, New York, 2004, p. 267.
11 Koselleck, *Futures Past*, p. 266.
12 Priya Satia, *Time's Monster*, Allen Lane, London, 2020.
13 Chakrabarty, *Provincializing Europe*, p. 8.
14 Satia, *Time's Monster*, p. 6.
15 Satia, *Time's Monster*, p. 261.
16 Samia Khatun, *Australianama*, Hurst & Company, London, 2018, p. 5.
17 Catherine Hall, *Macaulay and Son*, Yale University Press, New Haven, 2012.
18 Hall, *Macaulay and Son*, p. xv.
19 Satia, *Time's Monster*, pp. 264–71.
20 Anna Tsing, *The Mushroom at the End of the World*, Princeton University Press, Princeton, 2015, p. 20.
21 Katie Holmes, 'Generation Covid: Crafting History and Collective Memory', *Griffith Review*, no. 71, 2021, <www.griffithreview.com/articles/generation-covid>, accessed 11 August 2021; Tony Birch, 'Having Gone, I Will Come Back', in Muir, Wehner and Newell (eds), *Living with the Anthropocene*, p. 27.
22 Amitav Ghosh, *The Great Derangement*, University of Chicago Press, Chicago, 2016, p. 79.
23 Joëlle Gergis, 'The Great Unravelling', in Sophie Cunningham (ed.), *Fire, Flood, Plague*, Vintage, Sydney, 2020, p. 46.
24 Paul Kramer, 'History in a Time of Crisis', *Chronicle of Higher Education*, 19 February 2017, <www.chronicle.com/article/History-in-a-Time-of-Crisis/239208>, accessed 11 August 2021.
25 Rebecca Solnit, *Whose Story is This?*, Granta, London, 2019, p. 159.
26 Ursula K. Le Guin, 'Books aren't just commodities', *Guardian*, 21 November 2014, <www.theguardian.com/books/2014/nov/20/ursula-k-le-guin-national-book-awards-speech>, accessed 11 August 2021.

27 Satia, *Time's Monster*, p. 289.
28 Yves Rees and Ben Huf, 'Training Historians in Urgent Times', *History Australia*, vol. 17, no. 2, 2020, p. 275.
29 Rebecca Solnit, *Hope in the Dark*, Haymarket Books, Chicago, 2016, pp. 7, 26.
30 Speth quoted in Christine Wamsler, 'Contemplative Sustainable Futures', in Walter Leal Filho and Adriana Consorte McCrea (eds), *Sustainability and the Humanities*, Springer, Cham, 2019, p. 360.
31 Khatun, 'What You Look For is What You Find'.
32 Audre Lorde, *Sister Outsider*, Crossing Press, Trumansburg, 1984, p. 112.
33 Tyson Yunkaporta, *Sand Talk*, Text, Melbourne, 2019, p. 88.
34 Margo Neale and Lynne Kelly, *Songlines*, Thames & Hudson, Melbourne, 2020, p. 101.
35 Yunkaporta, *Sand Talk*, p. 57.
36 Satia, *Time's Monster*, p. 294.
37 Fiona Harvey, 'Major climate changes inevitable and irreversible', *Guardian*, 9 August 2021, <www.theguardian.com/science/2021/aug/09/humans-have-caused-unprecedented-and-irreversible-change-to-climate-scientists-warn>, accessed 11 August 2021.

5 Urban water policy in a drying continent

This chapter is based on research funded by the Australian Research Council (ARC DP180100807)

1 Commonwealth of Australia, 'National Water Reform', *Productivity Commission Inquiry Report*, no. 87, 19 December 2017, pp. 15–16.
2 Margaret Cook et al., *Cities in a Sunburnt Country: Water and the making of urban Australia*, Cambridge University Press, Cambridge, 2022.
3 Margaret Levi, 'A Model, a Method and a Map: Rational choice in comparative and historical analysis', in A.I. Lichbach and A.S. Zuckerman (eds), *Comparative Politics: Rationality, Culture and Structure*, Cambridge University Press, Cambridge, 1997, p. 28.
4 *Third Annual Report of the Board of Water Supply and Sewerage*, NSW, 1891, Appendix 7; 102nd Annual Report, Water Board, NSW, p. 88.
5 Andrea Gaynor, 'Lawnscaping Perth: Water supply, gardens, and scarcity, 1890–1925', *Journal of Urban History*, vol. 46, 2020, pp. 63–78.
6 F.L. Trelease, 'Policies for Water Law: Property rights, economic forces and public regulation', *Natural Resources Journal*, vol. 5, 1865, pp. 1–48; W. Musgrave, 'The Political Economy of Resource Use: Water', in J.A. Sinden (ed.), *The Natural Resources of Australia. Prospects and problems for development*, Angus and Robertson, Sydney, 1974; Ruth Morgan, *Running Out? Water in Western Australia*, University of Western Australia Press, Perth, 2015, pp. 104, 117–18.
7 In 2011 the Productivity Commission noted that while some of the desalination infrastructure was justified, other projects could have been

deferred, constructed on a smaller scale, or replaced with investment in lower cost sources of water, including recycled water. Commonwealth of Australia, 'Australia's Urban Water Sector', *Productivity Commission Inquiry Report*, Productivity Commission, Melbourne, 2011, pp. xxiii–xxiv, <www.pc.gov.au/inquiries/completed/urban-water/report>, accessed 27 August 2021. See also Patrick Troy (ed.), *Troubled Waters: Confronting the water crisis in Australia's cities*, ANU E Press, Canberra, 2008, <www.press-files.anu.edu.au/downloads/press/p20601/pdf/book.pdf>, accessed 16 June 2021.

8   Commonwealth of Australia, 'National Water Reform', *Productivity Commission Inquiry Report*, no. 87, 19 December 2017, pp. 2 & xvi.

9   J.I. Viggers, H.J. Weaver and D.B. Lindenmayer, *Melbourne's Water Catchments: Perspectives on a world-class water supply*, CSIRO Publishing, Melbourne, 2013, pp. 13–14.

10 Viggers, Weaver and Lindenmayer, *Melbourne's Water Catchments*, p. 17; L.E.D. Smith and K.S. Porter, 'Management of Catchments for the Protection of Water Resources: Drawing on the New York City watershed experience', *Regional Environmental Change*, vol. 10, 2010, pp. 311–26; Margaret Cook and Peter Spearritt, 'Water Forever: Warragamba and Wivenhoe Dams', *Australian Historical Studies*, vol. 52, no. 2, 2021, p. 215.

11 David Lindenmayer and Chris Taylor, 'Researchers allege native logging breaches that threaten the water we drink', *Conversation*, 26 November 2019, <www.theconversation.com/researchers-allege-native-logging-breaches-that-threaten-the-water-we-drink-127509>, accessed 27 August 2021.

12 Christopher Sheil, *Water's Fall: Running the risks with economic rationalism*, Pluto Press, Sydney, 2000; J.D. Spoehr et al., *State of Secrecy: Outsourcing – promise and performance*, Centre for Labour Research, Adelaide University, Adelaide, 2002; John Quiggin, 'Contracting Out: Promise and performance', *Economic and Labour Relations Review*, vol. 13, no. 1, 2002, pp. 88–104; K. Hartley, *Independent Audit of the Bolivar Wastewater Treatment Plant to Determine the Causes of a Major Odour Event*, Uniquest, Brisbane, 1997; Peter McClellan, *Sydney Water Inquiry: Final Report*, Sydney Water Inquiry Secretariat, Sydney, 1998.

13 Caroline Wenger, Karen Hussey and Jamie Pittock, *Living with Floods: Key lessons from Australia and abroad*, National Climate Change Adaptation Research Facility, Gold Coast, 2013, pp. 19–31; Margaret Cook, 'Vacating the Floodplain: Urban property, engineering and floods in Brisbane (1974–2011)', *Conservation and Society*, vol. 15, no. 3, 2017, pp. 344–54.

14 This resembles the argument made in relation to climate change by Mike Hulme, 'Am I a denier, a human extinction denier?', <www.mikehulme.org/am-i-a-denier-a-human-extinction-denier/>, accessed 16 June 2021.

15 Nick Dyrenfurth, *Getting the Blues: The future of Australian Labor*, Conor Court, Brisbane, 2019.

16 Water Corporation, *Water Forever: Towards climate resilience*, Water Corporation, Perth, 2009.
17 Samuel Alexander, 'Life in a "degrowth" economy, and why you might actually enjoy it', *Conversation*, 2 October 2014, <www.theconversation.com/life-in-a-degrowth-economy-and-why-you-might-actually-enjoy-it-32224>, accessed 16 June 2021.
18 Degrowth is defined by Jason Hickel as 'a planned reduction of energy and resource throughput designed to bring the economy back into balance with the living world in a way that reduces inequality and improves human well-being'. Jason Hickel, 'What does degrowth mean? A few points of clarification', *Globalizations*, 4 September 2020.
19 See, for example, this survey from the United States: Pew Research Center, 'What lessons do Americans see for humanity in the pandemic?', 8 October 2020, <www.pewforum.org/essay/what-lessons-do-americans-see-for-humanity-in-the-pandemic/>, accessed 27 August 2021.

6 War with China: What can history teach us?

1 Douglas Newton, *Hell-Bent: Australia's leap into the Great War*, Scribe, Melbourne, 2014; David Lee, *Stanley Melbourne Bruce: Australian internationalist*, Continuum, London, 2010; David S. Bird and J.A. Lyons, *The Tame Tasmanian: Appeasement and rearmament in Australia, 1932–39*, Australian Scholarly Publishing, Melbourne, 2008.
2 A.J.P. Taylor, *The Origins of the Second World War*, Hamish Hamilton, London, 1961, p. 7.
3 Tim Bouverie, *Appeasing Hitler: Chamberlain, Churchill and the road to war*, Bodley Head, London, 2019, p. xii.
4 For an important dissenting view, see John Charmley, *Mr Chamberlain and the Lost Peace*, Hodder & Stoughton, London, 1989.
5 Christopher Clark, *The Sleepwalkers: How Europe went to war in 1914*, Allen Lane, London, 2012.
6 See, for example, Yuen Foong Khong, *Analogies at War*, Princeton University Press, Princeton, 1992.
7 Coral Bell, *Negotiation from Strength: A study in the politics of power*, Alfred A. Knopf, New York, 1963.
8 'How Barbara Tuchman's *The Guns of August* influenced decision making during the Cuban Missile Crisis', Reader's Almanac: The official blog of the Library of America, 19 March 2012, <www.blog.loa.org/2012/03/how-barbara-tuchmans-guns-of-august.html>, accessed 24 January 2022.
9 Prime Minister Scott Morrison, 'Address – Launch of the 2020 Defence Strategic Update', 1 July 2020, <www.pm.gov.au/media/address-launch-2020-defence-strategic-update>, accessed 24 January 2022.
10 Winston S. Churchill, *The World Crisis*, volume II, T. Butterworth, London, 1923.
11 E.H. Carr, *The Twenty Years Crisis 1919–1939*, Macmillan, London, 1939, 1981.

12 Henry Kissinger, *A World Restored: Metternich, Castlereagh and the problem of peace 1812–22*, Houghton Mifflin, Boston, 1957, p. 1.
13 This question was explored in Niall Ferguson, *The Pity of War*, Basic Books, New York, 1998.

7 Past as prologue: Repairing Australia's trade relationship with China

The views expressed in this chapter are those of the authors and do not reflect the authors' involvements with specific organisations.

1 V.R. Panchamukhis, 'Complementarity and Economic Cooperation: A methodological discussion', *Foreign Trade Review: Quarterly Journal of Indian Institute of Foreign Trade*, vol. 39, no.1, 2004, pp. 5–18; M.Y. Hou, 'China-Australia Trade: How important and complementary is it?', *Journal of East Asian Affairs*, vol. 20, no. 1, 2006, pp. 155–79.
2 Observatory of Economic Complexity, 'Australia-China', <www.oec.world/en/profile/bilateral-country/aus/partner/chn?depthSelector=HS2Depth&dynamicBilateralTradeSelector=year1997>, accessed 29 August 2021.
3 UNICEF, *Children in China: An atlas of social indicators 2018*, UNICEF China, Beijing, 2018, p. 37, <www.unicef.cn/sites/unicef.org.china/files/2019-04/Atlas 2018 final ENG.pdf>, accessed 2 August 2021.
4 J.Y. Lin, 'Rural Reforms and Agricultural Growth in China', *American Economic Review*, vol. 82, no. 1, 1992, pp. 34–51.
5 China Power Team, 'How Well-off is China's Middle Class?', *China Power*, 26 April 2017, <www.chinapower.csis.org/china-middle-class/>, accessed 20 September 2021.
6 Ross Garnaut, *Australia and the Northeast Asian Ascendancy: Report to the prime minister and the minister for foreign affairs and trade*, AGPS, Canberra, 1989.
7 Laura Berger-Thomson, John Breusch and Louise Lilley, *Australia's Experience with Economic Reform*, The Treasury, Commonwealth of Australia, 2018.
8 Ann Kent, 'Australia-China Relations, 1966–1996: A critical overview', *Australian Journal of Politics and History*, vol. 42, no. 3, 2008, pp. 365–84; Australia–China Relations Institute (ACRI), *Whitlam and China*, UTS, Sydney, 2014.
9 ACRI, *Fraser and China*, UTS, Sydney, 2015.
10 Yi Wang, *Australia-China Relations Post 1949: Sixty years of trade and politics*, Ashgate Publishing Limited, Farnham, 2012; Roy Campbell McDowall, *Howard's Long March*, ANU Press, Canberra, 2009; and The Australia-China Story, 'The Gillard Government and Australia-China Relations', <www.aus.thechinastory.org/archive/the-gillard-government-and-australia-china-relations/>, accessed 29 August 2021.
11 The Australia-China Story, 'Kevin Rudd and Australia-China Relations', <www.aus.thechinastory.org/archive/kevin-rudd-and-australia-china-relations/>, accessed 29 August 2021.

12 Evan S. Medeiros, 'China's Foreign Policy Objectives', in *China's International Behavior: Activism, opportunism, and diversification*, RAND Corporation, Pittsburgh, 2009, p. 49.
13 Medeiros, 'China's Foreign Policy Objectives'.
14 Aaron L. Friedberg, *The Past, Present, and Future of US-China Relations* [A conversation with Aaron L. Friedberg hosted by the Institute for US-China Issues], 29 April 2021, <www.youtube.com/watch?v=KPrfjGtQf6M>, accessed 18 July 2021.
15 In 2019, the Morrison government established the National Foundation for Australia-China Relations, which built on the legacy of the Australia-China Council.
16 Edmund S.K. Fung, 'Australia's Relations with China in the 1980s', *Australian Journal of Politics and History*, vol. 32, no. 2, 1986, pp. 186–200.
17 McDowall, *Howard's Long March*, p. 22.
18 Wang, *Australia-China Relations*, p. 111.
19 Wang, *Australia-China Relations*, p. 112.
20 Australian Government Human Rights Delegation, *Report of the Australian Human Rights Delegation to China 14–26 July 1991*, AGPS, Canberra, 1991, p. viii; Australian Government Human Rights Delegation, *Report of the Australian Human Rights Delegation to China 8–20 November 1992*, AGPS, Canberra, 1992.
21 Wang, *Australia-China Relations*, p. 143.
22 The Howard government also initiated a bilateral human rights dialogue with China.
23 McDowall, *Howard's Long March*, pp. 10–12.
24 Geoff Raby, *China's Grand Strategy and Australia's Future in the New Global Order*, Melbourne University Press, Melbourne, 2020, p. 3.
25 Friedberg, *The Past, Present, and Future*.
26 The foreign relations law requires 'states and territories and their entities to seek approval from the Minister for Foreign Affairs if they propose to negotiate, or enter, or have entered a foreign arrangement'. See <www.foreignarrangements.gov.au/>, accessed 20 September 2021.
27 Ben Oquist, 'Australia's diplomatic approach needs a major revamp', *Canberra Times*, 28 November 2020.
28 The foregone goods export revenue from China was estimated to be A$6.6 billion between July 2020 and February 2021. Ron Wickes, Mike Adams and Nicolas Brown, *Economic Coercion by China: The impact on Australia's merchandise exports*, Institute for International Trade, Adelaide, July 2021.
29 Troy Bramston, 'Gough's man in China: Fix this mess', *Australian*, 2 March 2022.
30 Wang, *Australia-China Relations*.

8 Foreign aid: Australia's reputation at stake?

This research was supported (partially or fully) by the Australian Government through the Australian Research Council's Discovery Projects funding scheme (project DP17010229). The views expressed herein are those of the authors and are not necessarily those of the Australian Government or Australian Research Council. I would also like to acknowledge the assistance of Jacqui Baker, Anna Kent and Brad Underhill in data preparation for this chapter.

1. Ravi Tomar, 'The Ever-Shrinking Aid Budget', *Budget Review 2015–16*, Australian Parliamentary Library Research Paper, May 2015, <www.aph.gov.au/About_Parliament/Parliamentary_Departments/Parliamentary_Library/pubs/rp/BudgetReview201516/Aid>, accessed 2 July 2021.
2. Tim Costello, quoted in the *Sydney Morning Herald*, 17 December 2014.
3. Australian Department of Foreign Affairs and Trade (DFAT), 'Australian Aid: Promoting prosperity, reducing poverty, enhancing stability', June 2014, p. iii, <www.dfat.gov.au/sites/default/files/australian-aid-development-policy.pdf>, accessed 20 September 2016.
4. Jack Corbett, *Australia's Foreign Aid Dilemma: Humanitarian aspirations confront democratic legitimacy*, Routledge, Abingdon, 2017.
5. For the Colombo Plan, see David Lowe, 'Colombo Plans, Old and New: International students as foreign relations', *International Journal of Cultural Policy*, vol. 21, no. 4, 2015, pp. 448–62. For high levels of interest in, and support for, emergency and disaster relief in the early 1980s, see J.V. Remenyi, 'Australia's Foreign Aid Involvement: A report on a survey of the attitudes of Australians', *Australian Outlook*, vol. 38, no. 1, 1984, pp. 9–15; and for similar findings in 2009, see the report commissioned by AusAID, Instinct and Reason, *Community Attitudes Study: Segmentation Report*, 2009.
6. Remenyi, 'Australia's Foreign Aid Involvement'; Instinct and Reason, *Community Attitudes Study*.
7. Corbett, *Australia's Foreign Aid Dilemma*.
8. DFAT, *In the National Interest: Australia's foreign and trade policy (White Paper)*, DFAT, Canberra, 1997, p. 11.
9. DFAT, *In the National Interest*, p. 13.
10. US Whitehouse, Remarks by President Biden, Prime Minister Morrison of Australia, and Prime Minister Johnson of the United Kingdom Announcing the Creation of AUKUS (transcript), 15 September 2021, <www.whitehouse.gov/briefing-room/speeches-remarks/2021/09/15/remarks-by-president-biden-prime-minister-morrison-of-australia-and-prime-minister-johnson-of-the-united-kingdom-announcing-the-creation-of-aukus/>, accessed 20 September 2021.
11. Danielle Chubb and Ian McAllister, *Australian Public Opinion and Foreign Policy: Attitudes and trends since 1945*, Springer, Singapore, 2020, pp. 185–95.
12. Chubb and McAllister, *Australian Public Opinion*, p. 194.

13 A. Maurits van der Veen, *Ideas, Interests and Foreign Aid*, Cambridge University Press, Cambridge, 2011. Van der Veen's frames might not be quite the same as values, according to government pronouncements, and they are less abstract, but they have the advantages of usability for speakers, and recurrence over time. Another advantage of considering multiple frames that sit above the level of policy goals is that they allow multiplicity, overlap and measuring changes in emphasis.

14 Historic Hansard database, <www.historichansard.net/>, accessed 30 August 2021.

15 The method used to undertake this analysis involved compiling the times in which the term 'foreign aid' was used in Hansard (as per Historic Hansard), and then coding them to the most predominant frame (including, when several frames appeared in the same speech, the most emphasised one) as per Van der Veen's framework. The data was then analysed and the table on page 123 demonstrates the use of the term in the Australian Parliament over time.

16 William McMahon, House of Representatives, *Commonwealth Parliamentary Debates* (henceforth CPD), vol. 35, 31 August 1967, p. 651, <www.historichansard.net/hofreps/1967/19670831_reps_26_hor56/#subdebate-15-0-s1>, accessed 30 August 2021.

17 Len Reid, House of Representatives, *CPD*, no. 19, 9 May 1972, p. 2236, <www.parlinfo.aph.gov.au/parlInfo/download/hansard80/hansardr80/1972-05-09/toc_pdf/19720509_reps_27_hor78.pdf>, accessed 30 August 2021.

18 Terence Wood and Chris Hoy, 'Helping Us or Helping Them? What makes aid appeal to Australians', Devpolicy Discussion Paper 75, December 2018, Crawford School of Public Policy, ANU, Canberra, <www.papers.ssrn.com/sol3/papers.cfm?abstract_id=3302958>, accessed 3 August 2021

19 Terence Wood, 'Can Information Change Public Support for Aid?', *The Journal of Development Studies*, vol. 55, 2019, pp. 2162–76.

20 Terence Wood and Camilla Burkot, 'Want to Sell Aid to the Australian Public? Look to values not national interests', *Devpolicy Blog*, 23 March 2017, Crawford School of Public Policy, ANU, <www.devpolicy.org/want-sell-aid-australian-public-values-not-national-interests-20170323/>, accessed 1 August 2021.

21 Hasluck to Menzies, 17 September 1964, A1838 2020/1/24 part 3, National Archives of Australia (henceforth NAA).

22 Australian External Aid: Report to the Minister for External Affairs by the Interdepartmental Committee to Review Australian External Aid, p. 5, 25 March 1965, CRS A4311 item 147/1, NAA.

23 F.B. Hall, Acting High Commissioner, Karachi, to A. Tange, 24 November 1964, A1838 2020/1/24/1 part 1, NAA.

24 'Australia's External Aid: Report to the Minister of External Affairs by the Interdepartmental Committee to Review Australian Aid', 25 March 1965, CRS A 4311 item 147/1, NAA.

25 The 20 documents, from file series CRS A1838 2020/1/24 parts 1, 3, NAA, cover submissions from Australian overseas posts, and from officers based in the Department of External Affairs.
26 Official speeches and statements from *Current Notes on International Affairs*, vol. 26, nos 1–2 and vol. 36, nos 1–12. The number of predominant references to reputation/self-affirmation was 58; the number of predominantly security references was 47.
27 Aid Policy Section, Foreign Affairs 'External Aid and the Future Development of Papua New Guinea', no date (1972), CRS 1838 item 3080/10 4/3 part 1, NAA. Italics are mine.
28 Senator Gareth Evans, Minister for Foreign Affairs and Trade, Address to ACFOA 'One World or None' Conference, Canberra, 8 September 1989, <www.gevans.org/speeches/old/1989/080989_fm_australiasaidpr.pdf>, accessed 2 August 2021.
29 Van der Veen, *Ideas, Interests and Foreign Aid*, p. 231.

9 An open door? Foreign investment and multinational companies

1 Department of Foreign Affairs and Trade (DFAT), *Economic Activity of Majority Foreign Owned Businesses in Australia*, DFAT, Canberra, 2016.
2 R. Vernon, *Sovereignty at Bay: The multinational spread of U.S. enterprises*, Longman, London, 1971.
3 R. Fitzgerald, *The Rise of the Global Company: Multinationals and the making of the modern world*, Cambridge University Press, Cambridge, 2015.
4 Ann M. Carlos and Stephen Nicholas, '"Giants of an Earlier Capitalism": The chartered trading companies as modern multinationals', *Business History Review*, vol. 62, no. 3, 1988, pp. 398–419. For a recent broad ranging summary of the literature, see Teresa da Silva Lopes, Christina Lubinski and Heidi J. Tworek (eds), *The Routledge Companion to the Makers of Global Business*, Routledge, London, 2020.
5 DFAT, 'About foreign investment', n.d. <www.dfat.gov.au/trade/investment/Pages/about-foreign-investment>, accessed 8 August 2021.
6 Geoffrey Jones, 'Origins, Management and Performance', in Geoffrey Jones (ed.), *British Multinationals: Origins, management and performance*, Gower, Aldershot, 1986, p. 7.
7 Simon Ville and David T. Merrett, 'Investing in a successful resource-based colonial economy: International business in Australia before World War One', *Business History Review*, vol. 94, no. 2, 2020, pp. 321–46. Several earlier studies include Geoffrey Blainey, 'The History of Multinational Factories in Australia', in Akio Okochi and Tadakatsu Inoue (eds), *Overseas Business Activities*, University of Tokyo Press, Tokyo, 1984; Geoffrey Blainey, *Jumping over the Wheel: A centenary history of Pacific Dunlop*, Allen & Unwin, Sydney, 1993; Geoffrey Blainey, *White Gold: The story of Alcoa in Australia*, Allen & Unwin, Sydney, 1997; David T. Merrett, *ANZ Bank: A history of the Australia and New Zealand Banking Group Limited*, Allen & Unwin, Sydney, 1985. For a major study of Australian firms expanding overseas see, Howard W. Dick and David T. Merrett (eds),

The Internationalisation Strategies of Small-Country Firms: The Australian experience of globalisation, Edward Elgar, Cheltenham, 2007.

8   A forthcoming history of early international business: Simon Ville and David T. Merrett, *International Business in Australia before World War One: Shaping a multinational economy*, Palgrave.

9   Mira Wilkins, 'The Free-Standing Company, 1870–1914: An important type of British foreign direct investment', *Economic History Review*, vol. 41, no. 2, 1988, pp. 259–82.

10 Frances Steel, 'Re-routing Empire? Steam age circulations and the making of an Anglo Pacific, c.1850–90', *Australian Historical Studies*, vol. 46, no. 3, 2015, pp. 356–73.

11 Anne Rees, 'Travelling to Tomorrow: Australian Women in the United States, 1910–1960', PhD thesis, La Trobe University, 2016, pp. 11–13. (Note: Yves Rees formerly published as Anne.)

12 Alfred D. Chandler Jr, *Scale and Scope: The Dynamics of Industrial Capitalism*, Harvard Belknap Press, Cambridge MA, 1990.

13 Mira Wilkins, *The Emergence of Multinational Enterprise: American business abroad from the colonial era to 1914*, Harvard University Press, Cambridge MA, 1970, pp. 93–95.

14 Fitzgerald, *Rise of the Global Company*, p. 137.

15 A. Douglas Simmons, *Schweppes: The first 200 years*, Acropolis Books, Atlanta GA, 1983, p. 45.

16 Simon Ville and Claire Wright, 'Buzz and Pipelines: Knowledge and decision-making in a global business services precinct', *Journal of Urban History*, vol. 45, no. 2, 2019, pp. 199–203.

17 Pierre van der Eng, 'Beyond Liability of Foreignness: European firms in Australia, 1850s–1980s', World Economic History Congress, Boston, 2018.

18 The history of international business in Australia in the twentieth century is the subject of a current research project: Simon Ville, Pierre van der Eng, David Merrett and Andre Sammartino, 'A History of Foreign Multinational Enterprises in Australia since Federation', ARC Discovery Project DP 200101363.

19 Robert Conlon and John Perkins, *Wheels and Deals: The automotive industry in twentieth-century Australia*, Ashgate, Aldershot, 2001.

20 Jack Fahey, 'The Cultivation of an Australian Identity: New insights into public relations at General Motors-Holden in the interwar era', *Australian Historical Studies*, vol. 50, no. 4, 2019, p. 484.

21 Mira Wilkins, *The Maturing of Multinational Enterprise: American business abroad from 1914 to 1970*, Harvard University Press, Cambridge MA, 2013; Donald T. Brash, *American Investment in Australian Industry*, Australian National University Press, Canberra, 1966, pp. 289–327.

22 Pierre van der Eng, 'Turning Adversity into Opportunity: Philips in Australia, 1945–1980', *Enterprise & Society*, vol. 19, no. 1, 2018, p. 183.

23 Van der Eng, 'European Firms in Australia'.

24. Australian Trade and Investment Commission, *Japanese Investment in Australia*, Australian Government, Canberra, 2017.
25. Percentage in brackets. 1820–70 counts all firms that arrived in those years, while 1914 and 2010 are benchmark years that list firms in Australia during that year. 2010 'others' are 48 nations with four or less firms in Australia.
26. Bureau of Industry Economics (BIE) *Multinationals and Governments: Issues and Implications for Australia*, Australian Government Publishing Service (AGPS), Canberra, 1993; Peter Drysdale and Christopher Findlay, 'Chinese foreign direct investment in Australia: Policy issues for the resource sector', *China Economic Journal*, vol. 2, no. 2, 2009, pp. 133–58; Ross Garnaut, *Australia and the Northeast Asian Ascendancy*, AGPS, Canberra, 1989.
27. Greg Crough and Ted Wheelwright, *Australia: A Client State*, Penguin Books, Melbourne, 1982.
28. Brash, *American Investment*.
29. Fitzgerald, *Rise of the Global Company*, pp. 70–74.
30. Wilkins, *The Emergence of Multinational Enterprise*, p. 157.
31. Although Queensland sugar plantations and farms drew upon imported indentured cheap labour from the Pacific Islands from the 1860s to the 1900s.
32. David Tolmie Merrett, 'Paradise Lost? British banks in Australia', in Geoffrey Jones (ed.), *Banks as Multinationals*, Routledge, London & New York, 1990, pp. 62–84.
33. *Royal Commission of the Meat Export Trade*, Government Printer State of Victoria, Melbourne, 1914, Appendix D, p. 39.
34. Howard Cox, *The Global Cigarette: Origins and evolution of British-American Tobacco Company, 1880–1945*, Oxford University Press, Oxford, 2000, p. 104.
35. Christopher Pokarier, 'Australia's Foreign Investment Policy: An historical perspective', *International Journal of Public Policy*, vol. 13, no. 3–5, 2017, pp. 212–31.
36. OECD Centre for Tax Policy and Administration, 'The OECD'S Project on Harmful Tax Practices – 2006 Update on Progress in Member Countries', <www.oecd.org/tax/harmful/37446434.pdf>, accessed 9 October 2021.
37. OECD, 'Ending Offshore Profit Shifting', <www.oecd.org/about/impact/combatinginternationaltaxavoidance.htm>, accessed 9 October 2021.
38. KPMG and the University of Sydney, *Demystifying Chinese Investment in Australia*, Sydney, July 2021, pp. 10–11, <www.assets.kpmg/content/dam/kpmg/au/pdf/2021/demystifying-chinese-investment-in-australia-july-2021.pdf>, accessed 9 October 2021,
39. Drysdale and Findlay, 'Chinese Foreign Direct Investment', p. 152.

10 Tackling inequality: Lessons from the postwar reconstruction

1. Simon Ville and Glenn Withers (eds), *The Cambridge Economic History of Australia*, Cambridge University Press, Cambridge, 2015, Appendix 6.
2. Liam Byrne, 'Becoming John Curtin and James Scullin: Their early political career', Parliamentary Library Lecture delivered on 17 March 2021, Parliamentary Library, Canberra, 2021, p. 7.
3. Commonwealth of Australia, *Full Employment in Australia*, Australian Government Printer, Canberra, 1945.
4. David Graeber, *Bullshit Jobs*, Simon and Schuster, New York, 2018. Though note that Graeber's empirical findings for the modern labour market have been questioned: Magdalena Soffia, Alex J. Wood and Brendan Burchell, 'Alienation Is Not "Bullshit": An empirical critique of Graeber's Theory of BS Jobs', *Work, Employment and Society*, June 2021.
5. Diane Hutchinson, 'Manufacturing', in Ville and Withers (eds), *The Cambridge Economic History of Australia*, pp. 287–308.
6. Andrew Leigh, *Battlers and Billionaires: The story of inequality in Australia*, Black Inc., Melbourne, 2013, p. 37.
7. Unemployment figures for 1901–1965 are those compiled by N.G. Butlin, and published in Wray Vamplew (ed.), *Australians: Historical statistics*, Fairfax, Syme & Weldon Associates, Sydney, 1987. Figures for 1966–1977 are an average of ABS quarterly seasonally adjusted estimates. Figures for 1978–2020 are averages of ABS monthly seasonally adjusted estimates (ABS, Labour Force, cat. no. 6202.0, Table 1).
8. Tim Hatton and Glenn Withers, 'The Labour Market', in Ville and Withers (eds), *The Cambridge Economic History of Australia*, pp. 351–72.
9. Commonwealth Housing Commission, *Final Report of the Commonwealth Housing Commission*, 25 August 1944, Ministry of Post-War Reconstruction, Canberra, Commonwealth Government, 1944.
10. Quoted in Rae Dufty-Jones, 'A Historical Geography of Housing Crisis in Australia', *Australian Geographer*, vol. 49, no. 1, 2018, pp. 5–23.
11. Robert Freestone, 'Post-War Reconstruction and Planning Promotion in 1940s Australia', in 15th IPHS Conference Proceedings, International Planning History Society Conference, Sao Paolo, Brazil, 2012.
12. Home ownership figures are drawn from Advisory Council for Intergovernment Relations, *Australian Housing Policy and Intergovernment Relations*, Discussion Paper No. 14, 1981, Table B. 4 (in turn compiled from Census Reports); ABS, *A Picture of the Nation* (Catalogue no. 2070.0), Housing Overview, p. 211; ABS, *Housing: A Statistical Overview* (Catalogue No.1320), 1996; and ABS, *2011 Census QuickStats*, Dwelling – dwelling structure.
13. Martin Shanahan, 'Wealth and Welfare', in Ville and Withers, (eds), *The Cambridge Economic History of Australia*, p. 500. Note that Shanahan uses a slightly different measure of home ownership, being the share of all housing that was owner-occupied (rather than the share of people who owned their homes).

14 Australian Bureau of Statistics, *Yearbook 1960*, ABS, Canberra, 1960, p. 378.
15 Vehicle ownership data are drawn from ABS, *Motor Vehicle Census, Australia*, 1955–2020 and ABS, *Year Book Australia*, 1908–1996. Because the motor vehicle census figure is not available every year, I revert to the Year Book figure where using the vehicle census figure would imply an implausible drop in vehicle numbers. Household numbers are interpolated where missing, and extrapolated for 2017–2020 on the assumption that the average household size in these years is the same as in 2016 (2.9 persons). Vehicle ownership figures for 1910–1919 are drawn from state police reports, as compiled by Lester Hovenden, 'The Motor Car in New South Wales', MA(Hons) thesis, Department of History, University of Sydney, 1981, p. 57. Due to the absence of annual household counts for New South Wales in 1901–1919, I use state population figures to calculate the number of NSW households, assuming that NSW households are the same size as the national average in that year.
16 Henry Lawson, 'Since Then', in *When the World Was Wide*, Angus and Robertson, Sydney, 1900, p. 179.
17 Pamela Katic and Andrew Leigh ('Top Wealth Shares in Australia 1915–2012', *Review of Income and Wealth*, vol. 62, no. 2, 2016, pp. 209–22) estimate that the top 1 per cent held 34 per cent of all household wealth; a similar figure to that estimated by Shanahan (Martin Shanahan, 'Personal Wealth in South Australia', *Journal of Interdisciplinary History*, vol. 32, no. 1, 2001, pp. 55–80) for South Australia in the early twentieth century. The 2020 estimate for US wealth inequality is from Federal Reserve (2021).
18 Stuart Macintyre, *The Oxford History of Australia, Volume 4: 1901–1942, The Succeeding Age*, Oxford University Press, Melbourne, 1986, pp. 145–46.
19 The male Gini and top 1 per cent series were originally published in Anthony B. Atkinson and Andrew Leigh, 'The Distribution of Top Incomes in Australia', *Economic Record*, vol. 83, no. 262, 2007, pp. 247–61; and Andrew Leigh, 'Deriving Long-run Inequality Series from Tax Data', *Economic Record*, vol. 81, no. S1, 2005, pp. S58–S70; and updated in Andrew Leigh, *Battlers and Billionaires: The story of inequality in Australia*, Black Inc., Melbourne, 2013). Top 1 per cent estimates for the most recent years are calculated by Roger Wilkins, based on Richard V. Burkhauser, Markus H. Hahn and Roger Wilkins, 'Measuring Top Incomes Using Tax Record Data: A cautionary tale from Australia', *Journal of Economic Inequality*, vol. 13, no. 2, 2015, pp. 181–205. I use Wilkins' series excluding capital gains, which Wilkins argues is most consistent over time.
20 The Gini coefficient can be interpreted as half the mean difference between two randomly selected individuals, expressed as a fraction of the average. For example, a Gini of 0.3 means that the average gap between two people is 60 per cent of the average income.
21 Leigh, *Battlers and Billionaires*, p. 41.

22 William D Rubinstein, *The All Time Australian 200 Rich List*, Allen & Unwin, Sydney, 2004.
23 Walter Scheidel, *The Great Leveler: Violence and the history of inequality from the Stone Age to the twenty-first century*, Princeton University Press, Princeton, 2018, p. 444.
24 Jeff Borland and Michael Bernard Coelli argue that employment outcomes for the young deteriorated substantially from 2008 to 2019, and that the main explanation is increased labour market competition. Borland and Coelli, 'Is It "Dog Days" for the Young in the Australian Labour Market?', *Australian Economic Review*, vol. 54, no. 4, 2021, pp. 421–44.
25 Andrew Markus, *Mapping Social Cohesion: The Scanlon Foundation Surveys 2020*, Monash University, Melbourne, 2021, p. 9.
26 See Andrew Leigh, 'Finding Common Ground on China', in Genevieve Feely and Peter Jennings (eds), *After COVID-19*, vol. 3. Voices from Federal Parliament, Australian Strategic Policy Institute, Canberra, 2020, pp. 35–38.
27 For example, three out of five Australians would like to know their neighbours better, while four out of five people say that the decline of membership in organisations is not a positive development: Andrew Leigh and Nick Terrell, *Reconnected: A community builder's handbook*, Black Inc., Melbourne, 2020, pp. 18, 38.
28 Leigh and Terrell, *Reconnected*.

11 Electricity problems? Call a historian. Learning from the history of electricity reform in Australia

1 Climate Change Authority, *Australia's Climate Change Policies at the Australian and State and Territory Government Levels: A stocktake*, Australian Government, Canberra, 2019.
2 Martin Parkinson, *A Decade of Drift*, Monash University Publishing, Melbourne, 2021.
3 *National Electricity (South Australia) Act 1996*, Pt1, s.7.
4 Roger Morse, 'Energy', in *Technology in Australia 1788–1988*, Australian Academy of Technological Sciences and Engineering, Melbourne, 1988, p. 780.
5 See Ernst Boehm, 'Ownership and Control of the Electricity Supply Industry in Australia', *Economic Record*, vol. 32, no. 2, 1956, pp. 257–72; Guy Allbut, *A Brief History of Some of the Features of Public Electricity Supply in Australia*, Electricity Supply Association of Melbourne, Melbourne, 1958; Rob Linn, *ETSA: The story of electricity in South Australia*, ETSA Corporation, Adelaide, 1996; and Malcolm Thomis, *A History of the Electricity Supply Industry in Queensland*, vol. 1, 1888–1938, Boolarong Publications, Brisbane, 1987.
6 Cecil Edwards, *Brown Power: A jubilee history of the State Electricity Commission of Victoria*, State Electricity Commission of Victoria, Melbourne 1969, p. 14.

7   Thomis, *A History of the Electricity Supply Industry in Queensland*, vol. 1, p. 93.
8   Edwards, *Brown Power*, 1969, p. 78.
9   Allbut, *A Brief History*, p. 45.
10 Allbut, *A Brief History*, p. 45.
11 Linn, *ETSA*, chapter 2.
12 Allbut, *A Brief History*.
13 Edwards, *Brown Power*, 1969, p. 234.
14 G.J. McDonnell, *Reports of the Commission of Enquiry into Electricity Generation and Planning in NSW*, vol. 1, NSW Government, Sydney, 1986.
15 Aynsley Kellow, *Transforming Power: The politics of electricity planning*, Cambridge University Press, Melbourne, 1996, p. 155.
16 Industry Commission, *Energy Generation and Distribution*, vol. 1: Summary and Recommendations, AGPS, Canberra, 1991.
17 Industry Commission, *Energy Generation*, p. 2.
18 Independent Committee of Inquiry into Competition Policy in Australia, *National Competition Policy: Report by the Independent Committee of Inquiry into Competition Policy in Australia* (Professor F. Hilmer, Chairman), AGPS, Canberra, 1993.
19 See, for example, Graeme Hodge, Valerie Sands, David Hayward and David Scott (eds), *Power Progress: An audit of Australia's electricity experiment*, Australian Scholarly Publishing, Melbourne, 2004; John Quiggin, 'Electricity Reform', in Damien Cahill and Phillip Toner (eds), *Wrong Way: How privatisation and economic reform backfired*, Schwartz, Melbourne, 2018.
20 John Pierce, 'A Perspective on Australia's Microeconomic Reform Journey', Address to Australian Institute of Energy, Brisbane, 18 July 2019, p. 3.
21 Edwards, *Brown Power*, p. 206.
22 See, for example, Australian Competition and Consumer Commission, *Restoring Electricity Affordability and Australia's Competitive Advantage: Retail Electricity Pricing Inquiry – Final Report*, Commonwealth of Australia, Canberra, June 2018.
23 Alan Finkel, Chloe Munro, Terry Effeney and Mary O'Kane, *Independent Review into the Future Security of the National Electricity Market: Blueprint for the future*, Commonwealth of Australia, Canberra, 2017.
24 John Thwaites, Patricia Faulkner and Terry Mulder, *Independent Review into the Electricity and Gas Retail Markets in Victoria*, Victorian Government, Melbourne, 2017.
25 Australian Energy Markets Operator, Integrated System Plan, <www.aemo.com.au/en/energy-systems/major-publications/integrated-system-plan-isp>, accessed 20 September 2021.
26 See, for example, government announcements for NSW, <www.energy.nsw.gov.au/renewables/renewable-energy-zones>, accessed 20 September 2021; and for Victoria <www.lilydambrosio.com.au/media-releases/

new-projects-to-accelerate-victorias-renewable-energy-zones>, accessed 20 September 2021.
27   John Howard, *Lazarus Rising: A personal and political autobiography*, HarperCollins, revised ed., 2011, p. 662.
28   See Organisation for Economic Cooperation and Development, *Economic Surveys Australia*, OECD Publishing, Paris, 2021, p. 62.
29   Edwards, *Brown Power*, pp. 15–24.

12   Governing during economic crisis: The importance of memory

1   Scott Morrison, 'Coronavirus: Time for us to summon the Anzac spirit', *Australian*, 6 April 2020, <www.theaustralian.com.au/commentary/coronavirus-time-for-us-to-summon-the-anzac-spirit/news-story/f5d3a12daade1498a482ee65fb15d005>, accessed 24 January 2022.
2   This chapter draws on Joan Beaumont, *Australia's Great Depression*, Allen & Unwin, Sydney, 2022.
3   For further detail, see C.B. Schedvin, *Australia and the Great Depression*, Sydney University Press, Sydney, 1973, first published 1970, pp. 76–95.
4   Paul Hasluck, *The Government and the People 1939–1941*, vol. 1, series 4 (Civil), *Australia and the War of 1939–1945*, Australian War Memorial, Canberra, 1952, p. 109.
5   The definitive histories, on which this account draws, are Rob Watts, *The Foundation of the National Welfare State*, Allen & Unwin, Sydney, 1987; and Stuart Macintyre, *Australia's Boldest Experiment: War and reconstruction in the 1940s*, NewSouth, Sydney, 2015.
6   Quoted in National Museum of Australia, 'Unemployment insurance', <www.nma.gov.au/defining-moments/resources/unemployment-insurance>, accessed 24 January 2022.
7   Ian W. McLean, *Why Australia Prospered: The shifting sources of economic growth*, Princeton University Press, Princeton, 2013, p. 191.
8   Commonwealth of Australia, *Royal Commission Appointed to Inquire into the Monetary and Banking Systems*, Sydney, 1937, pp. 205–206.
9   Norman Abjorensen, 'Chifley Versus the Banks', *Australian Society for the Study of Labour History* (originally published in *Canberra Times*, 6 June 2017), <www.labourhistorycanberra.org/2017/08/ben-chifleys-botched-attempt-to-nationalise-australias-banks/>, accessed 24 January 2022.
10   Clause 11, *Reserve Bank Act 1959*, p. 206.
11   I owe this insight to Selwyn Cornish, Australian National University.
12   In the late 1960s and early 1970s, the unemployment rate stood at 2 per cent but over the 1970s rose gradually to 6 per cent. The early 1980s saw a sharp rise in the unemployment rate to 10 per cent in 1983. This declined to 6 per cent by 1989, but a further steep rise then occurred in the early 1990s, peaking at 11 per cent in 1993: Australian Bureau of Statistics, 4102.0 – Australian Social Trends, 2001, <www.abs.gov.au/ausstats/abs@.nsf/2f762f95845417aeca25706c00834efa/855e6f87080d2e1aca2570ec000c8e5f!OpenDocument>, accessed 24 January 2022.

13. The notion of 'postmemory' is fully developed in Marianne Hirsch's *The Generation of Postmemory: Writing and visual culture after the Holocaust*, Columbia University Press, New York, 2012.
14. Pierre Nora, *Realms of Memory: Rethinking the French past*, Columbia University Press, New York, 1992, pp. 18, 14.
15. Calla Wahlquist, 'Melbourne Renters Struggling in Lockdown Urge Government to Bring Back Eviction Moratorium', *Guardian Australia*, 4 June 2021, <www.theguardian.com/australia-news/2021/jun/04/melbourne-renters-struggling-in-lockdown-urge-government-to-bring-back-eviction-moratorium>, accessed 24 January 2022.
16. Senate, 4 August 2021.
17. House of Representatives, 6 October 2020.
18. Jennifer Duke, 'From the Great Depression to Coronavirus: How Australians survive hard times', *Sydney Morning Herald*, 15 April 2020, <www.smh.com.au/politics/federal/from-the-great-depression-to-coronavirus-how-australians-survive-hard-times-20200402-p54gaj.html>, accessed 24 January 2022; Amanda Horswill, 'Australian Economy: COVID-19 vs The Great Depression', *Canstar*, 23 July 2020, <www.canstar.com.au/home-loans/economy-now-vs-great-depression/>, accessed 24 January 2022.
19. James Morley and Richard Holden, 'It's Just Started: We'll need war bonds, and stimulus on a scale not seen in our lifetimes', *Conversation*, 29 April 2020, <www.theconversation.com/its-just-started-well-need-war-bonds-and-stimulus-on-a-scale-not-seen-in-our-lifetimes-137155>, accessed 24 January 2022.

13 We need to hear the voices of refugees: Citizen engagement for reforming refugee policy

1. 'Bring them Home', *ABC News*, 9 June 2021, <www.abc.net.au/news/2021-06-09/calls-intensify-for-the-release-of-biloela-family/13379904>, accessed 15 December 2021.
2. See Amnesty International, *Report of an Amnesty International Mission to Sri Lanka: 31 January–9 February 1982*, Amnesty International Publications, London, 1983, p. 19, <www.amnesty.org/download/Documents/200000/asa370011983en.pdf>, accessed 14 August 2018.
3. Judith Betts and Claire Higgins, 'The Sri Lankan Civil war and Australia's Migration Policy Response: A historical case study with contemporary implications', *Asia and the Pacific Policy Studies*, vol. 4, no. 2, 2017, p. 281.
4. The Ceylon Tamil Association became the Eelam Tamil Association in the mid-to-late 1980s. For consistency, I use Ceylon Tamil Association.
5. *Commonwealth Parliamentary Debates*, Hansard, no. 91, 18 September 1981, p. 817.
6. Author interview with Ceylon Tamil Association founding member, Melbourne, May 2016.

7   Alan Missen, 'Reports by Senator Alan Missen', Human Rights & Humanitarian Law, 1984/85, <www.tamilnation.org/humanrights/tamil/84missen.htm>, accessed 15 July 2021.
8   Missen, 'Reports', 1984/85.
9   Anna Arabindan-Kesson, 'Fragments of Memory: Writing the migrant story', in Deborah Willis, Ellyn Toscano and Kalia Brooks Nelson (eds), *Women and Migration: Responses in art and history*, Open Books Pub. Ltd, Cambridge, 2019, pp. 23–36.
10 Interview with Ceylon Tamil Association founding member.
11 Interview with Ceylon Tamil Association founding member.
12 Interview with Ceylon Tamil Association founding member.
13 NAA: A1838, 1690/1/18, Part 3.
14 NAA: A1838, 1690/1/18, Part 3.
15 NAA: A1838, 1690/1/18, Part 1.
16 NAA: A1838, 1690/1/18, Part 3.
17 NAA: A1838, 1690/1/18, Part 1.
18 Department of Immigration and Ethnic Affairs, *Annual Report 1987–88*, AGPS, Canberra, 1988.
19 NAA: A1838, 1690/1/18, Part 1.
20 *Commonwealth Parliamentary Debates*, Hansard, no. 136, 2 May 1984, p. 1626.
21 Interview with Ceylon Tamil Association founding member.
22 Frank Galbally, *Review of Post Arrival Programs and Services for Migrants*, Parliamentary Paper, no. 164, Canberra, AGPS, 1978, p. 29.
23 Author interview with Suthan, Sydney, December 2017.

14 The 'Muslim Problem' in Australia: The role of political leadership

1   Australian Army, 'Australian Army in Afghanistan', Australian Army, n.d., <www.army.gov.au/our-heritage/history/history-focus/australian-army-afghanistan>, accessed 27 August 2021.
2   Australian Bureau of Statistics, 'Census reveals Australia's religious diversity on World Religion Day', Australian Bureau of Statistics, 18 January 2018, <www.abs.gov.au/AUSSTATS/abs@.nsf/mediareleasesbyReleaseDate/8497F7A8E7DB5BEFCA25821800203DA4?OpenDocument>, accessed 18 January 2018.
3   Shahram Akbarzadeh, 'The Muslim Question in Australia: Islamophobia and Muslim alienation', *Journal of Muslim Minority Affairs*, vol. 36, no. 3, 2016, pp. 323–33.
4   Australian Human Rights Commission, *Sharing the Stories of Australian Muslims Report 2021*, Australian Human Rights Commission, Sydney, 2021, <www.apo.org.au/node/313236>, accessed 27 August 2021.
5   Jennifer E. Cheng, 'Exclusive and Inclusive Constructions of "Australia" in the Australian Parliament', *Critical Approaches to Discourse Analysis Across Disciplines*, vol. 7, no. 1, 2013, pp. 51–65, <www.lancaster.ac.uk/fass/journals/cadaad/wp-content/uploads/2015/04/Volume-7_Cheng.pdf>, accessed 23 September 2021; Imogen Richards, 'A Dialectical Approach to

Online Propaganda: Australia's United Patriots Front, right-wing politics, and Islamic State', *Studies in Conflict & Terrorism*, vol. 42, nos 1–2, 2019, pp. 43–69.
6   Scott Poynting and Linda Briskman, 'Islamophobia in Australia: From far-right deplorables to respectable liberals', *Social Sciences*, vol. 7, no. 11, article 213, 2018, pp. 1–17.
7   Poynting and Briskman, 'Islamophobia', p. 8.
8   Poynting and Briskman, 'Islamophobia', p. 2.
9   Mahsheed Ansari and Mirela Cufurovic, 'Collective Trauma and the Muslim Women of the Christchurch Attack: An observational and media study', in Ahmed A. Karim, Radwa Khalil and Ahmed Moustafa (eds), *Female Pioneers from Ancient Egypt and the Middle East*, Springer, Singapore, 2021, pp. 145–64.
10 Australian Human Rights Commission, *Sharing the Stories*, p. 69.
11 Melissa Davey, 'Bourke Street Attack: Morrison accused of "scapegoating" Muslim community', *Guardian Australia*, 12 November 2018, <www.theguardian.com/australia-news/2018/nov/12/bourke-street-attack-morrison-accused-of-scapegoating-muslim-community>, accessed 12 September 2021.
12 Paul Karp, 'Morrison urges Muslim community to be more "proactive" in tackling terrorism', *Guardian Australia*, 12 November 2018, <www.theguardian.com/australia-news/2018/nov/12/morrison-urges-muslim-community-to-be-more-proactive-in-tackling-terrorism>, accessed 12 September 2021.
13 Poynting and Briskman, 'Islamophobia', p. 6.
14 Alice Aslan, *Islamophobia in Australia*, Agora Press, Sydney, 2009, pp. 10–27.
15 Margaret Allen, 'Identifying Sher Mohamad "a good citizen"', in Ralph Crane, Anna Johnston and C. Vijayasree (eds), *Empire Calling: Administering Colonial Australasia and India*, Foundation Books, Bengaluru, 2013, pp. 103–19.
16 Allen, 'Identifying Sher Mohamad', pp. 103–19.
17 Hanifa Deen, *Ali Abdul v. the King: Muslim stories from the dark days of White Australia*, UWA Publishing, Perth, 2011, p. 2.
18 Paul Martin, 'Race, Colonial History and National Identity: Resident Evil 5 as a Japanese game', *Games and Culture*, vol. 13, no. 6, 2018, pp. 568–86.
19 Mark Francis, 'Social Darwinism and the Construction of Institutionalised Racism in Australia', *Journal of Australian Studies*, vol. 20, nos 50–51, 1996, pp. 90–105; Jeffrey R. Dafler, 'Social Darwinism and the Language of Racial Oppression: Australia's stolen generations', *ETC: A Review of General Semantics*, vol. 62, no. 2, 2005, pp. 137–50.
20 Edward Said, *Orientalism*, Vintage Books, New York, 1979.
21 See Jeremy Martens, *Empire and Asian Migration: Sovereignty, immigration restriction and protest in the British settler colonies, 1888–1907*, University of Western Australia Press, Perth, 2018, pp. 109–47.

22 Christine Stevens, *Tin Mosques and Ghantowns: A history of Afghan cameldrivers in Australia*, Paul Fitzsimons, Alice Springs, 2002; Regina Ganter, 'Remembering Muslim Histories of Australia', *La Trobe Journal*, vol. 89, 2012, pp. 48–62.
23 Katy Nebhan, 'Men on a Mission: Engaging with Islamophobia and radicalization in Australia 1863–1957', in John L. Esposito and Derya Iner (eds), *Islamophobia and Radicalization*, Palgrave Macmillan, Cham, 2019, pp. 225–44; Katy Nebhan, 'Revulsion and Reflection: The coloured and white Muslim in Australia's print media from the late 19th to the early 20th century', *Australian Journal of Islamic Studies*, vol. 3, no. 3, 2018, pp. 44–60.
24 Deen, *Ali Abdul v. the King*, pp. 111–28.
25 Marshall Clark and Sally K. May, '1. Understanding the Macassans: A regional approach', in Clark and May (eds), *Macassan History and Heritage: Journeys, encounters and influences*, ANU E Press, 2013, p. 1.
26 Kama Maclean, 'India in Australia: A recent history of a very long engagement', in Rick Hosking and Amit Sarwal (eds), *Wanderings in India: Australian perceptions*, Monash University Publishing, Melbourne, 2012, pp. 20–35; Mahsheed Ansari, 'Al-Mu'minah Down Under: The untold stories and legacies of Muslim women pioneers in Australia', in Ghena Krayem and Susan Carland (eds), *Muslim Women and Agency: An Australian context*, Brill, Leiden, 2021.
27 Richard Broome, *The Victorians Arriving*, Fairfax Syme & Weldon, Sydney, 1984, p. 78.
28 Deen, *Ali Abdul v. the King*, pp. 111–28.
29 Deen, *Ali Abdul v. the King*.
30 National Museum of Australia, 'End of the White Australia Policy', National Museum of Australia, 5 July 2021, <www.nma.gov.au/defining-moments/resources/end-of-white-australia-policy>, accessed 10 September 2021.
31 Deen, *Ali Abdul v. the King*.
32 Australian Human Rights Commission, 'Australia and the Universal Declaration on Human Rights', Australian Human Rights Commission, n.d., <www.humanrights.gov.au/our-work/publications/australia-and-universal-declaration-human-rights>, accessed 11 September 2021.
33 Louise C. Johnson, Tanja Luckins and David Walker, *The Story of Australia: A new history of people and place*, Routledge, New York, 2022, p. 159.
34 Lyndon Megarrity, 'Regional Goodwill, Sensibly Priced: Commonwealth policies towards Colombo Plan scholars and private overseas students, 1945–72', *Australian Historical Studies*, vol. 38, no. 129, 2007, pp. 100–101.
35 National Museum of Australia, 'End of the White Australia Policy'.
36 H. Deen, 'Muslim Journeys', National Archives of Australia, n.d., <www.naa.gov.au/collection/snapshots/uncommon-lives/muslim-journeys/arrivals.aspx>, accessed 18 January 2019.

37 Megarrity, 'Regional Goodwill, Sensibly Priced', pp. 88–105.
38 Mahsheed Ansari, 'The Muslim Student Associations (MSAS) and the Formation of the Australian Ummah', *Australian Journal of Islamic Studies*, vol. 3, no. 3, 2018, pp. 99–116.
39 Ansari, 'The Muslim Student Associations (MSAS)', p. 112.
40 Deen, 'Muslim Journeys'.
41 Megarrity, 'Regional Goodwill'.
42 Nahid Kabir, *Muslims in Australia: Immigration, race relations and cultural history*, Routledge, New York, 2005, p. 42.
43 Kabir, *Muslims in Australia*, p. 17.
44 Kabir, *Muslims in Australia*, p. 17.
45 Kabir, *Muslims in Australia*, p. 17. See also Kevin Dunn, 'Islam in Sydney: Contesting the discourse of absence', *Australian Geographer*, vol. 35, no. 3, 2004, pp. 333–53.
46 Dzavid Haveric, 'Muslim Memories in Victoria', *Australian Journal of Islamic Studies*, vol. 2, no. 3, 2017, pp. 20–39.
47 Ganter, 'Remembering Muslim Histories of Australia'.
48 Deen, *Ali Abdul v. the King*.

15 Why soldiers commit war crimes – and what we can do about it

1 Neil James, 'Special Forces Issues Have Deep Historical Roots', *Strategist*, 22 October 2019; Chris Masters and Nick McKenzie, 'Special Forces Chief Acknowledges War Crimes, Blames "Poor Moral Leadership"', *Sydney Morning Herald*, 28 June 2020; Paul Brereton, *Inspector-General of the Australian Defence Force Afghanistan Inquiry Report: Questions of Unlawful Conduct Concerning the Special Operations Task Group in Afghanistan* (hereafter IGADF Report), Australian Department of Defence, 2020, p. 325.
2 IGADF Report, p. 507.
3 Joanna Bourke, *An Intimate History of Killing: Face-to-face killing in twentieth-century warfare*, Granta Books, London, 1999, pp. 182–92.
4 Bourke, *Intimate History of Killing*, pp. 79, 99.
5 Tony 'Bomber' Bower-Miles and Mark Whittaker, *Bomber: From Vietnam to hell and back*, Macmillan, Sydney, 2009, pp. 85–86; Suel D. Jones, *Meeting the Enemy: A marine goes home*, self-published, 2008, p. 140.
6 Massilia Ali, 'Eighty Percent of Muslims in Australia Say They Have Experienced Discrimination', *SBS News*, 19 July 2021.
7 IGADF Report, pp. 334, 30–34.
8 Ben Wadham, 'The Dark Side of Defence: Masculinities and violence in the military', in Ross McGarry and Sandra Walklate (eds), *Palgrave Handbook of Criminology and War*, Palgrave, London, 2016, pp. 269–87.
9 Christian Appy, *Working-Class War: American combat soldiers and Vietnam*, University of North Carolina Press, Chapel Hill, 2000, p. 102.
10 John Akins, *Drowning Out the Drums: A marine comes home*, self-published, 2014, p. 166.

11. Nick Turse, *Kill Anything That Moves: The real American war in Vietnam*, Metropolitan Books, New York, 2013, p. 170, Gina Marie Weaver, *Ideologies of Forgetting: Rape in the Vietnam War*, State University of New York Press, New York, 2012, p. 35; Mark Baker, *Nam: the Vietnam War in the words of the men and women who fought there*, Berkley Books, New York, 1983, pp. 186, 321.
12. Geoff Dean, 'Right-Wing Extremism in Australia: The rise of the new radical right', *Journal of Policing, Intelligence and Counter-Terrorism*, vol. 11, no. 2, 2016, pp. 121–42.
13. Edward Said, 'The Clash of Ignorance', *The Nation*, 4 October 2001; Kathleen Belew, *Bring the War Home: The White Power movement and paramilitary America*, Harvard University Press, Cambridge, 2018; Cynthia Miller-Idriss, 'From 9/11 to 1/6', *Foreign Affairs*, September/October 2021.
14. Ben Wadham and Jason Pudsey, '(Un)masking Hegemony: Militarism, white masculinity and the logic of contemporary empire', *International Journal of Critical Psychology*, vol. 16, 2005, p. 147; Nick McKenzie, 'Fear of Neo-Nazis in Military Ranks after Ex-Soldier's Passport Cancelled', *Age*, 22 August 2021; Mark Willacy and Alexandra Blucher, 'Australian Special Forces Shown Posing with "Southern Pride" Confederate flag in Afghanistan', *ABC News*, 22 July 2020; '"Morally wrong": Official photo of Ben Roberts-Smith was altered to hide Crusader's Cross', *Age*, 26 July 2021.
15. Derek Gregory, *The Colonial Present: Afghanistan, Palestine, Iraq*, Wiley, Hoboken, 2004, pp. 10–11.
16. Laleh Khalili, 'Gendered Practices of Counterinsurgency', *Review of International Studies*, vol. 37, no. 4, 2011, p. 1481.
17. Turse, *Kill Anything That Moves*, p. 161; David Kushner, 'Casualty of Porn', *Rolling Stone*, 5 December 2005.
18. Small excerpts of interview data and analysis that appear in this section were adapted from the author's book, Mia Martin Hobbs, *Return to Vietnam: An Oral History of American and Australian Veterans' Journeys*, Cambridge University Press, Cambridge, 2021.
19. Bower-Miles and Whittacker, *Bomber*, p. 104.
20. Terry Burstall, 'Policy Contradictions of the Australian Task Force Vietnam, 1966', *Vietnam Generation*, vol. 3, no. 2, 1991, p. 44.
21. Dan Oakes and Sam Clark, '"What the f*** are you doing": Chaos over severed hands', *ABC News*, 11 July 2017.
22. Author's interview with Robert, Coburg, 1 July 2016.
23. Article 49, 33, 53, 68 respectively of Convention IV, Geneva Conventions, 12 August 1949. Civilians may only be temporarily displaced, under 'imperative' circumstances.
24. Author's interview with Mark, Da Nang, 14 April 2016.
25. IGADF Report, p. 41.
26. Heonik Kwon, *After the Massacre: Commemoration and Consolation at My Lai*, University of California Press, Berkeley, 2006, pp. 30–32.

27 Author's interview with James, Hanoi, 23 April 2016.
28 IGADF Report, p. 331.
29 Samantha Crompvoets, *Special Operations Command (SOCOMD) Culture and Interactions: Insights and reflections*, Rapid Context, Canberra, January 2016, pp. 4, 5.
30 Seymour Hersh, 'The Massacre at My Lai', *New Yorker*, 14 January 1972.
31 IGADF Report, pp. 29–31.
32 Mark Willacy, 'Australian SAS veteran says radios were planted on dead bodies to cover up unlawful killings', *ABC News*, 17 March 2020.
33 Crompvoets, *SOCOMD Culture and Interactions*, p. 4.
34 Darius Rejali, *Torture and Democracy*, Princeton University Press, Princeton, 2009, pp. 503–12.
35 Dan Taberski, 'The Hardest Thing', *The Line*, 4 May 2021.
36 Bob Buick and Gary McKay, *All Guts and No Glory: The story of a Long Tan warrior*, Allen & Unwin, Sydney, 2000, p. 113; 'Hero of Long Tan's "mercy killing" upsets comrades', *7.30 Report*, 17 August 2000.
37 Taberski, 'The Hardest Thing'.
38 Mark Nicol, 'Mercy Killing is "Part of the Job"', *Daily Mail*, 23 October 2016.
39 The literature on this stems from S.L.A. Marshall's *Men Against Fire: The Problem of Battle Command*, Peter Smith, Gloucester, 1947, but the original study is strongly disputed. Frederic Smoler, 'The Secret of the Soldiers Who Didn't Shoot', *American Heritage*, vol. 40, no. 2, 1989.
40 Bourke, *Intimate History of Killing*, pp. 192–93; Nick McKenzie, '"I Want to Say Sorry. And to tell them I should have done more": An Australian soldier and the Afghan man he couldn't forget', *Sydney Morning Herald*, 29 June 2020.
41 Alan Jones, '"War is a Messy Business": Brendan Nelson backs under fire war hero', 2GB radio, 15 August 2018; 'Stop the Witch Hunt. Support the SAS and Ben Roberts-Smith' online petition, <www.change.org/p/scott-morrison-stop-the-witch-hunt-support-the-sasr-and-ben-roberts-smith>, accessed 24 January 2022.
42 Dan Oakes and Jeremy Carter, '"Make Diggers Violent Again": Special Forces Instagram account makes light of killings', *ABC News*, 2 September 2020.
43 IGADF Report, p. 34.
44 David Chen, 'Chief of Army Bans Soldiers from Wearing "Arrogant" Death Symbols', *ABC News*, 19 April 2018.
45 McKenzie, 'An Australian Soldier and the Afghan Man He Couldn't Forget'; Turse, *Kill Anything That Moves*, pp. 161–62; Rory Callahan, 'Photo Reveals Australian Soldier Drinking Beer Out of Dead Taliban Fighter's Prosthetic Leg', *Guardian Australia*, 1 December 2020; IGADF Report, p. 29.
46 Crompvoets, *SOCOMD Culture and Interactions*, p. 4.
47 Ben Doherty, 'How the "Good" War Went Bad: Elite soldiers from Australia, UK and US face a reckoning', *Guardian Australia*, 1 June 2021.

48 Joan Beaumont (ed.), *Australia's War, 1914–18*, Allen & Unwin, Sydney, 1995, chapter 6.
49 McKenzie, 'An Australian Soldier'.
50 Anthony Bubalo and Susan Schmeidl, 'One Reason You Shouldn't Go to Afghanistan with a Beard', *Foreign Policy*, 3 November 2009. Regular army soldiers are not allowed to wear facial hair.
51 Crompvoets, *SOCOMD Culture and Interactions*, p. 3.
52 Charles Miller, 'ADF Views on Islam: Does cultural sensitivity training matter?', *Australian Army Journal*, vol. 13, no. 1, pp. 35–50, 1 June 2016.
53 IGADF Report, p. 31.
54 IGADF Report, p. 334.
55 'Taliban Captures Half of Afghanistan's Provincial Capitals as Insurgents Near the Capital Kabul', *ABC News*, 14 August 2021.
56 IGADF Report, p. 173.

16 How can we fight the far right?

1 For a discussion on the use of the term 'far right' as an umbrella term, see David Renton, *The New Authoritarians: Convergence on the Right*, Pluto Press, London, 2019, pp. 12–22; Aurelien Mondon and Aaron Winter, *Reactionary Democracy: How racism and the populist far right became mainstream*, Verso, London, 2020, pp. 18–19.
2 Nick McKenzie and Joel Tozer, 'Inside Racism HQ: How home-grown neo-Nazis are plotting a white revolution', *Age*, 16 August 2021, <www.theage.com.au/national/inside-racism-hq-how-home-grown-neo-nazis-are-plotting-a-white-revolution-20210812-p58i3x.html>, accessed 28 August 2021; 'Australian Neo-Nazi Leader Thomas Sewell Charged Over Alleged Armed Robbery', *ABC News*, 14 May 2021, <www.abc.net.au/news/2021-05-14/neo-nazi-thomas-sewell-arrested-melbourne/100140902>, accessed 28 August 2021.
3 Michael McGowan, 'Alleged Neo-Nazi Teenager Charged with Encouraging a "Mass Casualty" Terror Attack', *Guardian Australia*, 10 December 2020, <www.theguardian.com/australia-news/2020/dec/09/alleged-neo-nazi-teenager-arrested-in-nsw-to-face-terror-charges>, accessed 28 August 2021.
4 Tom Lowrey and David Lipson, 'Neo-Nazi Sonnenkrieg Division to Become First Right-Wing Terrorist Organisation Listed in Australia', *ABC News*, 2 March 2021, <www.abc.net.au/news/2021-03-02/sonnenkrieg-division-first-right-wing-terror-group-listed/13206756>, accessed 28 August 2021.
5 '[Australian Security Intelligence Organisation] Director-General's Annual Threat Assessment', 17 March 2021, ASIO website, <www.asio.gov.au/publications/speeches-and-statements/director-generals-annual-threat-assessment-2021.html>, accessed 28 August 2021.
6 Nick McKenzie, Jason Wilson, Joel Tozer and Heather McNeill, 'US Neo-Nazi Group Recruits Young Australians, Secret Recordings Reveal', *Sydney*

Morning Herald, 26 March 2021, <www.smh.com.au/national/us-neo-nazi-group-recruits-young-australians-secret-recordings-reveal-20210324-p57dqh.html>, accessed 22 September 2021.

7   Miki Perkins, 'Anti-Lockdown Protests a Coalition of the Alienated and the Far-Right', *Sydney Morning Herald*, 25 July 2021, <www.smh.com.au/national/anti-lockdown-protests-a-coalition-of-the-alienated-and-the-far-right-20210725-p58cqv.html>, accessed 28 August 2021.

8   Michael McGowan, 'Workers' Rights or the Far Right: Who was behind Melbourne's pandemic protests?', *Guardian Australia*, 25 September 2021, <www.theguardian.com/australia-news/2021/sep/25/workers-rights-or-the-far-right-who-was-behind-melbournes-pandemic-protests>, accessed 25 February 2022; Josh Roose, 'How "Freedom Rally" Protestors and Populist Right-Wing Politics May Play A Role in the Federal Election', *Conversation*, 15 February 2022, <www.theconversation.com/how-freedom-rally-protesters-and-populist-right-wing-politics-may-play-a-role-in-the-federal-election-176533>, accessed 25 February 2022.

9   Kristina Keneally, 'Canberra Must Crack Down on Right-Wing Terror', *Sydney Morning Herald*, 17 August 2021, <www.smh.com.au/national/canberra-must-crack-down-on-right-wing-terror-20210817-p58jg3.html>, accessed 28 August 2021.

10 Keneally, 'Canberra Must Crack Down'.

11 Katharine Murphy and Amy Remeikis, 'Dutton Says "Leftwing Lunatics" Must Be Dealt With As Asio Warns of Far-Right Threat', *Guardian Australia*, 25 February 2020, <www.theguardian.com/australia-news/2020/feb/25/dutton-says-leftwing-lunatics-must-be-dealt-with-as-asio-warns-of-far-right-threat>, accessed 28 August 2021; Christopher Knaus, 'Liberal Senator Tells Asio Chief His Use of Term "Rightwing" Can Offend Conservatives', *Guardian Australia*, 2 March 2020, <www.theguardian.com/australia-news/2020/mar/02/liberal-senator-tells-asio-chief-his-use-of-term-rightwing-can-offend-conservatives>, accessed 28 August 2021.

12 Daniel Hurst, 'Australia's Acting PM Says Capitol Attack "unfortunate" and Condemns Twitter "censorship" of Trump', *Guardian Australia*, 11 January 2021, <www.theguardian.com/australia-news/2021/jan/11/australias-acting-pm-says-capitol-attack-unfortunate-and-condemns-twitter-censorship-of-trump>, accessed 28 August 2021.

13 Andrew Zammit, 'Banning Extreme-Right Terrorism Organisations: The issues at stake', *Avert Research* Network, 10 April 2021, <www.avert.net.au/blog//banning-extreme-right-terrorist-organisations-the-issues-at-stake>, accessed 28 August 2021.

14 Osman Faruqi, 'Victoria Police and Extremism', *Saturday Paper*, 6–12 March 2021, <www.thesaturdaypaper.com.au/news/politics/2021/03/06/victoria-police-and-extremism/161494920011218>, accessed 16 September 2021.

15 For example, see discussion of the Christchurch shooter and Australia's settler colonial framework in Stuart Ward, '"Regular White Man": Reveries

of reverse colonization', in Daniel Geary, Camilla Schofield and Jennifer Sutton (eds), *Global White Nationalism: From Apartheid to Trump*, Manchester University Press, Manchester, 2020, pp. 53–70.
16 Keith Amos, *The New Guard Movement, 1931–1935*, Melbourne University Press, Melbourne, 1976, pp. 23–34.
17 Amos, *The New Guard*, pp. 37–38.
18 Andrew Moore, 'The New Guard and the Labour Movement, 1931–35', *Labour History*, no. 89, 2005, p. 60.
19 Moore, 'The New Guard', p. 60. For further discussion of this transition, see Phoebe Kelloway, 'Labour "Armies" in the 1930s Depression: From industrial disputes to anti-fascism', in Evan Smith, Jayne Persian and Vashti Jane Fox (eds), *Histories of Fascism and Anti-Fascism in Australia*, Routledge, London (forthcoming).
20 Moore, 'The New Guard', p. 61.
21 Stuart Macintyre, *The Reds: The Communist Party of Australia from origins to illegality*, Allen & Unwin Sydney, 1998, pp. 211–14; Moore, 'The New Guard', pp. 62–65.
22 Philip Mendes, 'From Protest to Acquiescence: Political movements of the unemployed', *Social Alternatives*, vol. 18, no. 4, 1999, p. 45.
23 For a discussion of the UWM's activism in Sydney in the early 1930s, see Drew Cottle and Angela Keys, 'Anatomy of an "Eviction Riot" in Sydney during the Great Depression', *Journal of the Royal Australian Historical Society*, vol. 94, no. 2, 2008, pp. 186–200.
24 Alex North, 'When Fascism Almost Came to Australia', *Jacobin*, 23 August 2020, <www.jacobinmag.com/2020/08/fascism-australia-old-guard-anticommunism>, accessed 9 September 2021.
25 David Rose, 'The Movement against War and Fascism, 1933–1939', *Labour History*, no. 38, 1980, p. 85.
26 See Robert Bozinovski, 'The Communist Party of Australia and Proletarian Internationalism, 1928–1945', unpublished PhD thesis, Victoria University, 2008.
27 Padraic Gibson, '"Stop the War on Aborigines": The Communist Party of Australia and the fight for Aboriginal rights, 1920–1934', unpublished PhD thesis, University of Newcastle, 2020.
28 Gianfranco Cresciani, *Fascism, Anti-Fascism and Italians in Australia*, ANU Press, Canberra, 1980; Gianfranco Cresciani, 'The Proletarian Migrants: Fascism and Italian anarchists in Australia', *Australian Quarterly*, March 1979, pp. 4–19; David Faber, 'The Italian Anarchist Press in Australia between the Wars', *Italian Historical Society Journal*, vol. 17, 2009, pp. 5–11.
29 Diane Menghetti, *The Red North: The Popular Front in North Queensland*, James Cook University of North Queensland, Townsville, 1981.
30 Menghetti, *The Red North*, pp. 84–88.
31 Menghetti, *The Red North*.
32 See Philip Mendes, 'The Cold War, McCarthyism, the Melbourne Jewish Council to Combat Fascism and Anti-Semitism, and Australian Jewry, 1948–1953', *Journal of Australian Studies*, vol. 24, no. 64, 2000,

pp. 196–206; Max Kaiser, '"Jewish Culture is Inseparable from the Struggle against Reaction": Forging an Australian Jewish antifascist culture in the 1940s', *Fascism*, vol. 9, nos 1–2, 2020, pp. 34–55; Evan Smith, 'Keeping the Nazi Menace Out: George Lincoln Rockwell and the border control system in Australia and Britain in the early 1960s', *Social Sciences*, vol. 9, no. 158, 2020, pp. 1–13.

33 David Harcourt, *Everyone Wants to be Fuehrer: National Socialism in Australia and New Zealand*, Angus & Robertson, Sydney, 1972, p. 42.
34 Barry York, 'Police, Students and Dissent: Melbourne, 1966–1972', *Journal of Australian Studies*, vol. 8, no. 14, 1984, pp. 58–77.
35 Harcourt, *Everyone Wants to be Fuehrer*, pp. 42–43; Philip Mendes, *The New Left, the Jews and the Vietnam War, 1965–1972*, Lazare Press, Melbourne, 1993, pp. 127–29.
36 Harcourt, *Everyone Wants to be Fuehrer*, pp. 46–50.
37 Harcourt, *Everyone Wants to be Fuehrer*, pp. 52–53
38 Mendes, *The New Left, the Jews and the Vietnam War*, p. 121.
39 Cited in Mika Benesh, 'Peeling Back the Mythology of the Australian Jewish Left', *New Voices*, 25 May 2021, <https://newvoices.org/2021/05/25/peeling-back-the-mythology-of-the-australian-jewish-left/>, accessed 12 September 2021.
40 Evan Smith, 'Exporting Fascism across the British Commonwealth: The case of the National Front of Australia', in Nigel Copsey and Matthew Worley (eds), *Tomorrow Belongs to Us: British Fascism since 1967*, London, Routledge, 2018, pp. 69–89.
41 Cabinet minute, 'Changed Pattern of Violence by Racist Groups in Australia', Memorandum 6766, 27 November 1989, A14039 6766, NAA.
42 Kristy Campion, 'A "Lunatic Fringe"? The persistence of right wing extremism in Australia', *Perspectives on Terrorism*, vol. 13, no. 2, 2019, pp. 8–10.
43 See Human Rights and Equal Opportunity Commission (HREOC), *Racist Violence: Report of National Inquiry into Racist Violence in Australia*, HREOC, Canberra, 1991, pp. 181–94.
44 Ghassan Hage, *White Nation: Fantasies of white supremacy in a multicultural society*, Pluto Press Australia, Sydney, 1998, p. 77.
45 See, for example, Nigel Copsey and Andrzej Olechnowicz (eds), *Varieties of Anti-Fascism: Britain in the inter-war period*, Palgrave Macmillan, Houndmills, 2010; Nigel Copsey, *Anti-Fascism in Britain*, Routledge, London, 2016; Anthony Ince, 'Anti-Fascist Action and the Transversal Territorialities of Militant Anti-Fascism in 1990s Britain', *Antipode*, August 2021, pp. 1–21.
46 HREOC, *Racist Violence*, p. 388.
47 Luke McNamara and Tamsin Solomon, 'The Commonwealth *Racial Hatred Act 1995*: Achievement or disappointment?', *Adelaide Law Review*, vol. 18, no. 2, 1996, pp. 259–88.
48 Vashti Jane Kenway, '"Never Again": Fascism and anti-fascism in Melbourne in the 1990s', *Labour History*, no. 116, 2019, pp. 227–29.

49 Kenway, '"Never Again": Fascism and anti-fascism in Melbourne', p. 227.
50 Suvendrini Perera and Joseph Pugliese, '"Racial Suicide": The re-licensing of racism in Australia', *Race & Class*, vol. 39, no. 2, 1997, pp. 1–19; Sigrid Baringhorst, 'Policies of Backlash: Recent shifts in Australian migration policy', *Journal of Comparative Policy Analysis*, vol. 6, no. 2, 2004, pp. 131–57.
51 Kurt Sengul, '"Swamped": The populist construction of fear, crisis and dangerous others in Pauline Hanson's Senate speeches', *Communication Research and Practice*, vol. 6, no. 1, 2020, p. 21.
52 Andy Fleming and Aurelien Mondon, 'The Radical Right in Australia', in Jens Rydgren (ed.), *The Oxford Handbook of the Radical Right*, Oxford University Press, Oxford, 2018, pp. 651–66.
53 Jeff Sparrow, *The Pocket Anti-Hanson*, Socialist Alternative, Melbourne, 1998, p. 18.
54 Sean Scalmer, *Dissent Events: Protest, the media and the political gathering in Australia*, UNSW Press, Sydney, 2002, pp. 155–60.
55 Scalmer, *Dissent Events*, p. 168.
56 Scalmer, *Dissent Events*, pp. 166–68.
57 Tony Abbott, 'The Feral Right', in Robert Manne et al., *Two Nations: The causes and effects of the rise of the One Nation Party in Australia*, Bookman Press, Melbourne, 1998, pp. 10–19.
58 Rae Wear, 'Permanent Populism: The Howard government 1996–2007', *Australian Journal of Political Science*, vol. 43, no. 4, 2008, pp. 617, 626–27.

17 The genie is out of the bottle: Self-determination and First Nations peoples of Australia

1 Megan Davis, 'Listening But Not Hearing', *Griffith Review*, no. 51, 2016; Patrick Sullivan, *Belonging Together: Dealing with the politics of disenchantment in Australian Indigenous Affairs policy*, Aboriginal Studies Press, Canberra, 2011; Stuart Bradfield, 'Separatism or Status-Quo? Indigenous Affairs from the birth of land rights to the death of ATSIC', *Australian Journal of Politics and History*, vol. 52, no. 1, 2006, pp. 80–97; Gary Foley, 'The Australian Labor Party and the Native Title Act', in Aileen Moreton-Robinson (ed.), *Sovereign Subjects: Indigenous sovereignty matters*, Allen & Unwin, Sydney, 2007, pp. 118–39; Jon Altman, 'Self-Determination's Land Rights: Destined to disappoint', in Laura Rademaker and Tim Rowse, *Self-Determination in Australia: Histories and historiography*, ANU Press, Canberra, 2020, pp. 227–46.
2 Gary Johns, 'The Failure of Aboriginal Separatism', *Quadrant*, vol. 45, no. 5, 2001; Peter Sutton, *The Politics of Suffering: Indigenous Australia and the end of the liberal consensus*, Melbourne University Press, Melbourne, 2009; Noel Pearson, *Up from the Mission: Selected writings*, Black Inc., Melbourne, 2009.

3   ATSIC's leadership also faced charges in the media of nepotism, corruption and improper conduct. Ian Anderson, 'The End of Aboriginal Self-Determination?', *Futures*, vol. 39, nos 2–3, 2007, pp. 137–54.
4   Noel Pearson, 'On the Human Right to Misery, Mass Incarceration and Early Death', *Quadrant*, vol. 45, no. 12, 2001, p. 9; Noel Pearson, 'Radical Hope: Education & equality in Australia', *Quarterly Essay 35*, Black Inc., Melbourne, 2009; Sutton, *The Politics of Suffering*.
5   Laura Rademaker and Tim Rowse, 'How Shall We Write the History of Self-Determination in Australia?', in Rademaker and Rowse (eds), *Indigenous Self-Determination in Australia: Histories and historiographies*, ANU Press, Canberra, 2020, p. 2.
6   Rademaker and Rowse, 'How Shall We Write the History of Self-Determination?', p. 11.
7   Anderson, 'The End of Aboriginal Self-Determination?', p. 143.
8   Johanna Perheentupa, *Redfern: Aboriginal Activism in the 1970s*, Aboriginal Studies Press, Canberra, 2020, p. 4; Maria K. John, 'Sovereign Bodies: Urban Indigenous health and the politics of self-determination in Seattle and Sydney, 1950–1980', PhD thesis, Columbia University, 2017, p. 28.
9   Johanna Perheentupa, 'Taking Control: Aboriginal organisations and self-determination in Redfern in the 1970s', in Rademaker and Rowse (eds), *Indigenous Self-Determination in Australia*, p. 193.
10 Perheentupa, *Redfern*, pp. 4–5.
11 Larissa Behrendt, foreword to Gary Foley (ed.), *The Aboriginal Tent Embassy: Sovereignty, Black power, land rights and the state*, Taylor & Francis, London, 2013, p. xxiii.
12 The first known example of Aboriginal demands for self-determination was Fred Maynard's speech launching the Australian Aboriginal Progressive Association in 1925. John Maynard 'The Origins of the Embassy', in Foley (ed.), *The Aboriginal Tent Embassy*, pp. 85–86.
13 Johanna Perheentupa, 'Whitlam and Aboriginal Self-Determination in Redfern', *Australian Journal of Public Administration*, vol. 77, no. 1, 2018, p. 14.
14 Perheentupa, 'Taking Control', p. 196; Perheentupa, *Redfern*, p. 7.
15 Perheentupa, 'Taking Control', p. 199; Perheentupa, 'Whitlam and Aboriginal Self-Determination', p. 14; Perheentupa, *Redfern*, 8; John, 'Sovereign Bodies', p. 258.
16 John, 'Sovereign Bodies', p. 258; Perheentupa, *Redfern*, p. 93.
17 Katherine Curchin and Tim Rowse, '"Taxpayers' Money"? ATSIC and the Indigenous sector', in Rademaker and Rowse (eds), *Indigenous Self-Determination in Australia*, p. 143.
18 John, 'Sovereign Bodies', p. 258.
19 Gary Foley in Olga Prokopovich, 'Aboriginal Health in Our Hands', *Black National Times*, 31 July 1975, cited in Perheentupa, *Redfern*, p. 93.
20 Tim Rowse, 'Democratic Systems Are an Alien Thing to Aboriginal Culture', in Marian Sawer and Gianni Zappala (eds), *Speaking for the*

People: Representation in Australian politics*, Melbourne University Press, Melbourne, 2001, p. 122.
21. Ian Anderson and Will Sanders, *Aboriginal Health and Institutional Reform within Australian Federalism*, Centre for Aboriginal Economic Policy Research, Discussion Paper no. 117, ANU, Canberra, 1996, p. 6.
22. Komla Tsey et al., *Improving Indigenous Community Governance through Strengthening Indigenous and Government Organisational Capacity*, vol. 10, Australian Government, Canberra, 2012, p. 3.
23. Aboriginal and Torres Strait Islander Social Justice Commissioner, *Social Justice Report 2005*, Australian Human Rights Commission, Sydney, 2005.
24. First Nations National Constitutional Convention, *Uluru Statement from the Heart*, 26 May 2017.
25. Coalition of Peaks, *Why We Formed*, <www.coalitionofpeaks.org.au/why-we-formed/>, accessed 16 July 2021.
26. Coalition of Aboriginal Peak Organisations, Letter to Prime Minister, Premiers and Chief Ministers, 4 October 2018, <www.coalitionofpeaks.org.au/wp-content/uploads/2020/05/First-Ministers-from-Aboriginal-Peaks-4-October.pdf>, accessed 16 July 2021.
27. Coalition of Aboriginal Peak Organisations, Letter to Prime Minister, Premiers and Chief Ministers, 4 October 2018, <www.coalitionofpeaks.org.au/wp-content/uploads/2020/05/First-Ministers-from-Aboriginal-Peaks-4-October.pdf>, accessed 16 July 2021.
28. National Cabinet, *National Agreement on Closing the Gap*, Australian Government, Canberra, 2020.
29. For discussion of forms of Indigenous representation see Elizabeth Ganter, 'Arguing about Indigenous Administrative Participation in the Whitlam Era: A representation theory analysis', *Australian Journal of Public Administration*, vol. 77, no. S1, 2018, pp. S19–S27.
30. See Megan Davis's critique of the Coalition of Peaks and the Agreement in Megan Davis, 'New Agreement Won't Deliver the Change Indigenous Australians Need', *Sydney Morning Herald*, 8 July 2020, <www.smh.com.au/national/new-agreement-won-t-deliver-the-change-indigenous-australians-need-20200705-p5593d.html>, accessed 16 July 2021.
31. Megan Davis, 'Gesture Politics', *Monthly*, December 2015, <www.themonthly.com.au/issue/2015/december/1448888400/megan-davis/gesture-politics>, accessed 16 July 2021.
32. Will Sanders, *Towards an Indigenous Order of Australian Government: Rethinking self-determination as Indigenous Affairs policy*, Centre for Aboriginal Economic Policy Research (CAEPR), Australian National University, Canberra, 2018.
33. Sanders, *Towards an Indigenous Order*, pp. 8–9.
34. Rowse, 'Democratic Systems are an Alien Thing', pp. 132–33.
35. Curchin and Rowse, '"Taxpayers' Money"?', p. 148.
36. Robynne Quiggin, 'What Does Democracy and Self-Determination Mean for Indigenous Australians?', *Australian Journal of Public Administration*, vol. 77, no. S1, 2018, p. 56.

37 Sanders, *Towards an Indigenous Order*, p. 5; Tim Rowse, 'The Political Dimensions of Community Development', in Frances Morphy and Will Sanders (eds), *The Indigenous Welfare Economy and the CDEP Scheme*, ANU Press, Canberra, 2001, p. 39.
38 Anderson, 'The End of Aboriginal Self-Determination?', p. 149.
39 Julie Lahn, *Aboriginal Professionals: Work, class and culture*, CAEPR, Canberra, 2018, p. 8.
40 Phillip Falk and Gary Martin, 'Misconstruing Indigenous Sovereignty: Maintaining the fabric of Australian law', in Moreton-Robinson (ed.), *Sovereign Subjects*, p. 41.
41 Sanders, *Towards an Indigenous Order*, p. 11.

18 Pipelines and catalysts: Lessons from the history of women in corporate leadership

1 Tony Boyd, 'Corporate Australia Needs to Get Serious about Diversity', *Australian Financial Review*, 8 September 2021, <www.afr.com/chanticleer/corporate-australia-needs-to-get-serious-about-diversity-20210907-p58pl0>, accessed 24 January 2022.
2 Georgie Dent, 'Is there an "impenetrable" girls' club in corporate Australia as Graeme Samuel says?', *Women's Agenda*, 27 March 2019, <www.womensagenda.com.au/latest/is-there-an-impenetrable-girls-club-in-corporate-australia/>; Patrick Durkin, '"Girls' club" unleash on Graeme Samuel', *Australian Financial Review*, 27 March 2019, < www.afr.com/work-and-careers/leaders/girls-club-unleash-on-graeme-samuel-20190327-p51852>, accessed 22 February 2022.
3 Anne Ross-Smith and Jane Bridge, '"Glacial At Best": Women's progress on corporate boards in Australia', in Susan Vinnicombe et al. (eds), *Women on Corporate Boards of Directors: International research and practice*, Edward Elgar, Cheltenham, 2008, pp. 67–78; Australian Institute of Company Directors (AICD), *30% by 2018: Gender diversity progress report, September–December 2018*, Sydney, AICD, 2015; AICD, *Board Diversity Statistics*, <www.aicd.companydirectors.com.au/advocacy/board-diversity/statistics>, accessed 24 January 2022.
4 Chief Executive Women (CEW), *Senior Executive Census*, CEW, Sydney, 2021, <www.cew.org.au/topics/cew-senior-executive-census/>, accessed 24 January 2022.
5 Jenny Cermak et al., *Women in Leadership*, McKinsey and Co./Workplace Gender Equality Agency/Business Council Australia, 2018.
6 Marion Hutchinson et al., 'Women in Leadership: An analysis of the gender pay gap in ASX-listed firms', *Accounting & Finance*, vol. 57, no. 3, 2017, pp. 789–813; Alison Cook et al., 'Gender Gaps at the Top: Does board composition affect executive compensation?', *Human Relations*, vol. 72, no. 8, 2019, pp. 1292–314.
7 Claire Wright, 'Good Wives and Corporate Leaders: Duality in women's access to Australia's top company boards, 1910–2018', *Business History*, published online ahead of print 9 December 2021.

8. David A. Matsa and Amalia R. Miller, 'Chipping Away at the Glass Ceiling: Gender spillovers in corporate leadership', *American Economic Review*, vol. 101, no. 3, 2011, pp. 635–39.
9. Corinne Post and Kris Byron, 'Women on Boards and Firm Financial Performance', *Academy of Management Journal*, vol. 58, no. 5, 2015, pp. 1546–71; Siri Terjesen et al., 'Does the Presence of Independent and Female Directors Impact Firm Performance? A multi-country study of board diversity', *Journal of Management & Governance*, vol. 20, no. 3, pp. 447–83; Gennaro Bernile et al., 'Board Diversity, Firm Risk, and Corporate Policies', *Journal of Financial Economics*, vol. 127, no. 3, 2018, pp. 588–612.
10. Jean Du Plessis et al., 'Multiple Layers of Gender Diversity on Corporate Boards: To force or not to force', *Deakin Law Review*, vol. 19, no. 1, 2014, pp. 1–50; Department of the Prime Minister and Cabinet, *Gender Balance on Australian Government Boards Report 2017–18*, Commonwealth of Australia, Canberra, 2018.
11. Adam Smith, *An Inquiry into the Nature and Causes of the Wealth of Nations*, Harriman House Limited, London, 1776, pp. 264–65; Josh Bendickson et al., 'Agency Theory: Background and epistemology', *Journal of Management History*, vol. 22, no. 4, 2016, pp. 437–49.
12. Amy J. Hillman et al., 'Resource Dependence Theory: A review', *Journal of Management*, vol. 35, no. 6, 2009, pp. 1404–27.
13. Post and Byron, 'Women on Boards', pp. 1546–71; D.J. Brass, 'A Social Network Perspective on Human Resources Management', *Research in Personnel and Human Resources Management*, vol. 13, no. 1, 1995, pp. 39–79.
14. Claire Wright and Hannah Forsyth, 'Managerial Capitalism and White-Collar Professions: Social mobility in Australia's corporate elite', *Labour History*, vol. 121, no. 1, 2021, pp. 99–127.
15. Wright and Forsyth, 'Managerial Capitalism'.
16. Grant Fleming et al., *The Big End of Town: Big business and corporate leadership in twentieth century Australia*, Cambridge University Press, Melbourne, 2004; F.L. Clarke et al., *Corporate Collapse: Regulatory, accounting and ethical failure*, Cambridge University Press, Cambridge, 1997.
17. Wright and Forsyth, 'Managerial Capitalism'.
18. Janet McCalman, *Journeyings: The biography of a middle-class generation 1920–1990*, Melbourne University Press, Melbourne, 1993; Anne Summers, *Damned Whores and God's Police*, NewSouth, Sydney, 2016 [first ed. 1975].
19. Anne Summers, *The Misogyny Factor*, NewSouth, Sydney, 2013; Hannah Forsyth, 'Reconsidering Women's Role in the Professionalisation of the Economy: Evidence from the Australian census 1881–1947', *Australian Economic History Review*, vol. 59, no. 1, 2019, pp. 55–79.
20. Wright, 'Good Wives'.

21 Ross-Smith and Bridge, '"Glacial At Best"'; AICD, 30%; Wright, 'Good Wives'.
22 Wright, 'Good Wives'.
23 Lucy Taksa and Dimitria Groutsis, 'Swings and Roundabouts: Reconsidering equal employment opportunity, affirmative action and diversity management in Australia from a historical perspective', in J.F. Chanlat and M. Ozbligin (eds), *Management and Diversity*, Emerald Publishing Limited, Bingley, 2017; Du Plessis et al., 'Multiple Layers'; Ross-Smith and Bridge, '"Glacial At Best"'; Summers, *The Misogyny Factor*.
24 Stephen Mayne, 'Meet Ilana Atlas: The People Person Lawyer Who Diverted to Banking, Then Boardrooms', *Eureka Report*, 4 June 2018, <www.eurekareport.com.au/investment-news/meet-ilana-atlas-the-people-person-lawyer-who-diverted-to-banking-then-boardroo/145557>, accessed 24 January 2022.
25 Catherine Fox, 'Sam Mostyn on Opening Doors to Women on Boards', *Board Level*, 3 December 2020, <www.aicd.companydirectors.com.au/membership/membership-update/sam-mostyn-on-opening-doors-to-women-on-boards>, accessed 24 January 2022.
26 Du Plessis et al., 'Multiple Layers'; Summers, *The Misogyny Factor*.
27 Du Plessis et al., 'Multiple Layers'; Karen Handley et al., 'The Same or Different: How women have become included in corporate leadership in Australia', in Sujana Adapa and Alison Sheridan (eds), *Inclusive Leadership: Negotiating gendered spaces*, Springer International Publishing, Cham, 2018, pp. 93–124.
28 AICD 2015.
29 AICD, 'ASX 200 hits 30% women on boards', *AICD media*, 19 December 2019, <www.aicd.companydirectors.com.au/media/media-releases/asx-200-hits-30-per-cent-women-on-boards>, accessed 24 January 2022.
30 Du Plessis et al., 'Multiple Layers'; Alison Sheridan et al., 'Institutional Influences on Women's Representation on Corporate Boards', *Equality, Diversity and Inclusion*, vol. 33, no. 2, 2014, pp. 140–59.
31 Summers, *The Misogyny Factor*; Sujana Adapa et al., '"Doing Gender" in a Regional Context: Explaining women's absence from senior roles in regional accounting firms in Australia', *Critical Perspectives on Accounting*, vol. 35, no. 1, 2016, pp. 100–10; Kieran Pender, 'Salary Transparency and Quotas: Will they solve law's gender inequality woes?', *LSJ Online*, 3 May 2021, <www.lsj.com.au/articles/an-act-of-parity-are-quotas-and-salary-transparency-the-solution-to-laws-gender-inequality-woes/>, accessed 24 January 2022; John Buckley, 'Male Accountants Paid Up to 50% More than Women: CA ANZ', *Accountants Daily*, 2 June 2021, <www.accountantsdaily.com.au/business/15760-male-accountants-paid-up-to-50-more-than-women-ca-anz>, accessed 24 January 2022.
32 Christopher Niesche, 'Nicola Wakefield Evans appointed to AICD board', *Company Director*, July 2016, <www.aicd.companydirectors.com.au/membership/company-director-magazine/2016-back-editions/july/time-for-change>, accessed 24 January 2022.

33 Smith-Gander cited in Anne Davies, 'Smith-Gander reveals how to conquer the boys club', *Sydney Morning Herald*, 19 February 2015, <www.smh.com.au/national/smithgander-reveals-how-to-conquer-the-boys-club-20150218-13ikgw.html>, accessed 24 January 2022.
34 Aileen Moreton-Robinson, *Talkin' Up to the White Woman: Aboriginal women and feminism*, University of Queensland Press, Brisbane, 2000.
35 Davies, 'Smith-Gander'.
36 Patrick Durkin, 'David Gonski, Master Mentor to Senior Corporate Women', *Australian Financial Review*, 13 February 2015, <www.afr.com/work-and-careers/management/david-gonski-master-mentor-to-senior-corporate-women-20150119-12tcu4>, accessed 24 January 2022.

19   Beyond productivity: Working mothers and childcare policy

This chapter draws upon research into the history of Australian mothering (1945–2020) funded by the Australian Research Council DE160100817.

1 Kristen interviewed by Carla Pascoe Leahy, 4 April 2017. All interviewees are referred to by pseudonyms. All interviews are in the possession of the author. Where agreed by the interviewee, interview material has been preserved in Museum Victoria's collections.
2 Catherine Kevin, 'Maternity and Freedom: Australian feminist encounters with the reproductive body', *Australian Feminist Studies*, vol. 20, no. 46, 2005, pp. 3–15.
3 Petra Bueskens, 'From Containing to Creating: Maternal subjectivity', in Camilla Nelson and Rachel Robertson (eds), *Dangerous Ideas about Mothers*, University of Western Australia Publishing, Perth, 2018, pp. 197–210.
4 For reasons of space the experiences of heterosexual women are the focus of this chapter, but interviews with lesbian mothers suggest they also often fall into breadwinner/homemaker patterns after having a child. Fathers and transgender parents have distinctive experiences which are adjacent to, but slightly outside, the scope of this chapter.
5 Deborah Brennan, *The Politics of Australian Child Care: From philanthropy to feminism*, Cambridge University Press, Melbourne, 1994; Carla Pascoe Leahy, 'From the Little Wife to the Supermom? Maternographies of feminism and mothering in Australia since 1945', *Feminist Studies*, vol. 45, no. 1, 2019, pp. 100–28.
6 John Murphy and Belinda Probert, 'Never Done: The working mothers of the 1950s', in Patricia Grimshaw, John Murphy and Belinda Probert (eds), *Double Shift: Working mothers and social change in Australia*, Melbourne Publishing Group/Circa, Melbourne, 2005, pp. 133–52.
7 Deborah Brennan, 'The Good Mother in Australian Child Care Policy', in Carla Pascoe Leahy and Petra Bueskens (eds), *Australian Mothering: Historical and sociological perspectives*, Palgrave Macmillan, Cham, 2019, pp. 339–58.
8 Sally interviewed by Carla Pascoe Leahy, 8 March 2014.

9   Miroslava interviewed by Carla Pascoe Leahy, 27 March 2017.
10 Sybil interviewed by Carla Pascoe Leahy, 6 April 2017.
11 Brennan, *The Politics of Australian Child Care*, pp. 174–77.
12 Jan Harper and Lyn Richards, *Mothers and Working Mothers*, 2nd ed., Penguin, Melbourne, 1986, p. ix.
13 Hazel interviewed by Carla Pascoe Leahy, 8 April 2017.
14 Genevieve interviewed by Carla Pascoe Leahy, 17 July 2017.
15 Carol interviewed by Carla Pascoe Leahy, 29 November 2016.
16 House of Representatives Standing Committee on Legal and Constitutional Affairs and Michael Lavarch, *Half Way to Equal: Report of the Inquiry into Equal Opportunity and Equal Status for Women in Australia*, AGPS, Canberra, 1992.
17 Belinda Probert, '"Grateful Slaves" or "Self-Made Women": A matter of choice or policy?', *Australian Feminist Studies*, vol. 17, no. 37, 2002, pp. 7–17.
18 Caitlyn interviewed by Carla Pascoe Leahy, 5 December 2016.
19 Katherine interviewed by Carla Pascoe Leahy, 30 November 2016.
20 Deborah Brennan, 'Babies, Budgets, and Birthrates: Work/family policy in Australia 1996–2006', *Social Politics: International Studies in Gender, State and Society*, vol. 14, no. 1, 2007, p. 32.
21 Brennan, 'The Good Mother in Australian Child Care Policy', p. 352.
22 Human Rights and Equal Opportunity Commission (HREOC), *It's About Time: Women, men, work and family* (Final Paper, 2007), HREOC, Sydney, 2007, p. 153.
23 Patricia Grimshaw, 'Mothers and Waged Work following Equal Opportunity Legislation in Australia, 1986–2006', in Pascoe Leahy and Bueskens (eds), *Australian Mothering*, pp. 359–80.
24 Lyn Craig, *Contemporary Motherhood: The impact of children on adult time*, Routledge, London and New York, 2007.
25 Kristen interview.
26 Brennan, 'The Good Mother in Australian Child Care Policy', p. 356.
27 Rowena interviewed by Carla Pascoe Leahy, 3 April 2017.
28 Ariana interviewed by Carla Pascoe Leahy, 5 April 2017.
29 Ariana interview.
30 Lyn Craig, 'Coronavirus, Domestic Labour and Care: Gendered roles locked down', *Journal of Sociology*, vol. 56, no. 4, 2020, pp. 1–9; Lyn Craig, and Brendan Churchill, 'Dual-Earner Parent Couples' Work and Care during COVID-19', *Gender Work & Organization*, vol. 28, no. S1, 2021, pp. 1–14.
31 Arlie Russell Hochschild, *The Second Shift: Working parents and the revolution at home*, Viking Penguin, New York, 1989. Sara Joiko referred to it as a 'third shift' in her research into how mothers in England and Chile have been affected by the COVID-19 pandemic: Sara Joiko, 'Schooling, Work and House Life: Women's triple shifts in times of a global health crisis', *Families, Relationships, Societies*, available online 25 September 2020, DOI: 10.1332/204674320X15990673690322.

32 Across several decades, feminist economist Marilyn Waring has persuasively analysed the ways in which women's work 'counts for nothing' in traditional economic theory: Marilyn Waring, *Still Counting: Wellbeing, women's work and policy-making*, Bridget Williams Books, Wellington, 2019.

33 Alistair Thomson, 'New Wave Fathers? Oral histories with Australian fathers from the 1970s to the 1990s', in Pascoe Leahy and Bueskens (eds), *Australian Mothering*, pp. 219–35.

34 Such views arose consistently in interviews conducted for this research and are discussed in my forthcoming book *Becoming a Mother: An Australian History 1945–2020*, Manchester University Press, Manchester.

35 Lyndall Strazdins, Jennifer Baxter and Jianghong Li, 'Long Hours and Longings: Australian children's views of fathers' work and family time', *Journal of Marriage and Family*, vol. 79, no. 4, 2017, pp. 965–82.

36 Bettina Cass, 'Citizenship, Work and Welfare: The dilemma for Australian women', *Social Politics: International Studies in Gender, State and Society*, vol. 1, no. 1, 1994, pp. 106–24.

37 Andrew Scott, *Northern Lights: The positive policy example of Sweden, Finland, Denmark and Norway*, Monash University Publishing, Melbourne, 2014, pp. 63–97; Andrew Scott and Rod Campbell (eds), *The Nordic Edge: Policy possibilities for Australia*, Melbourne University Press, Melbourne, 2021, pp. 124–46.

20 Too much talk, not enough action? Federal government responses to domestic violence

1 Anne Summers, 'International Women's Day keynote', online, 9 March 2021, <www.uts.edu.au/partners-and-community/initiatives/social-justice-uts/news/international-womens-day-2021-anne-summers-keynote>, accessed 24 January 2022.

2 Phoebe Hosier, 'Advocates say National Women's Safety Summit will be a "talkfest" unless it speaks to survivors of domestic violence', *ABC News* online, 8 April 2021, <www.abc.net.au/news/2021-04-08/domestic-violence-womens-safety-summit-qld/100053778>, accessed 24 January 2022.

3 Australian Institute of Health and Welfare, *Family, Domestic, and Sexual Violence in Australia: Continuing the National Story 2019*, AIHW, Canberra, 2019, p. ix.

4 Prime Minister, 'Address, Women's Safety Summit', 6 September 2021, <www.pm.gov.au/media/address-womens-safety-summit>, accessed 24 January 2022.

5 Delia Donovan, 'Women's Safety Summit missed the opportunity to really tackle domestic violence', news.com.au, 9 September 2021, <www.news.com.au/lifestyle/health/health-problems/womens-safety-summit-missed-the-opportunity-to-really-tackle-domestic-violence/news-story/48cbac8315637b90689f07a1b0fae40e>, accessed 24 January 2022.

6 Suellen Murray and Anastasia Powell, *Domestic Violence: Australian public policy*, Australian Scholarly Publishing, Melbourne, 2011, p. 23.
7 Suzanne E. Hatty, *National Conference on Domestic Violence, Volume 1*, Australian Institute of Criminology, Canberra, 1986, p. 4.
8 Lionel Bowen, *National Conference on Domestic Violence*, pp. 7–11.
9 Dawn Rowan, 'The Syndrome of Battered Women', *National Conference on Domestic Violence*, pp. 25–30.
10 Vivien Johnson, 'Love Will Tear Us Apart: Domestic violence and sexuality', *National Conference on Domestic Violence*, pp. 85–103.
11 Judith Allen, 'Desperately Seeking Solutions: Changing battered women's options since 1880', *National Conference on Domestic Violence*, pp. 119–36.
12 Phyllis Daylight and Mary Johnstone, *'Women's Business': Report of the Aboriginal Women's Task Force* for the Office of the Status of Women in the Department of the Prime Minister and Cabinet, AGPS, Canberra, 1986, pp. 56–57.
13 Wendy Weeks and Kate Gilmore, 'How Violence Against Women Became an Issue on the National Policy Agenda', in Tony Dalton et al. (eds), *Making Social Policy in Australia: An introduction*, Allen & Unwin, Sydney, 1996, p. 146.
14 Murray and Powell, *Domestic Violence*, p. 23.
15 Duncan Chappell, Peter Grabosky and Heather Strang (eds), *Australian Violence: Contemporary perspectives*, Australian Institute of Criminology, Canberra, 1991; Duncan Chappell and Sandra Egger (eds), *Australian Violence: Contemporary perspectives II*, Australian Institute of Criminology, Canberra, 1995.
16 Sandra Egger, 'Preface', *Australian Violence: Contemporary Perspectives II*, pp. xxxix–xl.
17 Maryanne Sam, *Through Black Eyes: A handbook of family violence in Aboriginal and Torres Strait Islander communities*, Secretariat of National Aboriginal and Islander Child Care Agencies, Canberra, 1992, p. ix.
18 National Committee on Violence, *Violence: Directions for Australia*, Australian Institute of Criminology, Canberra, 1990, p. xvii.
19 Jacqui Theobald and Suellen Murray, *From the Margins to the Mainstream: The domestic violence services movement in Victoria, Australia, 1974–2016*, Melbourne University Press, Melbourne, 2017, p. 83; Weeks and Gilmore, 'How Violence Against Women Became an Issue', pp. 149–50.
20 Anne Summers, *Unfettered and Alive: A memoir*, Allen & Unwin, Sydney, 2018, p. 297.
21 Heather Nancarrow and Karen Struthers, 'The Growth of Domestic Violence Responses in Australia: A "flash in the pan" or a sustainable program for change?', *Social Alternatives*, vol. 14, no. 1, 1995, p. 45.
22 National Committee on Violence Against Women, *National Strategy on Violence Against Women*, Office for the Status of Women, AGPS, Canberra, 1992, p. 4; Theobald and Murray, *From the Margins to the Mainstream*, p. 83.

23 Summers, *Unfettered and Alive*, p. 308.
24 Murray and Powell, *Domestic Violence*, pp. 25–26.
25 Louise Chappell, 'Federalism and Social Policy: The case of domestic violence', *Australian Journal of Public Administration*, vol. 60, no. 1, 2001, p. 64; Nancarrow and Struthers, 'The Growth of Domestic Violence Responses in Australia', p. 45.
26 Australian Bureau of Statistics (ABS), *Women's Safety Survey*, 1996.
27 Murray and Powell, *Domestic Violence*, p. 44.
28 Weeks and Gilmore, 'How Violence Against Women', p. 153; Chappell 'Federalism and Social Policy', p. 62. Theobald and Murray, *From the Margins to the Mainstream*, p. 114.
29 Chappell, 'Federalism and Social Policy', p. 62.
30 Chappell, 'Federalism and Social Policy', pp. 62–63.
31 Amy Webster, 'The Re-Conceptualism of Domestic Violence under the Howard Government since 1996', *Lilith*, vol. 16, 2007, pp. 57–68.
32 Chappell, 'Federalism and Social Policy', p. 65.
33 John Howard, 'Partnerships Against Domestic Violence', *PM Transcripts*, <www.pmtranscripts.pmc.gov.au/release/transcript-10605>, accessed 24 January 2022.
34 Murray and Powell, *Domestic Violence*, p. 27; *Partnerships Against Domestic Violence: Second Annual Report of the Taskforce, 1999–2000*, 2000, Commonwealth of Australia, 2000, p. 1; Suellen Murray, 'An Impossibly Ambitious Plan? Australian policy and the elimination of domestic violence', *Just Policy*, no. 38, 2005, p. 30.
35 Chappell, 'Federalism and Social Policy', p. 66.
36 Murray and Powell, *Domestic Violence*, p. 28.
37 Kevin Rudd, 'White Ribbon Foundation Address: Respecting women and leading men', 17 September 2008.
38 Murray and Powell, *Domestic Violence*, pp. 30–31.
39 The National Council to Reduce Violence against Women and their Children, *Time for Action: The National Council's plan for Australia to reduce violence against women and their children, 2009–2021: A snapshot*, Australian Government, Canberra, March 2009; National Council, *Time for Action: National plan to reduce violence against women and their children 2010–2022*, Australian Government, Canberra, February 2011.
40 Kate Ellis, 'Remarks at the launch of the National Plan to reduce Violence Against Women and Children', 15 February 2011, <www.formerministers.dss.gov.au/1118/remarks-at-the-launch-of-the-national-plan-to-reduce-violence-against-women-and-children/>, accessed 24 January 2022.
41 Judith Ireland (with Jane Lee), 'Malcolm Turnbull's Scathing Attack on Men who Commit Domestic Violence', *Sydney Morning Herald*, 24 September 2015.
42 Amy Greenbank and Jane Norman, 'Prime Minister Scott Morrison pledges $328 million to Combat Domestic Violence', *ABC News* online, 5 March 2019, <www.abc.net.au/news/2019-03-05/prime-minister-scott-

morrison-to-pledge-328-million-to-combat-dv/10869862>, accessed 24 January 2022.
43   Jess Hill, *See What You Made Me Do: Power, control, and domestic abuse*, Black Inc., Melbourne, 2019; Murray and Powell, *Domestic Violence*, p. 29.
44   National Summit on Women's Safety 2021, 'Statement from Delegates', <www.regonsite.eventsair.com/national-summit-on-womens-safety/>, accessed 24 January 2022.

21   The neglected north: Developing Northern Australia from the south since 1901

1   Mabel Forrest, 'Australia Undefended' (1909), cited in Patrick Buckridge, 'Roles for Writers: Brisbane and literature, 1859–1975', in Patrick Buckridge and Belinda McKay (eds), *By the Book: A literary history of Queensland*, University of Queensland Press, Brisbane, 2007, p. 39.
2   Much of the historical information in this chapter is drawn from Lyndon Megarrity, *Northern Dreams: The politics of northern development in Australia*, Australian Scholarly Publishing, Melbourne, 2018.
3   Russell McGregor, *Environment, Race, and Nationhood in Australia: Revisiting the Empty North*, Palgrave Macmillan, New York, 2016, p. 15. I rely on McGregor's population estimates for this section. See McGregor, *Environment, Race and Nationhood*, pp. 14–15.
4   W.H. Spooner, foreword, in W. Diesendorf (ed.), *The Snowy Mountains Scheme*, Horwitz Publications, Sydney, 1961, p. viii.
5   N.B. The National Party of Australia (also known as The Nationals) is the successor to the Country Party and largely retains its rural focus.
6   Liberal-National Coalition, *The Coalition's 2030 Vision for Developing Northern Australia*, Liberal-National Coalition, Canberra, 2013, p. 2.
7   Senator Murray Watt (Chair), *Select Committee on the Effectiveness of the Australian Government's Northern Australia Agenda: Final Report*, Commonwealth of Australia, Canberra, April 2021, pp. 24–25.
8   Catherine King (ALP, Ballarat), House of Representatives, *Commonwealth Parliamentary Debates*, 25 March 2021, p. 22.
9   Keith Pitt, Minister for Resources, Water and Northern Australia, Joint Media Release with Assistant Minister for Northern Australia Michelle Landry, 13 May 2021.
10   This section draws on Lyndon Megarrity, *Northern Australia and Foreign Investment: Challenges and opportunities*, Australian Policy and History website [Deakin University], online publication posted 16 October 2018: <www.aph.org.au/northern-australia-and-foreign-investment-challenges-and-opportunities/>, accessed 24 January 2022.
11   Andrew White and Amos Aikman, 'Chinese Outbid Funds to Buy Port of Darwin', *Australian*, 14 October 2015, p. 19.
12   Department of Defence, *2013 Defence White Paper*, May 2013, cited in Nathan Church, *The Australian Defence Force in Northern Australia*, Parliamentary Library, Canberra, 2015, p. 4.

13 See, for example, Mark Beeson, 'Issues in Australian Foreign Policy: July to December 2013', *Australian Journal of Politics and History*, vol. 60, no. 2, 2014, p. 271; Merriden Varrall, 'Australia's Response to China in the Pacific: From alert to alarmed', in Graeme Smith and Terence Wesley-Smith (eds), *The China Alternative: Changing regional order in the Pacific Islands*, ANU Press, Canberra, 2021, pp. 107–41.

14 Rolf Gerritsen, 'Pulse and Pause: Researching the economic future of Northern and remote Australia', in Ruth Wallace et al. (eds), *Leading from the North: Rethinking Northern Australia development*, ANU Press, Canberra, 2021, p. 118.

22   How to fix our federation

This chapter is based on research funded by the Australian Research Council (ARC DE190100677).

1 Anna Clark, *History's Children: History wars in the classroom*, NewSouth, Sydney, 2008.

2 Research conducted for the Council for the Centenary of Federation found that 43 per cent of Australians were unable to explain what a federation meant, see Clark, *History's Children*, p. 23. Recent research suggests young Australians lack sufficient civic knowledge: see *National Assessment Program – Civics and Citizenship 2019*, Australian Curriculum, Assessment and Reporting Authority, Sydney, 2020.

3 Chelsea Jones, 'Mark McGowan (Official Music Video)', <www.youtube.com/watch?v=-INs8dNK9cU&ab_channel=ChelsSingsThings>, accessed 6 September 2021.

4 Gladys Berejiklian, quoted in George Williams, 'We desperately need a genuine plan for federal reform', *Sydney Morning Herald*, 19 May 2017, <www.smh.com.au/opinion/we-desperately-need-a-genuine-plan-for-federal-reform-20170519-gw8pfe.html>, accessed 2 September 2021; Alan Fenna, 'Ideas for Australia: To really reform the federation, you must build strong bipartisan support', *Conversation*, 26 April 2016, <www.theconversation.com/ideas-for-australia-to-really-reform-the-federation-you-must-build-strong-bipartisan-support-56081>, accessed 8 September 2021.

5 Anne Twomey, 'Reforming Australia's Federal System', *Federal Law Review*, vol. 36, no. 1, 2008, n.p.

6 (Melbourne) *Herald*, 5 September 1900, p. 4.

7 *South Australian Register*, 19 July 1900, p. 4; (Sydney) *Daily Telegraph*, 18 September 1900, p. 4.

8 (Sydney) *Daily Telegraph*, 18 September 1900, p. 4.

9 *Coolgardie Miner*, 8 September 1900, p. 4; (Coolgardie) *Herald*, 10 September 1900, p. 3; (Sydney) *Daily Telegraph*, 18 September 1900, p. 4.

10 *Age*, 1 July 1901, p. 5.

11 (Launceston) *Daily Telegraph*, 24 December 1901, p. 3.

12 *Evening News*, 26 December 1901, p. 4.

13 (Sydney) *Daily Telegraph*, 2 January 1902, p. 3.
14 *Australian Star*, 1 January 1902, p. 5.
15 *Australian Star*, 1 January 1902, p. 5.
16 *Evening News*, 26 December 1901, p. 4; *Sydney Morning Herald*, 28 January 1902, p. 2.
17 Hansard, House of Representatives, 2 July 1901, p. 1831.
18 Hansard, Senate, 29 January 1902, p. 9323.
19 Hansard, Senate, 29 January 1902, p. 9323.
20 Hansard, Senate, 29 January 1902, p. 9323.
21 Hansard, Senate, 29 January 1902, p. 9323.
22 Hansard, House of Representatives, 29 May 1902, p. 1.
23 Hansard, House of Representatives, 29 May 1902, p. 1.
24 *Age*, 14 November 1902, p. 4.
25 *Sydney Morning Herald*, 19 December 1902, p. 5.
26 *Age*, 2 January 1903, p. 5.
27 (Adelaide) *Observer*, 10 January 1903, p. 38.
28 *Observer*, 10 January 1903, p. 38.
29 *Numurkah Leader*, 9 January 1903, p. 2.
30 (Launceston) *Examiner*, 1 January 1903, p. 4.
31 *Examiner*, 1 January 1903, p. 4.
32 Hansard, House of Representatives, 26 October 1910, p. 5185.
33 Hansard, House of Representatives, 25 November 1910, p. 6848.
34 John Hirst, *Australia's Democracy: A short history*, Allen & Unwin, Sydney, 2000, p. 329.
35 For a history of Anzac commemoration, see Carolyn Holbrook, *Anzac: The unauthorised biography*, NewSouth, Sydney, 2014.
36 See Carolyn Holbrook, '"Commemorator-in-chief": Australian politicians and the Anzac legend', in Tom Frame (ed.), *Anzac Day: Then and now*, UNSW Press, Sydney, 2016, pp. 214–31.
37 David Stephens, 'Why is Australia Spending So Much More on the Great War Centenary Than Any Other Country?', *Pearls and Irritations*, 20 June 2015, <www.johnmenadue.com/david-stephens-why-is-australia-spending-so-much-more-on-the-great-war-centenary-than-any-other-country/>, accessed 10 September 2021.
38 Carolyn Holbrook, 'Making Sense of the Great War Centenary', in Carolyn Holbrook and Keir Reeves (eds), *The Great War: Aftermath and commemoration*, NewSouth, Sydney, 2019, pp. 252–53.
39 Clark, *History's Children*, pp. 20–63.
40 Zareh Ghazarian, Jacqueline Laughland-Booy, Chiara De Lazzari and Zlatko Skrbis, 'How Are Young Australians Learning about Politics at School? The student perspective', *Journal of Applied Youth Studies*, no. 3, 2020, pp. 193–208.
41 David Donaldson, 'Cheryl Saunders: Ten principles for reforming the federation', *The Mandarin*, 15 July 2015, <www.themandarin.com.au/44286-ten-principles-reform-federation/>, accessed 15 July 2019.

Conclusion: The history of the future

1   Alix R. Green, *History, Policy and Public Purpose: Histories and historical thinking in government*, Palgrave Macmillan, London, 2016.

Index

Locators in *italics* refer to figures or illustrations. Locators followed by 'n' refer to footnotes, i.e., 352n1 refers to footnote 1 on page 352. This index uses letter by letter alphabetisation and set-out style. The introduction has been only partially indexed; the chapter summaries on pages 3 to 7 are omitted.

Abbott, Tony
    government of 107, 117, 167, 333–334
    in opposition 254, 325
Abdul, Ali 220, 222
Aboriginal and Torres Strait Islander Commission 254, 257, 266
Aboriginal Housing Company 259
Aboriginal Legal Service 259
Aboriginal Medical Service 259, 260
Aboriginal Tent Embassy 259
ABS *see* Australian Bureau of Statistics
ACCC *see* Australian Competition and Consumer Commission
accountability, of the government 33–34, 120, 264–265, 333, 344
activism
    anti-fascist 242, 244–245, 247, 251–252
    civic 7, 15–16, 44–46
    climate 57–59
    far-right 240, 241, 248–249
    feminist 42–43, 276, 300
    Indigenous 257, 259–260, 323
    refugee 221–222
    use of history in 53, 57–59, 347
Afghanistan
    military engagement in 36, 215, 342
    war crimes in 227–229, 231, 233–234, 236–238
Albert Lepage Center for History 3
Allen, Judith 302
Amos, Keith 243
analogy, historical
    use of appeasement as 15, 27, 35–38, 93–94
    use of by policy makers 13–15, 27, 36, 40, 58–59, 85–86
    use of Great Depression as 184–185, 197–199
    use of world wars as 37, 57, 93–94, 198
Andrews, Daniel 332
Anning, Fraser 216, 240
anti-fascism 242–248, 250–252
anti-Islamic attitudes 215–220, 228–229, 240
anti-lockdown protests 240
anti-Semitism 246, 247–248
anti-terrorism 203, 215–217, 239, 241
ANZAC myth 236, 341–342, 343
ANZUS security treaty 106
Aotearoa New Zealand 216–217
appeasement 15, 27, 35–38, 88–95
appliances
    manufacturing of 99–100, 138–139
    ownership of 74, 162, 172
Appy, Christian 229
Arabindan-Kesson, Anna 206–207
archives 48–49, 52–53
armed forces
    culture of 228–229, 235–238
    history of 13–14
    veneration of 228, 235–237, 341–342
    and war crimes 227–228, 230–238
    see also war
Armitage, David 10–11
Asia

Australian foreign policy and 83–85, 91–92, 123, 209, 223–224, 328–329
fear of invasion from 31, 316–318, 322
international students from 119, 224
migrants from 218–225, 252
trade with 33, 35, 322, 324
see also China
ASIO *see* Australian Security Intelligence Organisation
Atlantic Charter 190
Atlas, Ilana 277
ATSIC *see* Aboriginal and Torres Strait Islander Commission
AUKUS security pact 113–114, 120
Australia China Business Council 108
Australia-China Council 108
Australia Day 332, 340
Australian 49
Australian Agency for International Development 117
Australian Agricultural Company 134
Australian Aid: Promoting prosperity, reducing poverty, enhancing stability 117–118
Australian Bureau of Statistics 160, 306
Australian Competition and Consumer Commission 178, 182
Australian Institute for Criminology 300, 303
Australian Institute of Company Directors 272, 278–279
Australian Institute of Tropical Medicine 317
Australian Labor Army 243
Australian Nationalist Movement 249, 250, 252
Australian Policy and History network 3
Australian Securities Exchange 272, 278
Australian Security Intelligence Organisation 239, 249
Australian Settlement, the (narrative) 28–29
Australian Studies 42–43
Australian Violence: Contemporary Perspectives 303–304

Bacon, Francis 10
banking sector 134, 142–143, 188–189, 191–194, 196, 274–275, 277
see also Commonwealth Bank
Barnett, Oswald Frederick 155
Barton, Edmund 334–336, 338–339, 344
Batty, Rosie 310
Behrendt, Larissa 259
Bennett, Bruce 42
Berejiklian, Gladys 332
Biden, Joseph 113
bipartisan policies
economic 32–33
energy 167, 180–181
foreign 98, 115–116, 224
necessity for 98, 116, 311
welfare 190–191
Birch, Tony 63
Bird, David 85
Bishop, Julie 118
Black Theatre, The 259
Blainey, Geoffrey 28
Blewett, Neal 110
Boston, Ken 45
Bourke Street attack 216–217
Bowen, Lionel 300, 301
Brennan, Deborah 291
Brisbane
floods in 77
utilities infrastructure in 74–75, 169
Britain *see* United Kingdom
Bruce, Stanley 37–38, 85
Brunswick Against the Nazis 251–252
Bryne, Liam 149
building sector 152–153, 156–157
Burma 142
business *see* corporate boards; multinational enterprises

Calma, Tom 262
Calwell, Arthur 222

Index

cameleers 218, 220, 221
Campbell, Angus 236
Capitalism, Socialism and the Environment 21
carbon tax 167, 181
Carr, E.H. 93
cars
    manufacturing of 138–139, 152
    ownership of 158–159, *159*, 370n15
Casey, Richard 37, 38
Cass, Bettina 295
Ceylon Tamil Association 203–209, 375n4
Chakabarty, Dipesh 60
Chamberlain, Joseph 219, 334
Chamberlain, Neville 35
charities 164, 187, 221
Chief Executive Women 279
Chifley, Ben, government of 24, 149, 189–192, 318
childcare
    attitudes towards 285–286, 287–288, 291–297
    community provision of 259, 287
    funding for 276, 284–285, 287, 289, 290–291
    impact of on women's employment 280
Child Care Act (1972) 284, 285
China
    Australian diplomatic relationship with 95, 97–98, 105–107, 108–116, 164, 327–329
    economic reform in 101–103, *103*
    foreign policy of 107, 113
    multinationals in Australia 140, 145–146
    potential war with 83–86, 91–93
    trade with 97–101, *100*, 108–109, 114–115, 145
    US relationship with 107–108, 113, 327–328
China-Australia Senior Executive Forum 109
Chisholm, Caroline 221
Christchurch Mosque attack 216–217
Christensen, George 240

Chubb, Danielle 121
Churchill, Winston 35, 90
civic activism 7, 15–16, 44–46
civic community 46, 164–165, 331, 343–344
Civics Education Group 44, 45–46
Civics Expert Group 44–45
civilians, war crimes against 232–234
Clark, Christopher 87
climate activism 57–59
climate change
    crisis 21–22, 56–57, 163
    history and 10, 43, 57–60, 63–68
    policy related to 163, 164, 166–167, 181, 182–183
    and water 71, 80–81
Close the Gap movement 262–264
clothing industry 99, 152
Coalition of Aboriginal Peak Organisations 261, 263–266, 268
Coalition Party *see* Liberal National Coalition
Cold War 36, 90–91, 106
Colombo Plan 119, 125, 224
commemorations 150, 194–195, 338–345
commercialisation
    of childcare 289
    of Northern Australia 322–323
    see also corporatisation of utilities
Commonwealth Bank 186, 187–188, 191–192
Commonwealth Day 334–341
Communist Party
    of Australia 243–246
    in China 91–92, 145–146
community organisations
    anti-fascist 242, 251, 254, 255
    decline in 164–165, 372n27
    First Nations 258–264, 267–268
conferences
    constitutional 337–338
    on domestic violence 300–302, 303–304
construction industry 152–153, 156–157
    see also infrastructure

context, historical 2, 10–11, 15–17, 26–27, 36, 39, 58–59, 299–300
Coombs, H.C. 151, 260
Corowa 337–338
corporate boards
　culture of 273–275, 280–281
　women on 270–272, 275–286
corporations *see* multinational enterprises
corporatisation of utilities 70, 74–77, 174–175
　see also commercialisation
corpses, desecration of 231
Costello, Tim 117
Council of Australian Government 262–263
Country Party 37, 321, 397n5
COVID-19 pandemic
　and childcare 293
　as disruptive event 4, 5, 18, 22–24, 81, 162–163, 165
　economic response to 40, 47–48, 195–197
　and foreign policy 110, 114
　and Great Depression narratives 184–185, 195, 197–199
　and profile of state governments 332–333
　and protests 240
Crompvoets, Samantha 234
culture
　of armed forces 228–229, 235–238
　of corporate boards 273–275, 280–281
Curtin, John, government of 24, 38, 149, 189

Daniels, Kay 42–43
Darwin, Port of 146, 327–329
Davies, Alan 46
Davis, Megan 265
Davison, Graeme 49
Dawson, Emma 48
Daylight, Phyllis 302
Deakin, Alfred 29, 337
Dean, Fatteh Mohammed 222
Deen, Hanifa 218, 220, 226

defence policy 83–86, 91–92, 95–96
degrowth 81, 362n18
dehumanisation
　of ethnic minorities 217
　of military enemies 228–229, 237
democratic structure 343–345
Deng Xiaoping 101
Department of Aboriginal Affairs 259–260
Department of Foreign Affairs and Trade 117–118, 208, 209
Department of Home Affairs 337
desalination 72, 75, 80, 361n7
Dexter, Barrie 260
de Zylva, Quintus 208
dictation test 219, 223
digitisation, of records 49, 52–53
discrimination
　gender 229–230, 275–281, 283–284, 287–290
　racial 120, 217–222, 225–226, 228–230, 242, 249–255
Dixson, Miriam 42
domestic violence
　conferences on 299–302, 307, 310
　gender issues and 301–302, 303–304, 307, 311–312
　policy 303–304, 305–311, 312–313
　rates of 298–299, 305
Donovan, Delia 299
Downer, Alexander 36–37, 109
Dowse, Sarah 42
Drake, James George 337
Drysdale, Peter 145
Dutton, Peter 216–217, 241

economic history 47–48, 132–134, 193–194
economics
　driving decision making 76–77, 175, 180 *see also* commercialisation
　and Great Depression 148–149, 185–189
　and international trade 97–101, 100, 114–115, 118, 141–146

Index

    narrative of Australian decline 27–35
    reforms in Australia 33–34, 104–105, *105*, 151–154, 191–192, 274–275
    reforms in China 101–103, *103*
education
    in First Nations communities 262–263
    history within curriculum 343–344
    pandemic disruptions to 293
    of refugees 212
    travel services related to 100–101, 224
    for women 276, 277, 287
Edwards, Cecil 177–178
Egger, Sandra 303–304, 311
electricity
    corporatisation of 174–178
    future planning 166–167, 179–183
    government support for infrastructure development 168–173, 318
Elliott, Larry 47
Ellis, Kate 309
Elsie (women's refuge) 305
emission targets, for greenhouse gases 166–167, 181–182
Evans, Gareth 111, 128
Evans, Richard 15–16
Evatt, H.V. 190, 223
executives
    professionalisation of 273–275
    women as 270–272, 275–282
exports 99–101, *100*, 114
Extinction Rebellion 57–58

family violence *see* domestic violence
farming 30, 76, 102, 136, 142–143, 315–316, 324–325
far-right movements 216, 230, 239–243, 246–249, 252–255
federal government
    and childcare 284, 285, 287, 289, 290–291
    diplomatic relationships 85, 91, 106–107, 108–112, 209, 223–234, 327–329
    and domestic violence 299, 302–310
    and economic policy 32–34, 104–105, *105*, 143–146, 186–189, 191–194, 196–197
    and energy 166–167, 172, 175–176, 178–183
    and First Nations self-determination 257, 259–261, 266
    and Northern Australia 316–317, 321, 327–329
    and post-war reconstruction 149, 151–155, 189–191
    statements of Australian values and identity by 118, 120–123, *124*, 184, 299, 310
    and treatment of far-right movements 240–241, 249–250
    treatment of refugees 201–202, 203–206, 209, 211–214, 217, 219–220
    see also federation; legislation; *individual governments by name of Prime Minister*
federation
    attachment to 332–334, 343–345
    commemoration of 338–341
    inaugural celebration of 335–338
feminism
    and activism 42–43, 276, 300
    and contributions to domestic violence policy 300, 302, 305–307, 309, 311–312
Fierravanti-Wells, Concetta 241
finance industry *see* banking sector
Findlay, Christopher 145
Finnane, Mark 52–53
First Nations Australians
    and domestic violence 302, 304, 311–312
    and history 16–17, 43, 50–52, 67, 220–221

and land rights 17, 46, 256, 261, 264, 323
in Northern Australia 316, 322–323, 330–331
see also self-determination, Indigenous
First World War
commemorations of 150, 194, 341–343
and electricity 170
experiences in 148, 150
impact on business 137
lessons drawn from 85–88, 93–95
fiscal imbalance 333, 339
floods 71, 77–78
Foley, Gary 260
Ford 138
foreign aid
connection with values and reputation 117–120, 122, 125–130
goals of 118, 127–128
opinions on 121–122, 128–129
parliamentary debate on 122–123, *124*
foreign direct investment 102, 133, 144, 146–147, 327–329
Foreign Investment Review Board 144, 146–147
foreign multinational enterprises 131–132, 135–139, *140*, 141–147
foreign policy
Australian security agreements 84–85, 106–107, 113, 209, 327–329
and foreign aid goals 120, 128
future of 93–96, 98, 114–116
influencing far-right movements 215–216, 230
and trade 97–101, *100*, 105–106, 108–109, 135, 141–142
see also China; defence policy; foreign aid; immigration policy; USA
Forrest, John 335
Forrest, Mabel 314
Fox, Vashti Jane 251

frames, use in aid policy analysis 122–124, *124*, 126–127, 365n13
Fraser, Malcolm, government of 106, 108, 193, 203–204, 212, 285, 323
free trade 29–30, 31–32, 164, 192
frontier narratives 50–51, 314–316, 318–319, 324–325, 329–331
Frydenberg, Josh 49, 198, 327
future
use of history to visualise 11–14, 17–24, 25–26, 58–61, 66–67, 346–349
utilities planning 71–72, 166–167, 179–183
war with China 83–86, 91–93

Ganter, Regina 225
gardens 73
gender
discrimination 229–230, 275–281, 283–284, 287–290
domestic violence and 301–302, 303–304, 307, 311–312
United Nations goals on 272
see also masculinity
General Electric 136
General Motors 138
Gergis, Joëlle 63
Germany
and appeasement 35, 37–38
multinational enterprises from 136, 137, *140*
war against 87–90, 94–95, 96
Gerritsen, Rolf 331
Gibson, Padraic 245
Gibson, Robert 187–188
Gillard, Julia, government of 106–107, 109, 167, 278, 309, 328
Gini coefficient 160–161, 371n20
Glassey, Thomas 337
Global Financial Crisis 33–34, 40, 47
Gonski, David 281
government
accountability 33–34, 120, 264–265, 333, 344
systems of 332–334, 342–345
governments, federal *see* federal government

Index

governments, state *see* state governments
Graeber, David 152
Great Depression
  and the economy 148–149, 187–192
  narratives of 193–199
  unemployment during 155, 186–187, 244
  used as comparison event 184–185, 197–199
Green, Alix 347–348
Griffiths, Tom 15, 22
growth
  and Australian economy 34–35, 98, 104, 131–132, 144
  and Australian population 30, 70, 155, 172, 320, 326
  and progress narratives 60–65
  and sustainability 74, 79–82, 362n18
Guldi, Jo 10–11
Guterres, Antonio 68

Hage, Ghassan 250
Haigh, Gideon 48–49
Hall, Catherine 62
Hall, Peter 14
Hanlon, Ned 317
Hanson, Pauline 216, 239–240, 252–253
Harcourt, David 247
Harper, Jan 287
Harvard Kennedy School 3, 14
Hasluck, Paul 125, 189
Hawke, Bob, government of
  and ATSIC 257
  and economic policy 32–33, 104
  and foreign policy 106–107, 109
  and Gallipoli commemoration 342
  memory of depression 193
  and multiculturalism 249–250
  and policies to advance the status of women 277, 300, 302
  and refugee policy 203–204, 206, 208, 211
health, public 23–24, 155, 317
health care 261, 262–263, 344

Higgins, H.B. 29
Hill, Jess 312
Hirst, John 44, 45–46, 341
historians
  as activists 7, 47–49, 53, 347
  as educators 36, 39, 44, 50–53, 96
  engagement with public policy 2–4, 10–15, 17, 19–24, 25–27, 40–46, 53–54, 346–349
  and memory 11–13
  and narratives of progress 60–68
  and time 41–42, 59–60, 346
  and truth 15–17
historical analogy *see* analogy, historical
historical consciousness 26, 39, 41–42, 59, 62–64, 348–349
historical context 2, 10–11, 15–17, 26–27, 36, 39, 58–59, 299–300
history, as a discipline
  ability to contextualise 2, 10–11, 15–17, 26–27, 36, 39, 58–59, 299–300
  and creation of narratives 15–17, 50–53, 59–64, 66–68, 194–195, 341–345
  drawing 'lessons of the past' from 12–15, 39, 53–54, 85–87, 184–185
  strengths of 10, 19–21, 41–42, 346–349
  studying public policy within 3, 23–24
  see also analogy, historical; historians; time
History and Policy Network (UK) 3
History Manifesto, The 10–11
History of British India 61–62
History of England 62
Hitler, Adolf 89–90
Hobsbawm, Eric 14
Hochschild, Arlie 293
Holbrook, Carolyn 33
Holder, Frederick 334
home ownership 156–157, 157
Honest History website 16
Horne, Donald 19
housing 73, 155–157

Howard, John, government of
 anti-terrorism legislation 216
 and childcare legislation 289, 290
 and domestic violence 307–308, 309–310
 economic policy of 32–33, 104, 180, 193
 foreign policy of 106–107, 112
 and Indigenous self-determination 254, 257
 and national values 120, 254
 and use of history 40, 43
Howard, Michael 13
H.R. Nicholls Society 29
Hughes, Billy 340
Hu Jintao 107
human rights
 and Australian values 120
 and China 107, 110–112
 and far-right movements 250
 and First Nations health policy 262
 and refugee policy 206, 210, 223
 see also war crimes
Hussein, Saddam 37

IGADF report *see* war crimes
immigration policy
 development of 218–226
 opinions of 164, 216–217, 252, 254
 see also refugees
imperialism
 and industry 135–136, 142–143
 and narratives of progress 60–62
 and wars 38, 86–87, 91–92, 244–245, 248
imports 99–101, *100*
India 61–62
Indigenous Australians *see* First Nations Australians
inequality
 as current social problem 7, 10, 47, 79, 164
 in post-war period 149–150, 159–163, *161*
 see also Close the Gap movement
infrastructure 107, 143–144, 150, 316–318, 326–327, 330, 331
 see also electricity; water
Inman Grant, Julie 310
Inquiry into Equal Opportunity and Equal Status for Women 289
instrumentalism 2–3
Intergovernmental Panel on Climate Change reports 56–57, 68
international students 119, 196, 224
Intervention, The *see* Northern Territory Emergency Response
In the National Interest 120
Iraq War 36–37
Islamophobia 215–220, 228–229, 240
Italian Australians 245–246

Jackson Report 119, 128
Japan
 diplomatic relationship with 38, 114
 economic relationship with 103, 145
 multinational enterprises from 137, 139, *140*
Jayewardene, JR 203, 205
Jenkins, Kate 310
Jewish Australians 246–248
Jiang Zemin 112
JobKeeper and Seeker 196
Johnson, Vivien 302
Johnstone, Mary 302
Joint Committee on Social Services 155
Joint Ministerial Economic Commission 109, 110–111

Karskens, Grace 51–52
Katib, Samsudin bin 220, 222
Katter Jr, Bob 324
Keating, Paul, government of
 and domestic violence legislation 311
 and economic policy 33, 34, 104, 144, 193
 and foreign policy 106–107
 and multiculturalism 249–251
 and policies to advance the status of women 305, 342–343

Index

and use of history 40, 43, 45
Kelly, Bert 30
Kelly, Craig 240
Kelly, Paul 28–29
Kemp, David 45
Keneally, Kristina 240–241
Kennedy, John F. 90–91
Khalili, Laleh 230
Khatun, Samia 59–60, 66
Kingston, Beverley 42
Kissinger, Henry 93–94
Koselleck, Reinhart 60–61
Kwon, Heonik 233

Labor Party
  and childcare legislation 287, 289, 291
  and domestic violence policy 308–309
  economic policy of 34, 188–189
  and Northern Australia 319–322
  opposition to far-right movements 240, 243, 249
  perception of 37
  and White Australia Policy 219
  see also individual governments by name of Prime Minister
Landbridge Company 146, 327–329
land rights 17, 46, 256, 261, 264, 323
Lang, Jack 188, 243, 244
Lasswell, Harold 41
Latham, Mark 240
Laws of Armed Conflict 230–231, 234–235
Lawson, Henry 160
Lee, David 85
legislation
  anti-terrorism 215–216, 239, 241, 255
  on childcare 284, 285, 289
  on companies 137, 144, 274–275, 278–279
  on discrimination 251, 276–278, 287
  on electricity 169–170, 175
  on immigration 219–224
  on land rights and use 50, 76–77, 323
  military 230–231
Le Guin, Ursula K. 65
Lewis, Neil 335
Liberal National Coalition 37, 45, 254, 309–311, 324–325
  see also individual governments by name of Prime Minister
Lloyd George, David 87
Loan Council 191
Lorde, Audrey 67
Luskin Center for History and Policy 3
Lyons, Joseph, government of 37–38, 85, 188–189, 191

Macassar Trepang fishermen 220
Macaulay, Thomas 62
Macintyre, Stuart 44–45
Macmillan, Margaret 36
Malaya 142
Malay Pearl Divers 220, 222
manufacturing industry 99–100, 135–136, 138–139, 152
Markel, Howard 23
Marshall, Elizabeth 222
Marxists 14, 247
masculinity 229–230, 303–304, 305–306
massacres 50–51, 203, 205, 232–233
Masurel Fils 137
maternity leave 284, 287, 289–291, 295
  see also working mothers
Maynard, Fred 387n12
McAllister, Ian 121
McCalman, Janet 23–24, 48
McCarty, John 12
McCormack, Michael 241
McGowan, Mark 332–333
McGregor, Russell 316
McLean, Ian W. 30, 34–35
McMahon, William, government of 122–123, 129, 285
McMillan, William 338
media coverage
  of development in Northern Australia 319, 321, 324–325, 328–329

of far-right movements 246, 248–249, 251, 253–255
of Federation Commemorations 336–337, 339
of historical debates 27, 33, 39, 49, 51
of war crimes 236
of women in the workplace 279, 296
Melbourne
commemorations in 338
corporations based in 136–137
housing in 73, 149, 155
migrant communities in 208, 216–217, 225, 245
protests in 205, 240, 246–247, 251–252
utilities infrastructure in 76, 77, 78, 169–171
memory
of the Great Depression 184–186, 189–190, 193–199
historians and 11–13
institutional 17, 26
theory of 194–195
see also commemorations
Mendes, Philip 247
Menzies, Robert
biography of 40
government of 37–38, 125, 149, 318–319, 321
as opposition leader 190
military *see* armed forces; war
military history 13–14
Mill, James 61
mining industry 76, 134–135, 145, 315–316, 318, 323, 328–329
Ministry of Post-War Reconstruction 151–152, 153–156
misogyny 229–230
Missen, Alan 206
Monash, John 170
Moore, Andrew 243
Morrison, Scott, government of
and childcare 293
and defence policy 91, 120–121
and domestic violence 299, 310
and immigration 216

National Cabinet of 334
pandemic response of 11–12
use of history 184
Mostyn, Sam 270, 277, 279
motherhood, cultural perceptions of 283, 285–288, 296
multiculturalism 211–212, 224–226, 249–250, 252, 254
multinational enterprises
concerns over 131–132, 141–142
definitions of 132–134
establishment in Australia 134–139, *140*
policy regarding 142–147
Munich Agreement 1938 *see* appeasement
Murawing Preschool and Childcare Service 259
Murugappan family 200
Muslim Australians
immigration history 218–219, 222–225
political and physical attacks on 215–217, 225–226, 241
Myanmar 142
My Lai massacre 233, 234
Mylvaganam, Aran 200

narratives
about Great Depression 184–185, 193–199
about Northern Australia 314–315, 316, 324–325, 329–331
of Australian economic decline 27–35
creation of 15–17, 50–53, 59–64, 66–68, 194–195, 341–345
frontier 50–51, 314–316, 318–319, 324–325, 329–331
of progress 60–68
National Action 248–249, 251–253
National Agreement on Closing the Gap 264, 268
National Archives of Australia 49
National Committee on Violence 303, 304
National Committee on Violence Against Women 304–305

Index

National Competition Policy 176
National Electricity Market 176–177
National Energy Guarantee 167
National Front of Australia 248–249
National History Center (USA) 3
National Plan to Reduce Violence against Women and their Children 2010–2022 298, 309–310
National Socialist Network 239
National Socialist Party of Australia 246–247, 248
National Strategy on Violence Against Women 305–306, 311
National Summit on Women's Safety 298–299, 313
Nelson, Brendan 235
neoliberalism 32–34, 47, 77, 193–194, 346
Nestlé and Swiss Milk Company Australasia 136
New Guard 243–244
New South Wales
    far-right movements in 239–240, 243, 249
    utilities infrastructure in 168–169, 172–173, 181, 318
    see also Sydney
newspapers *see* media coverage
Newton, Douglas 85
New Zealand (Aotearoa) 216–217
Nicaragua 142
Nora, Pierre 195
North, Alex 244
Northern Australia
    narratives created about 314–315, 316, 324–325, 329–331
    plans for development 315–324, 326–329
    White Paper on 325–326
Northern Australia Infrastructure Facility 326–327
Northern Territory Emergency Response 257
nuclear war 84, 90, 92

O'Brien, Kerry 34
O'Dwyer, Kelly 272

Office for the Status of Women 302–303, 305, 307
One Nation 216, 239–240, 252–253
opinion polls 121, 123–124, 290
Opperman, Hubert 223
Ord irrigation scheme 321, 322
Organisation for Economic Cooperation and Development (OECD) 144–145, 181
Oscar, June 310

Page, Earle 37, 38
Palaszczuk, Annastacia 332
Papua New Guinea 119, 125, 126, 127, 128–129
parliamentary debates, analysis of 122–123, *124*
Partnerships Against Domestic Violence 308
Pascoe, Susan 45
pastoralism 30, 142, 315–316 *see also* farming
paternity leave 289, 291, 294–295
path dependency 26, 71–72, 75–78, 82, 346
Patterson, Rex 321–322
Pearson, Christopher 36–37
Pearson, Noel 257
Pereira, Dennis 208
Perth
    corporations based in 145
    protests in 253
    utilities infrastructure in 75, 76
Philips 139
policing, of far right movements 249–252, 255
politicians
    consultation of historians by 39, 42–46
    statements on Australian values 118, 120–123, *124*, 184, 299, 310
    statements on perceived threats 215–217, 241, 252–254
    using history for comparisons 27, 36–38, 40, 91, 184–185, 197–198, 347

see also individual politicians by name
population growth 30, 70, 155, 172, 320, 326
Port of Darwin 146, 327–329
Port Phillip and Colonial Mining Company 135
post-war reconstruction 149–159, 189–195
Poynting, Scott 216
primary production 99, 145, 185, 315–316, 318, 324–325
prisoners of war 234–235
progress, narratives of 60–68
Prosecution Project 52–53
protests
    about refugee rights 205, 209
    against domestic violence 298–299
    by and against far-right movements 240–241, 246–248, 253–254
public health 23–24, 155, 317
public inquiries 18, 143, 175–176, 182–183, 191, 256, 289
public opinion
    of foreign aid 121–122, 128–129
    shaped by historians 50–53, 347–348
public policy
    involvement of historians with 2–4, 10–15, 17, 19–24, 25–27, 40–46, 53–54, 346–349
    research into 3, 23–24
    see also individual policy areas by name, e.g., foreign aid

Qian Qichen 111
Qi Yuanjing 110
Queensland
    floods in 77
    industry in 136, 315
    infrastructure and development in 74–75, 168–170, 173, 317–318, 323–324
    politics in 245–246, 252–253, 319–321

    social welfare in 187
Quiggin, Robynne 267

racism 120, 217–222, 225–226, 228–230, 242, 249–255
rape 209, 229–230, 234
Read, Peter 51
recycling, of water 69, 75, 80, 361n7
Redfern 259
referendums 333–334
refugees
    attitudes towards 203–204, 218–219
    government policy on 201–202, 204, 209–210, 217, 254
    involvement of advocates with resettlement and policy 200–201, 204–208, 210–214, 221–222
refuges, women's 300, 302, 305
Reid, Elizabeth 42
Reid, George 29
Reid, Len 123
renewable energy 163, 167, 178–180
reputation, Australian 117–120, 122, 125–130
Reserve Bank of Australia 192
Returned Services League 246
Reynolds, Henry 16–17
Richards, Lou 12
Richards, Lyn 287
Rich List 162
Roberts, Malcolm 240
Roberts-Smith, Ben 235
Roosevelt, Franklin 90
Rowan, Dawn 301–302
Rowse, Tim 51, 266
Royal Commissions 18, 143, 182–183, 191, 256
    see also public inquiries
Rubinstein, William 162
Rudd, Kevin, government of 34, 107, 308–309
Rules of Engagement 230–231, 233, 237
Ryan, Lyndall 50–51
Ryan, Susan 42

Index

Sam, Maryanne 304
Samuel, Graeme 270
sanitation 69, 72–73
Santayana, George 13
Satia, Priya 61, 65
Saunders, Cheryl 344
Scalmer, Sean 253–254
Scheidel, Walter 162
Schweppes 136
Scullin, J.H. 188
Second World War
    and economic policy 188–189
    and electricity 172, 180
    experiences in 148
    lessons drawn from 85–91
    and Northern Australia 317–318
    used as comparison event 37, 57, 91, 198
    see also appeasement; post-war reconstruction
security concerns
    with far right terrorist groups 239
    with foreign aid 127–128
    with foreign company ownership 131, 146
security treaties and pacts 106, 113–114, 120
self-determination, Indigenous
    debates over 256–258
    government responses to 259–260, 262–263, 266–267
    Indigenous organisations and 258–268
service exports 100–101
settlement narratives 50–52
Sewell, Thomas 239
Seymour, Alan 341
Shann, Edward 29
Shergold, Peter 43
Shorten, Bill 216
simplicity, narrative appeal of 2, 13, 27–28, 94
Sinhalese community 208–209
Small, Ben 198
Smith, Adam 273
Smith, Bruce 29
Smith-Gander, Diane 280
Snowy Mountains Hydro-Electric Scheme 172, 184, 318, 320–321, 322
Socialist Alternative 253
social media 216, 241
solar energy 163, 179
Solnit, Rebecca 64, 66
Sonnenkrieg Division 239
South Australia
    far-right movements in 239
    migration to 220
    utilities infrastructure in 168, 169, 171, 172, 177
Soviet Union 36, 87, 90, 106
Special Humanitarian Program 204, 206–210, 214
Speth, Gus 66
Spooner, W.H. 319
Sri Lanka
    civil war in 201–203, 205–207, 208–209
    diplomatic relationship with 208–210
    see also Tamil refugees
Stalin, Joseph 90
Stanner, W.E.H. 67
State Electricity Commission, Victoria 170–171, 173, 175, 177–178, 182
state governments
    and domestic violence policy 300, 309
    and electricity sector 167, 169–176, 179
    responsibilities of 78, 332–333
    and welfare provision 187
    see also individual states by name
state-owned enterprises 102, 145–146, 170, 174
Stebbins, Roly 148, 149–150
Stewart, James 337
Stoll, Steven 1
Stretton, Hugh 18–21
Stretton, Leonard 18
suffrage movement 58–59
sugar industry 245, 315–316, 321–322, 369n31
Summers, Anne 42, 298, 305–306
Sutton, Peter 257

Sydney
    commemorations in 335, 336
    corporations based in 136–137
    far-right movements in 243
    housing in 155–156
    protests in 245, 247, 254
    utilities infrastructure in 73, 75, 77, 78, 169
Symon, Josiah 337

Tamil Language School 211, 212
Tamil refugees
    government policy on 201–202, 203–204, 206–210
    persecution in Sri Lanka 202–203, 205–206
    resettlement of 204–205, 210–213
Tange, Arthur 125
Tarrant, Brenton 216
Tasmania
    First Nations peoples in 50–51
    utilities infrastructure in 168, 170, 172–173, 174
taxation 144–145, 147, 160, 162, 333, 339
Taylor, A.J.P. 86
Tennyson, Hallam (Governor General) 338–339
terrorism 203, 215–217, 239, 241
Theodore, Edward 188
Through Black Eyes: A Handbook of Family Violence in Aboriginal and Torres Strait Islander Communities 303–304
Thunberg, Greta 58
Tiananmen Square 110–111
time
    historians and 41–42, 59–60, 346
    lack of, as barrier to historical consciousness 2, 41–42, 82, 348–349
    as part of historical context 58, 89
    and progress narratives 60–68
tobacco industry 143
Torres Strait Islanders *see* First Nations Australians
torture 203, 230–231, 234–236
trade
    with China 97–101, *100*, 108–109, 114–115, 145
    complementarity 98, 101, 115
    early Indigenous 220–221
    and foreign aid 118, 126, 127–128
    policies related to free 29–30, 31–32, 164, 192
trade unions *see* unions
Trump, Donald 113, 344
trust 33–34, 178, 191, 207, 212–213
truth 15–17, 27
Tsing, Anna 63
Tudor, Frank 337
Tune, David 49
Turnbull, Malcolm, government of 263, 310, 334
Turner, Pat 266

Uluru Statement from the Heart 16–17, 263
Unemployed Workers Movement 243–244
unemployment
    and activism 243–244
    levels of 47, 149–150, 153, *154*, 185, 372n24, 374n12
    memory of 34, 193–195, 198
    policies to address 151–154, 188
    welfare payments 187, 189–191, 196
unions 79, 153, 220, 242–246, 251–252, 255
United Australia Party 37, 188
United Kingdom
    economic policy of 24, 31
    foreign policy of 85, 87–89, 94–95, 120–121
    multinational enterprises 135, 137–138, 143
    see also imperialism
United Nations 90, 190, 223, 272, 306

Index

urbanisation 69–70, 102
urban planning 19, 70–71, 77, 156
urban water *see* water
USA
    Australian security agreements with 106, 113, 120, 327–329
    climate activism in 57
    electoral system in 343–344
    foreign policy of 36, 38
    multinational enterprises from 135–138, *140*
    relationship with China 83–85, 91–93, 107–108, 113
    research centres in 3

values
    and Australian identity 45–46, 159–160, 184–185, 198–199, 254, 310, 341–342, 346–347
    and foreign aid 117–120, 122, 125–130
van der Veen, Maurits 122, 129
Van Diemen's Land Company 134
veneration, of armed forces 228, 235–237, 341–342
vertical fiscal imbalance 333, 339
Victoria
    corporations based in 134–135, 136–137
    housing in 73, 149, 155
    politics in 239, 251–252
    utilities infrastructure in 76–78, 169–173, 175–178, 180–182, 318
    see also Melbourne
Vietnam War
    comparisons with 89, 90, 341
    protests against 246, 247
    war crimes in 228–229, 231–234
violence
    family *see* domestic violence
    by far-right movements 215–216, 241–242, 249–251
    against First Nations Australians 245, 259
    and the military 228–230, 235–238 *see also* war crimes
    against Tamils 203, 204–205

voting systems 343–345

Wakefield Evans, Nicola 280
Walter, James 33
war
    in Afghanistan 215, 227, 229, 233–235
    economic impact 31, 137, 151–154, 161, 189–190, 317
    and electricity sector 170, 172, 180
    lessons drawn from past 25, 35–38, 85–91, 93–95
    potential future 83–86, 91–93
    protests against 244, 246–248
    in Sri Lanka 201–203, 205–207, 208–209
    see also Cold War; First World War; Second World War; Vietnam War
war crimes 227–228, 230–238
Waring, Marilyn 394n32
water
    consumption levels 70–71, 73–75, 80–82
    infrastructure 71–73, 75–76, 318, 320, 325, 361n7
    management of supply 31, 69–73, 76–79, 81–82
    recycling 69, 75, 80, 361n7
Waters, Christopher 37
Watson, Don 43, 356n16
Wear, Rae 254
welfare, social 24, 186–187, 189–191, 196, 213
West, Stuart 206
Western Australia
    far-right movements in 249
    mining in 76, 110, 145
    as part of Northern Australia 315, 320
    utilities infrastructure in 75, 77, 80, 168, 172
    see also Perth
What Happens Next? 48
White Australia Policy 29, 216, 218–224, 316, 322
White Paper on Full Employment 151–152

white supremacy 216, 230, 239–240, 248–249 *see also* far-right movements; White Australia Policy
Whitlam, Gough, government and opposition of
    and childcare legislation 276, 285
    and development of Northern Australia 319–321, 322–323
    and multiculturalism 223, 225
    and relationship with China 106, 108
    and self-determination policies 256, 258–260, 266–267
Wilkins, Mira 135, 142
Wilson, Keith 223
women, on corporate boards
    actions to increase number of 276–279, 281–282
    barriers to appointment of 275–276, 279–281
    concerns over low number of 270–273
    rates of 270–271, 275–276
Women on Boards 279
women's refuges 300, 302, 305

Wood, George Arnold 25
wool industry 30, 99, 136–137
Workers Defence Corp 243
workers' defence groups 243
Worker Student Alliance 247
working mothers
    and gender balance 284, 289, 290–291, 293–295
    policies aimed at 284–285, 287, 289, 290, 291, 295–297
    societal attitudes towards 283, 285–288, 296
World Trade Organization 102–103
World Vision 117
world wars *see* First World War; Second World War

Xi Jinping 107, 164

Yan Yean water catchment 76
Young, Cass 246
Young, Katrina 246
Yunkaporta, Tyson 67

Zyngier, Davis 247–248